Belize

THE ROUGH GUIDE

There are more than one hundred Rough Guide titles
covering destinations from Amsterdam to Zimbabwe

Forthcoming titles include
Chile • New England
Toronto • New Orleans

Rough Guide Reference Series
Classical Music • European Football • The Internet • Jazz
Opera • Reggae • Rock Music • World Music

Rough Guide Phrasebooks
Czech • Egyptian Arabic• French • German • Greek • Hindi & Urdu
Hungarian • Indonesian • Italian • Japanese • Mandarin Chinese
Mexican Spanish • Polish • Portuguese • Russian • Spanish
Swahili • Thai • Turkish • Vietnamese

Rough Guides on the Internet
www.roughguides.com

ROUGH GUIDE CREDITS

Text editor: Caroline Osborne
Series editor: Mark Ellingham
Editorial: Martin Dunford, Jonathan Buckley,
Samantha Cook, Jo Mead, Amanda Tomlin, Kate
Berens, Ann-Marie Shaw, Paul Gray, Chris Schüler,
Helena Smith, Kieran Falconer, Judith Bamber, Olivia
Eccleshall, Orla Duane, Ruth Blackmore, Sophie Martin,
Jennifer Dempsey, Sue Jackson, Geoff Howard, Anna
Sutton, Gavin Thomas, Claire Saunders (UK); Andrew
Rosenberg, Andrew Taber (US)
Production: Susanne Hillen, Andy Hilliard, Link Hall,
Helen Ostick, James Morris, Julia Bovis, Michelle
Draycott, Cathy Edwards

Cartography: Melissa Flack, Maxine Burke, Nichola
Goodliffe
Picture research: Eleanor Hill
Online editors: Alan Spicer, Kate Hands (UK); Geronimo
Madrid (US)
Finance: John Fisher, Celia Crowley, Neeta Mistry, Katy
Miesiaczek
Marketing & Publicity: Richard Trillo, Simon Carloss,
Niki Smith, (UK); Jean-Marie Kelly, SoRelle Braun (US)
Administration: Tania Hummel, Alexander Mark
Rogers, Charlotte Marriott

ACKNOWLEDGEMENTS

Thanks above all to Maureen, who's been to Central America
with me many times and who'll be going on a long-awaited
return visit very soon; and to Caroline Osborne for her
speedy, accurate and good-natured editing, which has
helped make this first edition such enjoyable and rewarding
work. I'd also like to thank Kate Berens and Sam Cook, both
editing Belize chapters in other Rough Guides, and Maxine,
Nichola and Sam-Kirby for their work on my maps this year.
Thanks, too, go to Alexis Rosado, Maureen E. Roe and
Norma Best in the Belize High Commission for their help
and enthusiasm, and a welcome to Assad Shoman as High
Commissioner for Belize; to everyone at JLA and especially
Charlie Shepherd for knowing the answers to some tricky
airfare questions; to Dr Felicity Nicholson and Trailfinders
Travel Clinic for sharing the latest medical knowledge; to
Wendy Angrove at eXito and Layla Jazrawy at Travel Cuts
for their help; to Donna Childer at Continental Airlines; to
Dr Elizabeth Wood at the Marine Conservation Society for
advice on coral reefs; to Clark Werneke and Stephen
Houston for archeological advice; to Angelynn Rudd for the
first account of the Bay Islands; and the Toledo Maya
Cultural Council, Toledo Alcaldes Association and North

Atlantic Books for the Southern Toledo map. At Rough
Guides, thanks are also due to Helen Ostick, Terry Shannon
and Cathy Edwards for typesetting; Eleanor Hill for picture
research; Narrell Leffman and Melanie Ross for additional
Basics research; Jennifer Speake for proofreading; and Iain
Stewart for the index.

To select just a few out of the hundreds of people **in Belize**
who've helped in so many ways is the most difficult task.
Many of you are in the guide: you know who you are, so
thanks for everything. In addition, a very special mention
goes to Jean Shaw and everyone at the *Mopan*, and to
Captain Nick Sanchez in Belize City; to Lori Reed, Chris
Allnatt, Iraida Gonzales and everyone at Travel and Tour
Belize in San Pedro; Barbara Samoila in Orange Walk; Terry
and Doris Creasey in Caye Caulker; Derek and Debbie Jones
in Dangriga; Wende Bryan in Placencia; Ernesto and Aurora
Saqui and Julio Saqui in Maya Centre; and farewell to my
friends of many years, Homer Leslie and Winnel Branche,
who passed away during the last year. Finally, thanks to
Mark Whatmore, whose original idea it was all those years
ago to produce *The Rough Guide to Guatemala and Belize*.

PUBLISHING INFORMATION

This first edition published January 1999 by Rough
Guides Ltd, 62–70 Shorts Gardens, London WC2H 9AB.
Distributed by the Penguin Group:
Penguin Books Ltd, 27 Wrights Lane, London W8 5TZ
Penguin Books USA Inc., 375 Hudson Street, New York
10014, USA
Penguin Books Australia Ltd, 487 Maroondah Highway,
PO Box 257, Ringwood, Victoria 3134, Australia
Penguin Books Canada Ltd, 10 Alcorn Avenue, Toronto,
Ontario, Canada M4V 1E4
Penguin Books (NZ) Ltd, 182–190 Wairau Road,
Auckland 10, New Zealand
Typeset in Linotron Univers and Century Old Style to an
original design by Andrew Oliver.
Printed in England by Clays Ltd, St Ives PLC.
Illustrations in Part One and Part Three by Edward Briant.

Illustrations on p.1 & p.215 by Henry Iles.
© Peter Eltringham 1999.

288pp – Includes index
A catalogue record for this book is available from the
British Library.
ISBN 1-85828-351-5

Belize

THE ROUGH GUIDE

written and researched by

Peter Eltringham

with additional contributions by

Iain Stewart and Dominique Young

THE ROUGH GUIDES

TRAVEL GUIDES • PHRASEBOOKS • MUSIC AND REFERENCE GUIDES

We set out to do something different when the first Rough Guide was published in 1982. Mark Ellingham, just out of university, was travelling in Greece. He brought along the popular guides of the day, but found they were all lacking in some way. They were either strong on ruins and museums but went on for pages without mentioning a beach or taverna. Or they were so conscious of the need to save money that they lost sight of Greece's cultural and historical significance. Also, none of the books told him anything about Greece's contemporary life – its politics, its culture, its people, and how they lived.

So with no job in prospect, Mark decided to write his own guidebook, one which aimed to provide practical information that was second to none, detailing the best beaches and the hottest clubs and restaurants, while also giving hard-hitting accounts of every sight, both famous and obscure, and providing up-to-the-minute information on contemporary culture. It was a guide that encouraged independent travellers to find the best of Greece, and was a great success, getting shortlisted for the Thomas Cook travel guide award, and encouraging Mark, along with three friends, to expand the series.

The Rough Guide list grew rapidly and the letters flooded in, indicating a much broader readership than had been anticipated, but one which uniformly appreciated the Rough Guide mix of practical detail and humour, irreverence and enthusiasm. Things haven't changed. The same four friends who began the series are still the caretakers of the Rough Guide mission today: to provide the most reliable, up-to-date and entertaining information to independent-minded travellers of all ages, on all budgets.

We now publish over 100 titles and have offices in London and New York. The travel guides are written and researched by a dedicated team of more than 100 authors, based in Britain, Europe, the USA and Australia. We have also created a unique series of phrasebooks to accompany the travel series, along with an acclaimed series of music guides, and a best-selling pocket guide to the Internet and World Wide Web. We also publish comprehensive travel information on our Web site:

www.roughguides.com

HELP US UPDATE

We've gone to a lot of effort to ensure that this new edition of *The Rough Guide to Belize* is accurate and up to date. However, things change – places get "discovered", opening hours are notoriously fickle, restaurants and rooms raise prices or lower standards, extra buses are laid on or off. If you feel we've got it wrong or left something out, we'd like to know, and if you can remember the address, the price, the time, the phone number, so much the better.

We'll credit all contributions, and send a copy of the next edition (or any other Rough Guide if you prefer) for the best letters. Please mark letters: "Rough Guide Belize Update" and send to:
Rough Guides, 62–70 Shorts Gardens, London WC2H 9AB or Rough Guides, 375 Hudson St, 9th floor, New York NY 10014.
Or send email to: mail@roughguides.co.uk
Online updates about this book can be found on Rough Guides' Web site at www.roughguides.com

THE AUTHOR

Peter Eltringham's first visit to Belize was when he volunteered to do a tour of duty in what was considered a "hardship posting" by the Royal Air Force. Sailing, windsurfing and snorkelling on the barrier reef was only a hardship to anyone who didn't like being paid for that sort of thing, so after several more trips to Belize and a spell of living in North America he returned briefly to the UK before setting off once again for Central America to co-write the first edition of *The Rough Guide to Guatemala and Belize*. Since then he has researched and co-authored Rough Guides to Mexico, Central America and the Maya World, spending several months each year in the region and contributing articles on Belize to a number of newspapers and magazines. This year he promises to return to Portsmouth University to complete his Latin American Studies degree.

READERS' LETTERS

Thanks to everyone who has taken the time to write or email with suggestions, comments and information for this edition, including:

W. Iain MacKay; Jeremy Lea; Sara Lewis; John Powers; Jacob Moore; James Strachan; Raphael Birchmeier; Tom and Lucy Taylor; Hannah Roberts; James and Maureen Flatt; Kersty Hobson; John and Tanya Hortop; Melissa Flack; Rachel Blythe; Anne Barrett; Emily Kalep and Kevin Qazilbah; Melissa Werneke; Charlie Palmer; Brett Stewart; Louise McLaren; Ivan Danielewicz; Cate Heneghan; and Robert Williams.

HURRICANE MITCH

As this book goes to press much of Central America is suffering from the devastation caused by **Hurricane Mitch**, one of the most severe tropical storms of the twentieth century. On Saturday October 24, 1998, it was predicted that Mitch would pass directly over Belize, and by the following Monday the hurricane had become a category 5 storm – the highest level possible, with wind speeds in excess of 180mph – which would officially cause "catastrophic" damage to anything in its path. Residents and visitors on the cayes and coast began to move inland to higher ground, and hurricane shelters in Belmopan and inland resorts filled up with evacuees.

In the final event Mitch did not make landfall in Belize, though the storm surge that spread outward from the eye of the hurricane destroyed almost all the docks on the two main island destinations, Ambergris Caye and Caye Caulker, and any structures built over the sea were torn down by five-metre-high waves. The brunt of these enormous waves was borne by Belize's **barrier reef**, which amazingly suffered relatively slight damage, mostly in the first 10–15 metres of the outer reef wall; inside the reef, damage to coral was minimal. Two weeks after the storm struck, life was beginning to return to normal: docks were being rebuilt and divers were visiting the outer atolls. The only structural damage to buildings occurred on some of the remote cayes, particularly on Glover's Reef, and these were repaired relatively quickly. Belize had been spared a major disaster.

On the **Bay Islands of Honduras**, the picure was very different. Mitch hovered over Guanaja for over 24 hours and almost every building was destroyed. Damage, though much less severe, was still significant on Roatán, although most hotels were able to reopen. On Utila many buildings were torn down. If you intend visting the Bay Islands, particularly Guanaja and Utila, you should check current conditions first. For months after the hurricane many businesses and services will not be able to operate, though the infrastructure will gradually be rebuilt – updates will be posted on the Rough Guides Web site.

Peter would like to give special **thanks** to the many people who helped out with transport, accommodation and communications during the evacuation of Ambergris Caye, particularly Julia and Steve of the *Sunbreeze Hotel*; everyone at Tropic Air; Ray and Vicky at *Pook's Hill Lodge*; Matthew and Marga Miller at Monkey Bay; everyone at *Cheers*; Jean Shaw at the *Mopan*; and to Iris Velasquez of San Pedro for looking after the rest of her family in Belmopan. I couldn't have managed without any of you. Thank you.

CONTENTS

Introduction ix

LIST OF MAPS

MAP SYMBOLS

- Major highway (paved)
- Main road or highway (mostly unpaved)
- Road or track (unpaved)
- Ferry route
- International boundary
- Chapter division boundary
- District boundary
- River
- Airport
- Site of Interest
- Ruin
- Cave
- Mountain range
- Mountain peak
- Escarpment
- Coral reef
- Waterfall
- Immigration post
- Hotel
- Restaurant
- Gas station
- Church (regional maps)
- Lighthouse
- Information centre
- Telephone
- Post office
- Bus stop
- Building
- Church/cathedral (town maps)
- Cemetery
- Park
- National park or reserve
- Beach

INTRODUCTION

Wedged into the northeastern corner of Central America, **Belize** offers some of the most breathtaking coastal scenery – both above and below water – in the Caribbean. Add to this magnificent inland landscapes, archeological ruins and wildlife to rival any destination in the region, and it's easy to see why the number of visitors to this tiny country increases every year. Despite its small size – roughly that of Wales or Massachusetts – Belize has the lowest population density in Central America, a fact that contributes to its easygoing, friendly and, with the exception of bustling Belize City, noticeably uncrowded character.

Belizean territory comprises marginally more sea than land, and for most visitors it's the sea that's the main attraction. Lying just offshore is one of the country's, and the continent's, most astonishing natural wonders – the dazzling turquoise shallows and cobalt depths of the longest **barrier reef** in the Americas. Beneath the surface, a brilliant technicolour world of fish and corals awaits divers and snorkellers; while scattered along the entire reef like emeralds set in sapphire, a chain of islands, known as **cayes**, protects the mainland from the ocean swell and holds more than a hint of tropical paradise. Beyond the reef lie the real jewels in Belize's natural crown – three of only four **coral atolls** in the Caribbean. Dawn here is a truly unforgettable experience as the red-gold disk of the sun rises over the foaming white reef crest. These reefs and islands, among the most diverse marine ecosystems on the planet, are increasingly under threat; Belize, however, is at the forefront of practical research to develop effective protection for the entire coastal zone, which for visitors means a chance to explore some of the best **marine reserves** in the world.

In fact, Belizeans' recognition of the importance of their natural heritage means that the country now has the greatest proportion of protected land (over 35 percent) in the hemisphere. As a result, the densely **forested interior** with its plentiful natural attractions, including the highest waterfall in Central America and the world's only **jaguar reserve**, remains relatively untouched. The rich tropical forests support a tremendous range of **wildlife**, including howler and spider monkeys, tapirs and pumas, jabiru storks and scarlet macaws; spend any time inland and you're sure to see the national bird, the unmistakeable keel-billed toucan. Although it's the only Central American country without a volcano, Belize does have some rugged uplands – the **Maya Mountains**, situated in the south-central region and rising to over 1100m. The country's main rivers start here, flowing north or east to the Caribbean, and forming some of the largest **cave systems** in the Americas along the way. Few of these caves have been fully explored but each year more become accessible to visitors.

In addition to these natural attractions, Belize boasts a wealth of archeological remains. Rising mysteriously out of the forests are the ruins of the **ancient cities** of the **Maya**, the civilization that dominated the area from around 2000 BC until the arrival of the Spanish. Traces of this astonishing culture have been found all over the country; Maya ceremonial artefacts have even been discovered deep in caves. And although only a few sites in Belize have been as extensively restored as the great Maya cities in Mexico's Yucatán pensinsula, many are at least as large and in their forest settings you'll see more wildlife and fewer tour buses.

Culturally, Belize is as much a Caribbean nation as a Latin one, but with plenty of distinctively Central American features – above all, a blend of races and cul-

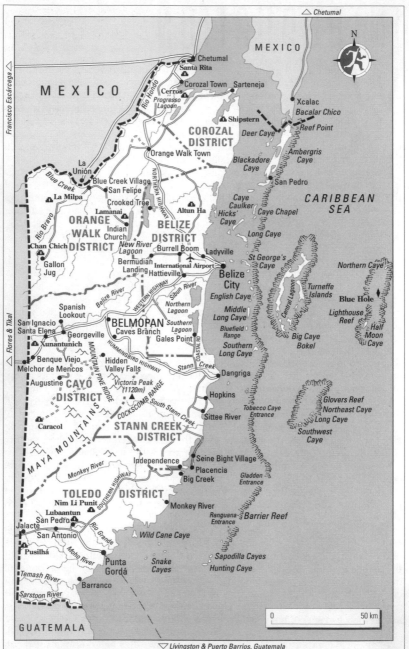

tures that includes Maya, Mestizo, African and European. English is the official language – Belize only gained full independence from Britain in 1981 – and Spanish is equally common, but it's the rich, lilting **Creole**, based on English but typically Caribbean, that's spoken and understood by almost every Belizean, whatever their mother tongue.

Where to go

With its wealth of national parks and reserves, numerous small hotels and reliable public transport, Belize is an ideal place to explore independently; even on a short visit you'll be able to take in both the little-visited Caribbean islands and the heartland of the ancient Maya. Almost every visitor will have to spend at least some time in **Belize City**, even if only passing through, as it's the hub of the country's transport system. First-time visitors may be shocked initially by the decaying buildings and the pollution of the river, but it is possible to spend several pleasant hours in this former outpost of the British Empire. In contrast, Belize's capital, **Belmopan**, is primarily an administrative centre, with little to offer visitors. Midway between the two, the **Belize Zoo** is easily the best in Central America and well worth making the effort to visit, to see the native animals close up and learn about the zoo's efforts towards their conservation.

Northern Belize is relatively flat and often swampy, with a large proportion of agricultural land, though still endowed, like everywhere in the country, with Maya ruins and nature reserves. **Lamanai**, near Orange Walk, is one of the most impressive Maya sites in the country, while the lagoons at **Sarteneja** (Shipstern Nature Reserve) on the northeast coast, and inland at **Crooked Tree** provide superb protected habitats for the country's abundant wildlife, particularly birds. In the northwest, adjacent to the Guatemalan border, is the vast **Rio Bravo Conservation Area**, where hunting has been banned for over a decade, allowing the possibility of close encounters with the wildlife.

The mainland coast is almost entirely low-lying and swampy – wonderful for wildlife, but for swimming and underwater activities you'll need to visit the **cayes**. The largest, **Ambergris Caye**, draws over half of all tourists to Belize, with the tiny resort town of **San Pedro** their main destination; **Caye Caulker**, to the south, is the most popular island for independent travellers. Many of the other cayes are now becoming easier to reach, and organized day-trips are available for divers and snorkellers to the wonderful atolls of the **Turneffe Islands** and **Lighthouse Reef**. Further south, off the coast of **Honduras**, the English-speaking, coral-fringed **Bay Islands** are a potential side-trip from Belize, offering a taste of Latin America in the Caribbean and some of the best-value diving in the world.

In the west of the country, **San Ignacio** and its environs offer everything the ecotourist could want: Maya ruins and rainforest, rivers and caves, and excellent accommodation in every price range. **Caracol**, the largest Maya site in Belize, is now a routine day-trip from here, while the magnificent ruins of **Xunantunich** lie en route to the Guatemalan border. Cross the border and a few hours later you can be in **Tikal**, one of the greatest of all Maya sites.

Dangriga, the main town of the south-central region, serves as a jumping-off point for visitors to the central cayes and atolls (little developed at present but more accessible every year) and for trips to the **Cockscomb Basin Wildlife Sanctuary**, home to the **jaguar reserve**. Further south, on the coast, the quiet Garífuna village of **Hopkins** sees more visitors with every year that passes, while the delightful, relaxed, fishing village of **Placencia**, at the tip of a long, curving peninsula, has some of the country's best **beaches**. Most visitors to **Punta Gorda**, the main town of Toledo District, are on their way to or from Puerto Barrios in Guatemala by boat. Venture inland, however, and you'll come across the villages of the **Mopan** and **Kekchí Maya**, set in some of the most stunning countryside in Belize and surrounded by the country's only true **rainforest**. Here are yet more caves, rivers and Maya ruins, including **Lubaantun**, source of the enigmatic Crystal Skull.

Climate – when to go

Belize lies in a **subtropical** latitude, so the weather is always warm by European standards, and often hot and humid. The immediate climate is largely determined by **altitude**: evenings in the forests of the Mountain Pine Ridge are generally pleasantly cool, while the lowland jungle is always steamy and humid. On the cayes, the sun's heat is tempered by near constant ocean breezes.

Although Belize has its dry and rainy seasons, you'll find that the sun shines most of the year, while rain can fall in any month. The **dry season** runs roughly from January to May, and the last couple of months before the rains come can be stiflingly hot. During the **rainy season** – officially May to November – mornings are generally clear and afternoons often drenched by downpours; this is when humidity is at its highest. During the heaviest of the rains rural roads can be flooded and journeys delayed, particularly in the south. There's often a break from the rains in August (called the mauger season in Belize), and even before then the rain is rarely persistent enough to ruin a holiday. The worst of the rains fall in September and October, which is also the height of the **hurricane season**, when wind speeds can exceed 120kph, though most severe storms follow a track to the north of Belize. If you're out on the cayes you'll need to leave, but rest assured that Belize has an efficient warning system and a network of shelters. The rain can continue into December, a time when **cold fronts** are sometimes pushed down from the north – lowering temperatures to 10°C for a couple of days – when you'll be grateful you brought a sweater or jacket.

With all this in mind, the **best time of year** to visit Belize is from late December to March, when the vegetation is still lush and the skies are clear. This is the main tourist season and therefore the priciest time to visit. Plenty of people visit during the summer months, too, a period that's appropriately promoted by the tourism industry as the "**green season**".

AVERAGE TEMPERATURES, HUMIDITY AND RAINFALL IN BELIZE CITY											
	Jan	Feb	Mar	Apr	May	Jun	Jul	Aug	Sep	Oct	Nov	Dec
Max temp (°C)	27	28	29	30	31	31	31	31	31	30	28	27
Min temp (°C)	19	21	22	23	24	24	24	24	23	22	20	20
Humidity (% at 7pm)	89	87	87	87	87	87	86	87	87	88	91	90
Rainfall (mm)	137	61	38	56	109	196	163	170	244	305	226	185
Rainy days	12	6	4	5	7	13	15	14	15	16	12	14

GETTING THERE FROM NORTH AMERICA

Getting to Belize is simplest and usually cheapest by air. There are daily scheduled flights to Belize City from the main departure "hubs" of Miami and Houston, and frequent departures from New Orleans, San Francisco and LA. From elsewhere in the US, and from Canada, you'll have to fly to one of these hubs first. From Canada you can get same-day connections from Vancouver, Toronto and Montréal; check box on p.4 for details on airlines serving Belize (including charters from Canada) and sample fares.

Travelling **via Mexico** (see also p.6) is another option – and one that can work out both cheaper and easier. There are excellent, often inexpensive, air connections from the US and Canada, particularly to Mexico City and Cancún. Although there aren't any flights to Belize from Mexico City, there are three or four flights a week from Cancún on Aerocaribe, though the quoted airline price of US$130 one way means you need to see a travel agent about special deals or an airpass. There are a couple of **airpasses** (see opposite) worth considering if you want to combine a visit to Belize with several other destinations in Mexico and Central America in a fairly short time. The potential route permutations are mind-boggling but the savings can be considerable.

SHOPPING FOR AIR TICKETS

The price you pay depends more on when and with whom you book your flight than on a particular "season". However, prices do go up in the high seasons of July and August, and Easter and Christmas. At these times **seat availability** can be a problem: flying mid-week and booking as far ahead as possible will pay dividends. If you plan to travel around the region you should consider buying an open-jaw ticket, which enables you to fly into one city and out of another and is particularly good value if combined with the "Visit Central America" airpass (see below).

Barring special offers, the cheapest of the airlines' published fares is usually an **Apex ticket**, although this will carry certain restrictions: you have to book – and pay – at least 21 days before departure, spend at least seven days abroad (maximum stay three months), and you tend to get penalized if you change your schedule. Many airlines offer youth or student fares to under 26s. If you qualify, you'll save perhaps eight to ten percent again but these tickets are subject to availability and can have eccentric booking conditions.

Generally, however, the best deals on flights are obtained by booking through a **specialist flight agent**, who, in addition to dealing with discounted flights, may also offer special student and youth fares and a range of other travel-related services. The only **charter flights** to Belize are the Canada 3000 flights (see box on p.4) from Toronto, which may be cheaper than anything available on a scheduled flight, but departure dates are fixed. The companies listed in the box on p.5 are a good place to begin your search; **eXito's Web site** is the best place to start on the Internet.

AIRPASSES

If you want to visit other cities in the region you can cut costs by using the "**Visit Central America Airpass**" offered by Grupo Taca (see p.4), which links gateways in North America with capitals and a few other cities in Central America. The pass consists of pre-booked, pre-paid coupons (minimum purchase of 3), is valid for 60 days (extendable to 90 for an extra payment), and must be bought outside Central America. For example, from Dallas, Houston, New Orleans or Miami to Belize City, on to Guatemala City, and back to any of the US cities listed uses three coupons and costs $539 (excluding departure taxes) in the low season, $589 in the high season. Prices from Toronto, Washington, New York, San Francisco or LA are $669/739.

AIRLINES AND SAMPLE AIRFARES

Aeroméxico (☎1-800/237-6639). *Direct flights from many US gateways to Mexico City. Tickets can be linked to the "MexiPass" for connections throughout Mexico, and onwards to Central and South America.*

American (☎1-800/433-7300). *Daily non-stops from Miami to Belize City and all Central American capitals.*

Canada 3000 (☎416/674-2661 ☎ & fax 1-877/973-3000 or ☎416/259-1118). *Inexpensive charter flights from Vancouver and Toronto to Belize and Cancún.*

Continental (☎1-800/231-0856). *Daily non-stops from Houston to Belize City and all Central American capitals. Route-sharing with Air Canada means good connections from Canada.*

Mexicana (☎1-800/531-7921). *Frequent flights from Chicago, Denver, LA, New York, San Francisco, Montréal and Toronto to Mexico City. Tickets can be linked to the "MexiPass" with flights on subsidiary airline Aerocaribe from airports in Yucatán to Belize City and Flores, Guatemala.*

Taca (☎1-800/535-8780). *Reservations for four of the national airlines of Central America: Aviateca, Lacsa, Nica and Taca. Daily flights from Houston and Miami to Belize City, several flights per week from New Orleans, LA and San Francisco, and good connections from New York and Chicago to Belize, Mexico City, and many other cities in Central America. Tickets can be linked to the "Visit Central America Airpass".*

SAMPLE AIRFARES TO BELIZE

These **prices** give a general idea of current "best-buy" fares from **discount agents** on scheduled flights between selected departure cities and Belize City in what the airline considers "high" and "low" seasons – exact dates vary. A typical charter flight is likely to be at least $100 cheaper. Flights to Cancún are included for travel via Mexico.

	low season	high season
From the US:		
Houston–Belize (Continental)	$460–540	$490–575
Houston–Cancún (Continental)	$399–499	$435–535
Miami–Belize (Taca)	$315–395	$357–435
Miami–Cancún (Continental)	$240–340	$290–380
New York–Belize (American, via Miami)	$520–595	$555–635
New York–Cancún (Continental)	$399–499	$440–540
San Francisco–Belize (Taca)	$495–575	$535–615
San Francisco–Cancún (Continental)	$354–454	$486–586
Seattle–Belize (Continental)	$550–695	$725–795
From Canada (prices in US$):		
Montréal or Toronto–Belize (Continental)	$470–555	$490–575
Montréal–Cancún (Continental)	$330–440	$360–460
Toronto–Cancún (Continental)	$320–420	$340–440
Vancouver–Belize (Air Canada/Continental)	$675–775	$715–815

If you're thinking of visiting Mexico en route to Belize you should consider the "**MexiPass International**", sold by Aeroméxico and Méxicana (see box above), both of which have an extensive network throughout the US, Canada and Mexico. This pass also consists of pre-booked, pre-paid coupons (minimum purchase of 3) at discount prices for travellers from outside Mexico, and is particularly good value if you're flying from Canada or Europe. It's valid for ninety days and you need to book routes and dates in advance. The real advantages are on the longer or multi-stop flights: for example Toronto–México–Oaxaca–Cancún–Belize–Toronto costs $700; a

NORTH AMERICAN FLIGHT SPECIALISTS AND COURIER TRAVEL COMPANIES

Air-tech 584 Broadway, Suite 1007, New York, NY 10012 (☎1-800/575-TECH or 212/219-7000, email *fly@airtech.com*; Web site *www.airtech.com*). Standby seat broker and courier flights. Good Web site.

Belize Transfer Service PO Box 1722, Palo Alto, CA 94302 (☎1-800 or 1-888/498-2282, fax 650/326-3775, email *mamimenlo@aol.com*). Small company with specialist knowledge of Belize, particularly adept at arranging travel to Cancún and then onward to Belize.

Close Encounters P.O. Box 1320 Detroit Lakes, MN 56502 (☎1-888-875-1822 or 218-817-4441, fax 847-4442, email *belizejq@tekstar.com*). Very experienced in arranging individual itineraries for all budgets to Belize.

Council Travel 205 E 42nd St, New York, NY 10017 (☎ & fax 1-800/226-8642, email *webmaster@ciee.org*; Web site *www.ciee.org/travel*). Student/budget travel specialists with a range of travel-related services and information. Arranges worldwide work/study programmes.

eXito 5699 Miles Avenue, Oakland, CA 94618 (☎1-800/655-4053 or ☎ 510/655-2154, fax 655-4566, email *exit@wonderlink.com*, Web site *www.wonderlink.com/exito*). North America's top specialists for travel to Belize and Latin America. The Web site has a particularly useful airfare finder.

Now Voyager 74 Varick St, Suite 307, New York, NY 10013 (☎212/431-1616; Web site *www.nowvoyager-travel.com*). Courier flight broker. Check Web site first if you can, then call for flight prices.

STA Travel 10 Downing St, New York, NY 10014 (☎1-800/781-4040 or 212/627-3111, Web site *sta-travel.com*). Worldwide discount travel specialists in student/youth fares and travel-related services such as student IDs. Offices throughout US.

Travel Cuts 187 College St, Toronto, ON M5T 1P7 (☎416/979-2406, email *mail@travelcuts.com*; Web site *www.travelcuts.com*). Foremost Canadian specialists in student fares, IDs, insurance and other travel services. Branches throughout Canada.

saving of between thirty and forty percent on the same flights bought separately. The best way to find out about if you'll benefit from an airpass is to call a recommended flight specialist (see box above).

PACKAGES AND ORGANIZED TOURS

The range of **tours** to Belize gets bigger every year with specialist companies organizing escorted group trips (often including other coun-

SPECIALIST TOUR OPERATORS IN CANADA

Eco-Summer Expeditions 1516 Duranleau St, Vancouver, BC, V6H 3S4 (☎1-800/465-8884 or 604/669-7741, fax 465-3244, email *trips@ecosummer.com*, Web site *www.ecosummer.com*). Rainforest wildlife tours and sea-kayaking expeditions in Belize for US$1400 a week; sailing through the atolls for around US$1300.

Gap Adventures 266 Dupont St, Toronto, Ontario, M5R IV7 (☎1-800/465-5600 or 416/922-8899, fax 922-0822, email *adventure@gap.org*, Web site *www.gap.ca*). Good group trips (some camping) with diving and kayaking in Yucatán, Belize and throughout Central America. Around C$1200 for 8 days in Belize (excluding airfare).

Island Expeditions 368–916 W Broadway, Vancouver, BC, V5Z 1K7 (☎1-800/667-1630 or

604/452-3212, fax 452-3433, email *info@island-expeditions.com*, Web site *www.islandexpeditions.com*). Expertly led sea- and river-kayaking expeditions. C$1200 for a week on a Belize atoll; C$1300 for a week exploring rainforest rivers in southern Belize.

Pacific Sun Spots Tours 196–201 W Third Ave, Vancouver, BC, V5Y 1E9 (☎1-800/663-0755 or 604/606-1750, email *res@pacsun.com*). Good-value hotel-based holidays in Belize and Costa Rica; C$520–1000 for a week in Belize (excluding airfare).

Quest Nature Tours 36 Finch Ave W, Toronto, Ontario, M2N 2G9 (☎416/221-3000). Wildlife tours to Belize and Costa Rica led by naturalists. C$1700 for eight days exploring reefs and rainforests in Belize.

SPECIALIST TOUR OPERATORS IN THE US

Far Horizons PO Box 91900, Albuquerque, NM 87199-1900 (☎1-800/552-4575; email *journey@farhorizon.com*, Web site *www.farhorizon.com*). Superb archeological trips to remote Maya sites in Belize, Guatemala and Honduras. Approx. $3000 for nine-day expedition.

Green Tortoise Adventure Travel 494 Broadway, San Francisco, CA 94133 (☎1-800/867-8647 or 415/956-7500, email *info@greentortoise.com*, Web site *www.greentortoise.com*). Bus trips through Mexico to Antigua and Guatemala, from where you could travel on independently to Belize. Twenty-three days for $900, including food.

Journeys 4011 Jackson Rd, Ann Arbor, MI 48103–1825 (☎1-800/255-8735 or 734/655-4407, fax 655-2945, email *info@journeys-intl.com*, Web site *www.journeys-intl.com*). Superb nature- and culture-oriented tours to Belize and the rest of Central America, some for women only. Around $1400–$1600 for a week, excluding airfare.

Magnum Belize PO Box 1560, Detroit Lakes, MN 56502 (☎1-800/447-2931, fax 218/847-0334, email *information@magnumbelize.com*, Web site *www.magnumbelize.com*). Representatives for over thirty hotels and resorts in Belize, specializing in tailor-made itineraries and airfares.

Monkey River Expeditions 1731 44th Ave SW, Suite 100, Seattle, WA 98116 (☎1-800/500-2175 or ☎206/660-7777, fax 938-0978, email *mre@halcyon.com*). Kayaking and nature expeditions along the Monkey River and the cayes of southern Belize. $1250 for nine days, excluding airfare.

Sea and Explore Belize 1809 Carol Sue Ave, Suite E, Gretna, LA 70056 (☎1-800/345-9786 or 504/366-9985). Specialists in tailor-made trips to Belize.

Slickrock Adventures PO Box 1400, Moab, UT 84532 (☎1-800/390-5715, fax 801/259-6996, email *slickrock@slickrock.com*, Web site *www.slickrock.com*). One of the very best companies, offering sea-kayaking, jungle and river (some white-water) expeditions in Belize, Guatemala and Honduras: $1800 for a nine-day adventure "week" in Belize.

Temptress Voyages 1600 NW LeJeune Rd, Suite 301, Miami, FL 33126 (☎1-800/336-8423, fax 305/871-2657, Web site *www.temptresscruises.com*). Small-scale cruises to Belize and Guatemala. Prices for a seven-day cruise departing from Belize City vary between $1500 and $2000, depending on season and cabin; shorter trips are available.

Toucan Adventure Tours PO Box 1073, Cambria, CA 93428 (☎805/927-5885, fax 927-0929, Web site *www.toucanadventures.com*). Inexpensive camping tours through the Maya region of Yucatán, Belize and Guatemala. Three-week 'Ruta Maya' trip; around $1150 for land costs.

Tread Lightly Limited PO Box 329, 37 Juniper Meadow Rd, Washington Depot, CT 06794 (☎1-800/643-0060 or 860/868-1710, fax 868-1718, email *info@treadlightly.com*, Web site *www.treadlightly.com*). Low-impact, high-quality natural history and cultural travel in Belize, Guatemala, Honduras and Panamá. Four days' reef and rainforest for $595 (excluding airfare).

Victor Emanuel Nature Tours PO Box 33008, Austin, TX 78764 (☎1-800/328-VENT or 512/328-5221, fax 328-2919, email *ventbird@aol.com*, Web site *www.ventbird.com*). The best birdwatching tours you can get, led by dedicated professionals. $3500 for twelve days at Chan Chich, Belize, with a trip to Tikal.

tries in the region) to the Maya ruins and nature reserves with options of biking, diving, birdwatching and the like. If time is short these can be very good value and give you the option of going to places or doing things that would be more difficult (or even impossible) to organize on your own, such as expeditions to remote jungle ruins and rivers, and sea-kayaking trips. In a group, you'll get expert leaders and emergency back-up. The best tour operators offering trips to Belize are listed in the box above; shop around to see what's included.

OVERLAND THROUGH MEXICO

It's a long haul **overland** to Belize from the US and Canada, but if you'd like to see something of Mexico on the way, it might be worth considering. Greyhound buses (☎1-800/231-2222) run regularly to all major border crossings; some will take you over the frontier and into the Mexican bus station. From every Mexican border crossing there are constant **buses to the capital** (generally 18–24 hours away) and also good bus connections to the border town of **Chetumal** into Belize. For possible routes and attractions on the way south see *The Rough Guide to Mexico*.

Travelling south **by car** may give you a lot more freedom, but it does entail a great deal of bureaucracy. You need separate insurance for Mexico, sold at the border by Sanborns (☎1-800/222-0158) for about $10 per day; they can arrange much more besides, such as legal assistance, road maps and guides and a 24-hour emergency hotline.

US, Canadian, EU, Australian and New Zealand **driving licences** are valid in Mexico and Belize, but it's a good idea to arm yourself with an International Driving Licence as well. If you run into problems with the traffic police for any reason, show that first, and if they abscond with it you at least still have your own licence. If you belong to a motoring organization at home you may find they'll offer advice, maps and even help from reciprocal organizations in Mexico. Unleaded petrol/gasoline is widely available in Mexico and Belize. See p.30 for details on driving in Belize.

GETTING THERE FROM THE UK AND IRELAND

There are no direct flights from the UK to Belize; flying there always involves a change of aircraft (and sometimes airline), and an overnight stay – usually in the US. From this side of the Atlantic the main destination hubs are Houston and Miami; flying to these cities will offer the least expensive connections to Belize. Fares to Mexico City or Cancún are lower than those to Belize so you might want to consider or travelling down overland from there. And, if you plan to spend any length of time travelling around the US or Central America you should look around at the various airpasses (see p.3) on offer.

Although flying from London gives you the greatest variety of flights to the US and Belize, you can often get flights from Manchester for the same price. A **scheduled flight** to Belize City booked through a **specialist flight or travel agent** (see box on p.8) will cost around £495–£545 return in the low season (Feb & Nov to mid-Dec), £565–£595 in the shoulder season (May, June, Sept & Oct), and £695 in the high season (July, Aug, mid-Dec to early Jan & Easter); prices do not include taxes of around £40. Official fares, quoted by the airlines, are generally higher. There's often some deal available for young people (usually under-26s) and students, but you'll need to book as far in advance as you can as seat availability at the discount prices is limited. Most tickets are valid for between three and six months, sometimes up to one year (though you can pay around ten percent more for a budget ticket that allows you to do this); some work out cheaper if you're away less than thirty days.

Besides the flight agents given on p.8, try the classified sections of the broadsheet papers or listings magazines. On the Internet, Campus Travel and STA's Web sites have reasonable fare-finders. Deciding which flight option is best for you can be a little complex; as always, a good flight specialist such as Campus, Journey Latin America or Trailfinders (see box on p.8) is the best first call to sort out the possibilities, whatever your route and ticket options.

An alternative is to **fly to Mexico** and continue overland (see p.6) or by air (see p.4). **British Airways** flies direct to Mexico City and Cancún – prices from around £429 – and several other European airlines fly to Mexico City from London via their European hubs: Air France via Paris,

AIRLINES

Aeroméxico ☎0171/734-9354 (Information and reservations only; no flights between UK and Mexico.)
Air France ☎0181/742-6600
American Airlines ☎0345/789789
British Airways ☎ 0345/222111
Continental ☎0800/776464
Delta ☎0800/414767
Iberia ☎0171/830-0011

Lufthansa ☎ 0345/737747
KLM ☎0990/750-900
Méxicana ☎ 0171/284-2550 (Information and reservations only; no flights between UK and Mexico.)
Taca Group ☎ 01293/23330 (Agents for four Central American airlines and their airpass.)
United ☎ 0845/844-4777
Virgin Atlantic ☎ 01293/747747

SPECIALIST FLIGHT AGENTS

Campus Travel 52 Grosvenor Gdns, London SW1W 0AG (☎0171/730-2101); 53 Forrest Rd, Edinburgh EH1 2QP (☎0131/668-3303); 166 Deansgate, Manchester M3 3FE (☎0161/833-2046); Web site *www.campustravel.co.uk*. *Student/youth travel specialists, with 45 branches on university campuses, in YHA shops and in cities all over Britain. Good Web site.*
Journey Latin America 14–16 Devonshire Rd, London W4 (☎0181/747-3108, fax 742-1312); Barton Arcade, 51–63 Deansgate, Manchester M3 2BH (☎0161/832-1441, fax 832-1551); email *sales@journeylatinamerica.co.uk.The leaders in the field on airfares and tours to Latin America, with some of the best prices on high-season flights.*
South American Experience 47 Causton St, London SW1P 4AT (☎0171/976-5511, fax 976-6908, email *sax@mcmail.com*). *Flight and tailor-*

made itinerary specialists; very good airfare prices.
STA Travel 86 Old Brompton Rd, London SW7 3LH (☎0171/361-6262, email *enquiries@sta.travel.co.uk*; Web site *www.sta-travel.co.uk*); other branches throughout the UK. *Student/youth travel specialists with an international help desk if you have problems while abroad.*
Trailfinders 42–50 Earls Court Rd, London W8 6FT (long-haul flights ☎0171/938-3366); 58 Deansgate, Manchester M3 2FF (☎0161/839 6969); 254–284 Sauchiehall St, Glasgow G2 3EH (☎0141/353 2224); 22–24 The Priory Queensway, Birmingham B4 6BS (☎0121/236 1234); 48 Corn St, Bristol BS1 1HQ (☎0117/929 9000). *Airfare specialists and tailor-made packages for independent travellers. Other offices in London,*

Iberia via Madrid, Lufthansa via Frankfurt and KLM via Amsterdam. From a discount agent you can get flights to Mexico City and Cancún from around £400. It may work out slightly cheaper to fly with BA to Cancún, spend the night there, then take the bus to Chetumal for a connection to Belize, but flying from Cancún to Belize is unlikely to save you any money and would still mean a next-day departure. A check through *www.cheapflights.co.uk* or *www.airtickets.co.uk* will allow some comparisons on fares to Mexico City and Cancún (Belize is not listed at present) from various UK airports, and there are good links to travel agents and other sources of information.

If you want to visit different areas of the US, travel to several countries in Central America, or continue into South America, then it's worth considering an **"open jaw"** ticket, which lets you fly into one city and out of another, often available at

little more than cost of an ordinary return ticket. It's also worth checking if your transatlantic carrier has an **airpass** which links flights in the US, Canada and Mexico (usually only Mexico City) – most major US airlines do. See p.3 for further details of airpasses.

PACKAGES AND INCLUSIVE TOURS

Many companies in the UK offer **package tours** to Belize and they can be especially good value if you're short of time. They're usually led by someone from the UK who knows the area, but in many cases you'll have a local guide too; travel varies from local buses to comfortable minibuses, fast launches to light aircraft. The box opposite covers the best and most experienced UK operators operating in Central America; all can provide detailed information sheets on each trip. Prices given are a guide only; some tours also require

SPECIALIST TOUR OPERATORS

Dragoman Camp Green, Kenton Rd, Debenham, Suffolk IP14 6LA (☎01728/861133, fax 861127, email *100344.1342@compuserve.com*, Web site *www.dragoman.co.uk*). Eight-week overland camping expeditions through Mexico and Central America to Panamá, around £1400, plus $550 food kitty.

Encounter Overland 267 Old Brompton Rd, London, SW5 9JA (☎0171/370-6845, fax 244-9737, email *adventure@encounter-overland.co.uk*). Three- to six-week overland camping and hotel trips through Mexico to Panamá; 42 days from Mexico City via Yucatán to Guatemala costs £1800 excluding airfare.

Exodus 9 Weir Rd, London, SW12 0LT (☎0181/673-0859, fax 673-0779, email *sales@exodustravels.co.uk*; Web site *www.exodustravels.co.uk*). Fifteen-day escorted tours, staying at hotels, through the Maya region for around £1400 including airfare.

Explore Worldwide 1 Frederick St, Aldershot GU11 1LQ (☎01252/344161, fax 343170, email *info@explore.co.uk*, Web site *www.explore.co.uk*). Wide range of two- to three-week hotel-based tours to Central America and Mexico. Some tours run year-round. Around £1200 for15 days in Mexico, Guatemala and Belize including airfare.

Global Travel Club 1 Kiln Shaw, Langdon Hills, Basildon, Essex SS16 6LE (☎01268/541732, fax 542275, email *info@global-travel.co.uk*; Web site *www.global-travel.co.uk*). Small company special-izing in individually arranged diving and cultural tours to Belize, Mexico and all of Central America.

Journey Latin America 12–13 Heathfield Terrace, London W4 4JE (☎0181/747-3108, fax 742-1312, email *sales@journeylatinamerica.co.uk*). Wide range of high-standard tours and individual itineraries from the acknowledged experts. Twenty-day trip through Guatemala, Belize and Yucatán from around £1350 including airfare.

Reef and Rainforest Tours Prospect House, Jubilee Rd, Totnes, Devon TQ9 5BP (☎01803/866965, fax 865916, email *reefrain@btinter-net.com*). Individual itineraries from a very experienced company, focusing on nature reserves, research projects and diving in Belize, Honduras and Costa Rica.

Travelbag Adventures 15 Turk St, Alton, Hants GU34 1AG (☎01420/541007, fax 541022, email *mail@travelbag-adventures.co.uk*; Web site *www.travelbag-adventures.co.uk*). Small-group hotel-based tours through Yucatán and Central America; eighteen-day "Realm of the Maya" trip, from Cancún through Belize and Guatemala for around £950 excluding airfare.

Trips 9 Byron Place, Clifton, Bristol BS8 1JT (☎0117/987-2626, fax 987-2627, email *trips@trips.demon.co.uk*; Web site *www.trips.demon.co.uk*). Friendly, experienced company with an inspired range of tailor-made itineraries to Belize, Mexico and all of Central America. Also agents for many other recommended tour operators.

---

local payment for some meals. Most operate only through the winter period but several run year-round.

BY CARGO SHIP FROM UK AND IRELAND

The days of working as a deck hand for your passage around the world may be over but you can still take the banana **boat to Belize** – though you won't be doing it to save money. A voyage on the *MV Auckland Star* from Waterford, Portsmouth and Flushing to Big Creek, near Placencia in Belize costs £1000 one way (£1850 return) and takes twelve days. Passengers (maximum six) stay in comfortable, a/c cabins on the upper deck, and meals are taken with the ships' officers. If you find the idea interesting contact Cargo Ship Voyages, Hemley, Woodbridge, Suffolk IP12 4QF (☎01473/736265).

BY AIR FROM IRELAND

No airline offers direct **flights from Ireland** to Belize. The cheapest way to get there is to take one of the numerous daily flights from Dublin or Belfast to London and then connect with one of the transatlantic flights covered in the previous section. Fares from Dublin and Belfast to Belize (via London and the US) start from IR£582/£525.

Alternatively you can fly direct from Ireland to the US or Europe and connect easily **to Mexico**, continuing on from there by air (see p.4) or overland (see p.6). Discount fares from Dublin or Belfast to Mexico City range from £430 to £588 return; Iberia often offers a good deal with flights from Dublin (via Madrid) to Mexico City and Cancún at around IR£422–467. There are plenty of other airlines to choose from: BA flies from Dublin to meet its con-

---

USEFUL ADDRESSES IN IRELAND

AIRLINES

Aer Lingus	☎01/844-4777	**Delta** Dublin	☎01-800/768080
British Airways		**Iberia** Dublin	☎01/677-9846
Belfast	☎0345/222-111	**KLM** Belfast	☎0990/750900
Dublin	☎01-800/626742	**Ryanair** Dublin	☎01/609-7800
British Midland			
Belfast	☎ 0345/554554		
Dublin	☎01/283-8833		

SPECIALIST FLIGHT AND TRAVEL AGENTS

Maxwell's Travel D'Olier Chambers, 1 Hawkins St, Dublin 2 (☎01/677-9479; fax 679-3948). *Very experienced in travel to Latin America and Ireland's representatives for many of the specialist tour operators in the box on p.9.*
Trailfinders 4–5 Dawson St, Dublin 2 (☎01/677-7888). *Irish branch of the airfare and indepen-*

dent travel experts. Very good flight and holiday deals.
USIT 19–21 Aston Quay, O'Connell Bridge, Dublin 2 (☎01/602-1700); Fountain Centre, College St, Belfast BT1 6ET (☎01232/324073; Web site www.usit.ie). *All-Ireland student travel agents: 17 offices (mainly on campuses).*

---

nections in London to Mexico City and Cancún; Delta has direct flights from Dublin (and several from Shannon) to JFK and Atlanta, with daily connections to Mexico City; and Aer Lingus flies from Dublin (and in some cases from Shannon), for same-day connections to Mexico City via New York

(JFK), or from Dublin to Amsterdam connecting with a KLM flight to Mexico City. From Belfast, KLM's flights connect with their services from Amsterdam to Mexico City.

To sort out the various possibilities, contact a reliable travel agent, such as USIT.

GETTING THERE FROM AUSTRALIA & NEW ZEALAND

There are no direct flights from Australasia to Belize, and consequently you've little choice but to fly via the US. Fares vary according to the time of year: for most airlines low season is mid-January to the end of February and October to the end of November; high season is mid-May to the end of August and December to mid-January. Seat availability on most international flights out of Australia and New Zealand is often limited, so it's best to book several weeks ahead. The best deals are with Air New Zealand–Continental and United Airlines, who fly daily via LA. Their scheduled low season fares are around A$2299/NZ$2499.

AIRLINES IN AUSTRALIA AND NEW ZEALAND

Air New Zealand Australia ☎13 2476; New Zealand ☎09/357 3000. *Daily from Sydney, Brisbane, Melbourne and Adelaide to LA, either direct or via Honolulu/Tonga/Fiji/Papeete.*

Cathay Pacific Australia ☎13 1747; New Zealand ☎09/379 0861. *Several flights a week to LA from Sydney, Brisbane and Cairns via Hong Kong.*

Continental Airlines Australia ☎02/9321 9242. *Team up with Qantas and Air New Zealand to offer a through service to Belize via LA.*

Garuda Australia ☎02/9334 9944 & 1800/800 873; New Zealand ☎09/366 1855. *Several flights a week to LA from major Australasian cities with a stopover in Denpasar or Jakarta.*

JAL Australia ☎02/9272 1111; New Zealand ☎09/379 9906. *Several flights a week from Sydney, Brisbane, Cairns and Auckland to LA and Mexico City with an overnight stopover in either Tokyo or Osaka included in the fare.*

Philippine Airlines Australia ☎02/9262 3333; no NZ office. *Several flights a week to LA from Sydney, Melbourne or Brisbane with a transfer or overnight stopover in Manila.*

Qantas Australia ☎13 1211; New Zealand ☎09/357 8900 & 0800/808 767. *Daily to LA from major Australian cities either non-stop or via Honolulu and daily from Auckland via Sydney.*

Singapore Airlines Australia ☎13 1011; New Zealand ☎09/379 3209. *Twice a week to LA from major Australian cities and once a week from Auckland via Singapore.*

United Airlines Australia ☎13 1777; New Zealand ☎09/379 3800. *Daily to LA and San Francisco from Sydney, Melbourne and Auckland either direct or via Honolulu.*

Alternatively, you could get a flight to LA or Mexico City, and then an add-on fare to Belize – A$630/NZ$699 from LA, A$313/NZ$345 from Mexico City (both year round flat rate). **From Australia**, the cheapest fares are on flights via Asia, with a stopover en route. JAL flies from Sydney, Brisbane and Cairns to LA or Mexico City with an overnight stop in Tokyo; fares range from A$1550 (low season) to A$1850 (high season).

Other options, though more expensive, are Garuda, via Jakarta or Denpasar, and Philippine Airlines via Manila; both fly to LA and prices start at around A$1750 low season. United Airlines, Qantas and Air New Zealand fly direct to LA from A$1850 low season.

From New Zealand, again the cheapest flight is on JAL via Tokyo, at NZ$1850 low season to NZ$2250 high season. Singapore

TRAVEL AGENTS IN AUSTRALIA AND NEW ZEALAND

Anywhere Travel 345 Anzac Parade, Kingsford, Sydney (☎02/9663 0411).

Brisbane Discount Travel 260 Queen St, Brisbane (☎07/3229 9211).

Budget Travel 16 Fort St, Auckland, plus branches around the city (☎09/366 0061 & 0800/808 040).

Destinations Unlimited 3 Milford Rd, Auckland (☎09/373 4033).

Flight Centres Australia: 82 Elizabeth St, Sydney, plus branches nationwide (☎13 1600). New Zealand: 205 Queen St, Auckland (☎09/309 6171), plus branches nationwide.

Northern Gateway 22 Cavenagh St, Darwin (☎08/8941 1394).

STA Travel Australia: 702 Harris St, Ultimo, Sydney; 256 Flinders St, Melbourne; other offices in state capitals and major universities (nearest branch ☎13 1776, fastfare telesales ☎1300/360 960). New Zealand: 10 High St, Auckland (☎09/309 0458, fastfare telesales ☎09/366 6673), plus branches in Wellington, Christchurch, Dunedin, Palmerston North, Hamilton and at major universities. Email: *traveller@statravelaus.com.au*, Web site *www.statravelaus.com.au*

Thomas Cook Australia: 175 Pitt St, Sydney; 257 Collins St, Melbourne; plus branches in other state capitals (local branch ☎13 1771, Thomas Cook Direct telesales ☎1800/063 913). New Zealand: 96 Anzac Ave, Auckland (☎09/379 3920).

Tymtro Travel Level 8, 130 Pitt St, Sydney (☎02/9223 2211 & 1300 652 969). *Competitive discounts.*

SPECIALIST TOUR AGENTS

Adventure Associates 197 Oxford St, Bondi Junction (☎02/9389 7466; toll-free 1800 222 141). *Two- to twelve-day jungle, archeological and cultural tours.*

Adventure Specialists 69 Liverpool St, Sydney (☎02/9261 2927). *Variety of adventure travel options in Belize.*

Adventure Travel Shop 164 Parnell Rd, Parnell (☎09/377 5770). *Offer a wide selection of adventure tours throughout Central America.*

Adventure World 73 Walker St, North Sydney (☎02/9956 7766 & 1800/221 931), plus branches in Brisbane and Perth; 101 Great South Rd, Remuera, Auckland (☎09/524 5118). *Variety of tours including reef-river cruises.*

Contours 466 Victoria St, N Melbourne (☎03/9329 5211). *Specialists in city stopover packages to Central America ranging from short stays to a 27-day cultural and archeological tour including Mexico.*

Padi Travel Network 4/372 Eastern Valley Way, Chatswood, Sydney (☎9417 2800 & 1800/678 100, email ptn_aust@padi.com.au) and agents throughout Australasia. *Dive packages to the prime sites of the Belize coast.*

Peregrine Adventures 258 Lonsdale St, Melbourne (☎03/9663 8611), plus offices in Brisbane, Sydney, Adelaide and Perth. *Extended overland-sea adventures through Belize.*

Airlines also offers a good connecting service via Singapore to LA for around NZ$2099 (low season) to NZ$2499 (high season); you'll pay around the same for a United Airlines or Air New Zealand flight direct to LA. All of the above fares are from Auckland; expect to pay an extra NZ$150 for Christchurch and Wellington departures.

You could also visit Belize on a **Round the World** fare: Cathay Pacific–UA's "Globetrotter" and *Air New Zealand–KLM-Northwest's* "World Navigator" offer open-jaw travel, limited back-tracking, side trips, and six stopovers worldwide, with additional stopovers at around A$100/ NZ$120 each; prices range from A$2699– 3299/NZ$3189–3699.

Tickets purchased direct from the airlines are usually at published rates; **travel agents** (see box on p.11) offer better deals on fares and have the latest information on limited special offers. If you intend to see something of Mexico or other Central American countries en route to Belize you may want to check out the various **airpasses** on offer; see p.3 for details.

RED TAPE AND ENTRY REQUIREMENTS

All visitors are required to fill in an immigration form on entry, and are generally allowed a stay of thirty days; the stamp can be renewed for Bz$25 each month, for a maximum of six months, after which you may have to leave the country for 24 hours. If you're flying in on a one-way ticket (providing the airline lets you board) be prepared to have to prove your intention to leave the country and show "sufficient funds" for your stay – estimated at US$50 per day – though these conditions are rarely, if ever, enforced upon arrival. Keep your passport with you at all times, or at least carry a photocopy, as you may be asked to show it.

The vast majority of foreign **embassies and consulates** are still in Belize City, with the exception of the UK, Venezuela, Chile, El Salvador and India, who are represented in Belmopan. Addresses of the main ones are given in the relevant chapters, and all current numbers are in the Diplomatic Listings in the green pages of the telephone directory.

Leaving Belize, you have to pay an exit tax (see p.25 for details).

Citizens of the US, Canada, the EU, Australia and New Zealand do not need visas to enter Belize as tourists. Swiss citizens, however, do need a visa (US$25) for which they have to apply to an embassy or consulate in advance – visas are not officially obtainable at the border. There is no charge to enter Belize.

BELIZE REPRESENTATIVES ABROAD

UK Belize High Commission, 22 Harcourt House, 19 Cavendish Sq, London W1M 9AD (☎0171/499 9728, fax 491 4139).

US Embassy of Belize, 2535 Massachusetts Ave NW, Washington DC 20008 (☎202/232-9636); Honorary Consuls throughout the US.

Canada (Honorary Consuls) Suite 3800, South Tower, Royal Bank Plaza, Toronto M5J 2JP (☎416/865-7000, fax 864-70480); in Quebec (☎514/871-4741).

Guatemala Embassy of Belize, Av Reforma, Edificio El Reformador 1–50, Zona 9, Suite 803, Guatemala City (☎334-5531).

Mexico Embassy of Belize, Bernado de Gálves 215, Col. Lomas de Chapultepec, Mexico DF 11000 (☎52-5/203-5642). In **Chetumal** (the border town with Belize) there's a Belize Consul on Av Alvaro Obregón 226/A (☎983/20100).

Switzerland Honorary Consul General, 1 Rue Pedro-Meylan, CP 251, Geneva 17 (☎786-38-89, fax 736-99-39).

In Australia and New Zealand contact the British High Commission, which represents Belize in these countries.

INSURANCE

Travel insurance, in particular medical cover, is a must for a trip to Belize and should include emergency treatment and repatriation by air ambulance. Although there is a modern private hospital in Belize City, in emergencies you may well need treatment in a hospital in the US, so ensure that your policy provides you with a 24-hour medical emergency contact number. Specialist travel policies also offer cover for loss or theft of personal possessions and travel delay, though on some this is optional. Whether you take this part depends on how valuable your equipment is; be warned that theft is common in Belize and expensive-looking luggage attracts attention.

Before shopping around for a policy check first to see what cover you already have. **Bank, credit and charge cards** (particularly American Express and Visa) often have certain levels of medical or other insurance included, especially if you use them to pay for your trip. This can be quite comprehensive, anticipating anything from lost or stolen baggage and missed connections to charter companies going bankrupt, but should still be considered supplementary to full travel insurance; the medical cover, in particular, is usually insufficient for Central America, so check the small print carefully.

If you plan to participate in **water sports**, including scuba-diving or rafting, you may have to pay an extra premium. Most companies can also arrange damage waiver and supplemental liability cover for car hire while abroad. Note also that very few insurers will arrange on-the-spot payments in the event of a major expense or loss; you will usually be **reimbursed** only after going home. In all cases of loss or theft of goods, you will have to contact the local police to have a **report** made out (make sure you get a copy) so that your insurer can process the claim.

NORTH AMERICAN COVER

Before buying an insurance policy, check that you're not already covered. **Canadian provincial health plans** typically provide some overseas medical coverage, although they are unlikely to pick up the full tab in the event of a mishap. Holders of official **student/teacher/youth cards** are entitled to accident coverage and hospital in-patient benefits – the annual membership is far less than the cost of comparable insurance. **Students** may also find that their student health coverage extends during the vacations and for one term beyond the date of last enrolment; if you need extra cover check with the student travel specialists STA or Travel Cuts (see box on p.5). **Homeowners' or renters'** insurance often covers theft or loss of documents, money and valuables while overseas.

After checking the possibilities above, you should still contact a specialist **travel insurance company** (see box opposite). **Policies** vary: some are comprehensive while others cover only certain risks (accidents, illnesses, delayed or lost luggage, cancelled flights, etc.). In particular, ask whether the policy pays medical costs up front or reimburses you later, and whether it provides for medical evacuation to your home country. It's also worth asking if you can extend your cover if you stay abroad longer than planned – World Access and Voyager (see box opposite) for example, allow this if you inform them before your cover expires. For policies that include lost or stolen luggage, check exactly what is and isn't covered, and make sure the per-article limit will cover your most valuable possession. Most North American travel policies apply only to items lost, stolen or damaged while in the custody of an identifiable, responsible third party – hotel porter, airline, lug-

TRAVEL INSURANCE COMPANIES IN NORTH AMERICA

IN THE US

Access America ☎1-800/284-8300

Carefree Travel Insurance
☎1-800/323-3149

STA Travel for International Student Insurance Service (ISIS) ☎1-800/781-4040

Travel Assistance International ☎1-800/821-2828

Travel Guard ☎1-800/826-1300

Travel Insurance Services ☎1-800/937-1387

World Access ☎1-800/955-4002

IN CANADA

Bon Voyage – from Travel Cuts (☎416/979-2406; *www.travelcuts.com*)

Desjardins Travel Insurance ☎1-800/463-7830

Voyager ☎905/799-4062

gage consignment, etc. Even in these cases you will have to contact the local police within a certain time limit to have a complete report made out.

The best **premiums** are usually to be had through student/youth travel agencies – ISIS policies (from STA Travel), for example, cost $48–69 for fifteen days (depending on level of coverage), $80–105 for a month, $149–207 for two months and $510–700 for a year. If you're planning to do any "dangerous sports" (e.g. scuba-diving, caving and mountaineering), be sure to ask whether these activities are covered: some companies levy a surcharge.

BRITISH COVER

Britain no longer has a reciprocal health agreement with Belize, so medical insurance is essential. Comprehensive travel insurance is sold by almost every travel agent (many will offer insurance when you book your flight or holiday), but

you'll almost certainly be better off arranging your own from a **specialist insurance company**. When getting a quote, ask about the level of cover and check if the price includes insurance premium tax – now 17 percent. **Premiums** depend on the level of cover, but work out at £26–40 for one month, £50–90 for three months and £190–300 for a year. If you have a good "all risks" home insurance policy it may well cover your possessions against loss or theft even when overseas; many private medical schemes also cover you when abroad. For any policy make sure you know the procedure and the emergency helpline number.

AUSTRALIAN AND NEW ZEALAND COVER

Travel insurance is put together by the airlines and travel agent groups (see box below) in conjunction with insurance companies, and all are comparable in premium and coverage. Adventure sports are covered, with the exception of mountaineering with ropes, bungee jumping (some policies), and unassisted diving without an Open Water licence; always check the policy first. For Belize, you can expect to pay around A$150/NZ$170 for one month, A$220/NZ$250 for two months and A$280/NZ$320 for three months.

TRAVEL INSURANCE COMPANIES IN THE UK

Club Direct Dominican House, St John's St, Chichester, W Sussex PO19 1TU (☎ 01243/817766).

Columbus Travel Insurance 17 Devonshire Sq, London EC2M 4SQ (☎0171/375 0011).

Endsleigh Insurance 97–107 Southampton Row, London WC1B 4AG (☎0171/436 4451).

Frizzell Insurance Frizzell House, County Gates, Bournemouth, Dorset BH1 2NF (☎01202/292333).

Marcus Hearn 65–66 Shoreditch High St, London E1 6JL (☎0171/739 3444).

TRAVEL INSURANCE COMPANIES IN AUSTRALIA AND NEW ZEALAND

Cover More Level 9/32 Walker St, North Sydney (☎02/9202 8000, toll-free 1800/251 881).

Ready Plan 141 Walker St, Dandenong, Melbourne (☎03/9791 5077, toll-free 1800/337 462); 10/63 Albert St, Auckland (☎09/379 3208).

INFORMATION AND MAPS

There's no shortage of information about Belize available from a variety of different

sources. The Belize Tourist Board offices (see box below) will send out some leaflets and details of travel agents specializing in Belize if you request them. It's also worth asking for a copy of the annual *Destination Belize* magazine, produced by the Belize Tourism Industry Association (BTIA). This useful publication contains information on each area of the country together with a list of all its members – ie, most tourism businesses in the country.

Increasingly however, it's the Internet, with several excellent **Web sites** dedicated to Belize (see box opposite), that provides the best place to start and refine your search for facts and practical details. For more in-depth information, especially if Belize is part of an extended trip to the region, it's a good idea to visit one of the organizations or

---

SOURCES OF INFORMATION ON BELIZE

BELIZE TOURIST BOARD OFFICES

BELIZE: The BTB's main office is in Belize City (listed on p.52): the email address is *btbb@btl.net* and the official Web site *www.belizenet.com* is the best one in the country.
US: 421 Seventh Ave, New York, NY 10001 (☎1-800/624-0686 or 212/563-6011, fax 563-6033).
GERMANY: Bopserwaldstrasse 40-G D-70184, Stuttgart (☎ 711/233-947, fax 233-954; *germany@t-online.de)*.
In **Canada** and the **UK** the consular/diplomatic offices listed on p.13 will be able to provide limited tourist information. There are no tourist offices in Australasia.

OTHER SOURCES OF INFORMATION

Canning House Library 2 Belgrave Sq, London SW1X 8PJ (☎0171/235 2303, Web site www.canninghouse.com). *Has the UK's largest publicly accessible collection of books and periodicals on Latin America, including a comprehensive section on Belize.*
Maya – The Guatemalan Indian Centre 94A Wandsworth Bridge Rd, London SW6 2TF (☎ & fax 0171/371 5291 for opening times, Web site *web.ukonline/jamie.marshall/index.html). For those also planning to visit the Maya areas of*

Guatemala and Mexico, the resource centre here will tell you all you need to know about Maya culture.
Expedition Advisory Centre at the Royal Geographic Society, 1 Kensington Gore, London SW7 2AR (☎0171/591 3030, email eac@rgs.org, Web site www.rgs.org/eac). *Information and advice for those planning an expedition to Belize and/or the rest of Central America from the UK. Publishes a range of specialist books and has reports on previous expeditions.*

SPECIALIST PUBLISHERS

Current political analysis and an interesting and informative overview of the society, economy and environment of Belize and all other Central American countries is provided by two specialist publishers (each can supply the other's publications):
UK: the Latin America Bureau (LAB), 1 Amwell St, London EC1R 1UL (☎0171/278 2829, fax 0171/278 0165, email *lab@gn.apc.org*, Web site *www.lab.org.uk). Publishes* Belize In Focus *(see p.256 for review).*
US: the Resource Center, PO Box 2178, Silver City, NM 88062-2178 (☎505/388-0208, fax 388-0619). *Publishes* Inside Belize *(see p.256 for review).*

BELIZE ON THE INTERNET

Belize must be one of the most online countries outside of (and perhaps even including) the Western world. The number of pages devoted to it increase daily and most organizations and tourist businesses have an email address. Any search engine, such as Alta Vista or Yahoo, will turn up thousands of possibilities; listed below are a few of the best sites to get you started. Other relevant Web sites and email addresses are published throughout the *Guide*.

Latin American Information Center (LANIC)

www.lanic.utexas.edu

The first place to look for detailed, authoritative information on Latin America, including Belize. Comprehensive, logically laid-out homepage and a seemingly never-ending series of superb links; you can reach almost anywhere and anything in Belize connected to the Net from here.

Newsgroup rec.travel.latin-america

The ever-helpful members of this newsgroup will answer any query about travel in Belize and the region. Most have been asked already so there's a huge (and generally accurate) information base for you to dip into.

General information

www.belizenet.com
www.belize.com
www.belizeit.com

Web sites designed and managed by professionals in Belize provide the real online highlights and these are the best – read the newspapers,

surf pages on everything from the Archaeology Department to the Zoo, visit Belize's national parks, look up hotel and tour operators, check email addresses in Belize . . . and for accurate daily TV news broadcasts have a look at www.channel5belize.com.

Belize First

www.turq.com/belizefirst/
and

Belize Report

www.belizereport.com

Two online magazines (most of the contents are free) dedicated to Belize and featuring accurate reviews and articles about hotels, restaurants and destinations. Their travel advice is definitely worth checking out before you go. You can subscribe to either magazine by contacting the editors: for Belize First, Lan Sluder, 280 Beaverdam Rd, Candler, NC 27815 (fax 704/667-1717, email:bzefirst@aol.com); for Belize Report, Pamella Picon, PO Box 1881, Belize City (fax (501) 09/32053, email: editor@belizereport.com).

---

centres (see box opposite) that specialize in Central American history, culture and politics. A comprehensive selection of **books** offering background on all aspects of Belize is listed on p.255; for a broader range of titles contact the specialist publishers detailed in the box below. Finally, for general information on independent travel, pick up a copy of the excellent *Everything You Need to Know Before You Go* by Mark Ashton (Abroadsheet Publications, from specialist bookshops), which packs an enormous amount of essential advice and travel tips on to one (large) glossy sheet.

In Belize, the main **BTB office** is in Belize City (see box on p.16 for details), with other offices in Corozal, San Pedro and Punta Gorda. The staff are very helpful, and will be able to give you a city/town map, a bus, boat and domestic airline schedule and a list of hotels – they may even call hotels for you. In addition there are local

representatives of the BTIA in all resort areas, and of course any tour and travel agents mentioned in the guide will be reliable sources of information. For the latest information on the growing number of reserves and national parks and their associated visitor centres, contact the **Belize Audubon Society** in Belize City (12 Fort St ☎02/35004), which administers many of the country's protected areas, or check with the Conservation Division of the Belize Forestry Department in Belmopan (☎08/22709), which has overall responsibility for Belize's conservation policy and management of protected areas. For in-depth information on social, cultural, political and economic matters concerning Belize, the **Society for the Promotion of Education and Research** (SPEAR; on the corner of Pickstock St and New Rd, Belize City ☎02/31668, fax 32367) has an excellent library and video collection open to all visitors.

MAPS

The best map is the **International Travel Map of Belize** (1:350,000), produced by International Travel Maps (345 West Broadway, Vancouver, BC V5Y 1P8, Canada). Specialist travel bookshops and map outlets should stock it; it's also available from several bookshops in Belize and from *Belize First*

magazine (see box on p.17). Topographic maps produced by Ordnance Survey in UK are available for Belize: two sheets at 1:250,000 cover the whole country, with 44 sheets at 1:50,000 scale providing greater detail, though many are out of date and not all are readily available; try Stanfords in the UK, or, in Belize, the Ministry of Natural Resources in Belmopan (see p.121).

MAP OUTLETS

US

Adventurous Traveler Bookstore PO Box 1468, Williston, VT 05495 (☎1-800/282-3963).

Central American Infocenter PO Box 50211, San Diego, CA 92105 (☎619/583-2925).

The Complete Traveler Bookstore 199 Madison Ave, New York, NY 10016 (☎212/685-9007).

Map Link 30 S La Petera Lane, Unit #5, Santa Barbara, CA 93117 (☎805/692-6777).

The Map Store Inc. 1636 1st St, Washington DC 20006 (☎202/628 2608).

Phileas Fogg's Books & Maps #87 Stanford Shopping Center, Palo Alto, CA 94304 (☎1-800/533-FOGG).

Rand McNally* 444 N Michigan Ave, Chicago, IL 60611 (☎312/321-1751); 150 E 52nd St, New York, NY 10022 (☎212/758-7488); 595 Market St, San Francisco, CA 94105 (☎415/777-3131).

*Call ☎1-800/333-0136 (ext 2111) for other locations, or for maps by mail order.

CANADA

Open Air Books and Maps 25 Toronto St, Toronto, ON M5R 2C1 (☎416/363-0719).

Ulysses Travel Bookshop 4176 St-Denis, Montréal (☎514/289-0993); 101 Yorkville Ave, Toronto, Ontario M5R 1C1 (☎1-800-268-4395).

World Wide Books and Maps, 1247 Granville St, Vancouver, BC, V6Z 1E4 (☎604/687-3320).

UK

Stanfords (see below) in London is the UK's largest map sellers. The UK-wide general book-

sellers Waterstone's and Dillons usually have comprehensive map departments.

Daunt Books 83 Marylebone High St, London W1M 3DE (☎0171/224 2295).

John Smith and Sons 57–61 St Vincent St, Glasgow G2 5TB (☎0141/221 7472).

National Map Centre 22–24 Caxton St, London SW1H 0QU (☎0171/222 2466).

Stanfords 12–14 Long Acre, London WC2E 9LP (☎0171/836 1321); 29 Corn St, Bristol BS1 1HT (☎0117/929 9966). Maps by mail or phone order are available from the London telephone number and via email: *sales@stanfords.co.uk.*

The Travel Bookshop 13–15 Blenheim Crescent, London W11 2EE (☎0171/229 5260).

IRELAND

Easons Bookshop 40 O'Connell St, Dublin 1 (☎01/873 3811).

Waterstone's Queens Bldg, 8 Royal Ave, Belfast BT1 1DA (☎01232/247355).

AUSTRALIA AND NEW ZEALAND

Bowyangs 372 Little Burke St, Melbourne (☎03/9670 4383).

The Map Shop 16a Peel St, Adelaide (☎08/8231 2033)

Perth Map Centre 891 Hay St, Perth (☎08/9322 5733).

Specialty Maps 58 Albert St, Auckland (☎09/307 2217).

Travel Bookshop 20 Bridge St, Sydney (☎02/9241 3554).

HEALTH

Belize has a high standard of public health and most visitors leave without suffering so much as a dose of diarrhoea. Tap water in all towns and many villages is safe to drink, though heavily chlorinated. As a general rule if you have tap water you're in a potable water area, though check first. In rural areas rainwater is collected; it's usually safe and delicious but you might want to treat it (see p.21), especially for children. Restaurants are subject to stringent hygiene regulations, and ice in drinks will almost certainly be made from treated water.

It's still essential to get the best **health advice** you can before you set off; always check with your doctor or a travel clinic (see box on p.20). Many travel clinics also sell travel-related medical supplies such as malaria tablets, mosquito nets and water filters. Regardless of how well prepared you are, **medical insurance** is also essential (see p.14). You might also want to take a travel **medical kit** – these range from a box of band-aids/plasters to a sterilized medical kit, complete with syringes and sutures and are available from clinics, pharmacies and specialist suppliers (see box on p.20).

VACCINATIONS

The only obligatory inoculation for Belize is **yellow fever** and that's only if you're arriving from a "high-risk" area (northern South America and equatorial Africa); carry your vaccination certificate as proof. However, there are several other **inoculations** that you should have anyway, particularly if you intend to spend time in remote rural areas. At least ten weeks before you leave (longer if you plan to be away for more than six months and need several immunizations) check that you are up to date with diphtheria, polio and tetanus jabs and arrange for **typhoid** and **hepatitis A** inoculations. Both typhoid and hepatitis A are transmitted through contaminated food and water. The former is very rare in Belize but the hepatitis A virus is common throughout Central America and can lay a victim low for several months with exhaustion, fever and diarrhoea, and possible liver damage. One dose (£50) of Havrix will give protection for up to a year; a further shot, one year later, gives up to ten years' protection.

Although the risk of contracting **hepatitis B** is low unless you receive unscreened blood products or have unprotected sex, travel clinics often recommend inoculation; a joint hepatitis A and B vaccine is now available from GPs. A course of three injections (£65), takes five weeks and gives up to five years' protection.

Though the risk of **cholera** is considered low in Belize, epidemics occur frequently throughout Central America, though with much less severity in Belize, due to generally good public health education. Spread via food and water, it's an acute bacterial infection recognizable by watery diarrhoea and vomiting. Symptoms (often only mild or even non-existent) are rapidly relieved by prompt medical attention and clean water. The cholera vaccine, which offers only brief and incomplete immunity, is not considered necessary and is no longer available from travel clinics.

Rabies exists in Belize, and vaccination (a course of three shots over a month; around £50) is recommended for anyone travelling to Latin America for over thirty days. If you're here for less time but intend to travel for days in rural areas you should also have the vaccine. The best advice is, as usual, prevention; give dogs a wide berth, and don't play with any animals at all, no matter how cuddly they look. Treat any mammal bite as suspect: wash any wound immediately with soap or detergent and apply alcohol or iodine if possible. Act immediately to get treatment – rabies is fatal once symptoms appear.

North Americans will have to pay for inoculations, available at any immunization centre or at most local clinics. Many GPs in the UK have a travel surgery where you can get advice and certain vaccines on prescription, though they may not administer some of the less common immunizations; most now charge for the service. Travel clinics tend to be cheaper and you can also get vaccinations almost immediately. In Australasia too, travel clinics tend to be less expensive than doctors' surgeries.

MALARIA AND DENGUE FEVER

Malaria, on the increase worldwide, is endemic in many parts of Central America, especially in the rural lowlands, and, though it poses no great threat in Belize – due to an effective nationwide

MEDICAL RESOURCES FOR TRAVELLERS

IN THE UK AND IRELAND

British travellers should pick up a copy of the excellent free booklet **Health Advice for Travellers**, published by the Department of Health and available from GPs' surgeries, many chemists, and most of the agencies listed below. **Nomad Traveller's Store and Medical Centre**, 3–4 Wellington Terrace, Turnpike Lane, London N8 0PX (☎0181/889 7014, email *nomad.travstore@virgin.net*) is the best and most experienced travel equipment shop in the UK, supplying all equipment and travel health needs; it also offers a mail-order service.

British Airways Travel Clinic 156 Regent St, London W1R 5TA (Mon–Fri 9am–4.15pm, Sat 10am–4pm; ☎0171/439 9584) and over 30 other clinics throughout UK: call ☎01276/685040 or check *www.british-airways.com* to find your nearest one. *Excellent medical advice, vaccinations and a comprehensive range of travel health items. No appointments necessary at Regent St; call ahead at other clinics.*

Hospital for Tropical Diseases Travel Clinic Mortimer Market Centre, Capper St, London WC1 (Mon–Fri 9am–5pm; ☎0171/530 3454). *Message service on %0839/337722 (49p per min) gives hints on hygiene, illness prevention and lists of appropriate immunizations; will fax back area-specific health information.*

Trailfinders Travel Clinic 194 Kensington High St, London W8 6BD (☎0171/338 3999); 254–284 Sauciehall St, Glasgow G2 3EH (☎0141/353 0066). *Expert medical advice and a full range of travel vaccines and medical supplies available; no appointments necessary in London. Discounts for Trailfinders clients.*

Travel Medicine Services PO Box 254, 16 College St, Belfast 1 (☎01232/315220). *Operates a travel clinic (Mon 9–11am & Wed 2–4pm) which can give inoculations after referral from a GP.*

Tropical Medical Bureau Grafton St Medical Centre, Dublin 2 (☎01/671 9200, email *tmb@iol.ie*); Dun Laoghaire Medical Centre, 5 Northumberland Ave, Dun Laoghaire, Co. Dublin (☎01/280 4996, email *tropical@iol.ie*, Web site *www.tmb.ie*). *Specialist travel medicine clinics and can give all immunizations.*

IN NORTH AMERICA

Canadian Society for International Health 170 Laurier Ave W, Suite 902, Ottawa, ON K1P 5V5 (☎613/230-2654). *Distributes a free pamphlet "Health Information for Canadian Travellers" containing an extensive list of travel health centres in Canada.*

Centers for Disease Control 1600 Clifton Rd NE, Atlanta, GA 30333 (☎404/639-3311, email *netinfo@cdc.gov*, Web site *www.cdc.gov/travel/camerica*). *Current information on health risks and precautions. Clear and comprehensive Web pages covering Mexico and Central America; check these first if you can.*

International Association for Medical Assistance to Travellers (IAMAT) USA 417 Center St, Lewiston, NY 14092 (☎716/754-4883); Canada 40 Regal Rd, Guelph, ON N1K 1B5 (☎519/836-0102). *Non-profit organization supported by donations. Provides climate charts and leaflets on various diseases and inoculations. IAMAT's list of English-speaking doctors in Central America may be useful if you travel beyond Belize.*

Travel Medicine 351 Pleasant St, Suite 312, Northampton, MA 01060 (☎1-800/872-8633). *Sells first-aid kits, mosquito netting, water filters and other health-related travel products.*

IN AUSTRALIA AND NEW ZEALAND

Auckland Hospital Park Rd, Grafton (☎09/797 440).

Travel-Bug Medical and Vaccination Centre 161 Ward St, N Adelaide (☎08/8267 3544).

Travel Health and Vaccination Clinic 114 Williams St, Melbourne (☎03/9670 2020).

Travellers' Medical and Vaccination Centre Level 7, 428 George St, Sydney (☎02/9221 7133); Level 3, 393 Little Bourke St, Melbourne (☎03/9602 5788); Level 6, 29 Gilbert Place, Adelaide (☎08/8212 7522); Level 6, 247 Adelaide St, Brisbane (☎07/3221 9066); 1 Mill St, Perth (☎08/9321 1977).

Travellers Immunization Service 303 Pacific Hwy, Sydney (☎02/9416 1348).

control programme – you should still take all the recommended precautions. The recommended prophylactic in Belize is Chloroquine; you need to start taking the tablets one week before arrival and continue for four weeks after leaving the area. **Avoiding bites** in the first place is the best prevention; sleep in screened rooms or under nets, burn mosquito coils containing permethrin, cover up arms and legs (especially around dawn and dusk when the mosquitoes are most active) and use insect repellent containing over 35 percent Deet. Keeping mosquitoes at bay is doubly important in the case of **dengue fever** – a viral infection transmitted by mosquitoes also active during the day – for which there is no vaccine or specific treatment. The first symptom is a fever, accompanied by severe joint and muscle pains, which subsides, only to recur a few days later, this time with a rash likely to spread all over the body. After this second outbreak the fever and rash subside and recovery is usually complete. Epidemic outbreaks of dengue are frequent in Belize.

INTESTINAL TROUBLES

Despite any dire warnings, a bout of **diarrhoea** is the medical problem you're most likely to encounter in Belize, generally caused by the change of diet and exposure to unfamiliar bacteria. Following a few simple precautions should help keep you healthy though; be sure to drink clean water (any bottled drinks, including beer and soft drinks are already purified; for more advice on water, see p.35), steer clear of raw shellfish and don't eat anywhere that is obviously dirty. If you do go down with a dose, the best cure is also the simplest: take it easy for a day or two, eat only the blandest of foods – papaya is good

for soothing the stomach and also crammed with vitamins – and, most importantly, ensure that you replace lost fluids and salts by drinking lots of bottled water and taking rehydration salts. If you can't get hold of rehydration salts, half a teaspoon of salt and three of sugar in a litre of water will do the trick. If diarrhoea lasts more than three or four days, is accompanied by a fever, or you see blood in your stools, seek immediate medical help.

If you're spending any time in rural areas you're also likely to pick up **parasitic infections**: protozoa – amoeba and giardia – and intestinal worms. These sound (and can be) hideous, but they're treatable once detected. If you suspect you may have an infestation take a stool sample to a pathology laboratory and go to a doctor or pharmacist with the test results. More serious is **amoebic dysentery**, endemic in many parts of the region. The symptoms are more or less the same as a bad dose of diarrhoea, but include bleeding. On the whole, a course of flagyl (metronidazole or tinidozole) will cure it; if you plan to visit the far-flung corners of Central America then it's worth carrying these, just in case, but get advice on their usage from a doctor before you go.

Finally, if you're using the Pill – or any other orally administered drug – bear in mind that severe diarrhoea can reduce its efficacy.

HEAT TROUBLE

Another common cause of discomfort and even illness is the sun. Build up exposure gradually, use a strong sunscreen and, if you're walking around during the day, wear a hat and try to keep in the shade. Be aware that overheating can cause **heatstroke**, which is potentially fatal. Signs are a very high

WATER PURIFICATION

Contaminated water is a major cause of illness amongst travellers in Central America, due to the presence of pathogenic organisms: bacteria, viruses and cysts. However, in Belize, water in most hotels and resorts will be treated, and bottled water is widely available; you will only need to consider treating the water if you travel to remote areas. While boiling water for ten minutes kills most micro-organisms, it's not the most convenient method. **Chemical sterilization** with iodine tablets is effective, but the resulting liquid

doesn't taste very pleasant (though it can be masked with lemon or lime juice) and you'll probably want to filter the water as well. (Iodine is unsafe for pregnant women, babies and people with thyroid complaints.) Portable **water purifiers**, which sterilize and filter the water, give the most complete treatment. Travel clinics (see box opposite) and good outdoor equipment shops will stock a range of water treatment products; their experts will give you the best advice for your particular needs.

body temperature without a feeling of fever, accompanied by headaches and disorientation. Lowering body temperature (a tepid shower, for example) is the first step in treatment. You should also avoid **dehydration** by taking plenty of fluids, especially water, and if you know you're going to be hiking in the jungle for days you might want to bring oral rehydration tablets or powder, though you'll still need pure water to reconstitute them.

BITES AND STINGS

Apart from the malaria-carrying mosquitoes, there are several other biting insects and animals whose nips could leave you in varying degrees of discomfort. **Sandflies**, often present on beaches, are tiny but their bites, usually on feet and ankles, itch like hell and last for days. Head or body **lice** can be picked up from people or bedding, and are best treated with medicated soap or shampoo. **Ticks**, which you're likely to pick up if you're walking or riding in areas with domestic livestock (and sometimes in the forests generally) need careful removal with tweezers – those in a Swiss Army knife are ideal.

Scorpions are common, but mostly nocturnal, hiding during the heat of the day under rocks and in crevices. You're unlikely to be stung but if you're camping, or sleeping in a rustic cabaña, shake your shoes out before you put them on and avoid wandering around barefoot. Their sting is painful (occasionally fatal) and can become infected, so you should seek medical treatment if the pain seems significantly worse than a bee sting. You're even less likely to be bitten by a spider, but the advice is the same – seek medical treatment if the pain persists or increases. You're unlikely to see any **snakes** and most are harmless in any case; if you're walking through undergrowth, wearing boots and long trousers will go a long way towards preventing a bite – tread heavily and they'll usually slither away. If you do get bitten remember what the snake looked like (kill it if you can), immobilize the bitten limb as far as possible and seek medical help: antivenins are available in most hospitals.

Swimming and snorkelling might bring you into contact with some potentially dangerous or venomous sea creatures. You're extremely unlikely to be a victim of a shark attack (though the dubious practice of shark-feeding as a tourist attraction is growing, and could lead to an accidental bite), but **jellyfish** are common and all corals will sting. Some, like the Portuguese man-o'-war jellyfish, with its distinctive purple, bag-like sail, have very long tentacles with stinging cells, and an encounter will result in raw, red weals. Equally painful is a brush against fire coral: in each case, clean the wound with vinegar or iodine and seek medical help if the pain persists or infection develops. See "rabies" (p.19) for advice on mammal bites.

GETTING MEDICAL HELP

Doctors in Belize will have received training abroad, often in the US, and are generally up to date with current treatments. Your embassy will have a list of recommended doctors, and a doctor is included in our "Listings" for Belize City (see p.61). A visit to a doctor will cost around Bz$30 and then you'll have to pay extra for medicines and treatment, which can be expensive. However, if you suspect all is not well with your insides, it might be worth heading straight for the local pathology lab (all the main towns have them) before seeing a doctor, as he/she will probably send you there anyway. **Pharmacists** are knowledgeable and helpful and sometimes sell drugs over the counter (if necessary) which are only available by prescription at home. Belize is also a centre for **herbal remedies**, and if you have confidence in complementary medicine you can seek advice from a number of respected practitioners – see p.132 for details of Ix Chel Tropical Research Centre.

Many rural communities have a health centre where health care is free, although there may be only a nurse or health-worker available and you can't rely on seeing a doctor immediately. Should you need an injection or transfusion, make sure that the equipment is sterile (it might be worth bringing a sterile kit from home) and ensure any blood you receive is screened. For anything serious you should go to the best hospital you can reach.

TRAVELLERS WITH DISABILITIES

The very nature of Belize's abundant natural attractions often makes much of the country inaccessible to anyone with a disability. Travelling around by public transport (with the possible exception of taxis which tend to be huge American saloon or estate cars) would be difficult: there's no provision for wheelchairs and much travel is by boat, with the attendant difficulty of getting in and out. Paved streets exist only in the towns, and even there sidewalks are virtually non-existent; you won't find either in coastal and caye resort locations.

Few hotels have smooth paths from the road and even in ground-floor rooms you often have steps to negotiate. Indeed many hotels have all **accommodation** upstairs – and only two have elevators. However, if you stay in places at the higher end of the range, it's more likely that there will be staff on hand to help out, and if you're determined, you can find a few places that are more suitable for disabled visitors, with accessible ground-floor rooms and other facilities. The only hotel which has specifically adapted rooms and facilities for disabled visitors is *Hok'ol K'in*, in Corozal (see p.83). Planning well ahead is essential; the organizations in the box below may be able to help with general information and advice.

CONTACTS FOR TRAVELLERS WITH DISABILITIES

US

Society for the Advancement of Travel for the Handicapped (SATH) 347 5th Ave, Suite 610, New York, NY 10016 (☎212/447-7284, Web site *www.sittravel.com*). *Non-profit travel-industry referral service that passes queries on to its members as appropriate; allow plenty of time for a response.*
Travel Information Service (☎215/456-9600). *Telephone information and referral service.*

UK

RADAR (Royal Association for Disability and Rehabilitation) 12 City Forum, 250 City Rd, London EC1V 8AF (☎0171/250 3222, Minicom ☎0171/250 4119). *A good source of advice on holidays and travel abroad. Produce a guide for long-haul holidays (both £5 inc. p&p).*

AUSTRALIA AND NEW ZEALAND

ACROD (Australian Council for Rehabilitation of the Disabled), PO Box 60, Curtin, ACT 2605 (☎02/6282 4333).
Disabled Persons Assembly 173–175 Victoria St, Wellington (☎04/811 9100).

MONEY, COSTS AND BANKS

Belize has the unfortunate but generally well-deserved reputation as the most expensive country in Central America; even on a tight budget you'll spend at least forty percent more than you would in say, Guatemala. And, if you've been travelling cheaply through Mexico to get here, many prices are going to come as a shock. Perhaps as compensation for the general cost of living you can travel in the sure knowledge that you'll be paying the same prices as the locals and you'll never have the mysterious (and sometimes illegal) charges levied that are sometimes imposed on foreigners elsewhere in the region.

CURRENCY AND EXCHANGE

Prices and exchange rates are fairly stable, with the national currency, the **Belize dollar**, firmly (and very conveniently) fixed at the rate of two to the US dollar **(Bz$2 = US$1)**. Because of the fixed exchange rate, US dollars (cash and travellers' cheques) are also accepted – and in some places even preferred – everywhere as currency. This apparently simple dual currency system can be problematic, however, as you'll constantly need to ask which dollar is being referred to; it's all too easy to assume the price of your hotel room or trip is in Belize dollars, only to discover on payment that the price referred to was in US dollars – a common cause of misunderstanding and aggravation. Prices in the *Guide* are usually quoted in Belize dollars – always preceded by the symbol Bz$.

The Belize dollar is divided into 100 cents. Bank notes come in denominations of 2, 5, 10, 20,

50 and 100 dollars; coins in denominations of 1, 5, 10, 25, 50 cents and 1 dollar. All notes and coins carry the British imperial legacy in the form of a portrait of Queen Elizabeth – and quarters are called "shillings".

For currency **exchange** on arrival, there's a branch of the Belize Bank at the international airport; a cash advance here will cost more than at other banks in the country, though all banks offer a lower rate than simply spending or exchanging US$ cash dollars. You'll find there's at least one **bank** (generally Mon–Thurs 8am–2.30pm, Fri 8am–4.30pm) in every town, and there's also one on Caye Caulker. **Cash US$** (very useful for leaving the country) can be bought easily from the banks; alternatively your hotel or restaurant may sell you some.

Mexican *pesos* and Guatemalan *quetzales* are easily exchanged at the airport and at land borders. There are no banks at either of the two land border crossings, though you can find them in the nearby towns of Corozal (for the Mexican border) and San Ignacio (for the Guatemalan border). **Changing money at borders** is no problem, however, as you'll be swamped by moneychangers, offering fair rates for travellers' cheques and cash and often at slightly higher rates than the standard Bz$2 for US$1, especially for larger sums; anywhere else beware of rip-offs. Heading for Honduras you'll find *lempiras* more difficult to get hold of, so again, cash US$ will come in handy. If you're leaving for good make sure you get rid of all your Belize dollars before you go.

TRAVELLERS' CHEQUES AND BANK CARDS

Travellers' cheques, formerly the safest and most popular way to carry your money, are rapidly being superseded by plastic, but it's always a good idea to have some for emergencies (perhaps 15–20 percent of your spending money). **Credit and debit cards** are widely accepted in Belize, and increasingly even in smaller hotels and restaurants, though always check what the charge will be for using it – many places add an extra five or even seven percent for the privilege. Visa is the most useful card in Belize but Mastercard is also accepted fairly widely. You can use cards (remember your PIN) to get cash in

Belize and US dollars (except when crossing land borders, which is where travellers' cheques and US$ cash come in handy) from some **ATMs** (only Barclays at present) and over the counter at banks.

Charges for using your card in Belize depend on both the card issuers' regulations – most charge a handling fee of one to two percent and perhaps a set fee of a few dollars each time you withdraw cash – and on which bank you use. At the time of writing, Barclays makes no additional local charge for cash withdrawals, whereas the Belize Bank charges Bz$15 per use: so check first. If you lose your card or it gets stolen, you'll have to get a replacement sent out by courier – the big banks and card issuers can get one to you within two days. A good security policy is to get another card for emergency use only.

COSTS

Costs in Belize are generally lower than those in North America and Europe, though not necessarily by very much and what you spend will obviously depend on where, when and how you choose to travel. Peak tourist seasons, such as Christmas and Easter, tend to push hotel prices up, and certain tourist centres are notably more expensive. VAT, introduced in 1996, increased costs, but the rate of inflation is low. Locally produced goods are cheap but anything imported is overpriced.

As a general rule, a solo budget traveller will need around US$25 per day to cover the basics (accommodation, food and transport); trips such as snorkelling or canoeing will be extra. Travelling as a couple will reduce the per-person costs slightly, but to travel comfortably and enjoy the best of Belize's natural attractions you need to allow at least US$35 per person per day.

A **basic room** will cost at least US$7.50 for a single, US$14 for a double; in many cases you'll pay more than this – a night in an upmarket lodge will set you back anything from US$65 to US$150. Food and drink are fairly pricey too, with an average breakfast costing around US$3–5, a simple lunch US$5–7 and dinner US$6–8. A small bottle of Belikin beer costs at least US$1.70 – well overpriced but it's the only local brew; imported beer costs over twice as much. **Bus travel** is much more reasonable with the longest bus ride in the

country, Belize City to Punta Gorda, costing US$11. A **taxi** ride within a town costs US$2.50 for one or two people. Travelling by car is expensive – the cost of rental is higher in Belize than it is in the US, as is the cost of fuel, though this is still often cheaper than in Europe.

MONEY PROBLEMS

Having **money wired** from home is never convenient or cheap, and should only be considered as a last resort. From the US and Canada, funds can be sent via **Western Union** (☎1-800/325-6000) or American Express MoneyGram (☎1-800/543-4080) to several offices in Belize. Both companies' fees depend on the destination and the amount being transferred, but you can expect a charge of around $75 to send $1000. The funds should be available for collection at Amex's or Western Union's local office within minutes of being sent. It's also possible to have money wired directly from a bank in your home country to a bank in Belize, although this is somewhat less reliable because it involves two separate institutions: from the UK, Barclays is the best option as they have branches in Belize. If you go this route, the person wiring the funds to you will need to know the routing number of the bank in Belize.

TAX AND TIPPING

In Belize, hotel rooms are subject to a seven percent **tax**. The fifteen percent VAT, which applies to most goods and services does not apply to hotel rooms, though some package operators may slap it on anyway; check carefully to see what you're paying for. Leaving Belize you must pay a Bz$22.50 **exit tax** at the international airport. In addition there's a conservation exit tax, the PACT, an extra Bz$7.50 payable at all exit points.

Tipping is by no means commonplace in Belize, and in most budget hotels and restaurants it's certainly not expected, though it's a nice gesture to leave some change if the staff have been helpful. When you get to the more expensive resorts you'll often find that they will impose a **service charge** of around ten percent on top of the bill. It's really up to you as to whether you pay it, as rates are quite high anyway. Check at the time of booking if you can, and only agree to accept this if you're satisfied.

ACCOMMODATION

Most accommodation in Belize is in the form of hotels and guest houses – generally small family-run places found mainly in towns – or cabaña-style rustic rooms, found in the countryside and on the more isolated parts of the cayes. In each category there is a wide range of choice and prices and it's generally easy to find somewhere reasonable. Towns in Belize are so small that you can usually walk to the majority of the hotels from the bus stop and see what's on offer; even in Belize City most places are within 1.5km of the Swing Bridge. For much of the year occupancy rates are very low, so you'll have no difficulty finding a room, even in the high season. Exceptions, when you'll almost certainly need to book ahead in resort areas, are Christmas, New Year and Easter.

The charming, often ramshackle, two-storey, clapboard buildings found throughout the former British Caribbean, and the lovely rustic **cabañas**, built of local hardwoods and often roofed with thatch, are among the most appealing places to stay, but for real holiday heaven, it's the small **guest houses**, often in beautifully restored colonial buildings in Belize City or on the cayes, that provide some of the best accommodation in the country. In some villages and rural areas you can also find inexpensive **bed and breakfast rooms** in private houses. Many of these are delightful and you'll be treated more as an extra member of the family than a guest, but others can be uncomfortable, with lumpy mattresses and poor ventilation – the best-value places are mentioned in the *Guide*. Note that serviceable insect proofing can make the difference here between misery and a good night's sleep. If money's no problem, you could try one of the delightful family-run **resorts and lodges**, usually set in spectacular locations. Finally, in Toledo, the Maya villages run a village guest house programme (see p.195), allowing you the opportunity to experience rural Belize in a very different way to most tourists.

The **cost** of accommodation in Belize is notably higher than that of surrounding countries, but there are bargains available and you'll soon get used to finding what's on offer in your preferred price and style of accommodation. A simple double room usually costs at least Bz$25 (just over half for a single). Many of the mid-range and more upmarket hotels are happy to give discounts to visitors using the *Rough Guide*, especially out of season. They may also offer you a discount for booking direct; don't be afraid to ask. Many of these hotels have an email address and even a homepage on the Internet: where an email

---

ACCOMMODATION PRICE CODES

All accommodation listed in this guide has been given a **price code** according to the following scale. The prices refer to the cost of **a double room in high season** (generally Dec to Easter) in Belize dollars (Bz$) but (unless otherwise stated in the text) do not include the government hotel tax of seven percent. Note that some establishments also add a service charge: make sure you realise you're agreeing to pay these charges in addition to the quoted price when you take the room. To get the equivalent price in US$ simply divide by two.

① under Bz$20	④ Bz$50–70	⑦ Bz$140–190
② Bz$20–30	⑤ Bz$70–100	⑧ Bz$190–240
③ Bz$30–50	⑥ Bz$100–140	⑨ over Bz$240

address exists we've given it in the listing for the hotel; you can find links to hotel homepages from the recommended Web sites on p.17.

It's always a good idea, especially in budget places, to have a look at the room before you take it; check that the light and fan work, and if you've been told there's hot water, see just what that means. There's no official hotel rating system in Belize, though all hotels are inspected by the Tourist Board before a licence is issued. If you have a complaint and the hotel owner or manager doesn't deal with it satisfactorily, you can take it to the BTB (see p.52) or the Belize Tourism Industry Association (BTIA), PO Box 62, 10 North Park St, Belize City (☎02/75717, fax 78710).

BUDGET AND MID-RANGE HOTELS

Most small **hotels** are family run, and the owners generally take pride in the cleanliness of the rooms. Check-in is typically informal – you'll usually have to pay in advance and sign the register. There may be a place to hand-wash clothes; ask first before you use it.

Budget hotels (①–③, see p.26) run the whole gamut of standards. As a rule, a basic room will have a bed, light and fan, and all but the most rock-bottom of places will supply a towel, soap and toilet paper. You'll often have the option of a private bathroom; worth paying a little extra for. In most places a fan will be more important than hot water, though nowadays even budget hotels have hot water at least some of the time.

In Belize City, you'll pay at least Bz$28 for a simple double room; add about Bz$10 for a private bathroom. Oddly enough, budget rooms in the popular tourist areas of Caye Caulker, San Ignacio and Placencia are usually less expensive, though you'll pay slightly more in San Pedro. You won't find any budget accommodation in Orange Walk or the capital, Belmopan, but both places have attractive, budget hotels less than an hour away.

Rooms in **mid-range hotels** vary from Bz$50 to Bz$190; they'll be more likely to have a private bathroom as standard and probably a private balcony. Many will have the option of air conditioning.

In towns it's sometimes better to get a room at the back, away from the street noise, although people-watching from the front balcony can be fascinating. In an upstairs room you're more likely to benefit from a breeze – arrive early at your destination to get the best selection of rooms.

In the countryside, especially in Cayo, you can occasionally get a good-value deal (around Bz$100) on a cabaña out of season, though most of them belong in the next section.

RESORTS AND LODGES

With more money to spend, you could stay in a very comfortable private cabaña at one of the **resorts**, many of which are family run and have spectacular beach or atoll locations. Alternatively, head inland to one of the beautiful **jungle lodges**, often in or near national parks and offering private, thatched cabañas, with a balcony overlooking the forest or a river. Expensive they may be, but the extra dollars will soon be forgotten as you watch the sun rise over the reef or hear the rainforest dawn chorus.

Resorts and lodges are often used by specialist diving, adventure and nature tour operators (pp.5, 6 & 9), and some only take guests on a complete package, which includes transport, meals and some activities. Rates start at US$85 for a double room per night, and can go up to over US$200 per person on some of the more expensive packages. Watch out for the service charge (see p.26), often added on top of the bill, which, combined with the seven percent hotel tax, can raise the price considerably.

CAMPING

Formal **camping** facilities are few and far between in Belize, and the country's only trailer park, in Corozal, is small and fairly basic in comparison with anything in the US or Canada. Specialist camping supplies are scarce or unobtainable, so don't expect to find camping gaz cartridges or Coleman fuel, though kerosene is widely available.

Generally, a tent will only really be of use if you're planning to hike off the beaten track; you'll probably have a guide who'll direct you to places where you can pitch a tent or sling a hammock. You might also want to take a tent if you're hiking around the Maya villages in southern Toledo, though many villages have a simple guest house. Some of the rural resorts in Cayo and in villages throughout Belize do have camping space but you won't find anywhere on Ambergris Caye or Caye Caulker. Places where you can pitch a tent are detailed in the text; the location is usually superb.

You can only camp in forest reserves and national parks if you obtain special permission from the Forestry Department in Belmopan. Two notable exceptions are the Jaguar Reserve (p.179), and the forestry village of Augustine in the Mountain Pine Ridge (p.137); you can also camp at the privately owned Black Cat reserve (p.180).

GETTING AROUND

Belize has a good public transport network. Buses along the paved Northern and Western highways are reliable, cheap, frequent and fairly fast; the south has fewer buses and paved roads, but scheduled services are improving all the time. Most places on the mainland are well served by buses; you can get to all the towns and most villages, though naturally it takes a while to get to some of the more distant corners of the country. At some point during your visit you'll probably travel by boat – out to and between the cayes obviously – but maybe along rivers too, or even further afield to Guatemala and Honduras.

If you can afford it, **flying** is a good way to travel around Belize – especially to the south, where buses take a while, or out to San Pedro, when you get superb views of the hills and the clear blue sea, skimming along at low altitude in a small plane. **Car rental** in Belize is very expensive, (US$60–100 per day), but it does enable you to visit more places in a short time than you could by bus. Cars and four-wheel-drive trucks are readily available from several companies in Belize City.

BUSES

The vast majority of **buses** in Belize are of the US schoolbus type (equivalent to a second-class service). Luxury, **express buses** operate along the Northern and Western highways but they stop only in the main towns. Non-express buses will stop anywhere along their route; tell the driver or conductor where you're heading for and they'll

usually know the best place to let you off. Details of bus services are given in the text; note that, on Sundays, some services are reduced, or, in the case of smaller local services, often non-existent.

Along the Northern Highway all buses cross the border and go into the Mexican town of Chetumal; on the Western Highway, though some buses terminate in San Ignacio or Benque, most continue to the border town of Melchor de Mencos in Guatemala. Services on both routes are particularly good, with departures at least every hour throughout the day. The Hummingbird and Southern highways, to Dangriga, Placencia and Punta Gorda, aren't quite as well served, though there are at least eight daily buses to Dangriga, three to Placencia and five to Punta Gorda (a good eight hours from Belize City).

Heading away from the main highways you'll be relying on the **local bus services** operated by smaller local companies. In many cases these own just one bus, so a breakdown can bring the whole service to a halt. Travelling by local bus tends to be a very slow business as it caters to the needs of the villagers – taking produce to the market, transporting building materials and so on – but it has its rewards; you're in contact with people who know the area well, and by the time you get to the village you'll have made friends who'll be only too pleased to show you around.

Fares are a bargain in comparison with the cost of most things in Belize: on the regular buses you'll pay Bz$5 from Belize City to San Ignacio; Bz$10 to Chetumal; and Bz$22 to Punta Gorda (the longest bus ride in the country). Tickets on express buses are about fifteen percent more. You'll always get an assigned seat if you board at the bus station; pay the conductor if you get on along the route. With the exception of holiday times when buses can get very crowded, there's usually no need to buy tickets in advance – just get to the bus station half an hour or so before departure to get your preferred seat. On the express services some tickets include a snack breakfast or lunch and there's usually a video to watch. Luggage usually goes inside the bus, at the back, though some buses have luggage compartments underneath: theft of luggage from buses in Belize is very rare indeed, but it still pays to keep your eyes on your belongings as people get in and out of the back door.

MAIN BUS COMPANIES IN BELIZE

See p.62 for addresses and telephone numbers.

Batty *The best bus company in the country, running the morning services (including expresses) on both the Northern Highway from Belize City to Chetumal (calling at Orange Walk and Corozal), and the Western Highway to San Ignacio and Melchor (calling at Belmopan), with return services in the afternoon. Also run to Crooked Tree.*

Novelos *Afternoon services (including expresses) on the Western Highway from Belize City to San Ignacio, Belmopan and Melchor, returning from early morning until midday.*

Venus *Afternoon services from Belize City to Chetumal, calling at Orange Walk and Corozal,*

returning from early morning until midday. Also runs buses to Sarteneja.

Z-Line *Services from Belize City on the Hummingbird and Southern highways to Dangriga and Punta Gorda, some calling at Belmopan, others using the Coastal Road shortcut. Also buses go to Placencia.*

Other bus companies serve the same destinations and various villages in Belize; the locations, schedules and telephone numbers of relevant companies are given in the *Guide.*

PLANES

The main towns and tourist destinations in Belize are linked by a reasonable network of **domestic flights** operated by two main scheduled carriers, Maya Island Air (☎02/31140, in US ☎1-800/422-3435) and Tropic Air (☎02/45671, in US ☎1-800/422-3435), and a number of charter airlines – Cari Bee Air Service (☎02/44253) and Javier's Flying Service (☎02/35360) are recommended. Together they provide up to eight or nine daily flights on each of the main routes – Belize City to Dangriga (Bz$55), Placencia (Bz$105) and Punta Gorda (Bz$135) – and literally dozens to San Pedro and Caye Caulker (Bz$47). There are no direct flights from Belize City to Corozal but you can fly there from San Pedro (Bz$74). Only charters fly to Belmopan and San Ignacio. The prices quoted above include tax and are for scheduled flights from Belize Municipal Airport (2km north of the city centre). All scheduled flights connect with Belize International Airport; departing from there you'll pay an extra Bz$30 for the destinations listed. Seat availability isn't usually a problem, except during the very busiest days of the peak season.

Flying is also the most convenient way to make side trips out of Belize to neighbouring countries. Domestic airlines and Aerovias operate **international flights** to **Flores and Guatemala City** – popular with those who can't face the rigours of the road. Chetumal and **Cancún** are served regularly by Aerocaribe and there are frequent departures and connections to **San Pedro Sula** in

Honduras. You can also make daily connections to **Roatán**, one of the Bay Islands (p.209), or fly there direct (Sat only) with Caribbean Air. Finally, the main international carriers fly daily from Belize to San Salvador, Taca's home base and the main hub for flights throughout Central America. If you think you're likely to need several flights it's worth considering an airpass (see p.3 for further details).

BOATS

Your first experience of water transport in Belize is likely to be aboard one of the fast **skiffs** that ferry passengers (around twenty at a time) from Belize City and other mainland destinations out to the **cayes**. Mostly open, though some have cabins, they provide a quick, reliable and safe service. If you're going in an open boat, always take some kind of light, waterproof coat – showers can occur at any time of year and you'll chill quickly as you speed along in the rain.

There are several scheduled services daily from the Marine Terminal next to the Swing Bridge in Belize City, to the most popular destinations: Caye Caulker and San Pedro on Ambergris Caye. A regular service operates between these two islands and most boats on the Caye Caulker/San Pedro run will also call at St George's Caye on request. There's no real need to book tickets in advance for these journeys, though it's worthwhile buying your ticket the day before for early departures *from* the cayes. From Dangriga there are daily boats to Tobacco Caye (no schedule) and the scheduled boat to Glover's

Reef (p.177) leaves on Sunday mornings. Times and destinations of all scheduled boats are detailed in the text. Travel to other cayes and atolls is usually done as part of a tour or package, such as the dive boats operating out of San Pedro.

Several daily **tour boats** leave Placencia for trips along the Monkey River (p.188) and others ply the New River from Orange Walk to visit the ruins of Lamanai (p.75). Alternatively, you could charter a boat for travel along the rivers and amongst the islands. If you're planning to explore the country's river network then San Ignacio is the ideal base, with **canoes** readily available to rent for an hour or a week; you can also rent canoes in Bermudian Landing and a growing number of other locations.

The only **international boat services** are the daily skiffs from Punta Gorda to Puerto Barrios in Guatemala and the weekly skiff from Dangriga to Puerto Cortés in Honduras; you'll need to book ahead for international departures by checking with the boat operator the day before.

DRIVING

Despite the fact that Belize has only four main roads, one of which (the Southern Highway) isn't yet surfaced along its entire length, **driving** is a popular option among visitors. The main roads, and even most unpaved side roads, are generally well maintained and usually passable except in the very worst rainstorms, though mud or dust can be a problem at any time. Traffic is generally light outside Belize City but driving standards are abysmal and fatal accidents are high in relation to traffic density. Under Belize's **seatbelt law**, you'll be fined Bz$25 for not belting up.

Driving in Belize is subject to the same limitations as bus travel. The Northern and Western highways offer easy motoring and smooth roads, as does most of the Hummingbird Highway – the first twenty kilometres south of Belmopan are in terrible condition but beyond that section you can enjoy some of the best road surface in the country. However, if you want to make your way down south or head off the beaten track, you'll need high clearance and possibly four-wheel drive. South of Dangriga, distances are long and the Southern Highway is mostly unpaved, though well graded. The first 25km section from Punta Gorda is now paved, with the rest scheduled for completion in the next few years. **Fuel** is about Bz$4.50 per gallon (which is how it's sold) and unleaded is available; bear in mind when planning your journey that filling stations are scarce outside the towns.

The best guide to Belize's roads is Emory King's *Driver's Guide to Beautiful Belize*, updated annually and sold at hotels and filling stations throughout the country. The slim volume contains recommendations heavily weighted towards advertisers, but the maps and distances are accurate and it offers a characteristically Belizean account of the road network. You'll also need a copy of the International Travel Map (see p.18).

If you've succeeded in getting your own car to Belize (see p.7) any further problems you face are likely to seem fairly minor. **Insurance** is available from an agent just inside either of the land border crossings or in Belize City. Note that some spare parts can be difficult to get hold of.

CAR RENTAL IN BELIZE

All the main **car rental companies** offer cars, jeeps and four-wheel drives for between Bz$150 and Bz$200 a day, plus Bz$30 per day for insurance. They have desks at the international airport, but you might prefer the convenience of booking ahead at an office in your home country (most major companies will offer a service in Belize); this can save money and gives you the certainty of a car waiting for you on arrival.

You'll probably have to leave a credit card imprint when you pick up the car, but before you belt up and drive off into the sunset, check exactly what the **insurance** covers, examine the car carefully for signs of existing damage (and make sure this is marked on the hire contract) and check what spares and equipment are included. A good spare wheel (and the tools to put it on) is essential – you'll get an average of one puncture a week from some heavy driving on Belize's roads. Most rental companies won't allow you to take their vehicles across borders but Crystal, which also offers some of the best rental prices, will let you take their cars to Tikal.

See Belize City "Listings" on p.61 for details of local car rental companies.

TAXIS

All **taxis** in Belize are licensed and easily identifiable by their green licence plates. They operate from ranks in the centres of towns and, particularly in Belize City, drivers will call out to anyone they suspect is a foreigner. There are no meters so you'll need to establish a rate in advance, though within the towns a fixed fare of Bz$5 for one or two people usually applies. From the international airport designated airport taxis charge Bz$30 to Belize City; taxis will almost certainly be waiting for all scheduled domestic flights.

HITCHING

In the more remote parts of Belize the bus service will probably only operate once a day, if at all, so unless you have your own transport, **hitching** is the only other option. The main drawback is the lack of traffic, but if cars or, more likely, pickup trucks, do pass, the driver will usually offer you a lift, though you may be expected to offer some money for the ride. On the plus side, seeing the countryside from the back of a pickup is a wonderful experience – provided you sit on some sort of padding.

CYCLING

Seeing Belize from a **bike** is fairly straightforward, particularly in the north and west where the roads are well surfaced. Cycling is popular; you'll find repair shops in all the towns and there's even a sponsored "Hike and Bike for the Rainforest" in Cayo every October in which visitors are welcome to take part. An increasing number of resorts and

shops have mountain bikes for **rent** (sometimes free for guests), but two of the best places to do it are San Ignacio, where you can ride along the forest roads in the Mountain Pine Ridge, and Placencia, for an enjoyable day riding on the flat, smooth sand road linking the peninsula's resorts. Renting a mountain bike in Punta Gorda will give you the freedom to get around the Maya villages and hills of Toledo.

Bikes can sometimes be carried on top of buses, though few Belizean buses have roof racks. Attitudes vary: if you're really lucky – and there's room – the driver might let you take the bike *onto* the bus; at other times you'll have to persuade the conductor to let you load the bike on at all.

If you've cycled into Belize from Mexico or Guatemala there's usually no problem bringing your bike over the border, though it may be recorded in your passport and you might then have difficulty leaving the country without it. In the UK, membership of the Cyclists' Touring Club, 69 Meadrow, Godalming, Surrey GU7 3HS (☎01483/417217, email *cycling@ctc.org.uk*, Web site *www.ctc.org.uk*), enables you to access information and trip reports from cyclists who've taken bikes to Belize and the region before.

CRIME AND PERSONAL SAFETY

Although Central America as a whole has earned a generally justified reputation for

criminal activities, violent crimes aimed at tourists were, until recently, extremely rare in Belize. But despite being on the increase, they're still low in comparison with other countries and while armed muggings of foreigners have occurred, you are very unlikely to become a victim, whatever you might hear to the contrary. Belize City does have a high crime rate but the place is nothing like as dangerous as you might think from its appearance and atmosphere, and it's now much less intimidating owing to the presence of the tourist police. On the whole petty crime is the only common pest.

That said, it pays to be aware of the dangers and if you've got valuables insure them properly (see p.15). Always take photocopies of your passport and insurance documents and try to leave them in a secure place. For British travellers an overview of the dangers of visiting Belize and Central America can be obtained from the Foreign Office Travel Advice Unit (Mon–Fri 9.30am–4pm ☎0171/238 4503, or ☎0374/500900 for automated service, Web site *www.foc.gov.uk/*). They also produce a good advice leaflet for independent travellers, which also explains what a consul can and cannot do for you when you're abroad. The US equivalent is the State Department's Consular Information Service (Web site *travel.state.gov/travel_warnings.html*) which publishes information sheets about each country, listing the main dangers to US citizens.

CRIME AND AVOIDING IT

The majority of crime is petty **theft** such as bag-snatching, pickpocketing and minor break-ins at hotels, though there's also a chance (albeit small) of being on the end of something more serious, such as **mugging** – take commonsense precautions everywhere; relax but don't get complacent. During the day there's little to worry about, so whenever possible, try to time your arrival in daylight. At night in **Belize City** you should stick to the main streets and, for women in particular, it's never a good idea to go out alone. If you arrive in Belize City at night take a taxi to a hotel, as the bus stations are in a particularly derelict part of town. Wherever you are, keep your most valuable possessions on you (but don't wear any expensive jewellery), preferably in a moneybelt under your outer clothes. Trousers with zipped pockets are also a good pickpocket-deterrent. Looking "respectable" without appearing affluent will go some way to avoiding unwanted attention.

Break-ins at hotels are one of the most common types of petty theft – something you should bear in mind when searching for a room. Make sure the lock on your door works; from the inside as well as out. In many budget hotels the lock will be a small padlock on the outside; for extra safety, it's a good idea to buy your own so you're the only one with keys. Many hotels will have a safe or secure area for valuables. It's up to you whether you use this; most of the time it will be fine, but make sure whatever you do put in is securely and tightly wrapped – a spare, lockable moneybelt does the job.

If you follow a few simple precautions, you shouldn't experience any trouble **at border crossings** – the presence of armed officials generally discourages thieves in the immediate area of the immigration post. Nevertheless, it's still advisable to do any transactions with money-changers out of sight of other people and, once away from the post, be on your guard. Watch out especially for people "helping" you to find a bus and offering to carry your luggage; most of the time they'll just be after a tip, but it's easy to get distracted – never let your belongings out of sight unless you're confident they're in a safe place. When you travel by bus, your main baggage will usually go in the luggage compartment underneath or at the back. It's generally safe (you have little option in any case) but keep an eye on it if you can – theft of bags is uncommon but opportunist thieves may dip into zippers and outer pockets.

Finally, don't let anyone without the official credentials talk you into being your "**guide**" – all legal tour guides in Belize are licensed and will have a photo ID. If you have doubts about using a guide don't go, and report the incident to the authorities.

POLICE AND REPORTING A CRIME

In addition to a regular police force, Belize has special **tourist police**, who are part of the Tourist Board. Easily identified by their shirts and caps emblazoned with "Tourist Police", they patrol Belize City, San Pedro and some other tourist destinations around the country. If you have anything stolen it's best to go to the tourist police first, if only to help you through the processes involved in **reporting a crime**. Police in Belize are poorly paid and, despite the campaign against criminals who prey on tourists, all too often you can't get them to do much more than make out the report – and you may have difficulty getting them to do even that; it helps to have the tourist police aware of your plight.

POLICE EMERGENCY NUMBER
The **police emergency number** in Belize is ☎911

Always report the crime to your embassy as well if you can – it helps the consular staff build up a higher-level case for better protection for tourists. Not that crime against tourists isn't already treated seriously in Belize; if the criminals are caught they are brought before the courts the next day, which is a much better system than most in the region.

DRUGS

Belize has long been an important transhipment link in the chain of supply between the producers in South and Central America and the users in North America, with minor players often being paid in kind, creating a deluge of illegal drugs. **Marijuana**, **cocaine** and **crack** are all readily available in Belize, and whether you like it or not you'll receive regular offers, particularly in San Pedro, Caye Caulker and Placencia. All such substances are **illegal**, and despite the fact that dope is smoked openly in the streets, the police do arrest people for possession of marijuana and

they particularly enjoy catching tourists. If you're caught you'll probably end up spending a couple of days in jail and paying a fine of several hundred US dollars. Practically every year foreigners are incarcerated for drug offences – the pusher may have a sideline reporting clients to the police, and catching "international drug smugglers" gives the country brownie points with the US Drug Enforcement Agency (DEA). Expect no sympathy from your embassy – they'll probably send someone to visit you, and maybe find an English-speaking lawyer, but certainly can't get you out of jail.

HARASSMENT

Verbal abuse is the most threatening aspect of life on the streets in Belize, though it's only really a problem in Belize City (and occasionally Dangriga), where there are always plenty of people hanging out on the streets, commenting on all that passes by. For anyone with a white face, the inevitable "Hey, white boy/white chick – what's happening?" will soon become a familiar sound. At first it can all seem very intimidating, but if you take the time to stop and talk, you'll find the vast majority of these people simply want to know where you're from, and where you're heading – and perhaps to scam you a deal on boat trips, money exchange, or bum a dollar or two. Once you realize that they generally mean no harm the whole experience of Belize City will be infinitely more enjoyable. Obviously, the situation is a little more serious for women, and the abuse can be more offensive. But once again, annoying though

it is, it's unlikely that anything will come of it and you can usually talk your way out of a dodgy situation without anyone losing face.

Women travellers may initially find the advances from local lotharios a nuisance, particularly in Belize City and on the busier cayes, but there's rarely any real menace. These men think it their duty to pass comments on any woman they consider attractive, but if you make it clear from the outset that you're not interested, they'll generally concentrate their attention on those who are. In rural areas, especially in the Maya villages in the south, you'll be treated with great courtesy – as would any outsider. Women travelling alone won't come across any particular problems, and are very likely to meet other solo women travellers. Additionally many foreign women come to Belize to work in VSO or the Peace Corps for instance, or to volunteer in NGOs; if you spend more than a few days you'll probably meet some of them, and get the chance to pick up useful information.

EATING AND DRINKING

Belizean food is a distinctive mix of Latin America and the Caribbean, with Creole "rice and beans" cuisine dominating the scene but plenty of other influences playing an important part. Central American *empanadas* are now as common as pizza, chow mein and hamburgers. At its best Creole food is delicious, taking the best from the sea and mixing it with the smooth taste of coconut – a favourite ingredient – and spices. Sadly though, in many places, it's a neglected art, and too often what you get is a stodgy, almost tasteless mass.

You'll soon become accustomed to the **lunch hour** (noon to 1pm), observed with almost religious devotion. Abandon any hope of getting anything else done and tuck in with the locals. This is often the main meal of the day, and, though most places naturally also serve dinner, dining late is not a Belizean custom; generally, getting to your table by around 8pm will mean you'll get a better choice – and possibly better service too.

WHERE TO EAT

There's a full range of **bars**, **cafés** and smart-looking **restaurants** around but bear in mind that the quality of the food rarely bears much relation to the appearance of the restaurant. Out on the islands and in small seashore villages some restaurants are little more than thatched shelters, with open sides and sand floors, though you'll just as often find upmarket hotels with polished floors, tablecloths and napkins. Only in Belize

City, San Pedro, Caye Caulker and possibly San Ignacio though, is there much choice: fast food and snack bars are springing up on street corners, and there's some surprisingly elegant restaurants too. Most places, however, lie somewhere between the two, serving up good food but with little concern for presentation.

The streetside **snack bars**, often run by former refugees from El Salvador or Honduras, serve up tasty *tamales*, *tacos* (rolled, filled corn tortillas, shallow fried), *empanadas* (similar to *tacos* but the tortilla is folded in half after filling, and deep fried) and other Latin staples, adding variety to the range of cuisine on offer. **Travelling**, you'll find that these snack foods, as well as the usual Belizean standby of "ham" burgers (literally a slice of canned ham in a bun), sometimes come to you as street traders offer them to waiting bus passengers, although the practice isn't nearly as common as elsewhere in Central America.

WHAT TO EAT

There are few surprises waiting at **breakfast**: you're likely to be offered eggs, usually accompanied by bread (sometimes toasted) or flour tortillas and stewed red beans, though in tourist areas you'll almost always be offered fresh fruit and somtimes pancakes, often served with yoghurt or locally produced honey.

The basis of any **Creole** main meal is **rice and beans**, and this features heavily in small restaurants. In some cases it means exactly that, with the rice and beans cooked together in coconut oil and flavoured with *recado* (a mild ground pepper) – often with a chunk of salted pork thrown in for extra taste – but usually it's served with stewed chicken or beef, or fried fish, and backed up by some kind of sauce. If you like your flavours full on, there'll always be a bottle of hot sauce on the table for extra spice. Vegetables are scarce in Creole food but on the side of the plate you'll often get a portion of potato salad or coleslaw, and sometimes **fried plantain** or **flour tortillas**.

Seafood is almost always excellent. **Red snapper** is invariably fantastic, and you might also try a **barracuda** steak, **conch fritters** or a plate of fresh (though usually farmed) shrimps. On

San Pedro and Caye Caulker the food is often exceptional, and the only worry is that you might get bored with **lobster**, which is served in an amazing range of dishes: pasta with lobster sauce, lobster and scrambled eggs, lobster chow mein, even lobster curry. Note: the closed season for lobster is from February to June, and it will not (or certainly should not) be served then. **Turtle** is still on the menu in a few places, in theory only during the short open season, but they're a protected species, threatened with extinction – avoid trying it, or indeed any animal taken from the wild.

When there's little else on offer, Belize's many Chinese restaurants are usually a safe bet and **Chinese food** will probably feature more in your trip than you anticipated. Other Belizean ethnic minorities are now starting to break into the restaurant trade; Dangriga has a good **Garífuna** restaurant, and there's an excellent **Sri Lankan** restaurant in San Ignacio, serving superb curries. Despite the proximity of Mexico and the Central American republics, their cuisine has had only a superficial influence on Belizean restaurant food. You might get *tamales* (a savoury cornmeal "pudding", usually with chicken cooked in a lightly-spiced sauce inside, wrapped in a banana leaf and steamed) or *ecsabeche* (a spicy onion soup) but without the familiar accompaniment of corn tortillas. However, you'll find several taco stands springing up in the main tourist places.

Vegetarians will find the pickings slim and there are no specifically vegetarian restaurants, though some places now offer a couple of vegetarian dishes. Note that in most Belizean restaurants if you say you don't eat meat you're likely to be offered chicken or ham (white meat is often not considered "meat" in the true sense). The fruit is good and there are some locally produced vegetables (thanks mainly to the Mennonites and Central American refugees) but they are rarely served in restaurants. Your best bet outside the main tourist areas, where there may be a meat-free choice on the menu, is to try a Chinese restaurant.

DRINKS

The most basic **drinks** to accompany food are water, beer and the oversweetened, but familiar, soft drinks. Belikin, the only brand of **beer** produced in Belize, comes in four varieties: regular, a lager-type bottled and draught beer; bottled stout (a rich, dark beer); and Premium and Supreme, more expensive bottled beers and often all you'll be able to get in upmarket hotels and restaurants. If you simply ask for a beer you'll usually be served a bottled Belikin. They're all overpriced at more than US$1.50 a bottle (more out on the cayes); imported European and American beers will cost you twice that. Mexican and Guatemalan beer is usually unavailable.

Cashew nut and berry **wines**, rich and full-bodied, are bottled and sold in some villages, and you can also get hold of imported wine, though it's far from cheap. Local **rum**, in both dark and clear varieties, is the best deal in Belizean alcohol. The locally produced gin, brandy and vodka are poor imitations – cheap and fairly nasty.

Non-alcoholic drinks include a predictable range of fairly cheap **soft drinks** including Sprite, Fanta, Coke and Pepsi. Despite the number of citrus plantations **fruit juices** are rarely available, though you can sometimes get orange juice. *Licuados*, the thirst-quenching blended fruit drinks, ubiquitous throughout Mexico and the rest of Central America, are almost never served in Belize. **Tap water**, in the towns at least, though safe, is highly chlorinated, and many villages (though not Caye Caulker) now have a potable water system. Filtered, bottled water and mineral water are sold almost everywhere and pure **rainwater** is usually available in the countryside and on the cayes.

Coffee, except in the best establishments, will almost certainly be instant. **Tea**, due to the British influence, is a popular hot drink, as are Milo and Ovaltine (malted milky drinks). One last drink that deserves a mention is **seaweed**, a strange blend of actual seaweed, milk, cinnamon, sugar and cream. If you see someone selling this on a street corner, give it a try.

COMMUNICATIONS: MAIL, PHONES AND EMAIL

Belize's excellent postal, telecommunications and Internet services are the best in Central America. Postal rates are relatively inexpensive and mail sent home almost invariably gets through. Local calls (and many long-distance internal calls) from payphones are fairly cheap, but international calls are comparatively more expensive than at home; you'll find a table of current charges in the Belize phone book, which is clearly laid out and easy to use. Many businesses in Belize are connected to the Internet and email is one of the best (and cheapest) means of making hotel bookings.

MAIL

Belizean postal services are the most efficient in Central America and **sending letters**, cards and parcels home is straightforward: a normal air-mail letter takes around 4–5 days to reach the US (Bz$0.60), a couple of days longer to Canada, 8–10 days to Europe (Bz$0.75) and two weeks to Australia (Bz$0.75). **Parcels** have to be wrapped in brown paper and tied with string; they may be inspected by customs. You can send parcels via surface mail but this takes literally months. **Registration** for mail isn't necessary but doesn't cost much extra above the postage and you'll get a certificate to give you some peace of mind. **Incoming mail** (have it sent to General Delivery) is kept at the main post office in Belize City (or any district town post office) for a couple of months; you'll need some kind of ID, preferably a passport, to pick it up. American Express card-

holders can have mail sent to them c/o AMEX at Belize Global Travel, 41 Albert St, Belize City.

There's a **post office** in all the towns and most villages, though in the latter it may be in a shop, or even someone's house. These very small ones are likely to be short of stamps, and may not have them in the correct denominations for overseas, so you're better off doing anything important at a main office. Post offices are generally open Monday to Friday 8am–noon and 1–5pm.

PHONES, FAX AND EMAIL

Belize's modern (albeit expensive) **phone system** is almost always easy to use. There's only one phone company, Belize Telecommunications Limited (BTL), which also controls access to the Internet, but competition is on the way. BTL's main office (for international calls, fax, email and Internet access) is at 1 Church St, Belize City (Mon-Fri 8am–6pm); other offices are given in the guide. **Payphones** (good for both local and international calls) are a common sight throughout the country, and you'll find them all over Belize City. Rural areas are served by **community telephones** (nowadays often fixed cellular phones) usually located in a private house; you pay the person who operates the phone. Two types of prepaid **phonecards** are in use: the **Telecard**, which you can use at any touch-tone phone (both pay and private phones), uses a PIN number, while the **Payphone card** is slotted into payphones. It's a good idea to pick up one of each as soon as you can; both can be purchased from BTL offices, and increasingly from hotels, shops and gas stations, and come in units of Bz$5, Bz$10, Bz$20, Bz$30 and Bz$50.

Local cash calls require a Bz$0.25 coin. Other domestic call charges from payphones are steep: between Bz$1.50 to Bz$3.50 for the first three minutes (with a three-minute minimum) – only Belize City has an off-peak discount (6pm–6am) of fifty percent. For **internal long distance** just dial the code for the town (given in the text) and the number.

It's easy enough to **dial home direct**: a call to Europe costs Bz$18, and to North America Bz$10, for the first three minutes, with night-time, off-peak discounts – if you use a phonecard you only pay per minute. **Calling home collect** is easy

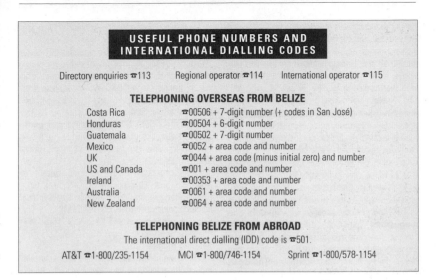

USEFUL PHONE NUMBERS AND INTERNATIONAL DIALLING CODES

Directory enquiries ☎113   Regional operator ☎114   International operator ☎115

TELEPHONING OVERSEAS FROM BELIZE

Costa Rica	☎00506 + 7-digit number (+ codes in San José)
Honduras	☎00504 + 6-digit number
Guatemala	☎00502 + 7-digit number
Mexico	☎0052 + area code and number
UK	☎0044 + area code (minus initial zero) and number
US and Canada	☎001 + area code and number
Ireland	☎00353 + area code and number
Australia	☎0061 + area code and number
New Zealand	☎0064 + area code and number

TELEPHONING BELIZE FROM ABROAD

The international direct dialling (IDD) code is ☎501.

AT&T ☎1-800/235-1154   MCI ☎1-800/746-1154   Sprint ☎1-800/578-1154

using Home Country Direct, available at BTL offices, most payphones and larger hotels. Simply dial the access code (on some payphones and in the phone book) to connect with an operator in your home country. To call Belize collect from North America use Belize Direct: contact AT&T, MCI or Sprint for the access number.

Cellular phones, both fixed and mobile, cover the whole country and visitors can easily rent a cell phone. The codes begin with 01, followed by one other number, or 021, then the phone number, and cost Bz$1.12 per minute to dial.

Most hotels and businesses now have **fax** machines and any BTL office will have a public fax you can use. Fax numbers are listed in the pink pages in the telephone directory. Belizean businesses and individuals are also avid users of **email** and the **Internet**, although at present there's only one Internet café: *Evas'*, in San Ignacio (see p.130). You can send and surf from BTL's Belize City office (Bz$6 for 30min); some of their other offices may also have public email by the time of publication. See the box on p.17 for some of the most useful **Web sites** covering Belize.

THE MEDIA

Although Belize, with its English-language media, can come as a welcome break in a world of Spanish, it doesn't necessarily mean that it's very easy to keep in touch with what's happening in the rest of the world. Local news, in the press particularly, but also on radio and television, is reported in a very nationalistic manner, taking pride of place over international stories which receive little attention.

NEWSPAPERS AND MAGAZINES

The four **national newspapers** – The People's Pulse, The Reporter, The Belize Times and The Amandala (all published on Fri) – stick mostly to a party line, and some of them exhibit racist and xenophobic tones that would make a British tabloid wince. That said, they do make entertaining reading, and you'll find some interesting articles in each edition. Belize has no independent, home-produced news magazine along the lines of *Newsweek*, but the government information service publishes *Belize Today*, a free monthly promoting official developments. There are also several private-enterprise occasional publications well worth looking at: *The Belize Review*, subtitled "News, Views and Ecotourism" is interesting, and sometimes controversial. *Belize Magazine*, a bi-monthly magazine published in the US and readily available in Belize, is expensive and aimed mainly at would-be property buyers, but has some excellent colour photography and interesting articles on Maya sites or Belizean wildlife.

In Belize City, Belmopan, San Pedro and occasionally in some other towns you should be able to get hold of some **foreign newspapers and magazines**, including copies of *The Miami Herald*, *Time* and *Newsweek*, usually next day, though the top hotels in Belize City get them same day in the incoming afternoon flights. **The Book Centre**, at 4 Church Street in Belize City, has the largest selection of magazines – and some newspapers – in the country.

TV, RADIO AND VIDEO

There are two more-or-less national **television** stations. Channel 5 is the best broadcaster in the country, producing superb news and factual programmes (you can access their daily news output on the Internet, see box on p.17). Channel 7, on the other hand, shows an almost uninterrupted stream of imported American shows, mixed in with some local news. Both show some educational programming and each broadcasts the main news programmes at 6.30pm. But it's Cable TV (mostly pirated from satellite) that gets most of the nation's viewers, with its saturation coverage of American soaps, talk shows, sports, films and CNN.

Two of the main **radio** stations – Radio Belize (91.1FM), mainly talk-based, with plays, cultural and educational programmes, and which transmits the BBC World Service from midnight to 6am, and Friends FM (89.9FM), primarily a music station – are operated by the Broadcasting Corporation of Belize and partly sponsored by the government. KREM (96.5FM), owned by *The Amandala* newspaper, plays mostly music, as does Love FM (95.1FM). Most stations broadcast some of their output in Spanish, and Estereo Amor (97.3FM) is a Spanish-language station. There's also a British Forces radio station, BFBS (93.1FM), and you can pick up Mexican and Caribbean stations – the latter wafting in across the sea and blasting out pure reggae.

There are no **cinemas** in Belize and unsurprisingly no local feature film industry as such, though it has provided the location for a few well-known films: *The Dogs of War*, *The Mosquito Coast* and *Heart of Darkness*. Great Belize Productions (17 Regent St, Belize City ☎02/77781; *gbtv@btl.net*) are the next best thing at the moment, producing an excellent series of locally made **videos**, which can make great souvenirs. These include: *The Best of Belize All Over*, showing slices of local life to the accompaniment of great Belizean music; *Belize – The Maya Heritage*, the first of a two-part history of Belize, including interviews with archeologists working in Belize; and *From Invasion to Nation – A History of Belize*, presented by Belizean historian Assad Shoman. They also produce several marvellous nature documentaries, the daily Channel 5 news programmes and an annual video anthology of news relevant to Belize.

OPENING HOURS, PUBLIC HOLIDAYS AND FESTIVALS

It's difficult to be specific about **opening hours** in Belize but in general most shops are open 8am–noon and 3–8pm. The lunch hour (noon to 1pm) is almost universally observed and it's hopeless to try and get anything done then. Some shops and businesses work a half-day on Wednesday and Saturday, and everything is liable to close early on Friday. Everybody takes it easy on Sundays; most shops, and sometimes restaurants, are closed, and fewer bus services and internal flights operate. Archeological sites, however, are open every day. The main **public holidays**, when virtually everything will be closed, are given in the box below.

You'll generally find plenty of entertainment at any time, as Belizeans are great party people and music is a crucial part of the country's culture. However, it's only in the outlying areas, such as around San Ignacio and Corozal, and in the Maya villages of the south, that you'll find traditional village **fiestas**, which in many ways resemble their counterparts in Guatemala. Elsewhere, any national celebrations – above all the Carnival and Independence Day, both in September, and marked by open-air dances – are the excuse for a fantastic, day-long party, with the rhythms of the Caribbean dominating the proceedings. **Dance** is very much a part of Creole culture and at these celebrations you'll feel less of an outsider and will always be welcome to dance and drink with the locals. The best time to see Garífuna drumming and dance is November 19, Garífuna Settlement Day, and the best places to see it are Dangriga and Hopkins. For more on Belizean music and dance see p.250.

PUBLIC HOLIDAYS

January 1 New Year's Day
March 9 Baron Bliss Day
Good Friday
Holy Saturday
Easter Monday
May 1 Labour Day

May 24 Commonwealth Day
September 10 National Day
September 21 Independence Day
October 12 Columbus Day (PanAmerica Day)
November 19 Garífuna Settlement Day
December 25–26 Christmas Day and Boxing Day

ARTS, CRAFTS, SHOPPING AND SOUVENIRS

Compared to its neighbours, Belize has less to offer in terms of traditional **crafts** or neighbourhood **markets**. The latter are purely for food, but in several places you'll come across some impressive local crafts. Craft and gift shops are now found throughout the country – the best ones are covered in the text – but you'll often get better prices from the artisans themselves, on the streets or in the villages. If time is short, the **National Handicrafts Center** in Belize City (see p.57), run by the Belize Chamber of Commerce, is the best place to buy souvenirs, with a wide range of good-quality, genuine Belizean crafts, including paintings, prints and music, as well as many of the items mentioned below. The craftspeople are paid fair prices for their work and no longer have to hawk it on the streets. Belizean artists often exhibit here too, but the best place for contemporary **Belizean art** is the Image Factory in Belize City (see p.57). For more on music and recordings, see p.250.

Wood carvings make beautiful and unusual souvenirs. The wood carvers are often found in Belize City and at the Maya sites; their often exquisitely executed carvings of dolphins, jaguars, ships etc, are made from *zericote* – a two-tone light-and-dark-brown wood which only grows in Belize and the surrounding areas. The best wood is kiln-dried — the items you buy on the streets may not be. Also at Maya sites you'll find **slate carvers**, creating wonderful, high-quality, reproductions of gods, glyphs and stelae; the **ceramics** aren't as good, but they're improving. In the Maya villages in southern Belize you'll also come across some attractive **embroidery**, though it has to be said that the quality of both the cloth and the work is better in Guatemala. Garífuna and Creole villages produce good basketware and superb **drums**; Dangriga, Hopkins and Gales Point are the places to visit if you want to see these.

For superb **videos** of Belizean wildlife, culture or history, have a look at the series produced by Great Belize Productions, which can be purchased from gift shops or from their office (see p.38). Those with a philatelic bent might appreciate a set of wildly colourful Belize **stamps**; relatively cheap and certainly easy to post home, they often feature the animals and plants of the country. You can get many of them from any post office but the one in Belize City has a special Philatelic Department. One tasty souvenir that finds its way into everyone's suitcase is a bottle (or three) of **Marie Sharp's Pepper Sauce**, made from Belizean *habañeros* and in various strengths ranging from "mild" to "fiery hot". This spicy accompaniment to rice and beans graces every restaurant table in the country – and visits to the factory near Dangriga can be arranged.

For **everyday shopping** you'll find some kind of shop in every village in Belize, however small, and there's a department store and several supermarkets in Belize City. If you have the time to hunt around, most things you'd find in North America and Europe are also available in Belize – at a price. Luxury items, such as electrical goods and cameras, tend to be very expensive, as do other imported goods. Film is a little more expensive than at home, but easy to get hold of.

SUSPECT SOUVENIRS

Some souvenirs you'll see are dependent on the destruction of the reef and wildlife, so think twice before you buy. They include black coral, often made into jewellery, turtle shells, which look far better on their rightful owners, and indeed marine curios of any kind. Many of the animal and plant souvenirs you may be offered in Belize are listed in Appendix 1 to CITES (The Convention on International Trade in Endangered Species) and their trade is prohibited, so you wouldn't be allowed to bring them into the US, Canada or Europe, and may face a fine for trying.

Even more of a black market item than animal curios are any archeological artefacts or remains; all such items belong to Belize and theft or trade is strictly prohibited; anyone attempting to smuggle these out could end up in jail in Belize or at home.

SPORTS AND OUTDOOR ACTIVITIES

Most of the **sports** on offer in Belize are connected to the water in some way, with sailing, diving and snorkelling extremely popular. **Diving courses**, for experts or beginners, are run in San Pedro, Caye Caulker, Placencia and some of the other cayes and the Bay Islands. **Sea kayaking**, too, is becoming more popular and a number of outfits organize trips.

Away from the coast, **canoeing**, **rafting** and **tubing** – floating down rivers in a giant inner tube – are extremely popular, particularly in the Cayo district, where there are plenty of people keen to arrange this for you. Back on land, or rather under it, Belize's amazing subterranean landscape is becoming ever more accessible, with several qualified **caving** guides leading tours and organizing specialist expeditions. Two caving instructors, Ian Anderson of Caves Branch and Pete Zubrzycki in San Ignacio are founder members of the Belize Cave Rescue Team, making safety a prime feature. **Horse-riding** is another possibility; there are some superb rides to be had through forested hills and to Maya ruins. Finally, an increasing number of places now rent **mountain bikes**. Details of the above activities and the companies organizing them are given where appropriate in the text.

The main **spectator sports** are **football** and **baseball**, which rank about equal as the national games, with avid reporting in the press. Softball is also popular, as is athletics, and American football and baseball have a devoted following on TV. As in the rest of Central America, **cycling** is closely followed and there are sometimes races in Belize, though scope for these is limited given the state of the roads. Finally, there are a number of **horse-racing** meets around New Year.

VOLUNTARY WORK AND STUDY

There's virtually no chance of finding paid temporary work in Belize as at least half of the population is underemployed. Work permits are only on offer to those who can prove their ability to support themselves without endangering the job of a Belizean.

There are, however, plenty of opportunities for **voluntary work** – mainly as a fee-paying member of a conservation expedition (see below and p.42) – or **study**, at an **archeological field school**. These options generally mean raising a considerable sum for the privilege and committing yourself to weeks (or months) of hard work, often in difficult conditions. Many of the expeditions are aimed at students taking time out between school and university, and arrange work on rural infrastructure projects – schools, health centres and so on, or building trails and visitor centres in nature reserves. These organizations will usually take expedition members from any country, regardless of where they are based; they also need some experienced technical and administrative staff who, while they may not always get paid, can at least go on the expeditions without raising a large sum first. At least twenty academic archeological groups undertake research in Belize each year, and many of them take paying students (and non-students) – for more on this see "Contexts" p.246.

If the cost deters you, you could contact the non fee-paying organizations in the box on p.42 or even volunteer independently; contact the **Belize**

VOLUNTARY WORK CONTACTS

NON FEE-PAYING PROJECTS

UK

Voluntary Service Overseas (VSO) 317 Putney Bridge Rd, London SW15 2PN (☎0181/780 7500; *www.oneworld.org/vso/). Recruits people with the required skills for long-term posts (usually a minimum of two years); mainly teachers but also agricultural and health specialists. You don't have to raise money and you get a small allowance.*

IRELAND

The Agency for Personal Service Overseas 29–30 Fitzwilliam Sq, Dublin 2 (☎01/661 4411).

Accepts specialist volunteers (with similar skills requirements to VSO) for long-term positions in Belize.

US

Peace Corps 1990 K St NW, Washington DC (☎703/235-9191).*Sends American volunteers to Belize to work in education, agriculture and conservation.*

FEE-PAYING CONSERVATION AND DEVELOPMENT PROJECTS

Earthwatch Earthwatch Headquarters, 680 Mount Auburn St, PO Box 9104, Watertown, MA 02272-9104, USA (☎617/926-8200; fax 926-8532); Earthwatch Europe, Belsyre Court, 57 Woodstock Rd, Oxford OX2 6HU, UK (☎01865/311600; fax 311383); Earthwatch Australia, 1st floor, 453–457 Elizabeth St, Melbourne 3000 (☎03/9600-9100; fax 03/9600-9066) (email *info@earthwatch.org*, Web site *www.earthwatch.org*.) *Matches volunteers with scientists working on several archeological and marine conservation projects in Belize. The cost per two-week stint is around US$1700.*

Coral Cay Conservation CCC 54 Clapham Park Rd, London SW4 7DE (☎0171/498-6248, fax 498-8447, email *ccc@coralcay.demon.co.uk*; Web site *www.coral.cay.demon.co.uk*). *Sends teams to Belize to research proposed protected marine areas. Approximate cost range from £650/US$1000 for two weeks to £2500/US$4100 for three months.*

Raleigh International Raleigh House, 27 Parsons Green Lane, London SW6 4HZ (☎0171/371 8585, fax 371 5116, email *info@raleigh.org.uk*; Web site *www.raleigh.org.uk*). *Operates youth development expeditions working on demanding community and environmental projects throughout Belize, with some time usually spent learning to dive. Applicants are expected to raise around £3000 and must be aged 17–25, be able to swim and speak English.*

Trekforce Expeditions Trekforce, 138 Buckingham Palace Rd, London SW1W 9SA (☎0171/824 8890, fax 824 8892, email *trekforce@dial.pipex.com*; Web site *www.ds.dial.pipex.com/town/parade/hu15*). *Runs projects in Belize ranging from surveys of remote Maya sites in the west, near Gallon Jug, and wildlife surveys and infrastructure projects in national parks. There are six-week expeditions for which volunteers need to raise £2350.*

Audubon Society (☎02/35004; PO Box 1001, Belize City) directly or ask at any of the reserves. You'll need to be self-motivated and self-supporting – no funding will be available – but you'll probably get accommodation in the field and it's a highly rewarding experience.

If you're thinking of working or volunteering in Belize or Central America it's worth looking at the **publications** of the Central Bureau for Educational Visits, 10 Spring Gardens, London SW1A 2BN (☎0171/389 4880, email: *books@centralbureau. org.uk*), particularly *Working Holidays* (updated annually) and *Volunteer Work*, both packed with essential information, including contacts in Mexico and other Central American countries. The Council on International Educational Exchange (see Council Travel entry on p.5 for address) also arranges and administers volunteer and study programmes and has information on Belize.

Green Arrow's Web pages (*www.greenarrow.com*), while concentrating on Costa Rica, are a good source of travel and environmental information and volunteering opportunities throughout Central America.

DIRECTORY

ADDRESSES In towns most streets are named and it's easy enough to find your way to a particular address despite there being no grid plan to follow, though numbering may be less prominent. Along Belize's main highways the official addresses are measured (in miles) from the start of the highway.

CONTRACEPTION Condoms are available from any drugstore in Belize, as are some brands of the Pill, though it's better to bring enough of the latter to last the trip.

ELECTRICITY The mains supply is 110 volts AC with American-style three-pin sockets. Electrical equipment made for the US and Canada should be OK – anything from Britain will need a transformer and a plug adaptor – but ask in your hotel before you do anything. The electricity supply is pretty dependable, but if you're bringing any delicate equipment, like a laptop, you'll need a good surge protector. Some hotels and small villages have their electricity supplied by local generators, and the voltage is then much lower.

GAY AND LESBIAN BELIZE Although homosexuality is still illegal in Belize things are easy-going here and you needn't expect any great hassle, though naturally, it's a good idea to be discreet in order to avoid possible verbal abuse. No one has been prosecuted for years and it's extremely unlikely that the authorities would begin proceedings against tourists. Given the legal status, however, it's no surprise to learn that there's no openly gay community and no exclusively gay bars in Belize.

LAUNDRY The only places that have any kind of laundry service are Belize City, Placencia, San Ignacio, San Pedro and Caye Caulker; addresses are listed in the *Guide*. Elsewhere you can usually find someone who takes in washing or possibly get away with doing your laundry in your hotel room.

TIME ZONES Belize is on Central Standard Time, six hours behind GMT and the same as Guatemala and Honduras. Belize does not observe Daylight Savings Time though the US, and, more importantly, Mexico do. This means that when DST is in operation (during the summer) the time in Belize is an hour earlier than Mexico – something to bear in mind when you're crossing the border.

TOILETS Public toilets are very rare indeed, though there is an excellent one in the new Belize City market. In hotels and restaurants standards are extremely variable, but toilets are never considered a high priority. On the whole toilet paper is provided, but it's always a good idea to travel with your own roll, just in case.

WEIGHTS AND MEASURES The imperial system is still used in Belize. This book is metric throughout, except when we refer to addresses on main roads outside towns that are commonly referred to in terms of their mile number. The small bottled drinks (especially beer) are referred to as "pints", though the measure is in fact much less.

IMPERIAL/METRIC WEIGHTS AND MEASURES

1 ounce = 28.3 grams	1 foot = 0.3 metre
1 pound = 454 grams	1 yard = 0.91 metre
2.2 pounds = 1 kilogram	1.09 yards = 1 metre
1 quart = 0.94 litre	1 mile = 1.61 kilometres
1 gallon = 3.78 litres	0.62 miles = 1 kilometre
1 inch = 2.54 centimetres	

PART TWO

THE

GUIDE

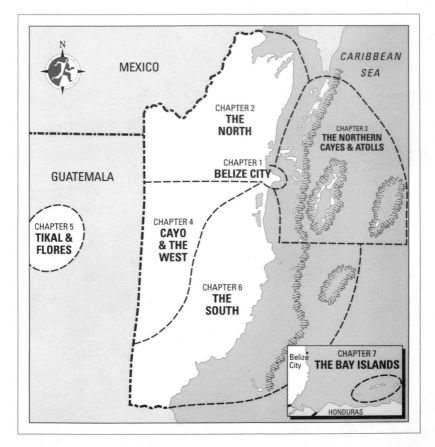

N

MEXICO

CARIBBEAN
SEA

CHAPTER 2
**THE
NORTH**

CHAPTER 3
**THE NORTHERN
CAYES & ATOLLS**

CHAPTER 1
BELIZE CITY

GUATEMALA

CHAPTER 5
**TIKAL &
FLORES**

CHAPTER 4
**CAYO
& THE
WEST**

CHAPTER 6
**THE
SOUTH**

Belize
City

CHAPTER 7
THE BAY ISLANDS

HONDURAS

CHAPTER ONE

BELIZE CITY

The narrow, congested streets of **BELIZE CITY** can initially be daunting to anyone who has been prepared by the usual travellers' tales of crime-ridden urban decay. Admittedly, at first glance the city can be unprepossessing and chaotic. Its buildings – many of them dilapidated wooden structures – stand right at the edge of the road, and few sidewalks offer refuge to pedestrians from the ever-increasing numbers of cars and trucks. Narrow bridges force the traffic to cross in single file over almost stagnant canals, which are still used for much of the city's drainage. Vultures circle overhead or sit with drooping wings on rotting riverside jetties. The overall impression is that the place has never recovered from some great calamity – an explanation that is at least partly true. Belize has suffered several devastating hurricanes, the latest in October 1961, when Hurricane Hattie tore the city apart with winds of 240kmph, leaving a layer of thick black mud as the storm receded. The hazards of Belize City, however, are often reported by those who have never been here.

Most visitors hurry through on their way to catch their next bus or a boat out to the cayes, but the city has a distinguished history, a handful of sights and an astonishing energy. The 60,000 people of Belize City represent every ethnic group in the country, with the **Creole** descendants of former slaves and Baymen forming the dominant element, generating an easy-going Caribbean atmosphere. If you approach the city with an open mind, meet the inhabitants, and take in the new museums and galleries, you may well be pleasantly surprised.

HASSLE

Walking in Belize City **in daylight** is perfectly safe if you observe common-sense rules. The introduction of specially trained **tourist police** in 1995 made an immediate impact on the level of hassle and this, coupled with the legal requirement for all tour guides to be licensed, drove away the hustlers and really reduced street crime. You'll soon learn to spot dangerous situations and in the city centre you can always ask the tourist police for advice or directions; they'll even walk you back to your hotel if it's near their patrol route. That said, it's still sensible to proceed with caution: most people are friendly and chatty, but quite a few may want to sell you drugs or bum a dollar or two. The best advice is to stay cool. Be civil, don't provoke trouble by arguing too forcefully, and never show large sums of money on the street, especially American dollars. Women wearing short shorts or skirts will attract verbal abuse from local studs.

The virtual absence of nightlife apart from the bars and discos in the more expensive hotels means there's little reason to walk the streets **after dark**; if you do venture out, bear in mind that anyone alone is in danger of being mugged. It's a good idea to travel by taxi at night, especially if you've just arrived by bus. For more on security and avoiding trouble see p.31.

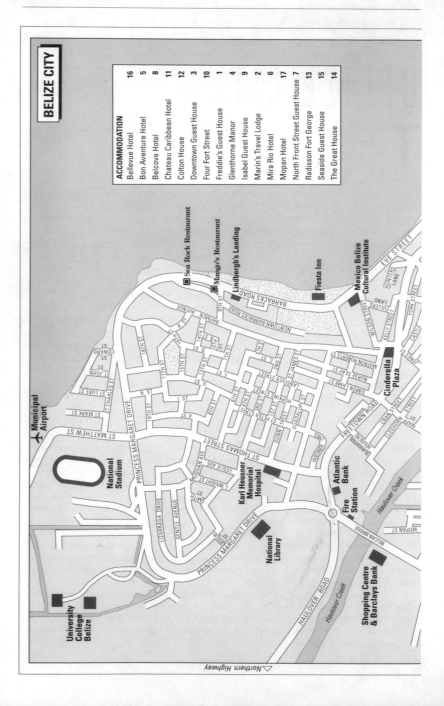

BELIZE CITY

ACCOMMODATION	
Bellevue Hotel	16
Bon Aventure Hotel	5
Belcove Hotel	8
Chateau Caribbean Hotel	11
Colton House	12
Downtown Guest House	3
Four Fort Street	10
Freddie's Guest House	1
Glenthorne Manor	4
Isabel Guest House	9
Marin's Travel Lodge	2
Mira Rio Hotel	6
Mopan Hotel	17
North Front Street Guest House	7
Radisson Fort George	13
Seaside Guest House	15
The Great House	14

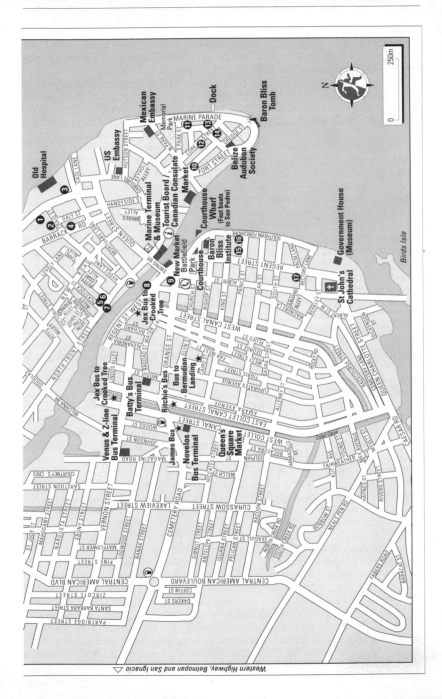

Western Highway, Belmopan and San Ignacio ▽

250m

0

N

Old Hospital

US Embassy

Mexican Embassy

Memorial Park

MARINE PARADE

Dock

Baron Bliss Tomb

HUTSON STREET

GAOL LANE

CRANBROOK LANE

KEYHOLE ALLEY

PARK ST

FORT STREET

CORK STREET

GEORGE ST

S PARK ST

11

12

13

14

Belize Audubon Society

HANDYSIDE ST

BARRACK RD

DALY ST

QUEEN STREET

BRIDES ALLEY

Marine Terminal & Museum

Tourist Board / Canadian Consulate

Market

Courthouse Wharf (Fast boats to San Pedro)

10

MORGAN LANE

HYDE LANE

SWING BR

New Market

Battlefield Park

Courthouse

Baron Bliss Institute

SOUTHERN FORESHORE

Government House (Museum)

Birds Isle

REGENT STREET

NORTH FRONT STREET

REGENT ST WEST

ALEXANDRIA ST

RICHARD ST

BAGDAD ST

WATER LANE

MOSUL ST

LINDOS ALLEY

Jex Bus to Crooked Tree

8

9

Court Tree

5

6

7

ALBERT ST

BISHOP ST

KING ST

CHURCH ST

PRINCE ST

DEAN ST

SOUTH ST

COMMANDANT LANE

MAGNESSA LA

PAYLANE

RECTOR LANE

17

15

16

St John's Cathedral

ALBERT ST W

WEST CANAL STREET

BELCANA BR

DOUGLAS

TARLTON ST

CURL ST

GYM ST

ORANGE ST

TIGRIS STREET

GEORGE ST

BASRA STREET

ROCK RD

BLUES ST

Jex Bus to Crooked Tree

Batty's Bus Terminal

Ritchie's Bus

Bus to Bermudian Landing

Venus & Z-line Bus Terminal

CEMETERY ROAD

SDOOW ST

JOHNSON ST

James Bus

Novelos Bus Terminal

MAGAZINE ROAD

EAST COLLET CANAL STREET

WEST COLLET CANAL STREET

CANAL STREET

EUPHRATES AVENUE

AMARA AVENUE

ALLEN ST

Queen's Square Market

HICCATEE STREET

WELCH ST

BOCATORA ST

DOLPHIN ST

ARMADILLO ST

Collet Canal

FAIRWEATHER ST

CAESAR RD

QUEEN CHARLOTTE STREET

CEMETERY LANE / MAY LANE

BARRACKS LANE

COURTNEY'S CRES

SARSTOON STREET

VERNON STREET

LAKEVIEW STREET

CURASSOW STREET

BANAK STREET

GIBNUT STREET

ANTELOPE STREET

IGUANA STREET

PELICAN STREET

SEAGULL ST

KUT AVE

NEAL'S PEN RD

BENBOW ST

SOUTH CREEK RD

RIVERO STREET

HAYNES ST

MCNEE AVENUE

MYVETTE ST

MAHOGANY STREET

MARGUSTA STREET

EBONY STREET

MAYFLOWER ST

LOGWOOD STREET

PINE STREET

ST JUDE ST

CENTRAL AMERICAN BLVD

ZIRICOTE STREET

COFFIN ST

CENTRAL AMERICAN BOULEVARD

DAKERS ST

SANTA BARBARA STREET

PARTRIDGE STREET

KING FISHER RD

FABERS ROAD

BARRACAT ST

A brief history

Exactly how Belize came by its name is something of a mystery, but there are plenty of possibilities. It could be a corruption of "Wallace"; the name either of a notorious English pirate reputed to have landed here in 1638 or of Peter Wallace, a Scotsman who may have founded a colony here in 1620. Another possibility is that it is a corruption of the French word *balise* (beacon), as there may have been a light marking the mouth of the **Belize River** – a vital trade route throughout Maya times up to the arrival of the Spanish in the sixteenth century. Those preferring a more ancient origin believe the name to be derived from *beliz*, a Maya word meaning "muddy water", or from the Maya term *belekin*, meaning "towards the east".

Historians estimate that when the **Spanish** conquered southern Yucatán and Belize in 1544 there were around 200,000 Maya living in Belize (a close approximation of the country's total population today) and, even if there is scant proof of a Maya settlement beneath the present-day city, there is abundant evidence that Moho Caye, just off the river mouth, was a Maya fishing and transhipment port. Although Spanish friars founded missions inland and the secular authorities sent military expeditions upstream to force the scattered Maya villages into paying tribute to *encomenderos* (colonial landlords) in Yucatán, they built no large towns in Belize, and the Maya population along the coast was decimated by disease and enslavement during the century after the conquest. The area that became Belize was administered from Mérida, via Bacalar, as part of colonial Yucatán, itself a remote province of New Spain: the imperial Spanish power may have reigned but it exercised little effective rule in this far frontier.

By the late sixteenth century the Spanish treasure fleets in the Caribbean attracted British (and other European) pirates, or **buccaneers**, who took advantage of the refuge offered by the reefs and shallows of Belize, using the cayes as bases for further plundering raids. Ever the opportunists, the buccaneers made money between raids by cutting the valuable logwood (used for textile dyes) that grew abundantly in the tropical swamps, building a number of camps from Campeche to Honduras. The settlement at the mouth of the Belize River, constructed by consolidating the mangrove swamp with wood chips, loose coral and rum bottles gradually became more permanent, and by the 1700s **Belize Town** was well established as a centre for the **Baymen** (as the settlers called themselves), their families and their slaves, though the capital of the Bay settlement was on St George's Caye. After the rains had floated the logs downriver the men returned to Belize Town to drink and brawl, with huge Christmas celebrations going on for weeks. The seafront contained the houses of the logwood cutters; the slaves lived in cabins on the south side of Haulover Creek, with various tribal groups occupying separate areas.

Spain was still the dominant colonial power in the region, however, and mounted several expeditions aimed at demonstrating control over the territory. In 1779 a Spanish raid captured many of the settlers and the rest fled, but most returned in 1783, when Spain agreed to recognize the rights of the British settlers, and Belize Town grew into the main centre of the logwood and mahogany trade on the Bay of Honduras. Spanish raids continued until the Battle of St George's Caye in 1798, when the settlers achieved victory with British naval help – a success that reinforced the bond with the British government. The nineteenth century saw the increasing influence of **British expatriates**, colonial-style wooden housing dominating the shoreline as the "Scots clique" began to clean up the town's image and take control of its administration. Belize also became a base for Anglican missionaries: in 1812 the Anglican cathedral of St John was built to serve a diocese that stretched from Belize to Panamá.

Fires in 1804, 1806 and 1856 necessitated extensive rebuilding, and there were epidemics of cholera, yellow fever and smallpox in this period too. Despite these reversals, the town grew with immigration from the West Indies and refugees from the Caste Wars in the Yucatán. In 1862 Belize became the colony of **British Honduras**, with Belize City as the administrative centre, and in 1871 Belize was officially declared a Crown Colony, with a resident governor appointed by Britain.

For the people of Belize the twentieth century has been dominated by uncertainty over their relationship with the "mother country". In 1914 thousands of Belizeans volunteered to assist the war effort, but when they arrived in the Middle East they were confronted by a wall of prejudice and racism, and consigned to labour battalions. In 1919 the returning soldiers rioted in Belize City, an event that marked the onset of Black consciousness and the beginning of the **independence movement**.

On September 10, 1931, the city was celebrating the anniversary of the Battle of St George's Caye when it was hit by a massive **hurricane** that uprooted houses, flooded the entire city and killed about a thousand people – 10 percent of the population. Disaster relief was slow to arrive and many parts of the city were left in a state of squalid poverty. This neglect, together with the effects of the Depression, gave added momentum to the campaign for independence, and the city saw numerous rallies and marches in an upsurge of defiance against the British colonial authorities. In 1961 the city was again ravaged by a hurricane: 262 people died, and the damage was so serious that plans were made to relocate the capital inland to Belmopan. (Hattieville, on the Western Highway, began life as a refuge for those fleeing the hurricane.) The official attitude was that Belize City would soon become a redundant backwater as Belmopan grew, but in fact few people chose to leave for the sterile "new town" atmosphere of Belmopan, and Belize City remains by far the most populous place in the country.

Belize gained internal self-government in 1964, and the goal of **full independence** was reached in 1981, with Belize joining the Commonwealth as a sovereign state. Loyalty to the monarchy remains strong, though – as shown by the tumultuous welcome given to Queen Elizabeth on her visits in 1985 and 1994. Since independence the rise of foreign investment and tourism has made an impact, and Belize City is now experiencing a major construction boom.

Arrival and orientation

Although Belize City is by far the largest urban area in the country (the capital, Belmopan is less than one tenth the size), it's small enough to make **walking** the easiest way to get around. The city is divided neatly into north and south halves by the **Haulover Creek**, a delta branch of the Belize River. The pivotal point of the city centre is the **Swing Bridge**, always busy with traffic and opened twice a day to allow larger vessels up and down the river. **North** of the Swing Bridge things tend to be slightly more upmarket; here you'll find the most expensive hotels, most of the embassies and consulates, and – in the King's Park area – some very luxurious houses. **South** of the Swing Bridge is the market and commercial zone, with banks, offices and supermarkets; the foreshore is the prestige area, home to the colonial governor's residence, now a museum. The area west of the main thoroughfares of Regent and Albert streets is unsafe after dark.

Getting from the transport terminals to the centre is very easy, and once you get downtown you'll find that almost everything you need is within a kilometre of the Swing Bridge. **Taxis**, identified by green licence plates, cost Bz$5 for one or two passengers within the city (including to and from the municipal airport), and Bz$30 to the international airport; for other journeys agree the fare in advance. They'll be waiting for passengers at all the transport terminals given below, or you can call one on ☎32916; you should definitely take a **taxi** if you arrive anywhere at night. A **city bus** operates to a few residential areas but is of little use to the visitor.

Points of arrival

Belize City has two **airports**. International flights land at the **Philip Goldson International Airport**, 17km northwest of the city at Ladyville, just off the Northern Highway. Arriving here can be chaotic, with a crush of people waiting anxiously for trolleys to trundle in with their luggage. Not infrequently, baggage is left on board, to return from San Salvador or Tegucigalpa in a couple of days. The new terminal, opened in 1990, initially alleviated some of the overcrowding but even this is sometimes swamped by the huge increase in visitor numbers; a further extension is currently under construction. It's worth knowing that incoming passengers can pick up a large **duty-free** allowance at far cheaper prices than the duty-free shops at departure airports in North America or Europe. Belize's **domestic airlines** also make stops at the international airport, so you might want to pick up an onward flight right away: prices to all destinations are Bz$30 more than from the main domestic base at the **municipal airport**, a few kilometres north of the city centre, by the sea.

From the international airport, the only way into the city is by taxi (Bz$30), or walk to the Northern Highway (25min) and flag down one of the frequent passing buses. If you're heading straight to San Ignacio, Cayo District, go to the Discovery Expeditions kiosk just outside the entrance, where you can pick up their **limo service**; pricey at Bz$58 but worth it if you're in a hurry. From the municipal airport take a taxi to town; walking takes 25 minutes.

The four main **bus companies** in Belize have their terminals in the same western area of the city, around the Collet Canal and Magazine Road, a fairly derelict part of town known as Mesopotamia. It's only 1km from the centre and you can easily walk – or, especially at night, take a taxi – to any of the hotels listed below. Most scheduled **boats returning from the cayes** pull in at the Marine Terminal on the north side of the Swing Bridge, though some use Courthouse Wharf on the south side; from either it's a fairly short walk or taxi ride to any of the hotels or bus depots.

Information and tours

The Belize **Tourist Board** main office is at 83 N Front St (Mon–Fri 8am–noon & 1–5pm; ☎77213). Here, you can pick up free bus timetables, a hotel guide and city map, nature reserve brochures and copies of the free tourist **newspapers**. Superb topographical **maps** of Belize are sold at the Lands Office, above the post office (entrance on N Front St). A two-sheet map covering the whole country (1:250,000) costs Bz$10 per sheet, and there is a series of 44 sheets covering the whole country (1:50,000), for Bz$3 each. They also have geological maps and a land-use map.

If walking around the city sights sounds too tiring then take a **city bus tour** with Captain Nicolas Sanchez (☎014/8777), whose historical knowledge is phenomenal: daily tours (2hr 30min; Bz$25) leave punctually from the Marine Terminal at 9am and 3pm. Should you want to escape the city for a day or two, you can take one of the **day tours** inland. Most visit at least two of the following: the Belize Zoo, Bermudian Landing Baboon Sanctuary, Crooked Tree Wildlife Sanctuary, Altun Ha ruins and Lamanai ruins. All but the last two are very easy to visit independently, though, with the exception of the zoo, you'll need to stay overnight. However, even with the extra cost of accommodation, it's still likely to work out less expensive than a tour. If time is short and you'd prefer a **guided tour** contact one of the following: Belize Travel Adventures, 168 N Front St (☎33064, fax 33196); Discovery Expeditions, 126 Freetown Rd (☎30748, fax 30750); Melmish Mayan Tours (☎35399, fax 31531); or David Cunningham, an independent naturalist tour guide (contact through the *Mopan Hotel* or ☎ & fax 24400; mobile ☎014/9892).

> The **telephone code** for Belize City is ☎02

Accommodation

There are about fifty **hotels** in Belize City, around a third of which cost between Bz$30–50 double, with at least another half-dozen in the range of Bz$50–75. The selection below covers all price ranges. For a more comprehensive list, pick up a copy of *Destination Belize* from the tourist board or any hotel. There's usually no need to book (unless you're eager to stay in a particular hotel) as you'll almost always find something in the price range you're looking for — though a phone call can save time and effort.

The north side
Most of the budget hotels north of the river are clustered on or near **N Front St**; those listed below also have good rates for singles. The more upmarket hotels (most take credit cards) are generally located in the historic **Fort George area** or along the **seafront**, where the residents can benefit from the sea breezes.

BUDGET ACCOMMODATION
Bon Aventure, 122 N Front St (☎44248). Next door to the *North Front Street Guest House* and equally good value at very similar prices. ②.

> ## ACCOMMODATION PRICE CODES
>
> All accommodation listed in this guide has been given a **price code** according to the following scale. The prices refer to the cost of **a double room in high season** (generally December to Easter) in Belize dollars (Bz$), but usually do not include the government hotel tax of seven percent. For more details see p.26.
>
> | | | |
> |---|---|---|
> | ① under Bz$20 | ④ Bz$50–70 | ⑦ Bz$140–190 |
> | ② Bz$20–30 | ⑤ Bz$70–100 | ⑧ Bz$190–240 |
> | ③ Bz$30–50 | ⑥ Bz$100–140 | ⑨ over Bz$240 |

Downtown Guest House, 5 Eve St, near the end of Queen St (☎ & fax 32057). Best-value budget place in the city. Small, very friendly, clean and secure; even the shared bathrooms have reliable hot water. You can receive a fax, get laundry done and the owner, Miss Kenny, will cook a bargain breakfast. ②.

Marin's Travelodge, 6 Craig St, towards the old hospital (☎45166). Another very good budget option; comfortable, clean and really quiet. The rooms are well furnished and the showers excellent. ②.

Mira Rio, 59 N Front St (☎34147), across the road from the *North Front Street Guest House*. Reasonable rooms, overlooking the river, with washbasin and toilet; shared bathroom. The bar below is good for information, as boat owners often call in for a beer (but there's no late-night noise) and there's also simple but tasty Creole food available. ②.

North Front Street Guest House, 124 N Front St (☎77595). A budget travellers' favourite: friendly, helpful and just two blocks from the boats to Caye Caulker. New management has improved the whole place; you may need to book. ②.

MODERATE TO EXPENSIVE

Chateau Caribbean, 6 Marine Parade (☎30800, fax 30900, email *chateaucar@btl.net*). Comfortable, colonial-style hotel with a/c, cable TV, some sea views and a good restaurant (see p.59). The Chateau featured in several movies – the spacious public areas, with wicker furniture and balconies overlooking the sea, are a favourite of visiting film crews. ⑦.

Colton House, 9 Cork St (☎44666, fax 30451, email *coltonhse@btl.net*). Beautifully kept colonial house in the Fort George area, dating from the 1920s; easily the best guest house in Belize. The five rooms are individually decorated in English country-house style, each with an immaculate bathroom and balcony (a/c is available and the downstairs garden room has a fridge, microwave and TV). No meals are served but there's free coffee in the mornings and you can enjoy tea on the veranda. Owners Alan and Ondina Colton keep an extensive book and video library on Belize and can arrange substantial discounts on tours. No children under 9. ⑤.

Four Fort Street (☎30116, fax 78808, email *fortst@btl.net*). Large rooms with ceiling fans in an expertly restored colonial house. Beds are comfortable four-posters, draped with mosquito nets, and the upstairs sitting room is furnished with wicker couches. A/c rooms are available but there are no private bathrooms. There's also a popular (but pricey) restaurant. Breakfast included. ⑥.

Freddie's Guest House, 86 Eve St, on the city edge near the waterfront (☎33851). Three clean, secure and peaceful rooms (one with immaculate private bathroom); the shared bathrooms also gleam. Best value in this price range. ④.

The Great House, 13 Cork St (☎33400, fax 33444, email *greathouse@btl.net*). Six spacious and well-equipped a/c rooms in a recently modernized and expanded private house, originally built in 1927. All rooms have a balcony, private bathroom, coffee-maker, TV, phone and dedicated fax line. There's also a fine restaurant in the courtyard. ⑦.

Glenthorne Manor, 27 Barrack Rd, off Queen St (☎44212). Lovely, individually designed (and named) rooms with balconies in a large, very comfortable colonial-style house. A delicious "Belizean-style" continental breakfast is included, and guests can use the kitchen. There's secure parking, an upstairs sitting room and you can do laundry; a/c rooms available. ⑤.

Radisson Fort George, 2 Marine Parade, north side of the harbour mouth (☎33333, fax 73820, email *rdfgh@btl.net*). Luxurious flagship of the city's hotels, and by far the most expensive at around Bz$300, though you can expect substantial discounts on the "rack rates". All rooms have huge cable TV, fridge and minibar and those in the Club Wing, reached by the only glass elevator in Belize, have unbeatable sea views. There's an excellent restaurant and the grounds are an oasis of calm on the edge of the sea, with a sea-facing pool and a private dock. ⑨.

The south side

Belcove Hotel, 9 Regent St West (☎73054). You pay for the luxury of a balcony over the r. with a view of the Swing Bridge. There's a certain thrill of being on the edge of the dangerous part of town, though the hotel itself is quite secure and the rooms have been recently renovated. The friendly, knowledgeable owner, Danny Weir, organizes day-trips to the reef at Gallows Point. ④.

Bellevue Hotel, 5 Southern Foreshore (☎77051, fax 72353, email *fins@btl.net*). The top hotel on the south side of the Swing Bridge, right on the seafront with a private dock. Modern, a/c rooms in a converted colonial house with a relaxing courtyard, adorned with palms and pool. The upstairs Harbour Room bar is a popular meeting place; especially during the Friday evening happy hour, and the Mayan Tavern disco is a focal point of the city's nightlife, with live music at weekends. Good restaurant. ⑥.

Isabel Guest House, across Swing Bridge, above and behind *Central Drug Store* (☎73139). Small, friendly, Spanish-speaking guest house, with large rooms and private showers. ③.

Mopan Hotel, 55 Regent St (☎77351, fax 75383, email *hotelmopan@btl.net*). Large wood-fronted building at the quiet end of the street near Government House Museum. Run by avid conservationist Jean Shaw, it's popular with naturalists, writers and scientists. Rooms have private bath and some have a/c, but some are dimly lit. Jean is a mine of information on Belize; she runs Mopan Travels and can arrange flights to Guatemala. Very good-value breakfasts, and you can order lunch and dinner. ⑤.

Seaside Guest House, 3 Prince St (☎78339, email *friends@btl.net*), half a block from the southern foreshore. A clean, well-run and very secure hotel that's become a bustling meeting place for travellers – and you really can see the sea. One room has seven hostel-style dorm beds (Bz$18). Good hot showers (shared), a payphone, tons of accurate information and a relaxing, orchid-filled garden make it a great budget option. Meals can be ordered, and there's a beer and wine licence. You get a key for access at all times – a rarity in budget hotels. ③.

The City

Richard Davies, a British traveller in the mid-nineteenth century, wrote of the city: "There is much to be said for Belize, for in its way it was one of the prettiest ports at which we touched, and its cleanliness and order... were in great contrast to the ports we visited later as to make them most remarkable." Many of the features that elicited this praise have now gone, though some of the distinctive **wooden colonial buildings** have been preserved as heritage showpieces, or converted into hotels, restaurants and museums. Yet even in cases where the decay is too advanced for the paintwork, balconies and carved railings to be restored, the old wooden structures remain more pleasing than the concrete blocks that have replaced so many of them.

Before the construction of the first wooden bridge in the early 1800s, cattle were winched over the waterway that divides the city – hence the name **Haulover Creek**. Its replacement, the **Swing Bridge**, made in Liverpool and opened in 1923, is the only manually operated swing bridge left in the Americas. Every day at 5.30am and 5.30pm the endless parade of vehicles and people is halted by policemen, and the process of turning begins. Using long poles inserted into a capstan, four men gradually lever the bridge around until it's pointing in the direction of the harbour mouth. During the few minutes that the bridge is open, the river traffic is busier than that on the roads, and traffic is snarled up across the whole city. There's a possibility, however, that the bridge may be demolished, since a drawbridge has been built a few blocks upriver, relieving some of the congestion. A vocal preservation campaign has been mobilized.

The north side

Immediately on the **north side** of the Swing Bridge is the **Marine Terminal**, the place to catch boats for the northern cayes. In the same building – the beautifully restored former Belize City Fire Station, built in 1923 – are two of Belize's new museums, both superbly designed. The **Coastal Zone Museum** contains fascinating displays and explanations of reef ecology, the highlight being a 3-D model of the entire reef system including the cayes and atolls; upstairs, the **Marine Museum** exhibits an amazing collection of models and documents relating to Belize's maritime heritage (both Mon–Sat 8am–4.30pm; Bz$4). Opposite the Marine Terminal, the three-storey wooden **Paslow Building** (named after Thomas Paslow, a controversial hero of the Battle of St George's Caye) houses the post office on the ground floor. A block east of the Marine Terminal, at 91 N Front Street, **The Image Factory** (Mon–Fri 9am–6pm; ☎34151; free but donations welcome) is home to Belize's hottest contemporary artists. The gallery holds outstanding, sometimes provocative exhibitions and you often get a chance

---

EMORY KING

Any sailor shipwrecked on a foreign shore would doubtless be grateful to the land that saved them, but while for many such salvation might leave a lifelong impression, few would be so impressed that they would want to spend the rest of their lives there. Nevertheless, that's exactly what happened to **Emory King**, American-born wit, raconteur, realtor, historian, broadcaster, writer, film extra and businessman, when his schooner *Vagabond* crashed onto the coral off English Caye, British Honduras in 1953. Realizing almost immediately that the colony presented unrivalled opportunities to a young man of limited means but boundless entrepreneurial spirit, he stayed on, convinced he could play a major role in the development of this colonial backwater.

Finding the **Belize City** of the early 1950s much like a nineteenth-century village, with only a handful of cars (which, to his astonishment, drove on the left), a sickly electric power system and a few telephones to represent the twentieth century, he set about trying to change it. Within a year he managed to get appointed as the Secretary of the Chamber of Commerce, and then Secretary of the Tourist Committee — at a time when tourists were counted in dozens rather than hundreds of thousands. Believing that what the moribund colony needed to prosper was investment, and that the best way to attract investors was to offer them a land with low (or no) taxes, he waged a (so far still unsuccessful) campaign to abolish income tax. But although he advised investors and found land for American farmers who no longer had a frontier of their own to conquer, Emory King's most enduring gift to his adopted country was persuading the **Mennonites** (see box on p.74) to settle here in 1958; their back-breaking pioneer work is probably Belize's greatest agricultural success story.

Emory King's involvement in Belize extends to **film appearances**: he has had cameo roles in all the Hollywood movies filmed here (see p.38). In perhaps the best-known, *The Mosquito Coast*, he played a down-at-heel, drunken landowner offering to sell Harrison Ford a piece of land – a part he claims is not typecasting. Emory's **books** on or about Belize and Belize life are on sale all over the country; a good one to start with is *Hey Dad, This Is Belize*, a whimsical account of family life (see pp.225–6 for further titles). Most days he can be found in his office, in the forecourt of the *Radisson Fort George*, and will usually have time to sign a book or two — and without the markup charged by hotel gift shops.

to discuss the work with the artists themselves. Continuing east along N Front Street, past the "temporary" market (which often has a greater variety of produce than the official market south of the Swing Bridge), you pass the **National Handicraft Center** (Mon–Fri 8am–5pm), which sells high-quality Belizean crafts at fair prices.

Beyond, the road follows the north shore of the river mouth – an area that was Fort George Island until the narrow strait was filled in in 1924 – reaching the point marked by **Bliss Lighthouse**, the tomb of and memorial to Baron Bliss, Belize's greatest benefactor (see p.58). Walking around the shoreline you pass the *Radisson Fort George* hotel, in whose forecourt is the office of Emory King, one of Belize's most famous characters (see box opposite), and **Memorial Park**, which honours the Belizean dead of World War I. In this area you'll find several **colonial mansions**, many of the best-preserved now taken over by embassies and upmarket hotels; a fine example is the Mexican embassy on the north corner of the park.

Natural history enthusiasts will benefit from a visit to two of Belize's foremost conservation organizations in the Fort George area: the **Belize Audubon Society** at 12 Fort St (☎35004), has information, books, maps and posters relating to all the country's wildlife reserves, and is very prominent in conservation education; nearby, at 2 S Park St (☎75616), facing Memorial Park, are the offices of the **Programme for Belize**, which manages the Rio Bravo Conservation Area (p.77); call in for news on access and progress from the enthusiastic staff. A little to the north, at the corner of Hutson Street and Gabourel Lane and set back one block from the sea, is the **US Embassy**; this superb "colonial" building was actually constructed in New England in the nineteenth century from American timber, before being dismantled and shipped to Belize. About 750m north along the shore, at the far end of Eve Street, a new sea wall and promenade have been built, leading to the landmark *Fiesta Inn*. The attractive new park beyond was built on reclaimed land. It was in this area that Charles Lindbergh landed the *Spirit of St Louis* in 1927, the first aircraft to land in Belize. Today the approximate spot is marked by **Lindbergh's Landing** bar, decorated with photographs of the famous aviator.

The south side

The **south side** is generally the older section of Belize City: in the early days the elite lived in the seafront houses while the backstreets were home to the slaves and labourers. These days it's the city's commercial centre, containing the main shopping streets, banks and travel agencies. Right by the Swing Bridge is the three-storey **covered market**, which opened in 1993 on the site of the rather decrepit old market from 1820. Though the new one is much cleaner, it's not popular with either traders or shoppers, most of whom have carried on using the "temporary" market, on the north side of the river.

Albert Street, running south from the Swing Bridge, is the main commercial thoroughfare, with banks, supermarkets and good value T-shirt and souvenir shops – Sings, at number 35, has some of the best bargains. On the parallel **Regent Street**, a block closer to the sea, are the former colonial administration and court buildings, known together as the **Court House**. These well-preserved examples of colonial architecture, with their columns and fine wrought iron, were completed in 1926 after an earlier building on the same site was destroyed by fire. The Court House overlooks a patch of grass and trees with an ornamental fountain in the centre, ambitiously known as Central Park until it was renamed **Battlefield Park** in the early 1990s, commemorating the heated political meetings which took place there before independence.

A block south of the Court House, on the waterfront and resembling a squat airport control tower, the **Bliss Institute** is in fact the cultural centre of Belize City (Mon–Fri 8.30am–noon & 2–8pm, Sat 8.30am–noon). The Institute was funded by the legacy of Baron Bliss, a moderately eccentric Englishman with a Portuguese title. A keen fisherman, he arrived off the coast of Belize in his yacht *Sea King* in 1926 after hearing about the tremendous amount of game fish in local waters. Unfortunately, he became ill and died without ever having been ashore, but he must have been impressed by whatever fish he did catch, as he left most of his considerable estate to benefit the people of the colony. This became the Bliss Trust, which has been used on various projects, helping to build markets and improve roads and water supplies. In gratitude the authorities declared March 9 (the date of his death) an official public holiday – Baron Bliss Day – commemorated by boat races funded partly by his legacy. The Bliss building is the home of the **National Arts Council** and there's a small exhibition from the National Art Collection. The Institute also hosts many other exhibitions, concerts and plays; it's worth checking with the tourist board if there's anything on during your visit. Just inside the entrance are stelae and altars from Caracol, priceless examples of Maya art that seem to have been dumped in a corner while somewhere is found to display them; a small plaque gives an account of the scenes depicted on the stones.

At the southern end of Albert Street is **St John's Cathedral**, the oldest Anglican cathedral in Central America and one of the oldest buildings in Belize. Work began in 1812 and was completed in 1820, the red bricks for its construction brought over as ballast in British ships. With its square, battlemented tower, it looks more like a large English parish church than anything you might expect to find in Central America; the main structure, roof and mahogany beams have survived almost 180 years of tropical heat and hurricanes. Here, between 1815 and 1845, the kings of the Mosquito Coast were crowned amid great pomp, taking the title to a British Protectorate that extended along the coast of Honduras and Nicaragua. The Miskito Indians, keen to keep their links with Britain to avoid Spanish colonial rule, had their kings crowned and children baptized in Belize's cathedral.

Opposite the cathedral, in a beautiful, breezy seafront setting and shaded by palms is the well-preserved, white-painted **Government House Museum** (Mon–Fri 8.30am–4pm; Bz$5), complete with green lawn. Built in 1814, it was the governor's residence when Belize was a British colony: at midnight on September 20, 1981 the Belize flag was hoisted here for the first time as the country celebrated independence. Government House is still used for some official receptions, particularly on Independence Day, but the present governor general, Sir Colville Young, wanted to make this superb example of Belize's colonial heritage open to everyone, with the result that in 1996 it was designated a museum. The collection includes silverware, glasses and furniture used during the colonial period, as well as colonial archives. A plush red carpet leads down the hall to the great mahogany staircase, the walls lined with prints of sombre past governors; upstairs some of the grandeur is lost – the bedroom furniture on show wouldn't have looked out of place in a 1960s middle-class British house. In the grounds, the carefully restored *Sea King*, the tender of Baron Bliss's yacht of the same name, stands as testimony to the craftsmanship of Belizean boatbuilders.

Yarborough Cemetery, just west of the cathedral, was named after the magistrate who owned the land and permitted the burial of prominent people here from 1781 – commoners were admitted only after 1870. Although the graves have fallen into disrepair, a browse among the stones will turn up fascinating snippets of history. At the seaward end of this strip of land, connected to the mainland by a narrow wooden causeway, **Bird's Isle** is a venue for reggae concerts and parties.

Eating, drinking and nightlife

The multitude of **restaurants** in Belize City don't offer very much in the way of variety. There's the tasty but monotonous **Creole** fare of rice and beans, plenty of seafood and steaks, and a preponderance of **Chinese** restaurants, usually the best bet for **vegetarians**. Vegetables other than cabbage, carrots, onions and peppers are rarely served in restaurants and these are likely to be the main components of any salad. As always, the **market**, and particularly the "temporary" market on the north bank of the river, are the best places to eat cheaply, with basic dishes of rice and beans, beef, fish and chicken. Greasy fried chicken is available as takeaway from small restaurants all over the city: a Belizean favourite known as **"dollar chicken"**, whatever the price. If you're really in a hurry, *HL's Burger*, Belize City's answer to *McDonald's*, has a growing number of outlets, serving standard but safe fast food fare. The big **hotels** have their own restaurants, naturally quite expensive but with much more varied menus and good service.

If you're **shopping for food**, the main **supermarkets** – Brodie's and Romac's – are worth a look; they're on Albert St, just past the park, and their selection of food is good if expensive, reflecting the fact that much is imported. Milk and dairy products, produced locally by Mennonite farmers (see p.74), are delicious and good quality. Naturally enough, local **fruit** is cheap and plentiful, though highly seasonal – Belizean citrus fruits are among the best in the world.

In the listings below we have quoted a phone number in places where it is recommended you should **reserve a table** or for those places which offer **delivery service**.

Restaurants and cafés north of the river

The Ark, 109 N Front St (☎77820). Very tasty Belizean dishes at great prices; already cooked so it's a good choice for a quick meal. Also does deliveries. Mon–Sat 7am–11pm.

Chateau Caribbean, 6 Marine Parade. For undisturbed views of blue sea and offshore islands, head up the steps to this cool first-floor restaurant, where prices are more reasonable than you'd guess from the gleaming white linen and cutlery.

Chon Sing, N Front St, opposite the Texaco station. Large portions of Chinese food, unfortunately accompanied by violent Chinese kung-fu fighting videos.

Fort Street Restaurant, 4 Fort St (☎30116). High-quality Creole and American food in the relaxed surroundings of a restored colonial house. Popularity has led to an increase in prices, but the daily lunch special remains reasonable value.

Mango's, 164 Newtown Barracks Rd (☎34021). Away from the centre, near the *Fiesta Inn*, this was formerly *The Grill*, and continues to be one of the best restaurants in the city. Seafood is a speciality but, also serves well-prepared steak and pasta dishes and there's always a vegetarian option.

Mar's Belizean Restaurant, 118 N Front St. Great, clean place serving really tasty Belizean food at good prices. Handy for anyone at *N Front St Guest House*; opens at 6am.

Pepper's Pizza, 2215 Baymen Ave. Decent pizza restaurant that delivers. Mon–Thurs 5–11pm, until midnight Fri & Sat.

Sea Rock, 190 Newtown Barracks Road. Extremely good Indian food in a quiet, clean restaurant. It's a long way from the centre so you'll need to take a taxi.

Restaurants and cafés south of the river

La Cocinita, 56 Regent St. Wonderful Belizean restaurant, with great daily breakfast and lunch specials. Eat indoors or at a table on the veranda overlooking the street. Mon–Fri 7.30am–2.30pm.

Dit's, 50 King St. Great pastries and inexpensive Creole food such as cowfoot soup.

Macy's, 18 Bishop St (☎73419). Long-established, reasonably priced Creole restaurant that's popular with locals and extremely busy at lunchtimes. They also serve traditional game: armadillo, deer and gibnut (a type of large rodent), but thankfully turtle is no longer on the menu.

Marlins, 11 Regent St West, next to the *Belcove Hotel*. Good, inexpensive, local food in large portions – and you can eat on the veranda overlooking the river.

Pop'n'Taco, corner of King St and Regent St. Chinese-run restaurant, serving cheap Chinese food, despite the name.

River Side Patio, at the rear of the market. Good place to relax with a drink as you watch the bridge swing. Mexican-style food, and entertainment on Fri and Sat evenings.

Drinking, nightlife and entertainment

Belize City's more sophisticated, air-conditioned **bars** are found in the most expensive establishments, and there aren't many of those. At the lowest end of the scale are dimly lit dives, effectively men-only, where, though there's the possibility that you'll be offered drugs or be robbed, it's more likely that you'll have a thoroughly enjoyable time meeting easy-going, hard-drinking locals. There are several places between the two extremes, most of them in restaurants and hotels – for example, *Marlins* restaurant (see above) and *Mira Rio* hotel (see "Accommodation" p.54). One of the best is *Lindbergh's Landing* (see p.57), a quiet, open-air bar with sea views. The *Calypso Bar* at the *Fiesta* frequently hosts top local bands.

Nightlife, though not as wild as it used to be, is becoming more reliable and the quality of live bands is improving all the time. The *Radisson Fort George* and the *Bellevue* hold regular dances, and if you're after **live music**, there's reggae at the *Lumba Yaad Bar*, on the riverbank just out of town on the Northern Highway. It can get out of hand – best go at lunchtime on Saturdays.

Listings

Airlines Aerocaribe, Belize Global Travel, 41 Albert St (☎77185); Aerovias, Mopan Travels, 55 Regent St (☎75446); American, corner of New Rd and Queen St (☎32522); Continental, 32 Albert St (☎78309); Maya Island Air, Municipal Airport (☎31140 or 026/2345); TACA, Belize Global Travel (☎77185); Tropic Air, Municipal Airport (☎45671 or 026/2012).

American Express in Belize Global Travel, 41 Albert St (☎77363).

Banks and exchange The main branches of Atlantic, Barclays, Belize and Scotia Bank are on Albert St (Mon–Thurs 8am–2pm, Fri 8am–4.30pm). Barclays, opposite the park, does cash advances on Visa and Mastercard (Belize Bank charge Bz$15), and has an ATM. Cash in US$ is usually readily available from the banks. Many shops, hotels and restaurants change travellers' cheques and cash, and money can sometimes be changed on the streets at a slightly better rate, but take care.

Books In addition to the bookshops listed here, many of the larger hotels also sell books, magazines and papers (including Caribbean editions of US newspapers and *Time, Newsweek* etc.), and some budget hotels operate book exchanges. The Book Centre, 2 Church St (opposite the BTL office) has the best selection of titles, including Rough Guides. The Belize Book Shop, Regent St opposite the *Mopan Hotel*, also has a good selection. For informed reading on Belize check out the SPEAR library on Pickstock St and New Rd (☎31668).

Car rental The following companies are in Belize City and will arrange vehicle pickup and drop-off anywhere in the city or at the Municipal or International Airports at no extra charge: Avis ☎34619; Budget ☎23435; Crystal ☎31600; National ☎31650; Pancho's ☎45554; Safari ☎35395.

Embassies and consulates Though the official capital is at Belmopan, some embassies remain in Belize City and are normally open Mon–Fri mornings. Several EU countries have (mainly honorary) consulates in Belize City; current addresses and phone numbers are listed in the green pages of the telephone directory. Canada (cannot issue passports), 83 N Front St (☎31060); Guatemala, 8 A Street, Kings Park (☎33150); Honduras, 91 N Front St (☎45889); Mexico, 20 Park St (☎31388); US, 29 Gabourel Lane (☎77161).

Film developing For prints, slides and fast passport photos, try Spooners, 89 N Front St.

Immigration The Belize Immigration Office is in the Government Complex on Mahogany St, near the junction of Central American Blvd and the Western Highway (Mon–Thurs 8.30–11.30am & 1–4pm, Fri 8.30–11.30am & 1–3.30pm; ☎24620). Thirty-day extensions of stay (the maximum allowed) cost Bz$25.

Laundry Central America Coin Laundry, 114 Barrack Rd (Mon–Sat 8.30am–9pm; reduced hours Sun), and in many hotels.

Medical care Dr Gamero, Myo-On Clinic, 40 Eve St (☎45616); Karl Heusner Memorial Hospital, Princess Margaret Drive, near the junction with the Northern Highway (☎ 31548).

Police The main police station is on Queen Street, a block north of the Swing Bridge (☎72210). Or contact a member of the Tourist Police (see p.32) or the Tourist Board (see p.52) during opening hours.

Post office The main post office is in the Paslow Building, on the corner of Queen St, immediately north of the Swing Bridge (Mon–Fri 8am–noon & 1–4.30pm). The parcel office is next door on N Front St.

Telecommunications There are payphones and cardphones dotted around the city; or use the main BTL office, 1 Church St (Mon–Sat 8am–6pm), where there are also fax and email services.

Travel and tour agents The following travel agents are the best for information and bookings on flights and connections throughout the region; all can arrange tours within Belize: Belize Global Travel, 41 Albert St (☎77363, fax 75213); JAL's Travel and Tours, 184 North Front St (☎45407, fax 30792); Universal Travel, 14 Handyside St (☎30963, fax 32120).

Western Union Belize Chamber of Commerce, 63 Regent St (☎75924, fax 74984).

MOVING ON FROM BELIZE CITY

Moving on from Belize City is easy, with regular departures by plane, bus or boat to all parts of the country, across the borders to Chetumal in Mexico and Melchor in Guatemala, and to the main northern cayes. Most transport tends to peter out at dusk.

BY BUS

Most of the **bus companies** and bus departure points are in the same area, along the Collet Canal and Magazine Road, a short walk from the centre of town. While the main bus companies have their own depots, there are numerous smaller operators with regular departures but no contact address or telephone number. The abbreviations used below follow the name of the company.

Bus companies and depots

Batty (BA), 15 Mosul St (☎72025); for the Northern and Western highways.

James Bus (JA), leaves for Punta Gorda (via Belmopan) from Shell station, Cemetery Rd, near Collet Canal, at 7am daily.

Jex Bus (JX; ☎025/7017) leaves for Crooked Tree from Regent St West and Pound Yard, Collet Canal.

McFadzean's Bus (MF), leaves for Bermudian Landing (via Burrell Boom) from the corner of Cemetery Rd and Mosul St, near the Batty bus depot, at noon.

Novelos (NV), 19 West Collet Canal (☎77372); for the Western Highway.

Perez Bus (PE), leaves for Sarteneja from the Texaco station on North Front St at noon.

Ritchie's Bus (RI), leaves from Collet Canal, near Cemetery Rd. Direct bus for Placencia at 2.30pm.

Russell's Bus (RU), leaves for Bermudian Landing from Cairo St, near the corner of Cemetery Rd and Euphrates Ave at noon & 4.30pm.

Venus (VE), Magazine Rd (☎73354); for the Northern Highway.

Z-Line (ZL), Magazine Rd (☎73937); for the Hummingbird and Southern highways and Coastal Road to Dangriga, Placencia and Punta Gorda.

Bus services from Belize City

Where express services (exp), are available these are faster and a fraction more expensive than regular services.

DESTINATION	FREQUENCY	BUS CO	DURATION
Belmopan	hourly 5am–8pm (exp)	BA, NV	1hr 15min
Bermudian Landing	Mon–Sat noon & 4.30pm	MR, RU	1hr 15min
Chetumal, Mexico	hourly 4am–7pm (exp)	BA, VE	3hr 30min
Corozal	hourly 4am–7pm (exp)	BA, VE	2hr 30min

Crooked Tree	Mon–Sat 4 daily, 1 on Sun:	BA	Mon–Fri 4pm, Sat noon, Sun 9am;
		JX	Mon–Sat 10.30am, 4.30pm & 5.30pm
		BA, JX	1hr 30min
Dangriga	10 daily 6am–5pm	RI, JA, ZL	2hr via Coastal Road; 3hr 30min via Belmopan
Gales Point	few direct; buses pass junction 3km away	RI, ZL	1hr 40min to junction
Melchor, Guatemala	hourly 5am–6pm	BA, NV	3hr 30min
Orange Walk	hourly 4am–7pm	BA, VE	1hr 30min
Placencia	3–4 daily, all via Dangriga	RI, ZL	4hr 30min; 6–7hr direct at 2.30pm via Belmopan
Punta Gorda	5 daily, all via Dangriga	JA, ZL	8–10hr
San Ignacio	hourly 5am–8pm (exp), all via Belmopan	BA, NV	3hr
Sarteneja	2 daily, via Orange Walk; PE noon, VE 12.30pm	PE, VE	3hr 30min

BY AIR
See "Listings" p.4 for details of international and domestic airlines.

International flights
Belize City International Airport to: Cancún, San Salvador, Guatemala City, Flores, San Pedro Sula and Roatán (see p.29).

Domestic flights
Domestic flights originate from Belize City's Municipal Airport, with dozens of scheduled flights to many destinations. Maya Island Air and Tropic Air operate flights to: Caye Caulker (15–20min) and San Pedro (10min from Caye Caulker), at least hourly from 7am–5pm; Dangriga (8–10 daily; 25min), Placencia (a further 20min) and Punta Gorda (another 25min). See "Basics" p.29 for further destinations.

BY BOAT
Scheduled **boats** to Caye Caulker leave from the Marine Terminal (☎31969) on N Front St, by the Swing Bridge (every two hours from 9am–5pm; 45min; Bz$15). For San Pedro on Ambergris Caye, scheduled boats leave from Courthouse Wharf, south of the Swing Bridge (3 daily, calling at Caye Caulker; 1hr 25min; Bz$25). Any scheduled boat will also stop on request at St George's Caye.

CHAPTER TWO

THE NORTH

Northern Belize is an expanse of relatively level land, where swamps, savannahs and lagoons are mixed with rainforest and farmland. For many years this part of the country was largely inaccessible and had closer ties with Mexico than Belize City – most of the original settlers were refugees from the Caste War in Yucatán, and brought with them the sugar cane which formed the basis of the economy for much of the twentieth century. The Indian and Mestizo farming communities were connected by a skeletal network of dirt tracks, while boats plied the route between Belize City and Corozal. In 1930, however, the Northern Highway brought the region into contact with the rest of the country, opening up the area to further waves of settlers.

The largest town in the north is **Orange Walk**, the main centre for sugar production. Further to the north, **Corozal** is a small and peaceful Caribbean town

ACCOMMODATION PRICE CODES

All accommodation listed in this guide has been given a **price code** according to the following scale. The prices refer to the cost of **a double room in high season** (generally December to Easter) in Belize dollars (Bz$), but usually do not include the government hotel tax of seven percent. For more details see p.26.

① under Bz$20   ④ Bz$50–70   ⑦ Bz$140–190
② Bz$20–30   ⑤ Bz$70–100   ⑧ Bz$190–240
③ Bz$30–50   ⑥ Bz$100–140   ⑨ over Bz$240

---

with a strong Mexican element – scarcely surprising as it lies just fifteen minutes from the border. Throughout the north Spanish is as common as Creole, and there's a mild Latin flavour to both of these places.

Most visitors to northern Belize are here to see the **Maya ruins** and wildlife reserves. The largest site, **Lamanai**, features some of the most impressive pyramids in the country; it's served by regular boat tours along the **New River** and a good road to the nearby village of **Indian Church**. East of Lamanai, **Altun Ha**, reached by the old Northern Highway, is usually visited as part of a day-trip from Belize City or San Pedro. Other sites include **Cuello** and **Nohmul**, respectively west and north of Orange Walk, and **Santa Rita** and **Cerros**, both near Corozal.

The four main **wildlife reserves** in the region each offer a different approach to conservation and an insight into different environments. At the **Bermudian Landing Community Baboon Sanctuary** in the Belize River Valley a group of farmers have combined agriculture with conservation, much to the benefit of the black howler monkey, while at the **Crooked Tree Wildlife Sanctuary** a network of rivers and lagoons offers protection to a range of migratory birds, including the endangered jabiru stork. By far the largest and most ambitious conservation project, however, is the **Rio Bravo Conservation Area**, comprising 970 square kilometres of tropical forest and river systems in the west of Orange Walk district. This vast, practically unspoilt area, containing several Maya sites, adjoins the borders with Guatemala and Mexico. The most northerly protected area is the Shipstern Nature Reserve, where a section of tropical forest and wetland is preserved with the help of the income from a butterfly farm.

Travelling around the north is fairly straightforward if you stick to the main roads. Batty and Venus between them operate bus services every hour from 4am to 7pm along the Northern Highway between Belize City and Santa Elena on the Mexican border, calling at Orange Walk and Corozal, and continuing across the border to the market in Chetumal. Smaller roads and centres are served by a fairly regular flow of buses and trucks; in addition, several companies operate tours to the Maya sites and nature reserves, though these can be expensive.

Belize City to Orange Walk

Regular, fast buses run the 88km along the **Northern Highway** from Belize City to Orange Walk in less than an hour and a half. To get to the **Bermudian Landing Baboon Sanctuary**, **Crooked Tree Wildlife Sanctuary** or the ruins of **Altun Ha** by public transport, you'll need to take one of the local buses detailed in the text.

Leaving Belize City you pass spreading suburbs, where expensive houses are constructed on reclaimed mangrove swamps; look to the east and you'll get a glimpse of the sea. Seven kilometres from the city a bridge carries the road over the mouth of the Belize River at the point where the Haulover Creek branches away to the south. For the next few kilometres the road stays very close to the river and this stretch is prone to flooding after heavy rain. If you notice a large, brightly painted, concrete building on the right-hand side of the road called Raul's Rose Garden you may care to know that it's not a nursery in the horticultural sense but a brothel. At **Ladyville**, 15km from Belize City, you pass the turning to the International Airport; another kilometre brings you to the branch road to Airport Camp, now run by the Belize Defence Force, and the main base of the British Forces in Belize.

The Bermudian Landing Community Baboon Sanctuary

The **Community Baboon Sanctuary**, established in 1985 in collaboration with primate biologist Rob Horwich and a group of local farmers (with help from the Worldwide Fund for Nature), is one of the most interesting conservation projects in Belize. A mixture of farmland and broad-leaved forest, the sanctuary stretches along 30km of the Belize River valley – from Flowers Bank to Big Falls – and comprises a total of eight villages and over a hundred landowners. Farmers here have adopted a voluntary code of practice to harmonize their own needs with those of the wildlife in a project combining conservation, education and tourism; visitors are welcome and you'll find plenty of places where you can rent canoes or horses.

The main focus of attention is the **black howler monkey** (locally known as a baboon), the largest monkey in the New World and an endangered subspecies of howler that exists only in Belize, Guatemala and Mexico. They generally live in troops of between four and eight, and spend the day wandering through the leafy canopy feasting on leaves, flowers and fruits. You're pretty much guaranteed to see them close-up, feeding and resting in the trees along the riverbank and they're often as interested in you as you are in them. At dawn and dusk they let rip with the famous howl, a deep and rasping roar that carries for miles.

The conservation programme has proved so successful that conservationists agreed that the existing troops were stable enough to permit some to be relocated to reserves elsewhere in Belize, with the aim of replacing populations formerly wiped out by hunting or disease: in 1992 eighteen black howler monkeys were successfully relocated to the Cockscomb Basin and in 1996 eight monkeys were transferred to the Macal River valley. Both relocations have resulted in howler monkeys breeding in these former parts of their range, and Belize is now considered to be at the forefront of successful primate relocation techniques. Howler numbers in the sanctuary now stand at around 1500.

The sanctuary is also home to around two hundred bird species, plus anteaters, deer, peccaries, coatis, iguanas and the endangered Central American river turtle. Special **trails** are cut through the forest so that visitors can see it at its best; you can wander these alone or with a guide from the village. You can also take a guided canoe trip from *Jungle Drift Lodge* (see opposite).

Practicalities: Bermudian Landing and Burrell Boom

The village of **BERMUDIAN LANDING**, 43km northwest of Belize City, lies at the heart of the area, a Creole village and former logging centre that dates back to the seventeenth century. The turn-off to the village is 23km along the Northern Highway; the rest of the journey is along a good unpaved road, also used to access Hill Bank Field Station (see p.79). Regular buses run from Belize City to the village. Some of the other villages in the sanctuary now have their own bus services, also departing from Belize City. Bear in mind that all buses for Belize City leave Bermudian Landing early – between 5.30 & 6.30am.

Visitors are asked to register at the **visitor centre** (8am–4pm; Bz$10) at the western end of the village. The fee includes a short guided trail walk and inside the centre is Belize's first natural history museum, with exhibits and information on the riverside habitats and animals you're likely to see. Plans are afoot to expand the visitor centre to become the Belize River Valley Museum.

On the way to Bermudian Landing, 6km after the Northern Highway turn off, you'll pass **BURRELL BOOM**, also on the Belize River. In logging days a huge, heavy metal chain (a boom) was placed across the river to catch the logs floating down — you'll see the chain and the anchors that held it by the roadside on the right as you pass through the village. Though nowhere near as attractive as Bermudian Landing, Burrell Boom does have a good hotel, *El Chiclero* (☎028/2005, ⑥), with large, tiled, a/c rooms, very comfortable beds and a good restaurant. If you get the chance, have a chat with the owner, Carl Faulkner, an American ex-pat who can regale you with amazing tales of life in Belize. If you have your own vehicle and are heading directly west you can save time and considerable distance by cutting down through Burrell Boom to Hattieville.

BERMUDIAN LANDING: ACCOMMODATION, EATING AND DRINKING

You can **camp** at the visitor centre (Bz$10) but check first with manager Iola Joseph. Alternatively, a number of local families offer **bed and breakfast** rooms (③), a wonderful way to experience village life; check at the visitor centre or ask the sanctuary manager, Fallet Young, who lives nearby, though you'll always get somewhere to stay if you just turn up. The *Baboon Guest House*, behind the visitor centre (☎014/9286; ③), has two beautiful rooms, with electric lights, fan and coffee maker, in a simple thatched cabin with hammocks on the porch; there's a separate, clean tiled bathroom.

The best place to stay in the village however, is the very friendly *Jungle Drift Lodge* (☎014/9578, fax 02/78160, email *jungled@btl.net*; ③–⑤; Visa and M/C accepted), set right above the riverbank, shaded by trees festooned with howler monkeys, and surrounded by a profusion of tropical plants in the gardens. It's a budget travellers' paradise, children are welcome, and the bus stops just 75m from the entrance. Accommodation is in neat wooden, thatched cabañas, each with a porch, electric light and fan. Some have private bathrooms and even those with shared bath have hot water; camping is Bz$10. Meals (vegetarian and vegan if required) are eaten with the family, and the food, some of the best you'll find anywhere in the country, is plentiful. There's a trail along the riverbank, and *Jungle Drift* also rents out canoes and kayaks, and organizes superb river floats and night trips to spot crocodiles in nearby Mussel Creek.

There are a few **restaurants and bars** in the village: *Russell's Restaurant*, in the centre on the left-hand side (also the place where the bus parks for the night), and *Edna's Cool Spot* on the right, both serve simple meals of beans and rice. *Jeff's Gifts*, next to *Edna's*, has an amazing selection of souvenirs and postcards.

The ruins of Altun Ha

Fifty-five kilometres north of Belize City and just 9km from the sea is the impressive Maya site of **Altun Ha** (daily 8am—4pm; Bz$10), occupied for around twelve hundred years until the Classic Maya collapse between 900 and 950 AD. Its population peaked at about 10,000 inhabitants. The site was also occupied at various times throughout the Postclassic, though no new monumental building took place during this period. Its position close to the Caribbean coast suggests that it was sustained as much by trade as agriculture – a theory upheld by the discovery of trade objects such as jade and obsidian, neither of which occurs naturally in Belize and both very important in Maya ceremony. The jade would have come from the Motagua valley in Guatemala and much of it would probably have been shipped onwards to the north.

Around five hundred buildings have been recorded at Altun Ha but the core of the site is clustered around two Classic period plazas, both dotted with palm trees. Entering from the road, you come first to **Plaza A**. Large temples enclose it on all four sides, and a magnificent tomb has been discovered beneath Temple A-1, **The Temple of the Green Tomb**. Dating from 550 AD, this yielded a total of three hundred pieces, including jade, jewellery, stingray spines, skin, flints and the remains of a Maya book. Temple A-6, which has been particularly badly damaged, contains two parallel rooms, each about 48m long and with thirteen doorways along an exterior wall.

The adjacent **Plaza B** is dominated by the site's largest temple, B-4, **The Temple of the Masonry Altars**, the last in a sequence of buildings raised on this spot. If it seems familiar, it's because you might already have seen it on the Belikin beer label. The temple was probably the main focus of religious ceremonies, with a single stairway running up the front to an altar at the top. Several priestly tombs have been uncovered within the main structure, but most of them had already been desecrated, possibly during the political turmoil that preceded the abandonment of the site. Only two of the tombs were found intact; in 1968 archeologists discovered a carved jade head of **Kinich Ahau**, the Maya sun god, in one of them. Standing just under 15cm high, it is the largest carved jade found anywhere in the Maya world; today it's kept hidden away in the vaults of the Belize Bank, as there's no national museum to display it.

Outside these two main plazas are several other areas of interest, though little else has been restored. A short trail leads south to **Rockstone Pond**, a literal translation of the Maya name of the site and also the present-day name of a

nearby village. The pond was dammed in Maya times to form a reservoir (today it's home to a large crocodile); at the eastern edge stands another mid-sized temple. Built in the second century AD, this contained offerings that came from the great city of Teotihuacán in the Valley of Mexico.

Practicalities

Altun Ha is fairly difficult to reach independently as the track to the site is located along the Old Northern Highway, but there is a daily afternoon bus from Cinderella Plaza in Belize City (call ☎03/22041 to check times) to the village of **MASKALL**, passing the turn-off to the site at the village of **LUCKY STRIKE** (community phone ☎02/44249), just 3km from Altun Ha. However, you should only do it this way if you're really dedicated.

There's no **accommodation** at the site but you can ask the caretaker for permission to camp nearby, or press on 15km to Maskall, where you may be able to get a room. Any travel agent in Belize City will arrange a tour (see "Listings" p.61) and increasing numbers make the visit as part of a day-trip from San Pedro (p.98).

If money's no object, you can submit to the hedonistic (and undoubtedly therapeutic) pleasures of the outrageously Californian-style *Maruba Resort and Jungle Spa*, near Maskall at Mile 40, Old Northern Highway (☎03/22199, in US ☎713/799-2031, fax 795-8573; ⑨). Each room and cabin is luxurious, verging on the opulent, with hand-built wooden furniture and feather beds (there are alternatives if you're allergic). All are decorated individually; one does boast larger-than-life carved wooden penises for door handles, but they're not obtrusive. The food is excellent, and you'd need to stay a week to take advantage of all the body treatments. If the African honey bee pat or seaweed body wrap sound just too decadent then perhaps a jungle sand scrub would be more to your liking.

Crooked Tree Wildlife Sanctuary and village

Further along the Northern Highway, roughly midway between Belize City and Orange Walk, you pass the well-signed branch road which heads west 5km to **Crooked Tree Wildlife Sanctuary**, a reserve that takes in a vast area of inland waterways, logwood swamps and lagoons. Founded in 1984 by the Belize Audubon Society and covering four separate lagoons and twelve square kilometres, it was designated Belize's first Ramsar site (after the Ramsar conference in on wetlands in Iran) in 1998, as a "wetland habitat of international importance for waterfowl". It's an ideal nesting and resting place for the sanctuary's greatest treasure: the tens of thousands of migrating and resident **birds**, including snail kites, tiger herons, snowy egrets, ospreys and black-collared hawks. Representatives of over 250 bird species (two-thirds of Belize's total) have been recorded here.

The reserve's most famous visitor is the **jabiru stork**, the largest flying bird in the New World, with a wingspan of 2.5m. Belize has the biggest nesting population of jabiru storks at one site; they arrive in November, the young hatch in April or May, and they leave just before the summer rainy season gets under way. The **best time to visit** for bird-watchers is from late February to June, when the lagoons shrink to a string of pools, forcing wildlife to congregate for food and water. In an average day's bird-watching you can expect to see up to a hundred species. Visitors are welcome to participate in the May jabiru census; contact the Belize Audubon Society (see pp.41–2) for details. If you set off to explore the lagoons you might also catch a glimpse of howler monkeys, crocodiles, coatis, turtles or iguanas.

The village

In the middle of the reserve, connected to the mainland by a causeway, the village of **CROOKED TREE** straggles over a low island in the wetlands. One of the oldest inland villages in the country, its existence is based on fishing, farming and, more recently, tourism. Although the main attraction at Crooked Tree – taking guided boat trips through the lagoon and along sluggish, forest-lined creeks – can work out quite expensive (upwards of Bz$75, even in a group), it's still worth coming just to enjoy the unbelievably tranquil pace of life in the village. Strolling through the sandy, tree-lined lanes, and along the lakeshore you'll see plenty of birds. Villagers are courteous to strangers, and always have time to chat. Guides in the village are supremely knowledgeable, particularly about the many birds you'll encounter in the sanctuary, and impart their expertise with enthusiasm; even the children vie with each other to show off their bird-spotting expertise.

Some of the mango and cashew trees here are reckoned to be more than a hundred years old, and during January and February the air is heavy with the scent of cashew blossom. Since 1993 villagers and visitors have celebrated a **Cashew Festival** during the first week of May (hardly a tradition in itself, as it was started by a US tour company), but it does aim to highlight the economic importance of the famous nut, and it's a good chance to get a glimpse of village traditions and culture through the music, dance, storytelling and crafts that take place during the festival. The Bz$8 visitor fee is payable in the **Sanctuary Visitor Centre** near the end of the causeway. Steve and Donald Tillet and the other reserve wardens are excellent guides, providing a wealth of information on the area's flora, fauna and rural culture. They also sell trail maps and give information on accommodation and camping and canoe trips.

Practicalities

There are four daily buses to Crooked Tree from Belize City. The Jex service leaves once daily from Regent St West (Mon–Sat 10.30am), and twice daily from the Pound Yard bridge (Mon–Fri 4.30pm & 5.30pm); there's also a daily Batty service (Mon–Fri 4pm, Sat noon & Sun 9am). As always it's a good idea to check the times with the company (details on p.62), or by calling the village community phone on ☎02/44101 or ☎021/2084. There's enough traffic along the side road from the Northern Highway to make hitching an option; any non-express bus along the highway will drop you off at the junction. Returning buses leave daily for Belize City (Mon–Sat between 6am & 7am; Sun 4pm).

Private telephones are just coming online in Crooked Tree, so some numbers may change. At present you can use the **telephone** at the Jex store – the best stocked in the village – just past the end of the causeway, and there's a payphone in the centre of the village. There are a number of quiet, friendly restaurants and bars in the village – the liveliest is the *Riverview*, on the side of the lagoon, which has a disco most weekends and sometimes there's live music.

ACCOMMODATION

Most of the accommodation at Crooked Tree is in resort-type lodgings. If this is not your scene, there is reasonably priced **bed and breakfast** accommodation (*Molly's* is recommended) available through the Belize Audubon Society

(☎02/35004; ③) or check at the visitor centre. Otherwise, there's a dorm room at Bird's Eye View Lodge (below), and most of the resort lodges also have space for camping (Bz$10 per person). All the places listed can arrange superb guided boat tours through the reserve.

Bird's Eye View Lodge (☎02/32040, fax 24869; in US ☎718/845-0749). Comfortable, if incongruous-looking concrete building, right on the lakeshore. All rooms have private bath and there's a dorm (Bz$20 per person). The food is excellent and the tiny bar on the upstairs deck is a good place to catch the evening breeze. Camping available. Room rates include breakfast. ⑥.

Chau Hiix Lodge (☎02/73787; in US ☎407/322-6361, fax 322-6389). Five well-appointed cabins set in comfortable isolation amid four thousand acres of forest and wetlands at Sapodilla lagoon on the southern edge of the sanctuary. Just getting here is an adventure, as the boat (no road access) navigates broad lagoons and tiny creeks. Book in advance; packages include transport from the airport, meals, guided trips and use of boats and canoes. Two people each pay US$525 for three nights; US$935 for a week.

Crooked Tree Resort (☎02/75819, fax 74007). Neat wood-and-thatch cabins on the lakeshore. ⑤

Paradise Inn (☎021/2084, fax 02/32579; in US ☎888/875-8453; email *wildsident@aol.com*). Simple but beautiful thatched cabins at the north end of the village just paces from the lake, built by the owner Rudy Crawford. The bus stops about 500m from the cabins; just let the driver know where you're going. Rudy's sons, Glen and Robert, are two of the best guides in the village. The hospitality is wonderful and the home-cooked food is great. Camping available. ⑤.

Sam Tillet's Hotel (☎ & fax 021/2026; in US ☎1-800/765-2611, fax 407/322-6389). Near the village centre, on the bus route. Though not on the lagoon, this is the best-value hotel in the village. Rooms (including a budget room downstairs) are in a large, thatched cabaña; each has a private bathroom and the deck is a good place to relax in the evenings. Sam, known locally as the "king of birds" for his knowledge, is a great host. The garden attracts an amazing variety of birds and there's a shelter for camping. The restaurant serves superb food. ④.

Around Crooked Tree: Chau Hiix

Visitors to Crooked Tree can benefit from a couple of projects carried out nearby by volunteers from two British-based conservation development organizations, each aiming to promote bird-watching around the lagoon. Both are accessible by boat only. The first, 3 km north of the village, is an amazing 700m long **boardwalk** supported 1.5m above the swamp on strong logwood posts. Built in 1997 by an Operation Raleigh team, the walkway allows access through the otherwise impenetrable low forest at the edge of the lagoon and a 7m high observation tower affords panoramic **views** – a great place to enjoy the sunset.

Chau Hiix ("small cat"), a Maya site on the western shore of the lagoon, has escaped looting and therefore offers potentially revolutionary discoveries to the University of Indiana team currently excavating here. Climbing the nearby **observation tower** (also with a boardwalk), built in 1998 by volunteers from Trekforce Expeditions, will give you a clearer idea of the site, though admittedly much of what you see are just great, forested mounds. A number of burials have been discovered and the findings are currently being analysed. You experience a real thrill of discovery as you wander around the site, particularly if you're with a guide from the village (many have worked on the excavations) as they point out sites of recent finds. Most exposed stonework is covered over at the end of the season, but there are plans to consolidate the structures, and make them more accessible to visitors.

Orange Walk and around

With a population approaching 20,000, **ORANGE WALK** is the largest town in the north of Belize and the centre of a busy agricultural region. Though not unattractive, the town boasts few tourist attractions; Corozal (see p.81), less than an hour to the north, is a preferable place to spend the night. The centre of town is marked by a distinctly Mexican-style formal plaza, shaded by large trees, and the town hall across the main road is called the Palacio Municipal, reinforcing the strong historic links to Mexico. The tranquil, slow-moving **New River**, a few blocks east of the centre, was a busy commercial waterway during the logging days; now it provides a lovely starting point for a visit to the ruins of Lamanai, and several local operators now offer tours (see pp.76–7).

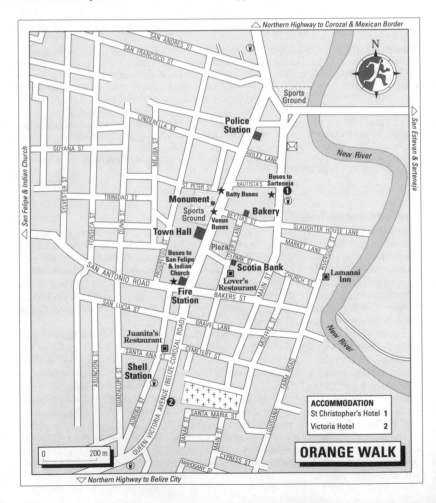

Like Corozal, Orange Walk was founded by Mestizo refugees fleeing from the Caste Wars in Yucatán in 1849, who chose as their site an area that had long been used for logging camps and was already occupied by the local Icaiché (Chichanha) Maya. Throughout the 1850s and 1860s the Icaiché Maya were in conflict with both the Cruzob Maya, who were themselves rebelling against Mestizo rule in Yucatán (and supplied with arms by British traders in Belize), and with the British settlers and colonial authorities in Belize. The leader of the Icaiché, Marcos Canul, organized successful raids against British mahogany camps, forcing the logging firms to pay "rent" for lands they used, and Canul even briefly occupied Corozal in 1870. In 1872 Canul launched an attack on the barracks in Orange Walk. The West India Regiment, which had earlier retreated in disarray after a skirmish with Canul's troops, this time forced the Icaiché to flee across the Rio Hondo, taking the fatally wounded Canul with them. This defeat didn't end the raids, but the Maya ceased to be a threat to British rule in northern Belize; a small monument opposite the park in Orange Walk commemorates the last (officially the only) battle fought on Belizean soil. Nowadays, the few remaining Icaiché Maya live in the village of Botes, on the Mexican border near the Rio Hondo.

Orange Walk has traditionally thrived on its crops, first with the growth of the sugar and citrus industries, and after the fall in sugar prices, with the profits made from marijuana. Recently, however, pressure from the US government has forced Belizean authorities to destroy many of the marijuana fields, and today the town has less of a Wild West atmosphere than just a few years ago. The land around Blue Creek and Shipyard has been developed by **Mennonite** settlers, members of a Protestant religious group who choose to farm without the assistance of modern technology (see box on p.74).

> The **telephone code** for Orange Walk is ☎03

Practicalities

Hourly **buses** from Belize City and Corozal pull up on the main road in the centre of town, officially Queen Victoria Avenue but always referred to as the Belize–Corozal Road, and head north on the hour and south on the half-hour. Services to and from Sarteneja (see below) stop at Zeta's store on Main Street, two blocks to the east, while local buses to the surrounding villages (including Indian Church, for Lamanai) leave from the crossroads by the fire station in the centre of town.

The Belize–Corozal Road is lined with hotels, restaurants and filling stations, so there's no need to walk far. There are no recommended budget **hotels**; if you do have to stay, then the best options are either the *Victoria*, 40 Belize–Corozal Rd, at the southern end of town (☎22518, fax 22847; ④), where most of the rooms have balconies, some are a/c, and there's a pool, or the new *St Christopher's*, 10 Main St (☎ & fax 21064; ④), which has beautiful rooms (some a/c) with private bathrooms, set in grounds sweeping down to the river. You could also stay near the toll bridge over the New River (see p.77).

The best place to **change money** and get cash advances is the Scotia Bank, just east of the plaza. Caribbean Holidays, on Beytias Lane (☎22803), is able to book international flights. The **post office** is on the right of the main road at the north end of town.

The majority of **restaurants** in Orange Walk are Chinese, though there are a few Belizean-style places serving simple Creole or "Mexican" food. *Lover's Restaurant*, tucked away in the far corner of the park at 20 Lover's Lane, offers the best Belizean food (and is the meeting place for the Novelos' Jungle River Tours; see p.76), while *Juanita's*, on Santa Ana Street, by the Shell station towards the south end of town, has the best Mexican dishes. For Mexican-style *pan dulces* (sweet bread and pastries) and fresh bread, try the Panificadora la Popular, on Beytias Street, off the northeast side of the park. The *Lamanai Inn*, on Riverside Street, is a pleasant waterside **bar** and restaurant. Nightlife boils down to either the weekend **discos** in the *Mi Amor* or *Victoria* hotels or the numerous bars and clubs dotted around town, some of which serve as brothels.

Maya sites around Orange Walk

Although the **Maya sites** in northern Belize have been the source of a number of the most important archeological finds anywhere in the Maya world, they are not (with the notable exception of Lamanai) as monumentally spectacular as some in Yucatán. The area around Orange Walk has some of the most productive arable farmland in Belize, and this was also the case in Maya times; aerial surveys in the late 1970s revealed evidence of raised fields and a network of irrigation canals, showing that the Maya practised skilful intensive agriculture. In the Postclassic era this region became part of the powerful Maya state of Chactemal (or Chetumal), controlling the trade in cacao beans (used as currency) grown in the

MENNONITES IN BELIZE

The **Mennonites** arose from the radical Anabaptist movement of the sixteenth century and are named after the Dutch priest Menno Simons, leader of the community in its formative years. Recurring government restrictions on their lifestyle, especially regarding their pacifist objection to military service, forced them to move repeatedly. Having removed to Switzerland they travelled on to Prussia, then in 1663 to Russia, until the government revoked their exemption from military service, whereupon some groups emigrated to North America, settling in the prairies of Saskatchewan. World War I brought more government restrictions, this time on the teaching of German (the Mennonites' language). This, together with more widespread anti-German sentiments in the Dominion and the prospect of conscription, drove them from Canada to Mexico, where they settled in the arid northern state of Chihuahua. When the Mexican government required them to be included in its social security programme it was time to move on again. An investigation into the possibility of settling on their own land in British Honduras brought them to the British colony of Belize in 1958.

They were welcomed enthusiastically by the colonial authorities, eager to have willing workers to clear the jungle for agriculture. Perseverance and hard work made them successful farmers, and in recent years prosperity has caused drastic changes in their lives. The Mennonite Church in Belize is increasingly split between the *Kleine Gemeinde* – a modernist section who use electricity and power tools, and drive trucks, tractors and even cars – and the *Altkolonier* – traditionalists who prefer a stricter interpretation of their beliefs. Members of the community, easily recognizable in their denim dungarees, can be seen trading their produce and buying supplies every day in Orange Walk and Belize City.

valleys of the Hondo and New rivers. For a while the Maya here were even able to resist the conquistadors, and long after nominal Spanish rule had been established in 1544 there were frequent Maya rebellions: in 1638 they drove the Spanish out and burned the church at Lamanai.

Cuello and Nohmul

Cuello is a small site 5km west of Orange Walk. Discovered in 1973 by Norman Hammond, until recently the site was thought to be one of the earliest in the Maya area originating in 1500 BC. However, new ideas suggest that it in fact dates back to 1000 BC, still making it one of the earliest sites from the Middle Preclassic Maya lowlands. The site is more interesting to archeologists than the casual visitor; there's not much to look at except a single small stepped pyramid (structure 350), rising in nine tiers – a common feature of Maya temples – and several earth-covered mounds.

The ruins are behind a factory where Cuello rum is made; the site is on the Cuello family land, so you should ask permission to visit by phoning ☎22141. You can also get a tour of the distillery if you ask. Cuello can be reached by simply walking west from the plaza in Orange Walk for a little under an hour; a taxi to the site costs around Bz$10 each way.

Situated on the Orange Walk–Corozal boundary, 17km north of Orange Walk and just west of the village of San Pablo, **Nohmul** (Great Mound) was a major ceremonial centre with origins in the early Preclassic period, perhaps as early as 900 BC. The city was abandoned before the end of the Classic period, to be reoccupied by a Yucatecan elite during the Early Postclassic (known here as the Tecep phase, around 800–1000 AD). The ruins cover a large area, comprising the East and West groups connected by a *sacbe* (causeway), with several plazas around them. The main feature (structure 2) is an acropolis platform surmounted by a later pyramid which, owing to the site's position on a limestone ridge, is the highest point in northern Belize. As at so many of Belize's Maya sites, looters have plundered the ruins and, tragically, at least one structure has been demolished for road fill – that said, as it is one of the sites earmarked for tourism, some structural restoration has taken place.

Nohmul lies amid sugar-cane fields, 2km west of **San Pablo**, on the Northern Highway. Any bus between Corozal and Orange Walk goes through the village. To visit the site, contact Estevan Itzab, whose land it's on and who lives in the house on the west side of the highway, across from the village water tower at the north end of the village; his son Guillermo will probably be your guide.

Lamanai

Though they can't match the scale of the great sites in Mexico and Guatemala, the **ruins of Lamanai** (daily 8am–4pm; Bz$10) are perhaps the most impressive in Belize, and their setting on the New River Lagoon – in the 950-acre Archeological Reserve, now the only jungle for miles around – gives them a special quality that is long gone from sites served by a torrent of tourist buses.

Lamanai is one of only a few sites whose original Maya name – Lamanyan – is known; it translates as "Submerged Crocodile", hence the numerous representations of crocodiles. *Lamanai*, however, the seventeenth-century mistransliteration, actually means "Drowned Insect". The site was continually occupied from around 500 BC up until the sixteenth century, when Spanish missionaries built a church alongside to lure the Indians from their heathen ways. More than seven hundred structures have been mapped by teams led by David Pendergast of the Royal Ontario Museum, the majority of them still buried beneath mounds of earth. Seven troops of black howler monkeys make Lamanai their home and you'll certainly see a couple of them peering down through the branches as you wander the trails.

The site

The most impressive feature at Lamanai, prosaically named N10-43 (informally called "El Castillo", the castle), is a massive **Late Preclassic temple**, towering 35m above the forest floor. When first built, around 100 BC, it was the largest structure in the entire Maya world, though one which was extensively modified later. The view across the surrounding forest from the top of the temple is magnificent. On the way to El Castillo you pass N10-27, a much smaller, unreconstructed pyramid, at the base of which lies **Stela 9**, bearing some of the best-preserved carvings at Lamanai. Dated to 625 AD, it shows the magnificently attired Lord Smoking Shell participating in a ceremony – probably his accession. This glyph has become emblematic of Lamanai and features on many of the T-shirts on sale here. At the northern end of the site, structure N9-56 is a sixth-century pyramid with two stucco masks of a deity (probably Kinich Ahau, the sun god) carved on different levels. The lower mask, 4m high, is particularly well preserved, showing a clearly humanized face wearing a crocodile headdress and bordered by decorative columns. The temple overlies several smaller, older buildings, the oldest of which is a superbly preserved temple from around 100 BC, and there are a number of other well-preserved and clearly defined glyphs.

Traces of later settlers can be seen around the nearby village of **INDIAN CHURCH**: to the south of the village are the ruins of two churches built by Spanish missionaries, and to the west are the remains of a nineteenth-century sugar mill, built by Confederate refugees from the American Civil War.

The small **archeological museum** at the site, so far the only one of its kind in Belize, houses an amazing collection of artefacts, arranged in chronological order, mostly figurines depicting gods and animals, particularly crocodiles. The most beautiful exhibits are the delicate eccentric flints – star and sceptre-shaped symbols of office – skilfully chipped from a single piece. The most unusual item is a drum the size and shape of a pair of binoculars. Nazario Ku, the friendly head caretaker at the site, is very knowledgeable about Maya culture and is the best guide at the site.

Practicalities

Getting to Lamanai is relatively easy. Three buses a week (Mon, Wed & Fri; 2hr) leave at 4pm from the side of the fire station in Orange Walk for **Indian Church**. The bus is based in the village, leaving for Orange Walk at 6am on the same days, so you'll have to stay overnight; you can check bus times by calling the community phone in Indian Church on ☎031/2015. The most pleasant way to get here though is by river, and a number of operators organize **day-trips** for US$30–50 per person. By far the most informative are those of Jungle River Tours, run by Antonio, Wilfrido and Herminio Novelo and based in Orange Walk at the *Lover's Restaurant* (☎22293, fax 23749). In addition to their extensive knowledge of Maya sites, the Novelos are also wildlife experts, and will point out the lurking crocodiles and dozens of species of bird, including snail kites, that you might otherwise miss. Another good, regular tour is aboard the *Lamanai Lady*, which departs daily at 9am from the toll bridge 11km south of Orange Walk; book through Discovery Expeditions in Belize City (☎02/31063). To get to the bridge take the Batty bus that leaves Belize City at 7am for Chetumal; the driver will drop you at the right place to catch your trip for the 9am start. For independent travellers on a budget, the best bargain can usually be arranged by Barbara or Tanya at Tower Hill Maya Tours (☎23839), on the right immediately north of the toll bridge; call ahead to check availability. There's a reasonable hotel by the bridge should you need to stay; the *New River Park Hotel* (☎ & fax 23987; ④–⑤), with large rooms (some a/c, all have private bathrooms), pleasant gardens and a good restaurant.

To get to Lamanai **by road** in your own vehicle, head to the south end of Orange Walk and turn right (west) by Dave's Store, where a signpost gives the distance to Lamanai as 35 miles. Continue along the Yo Creek road as far as San Felipe, where you should bear left for the village of Indian Church, 2km from the ruins.

If you want **to stay** in Indian Church (and you'll have to if you're travelling by bus), there are a couple of places offering **rooms** (③), though they're rather over-priced. Speak to Nazario Ku at the site and he'll let you **camp** at his house or rent you a hammock very cheaply; you can eat with the family. In his grounds you can visit the Xochil Ku (Sacred Flower) project (daily; donation only), a butterfly-breeding educational centre, designed to raise awareness of the natural world amongst local people; you're welcome to watch the butterflies develop through the stages of their life-cycle. More **upmarket accommodation** is available near-by in the thatched cabañas at *Lamanai Outpost Lodge* (☎ & fax 02/33578, in US ☎1-888/733-7864, email *lamanai@btl.net*; ⑧), set in extensive gardens sweeping down to the lagoon. The restaurant, *Bushey's Place*, serves superb meals. Guests can use canoes or take a "moonlight safari" to spot nocturnal wildlife, or even take part in some Maya research under the supervision of archeologist Laura Howard, who is based at the lodge.

The Rio Bravo Conservation Area

In the far northwest of Orange Walk district is the **Rio Bravo Conservation Area**, a 240,000-acre tract designated for tropical forest conservation, research and sustained-yield forest harvests. This astonishing conservation success story actually began with a disastrous plan in the mid-1980s to clear the forest, initially to fuel a wood-fired power station and later to provide Coca-Cola with frost-free land to grow citrus crops. Environmentalists were alarmed, and their strenuous objections forced Coca-Cola to drop the plan, though the forest remained threatened by agriculture.

An imaginative project to save the threatened forest by purchasing it, the **Programme for Belize**, was initiated by the Massachusetts Audubon Society and launched in 1988. Funds were raised from corporate donors and conservation organizations but the most widespread support was generated through an ambitious "adopt-an-acre" scheme, enthusiastically taken up by schools and individuals in the UK and North America. Coca-Cola itself, anxious to distance itself from the charge of rainforest destruction, has donated more than 90,000 acres. Today rangers with powers of arrest patrol the area to prevent illegal logging and to stop farmers encroaching on to the reserve with their *milpa*s (slash and burn fields). The guarded boundaries also protect dozens of Maya sites, most of them unexcavated and unrestored, though many have been looted.

The **landscape** ranges from forest-covered limestone escarpments in the northwest, near the Guatemalan border, eastwards through the valleys of several rivers, to palmetto savannah, pine ridge and swamp in the southeast around the New River Lagoon. The forest teems with **wildlife**: including all five of Belize's cat species, tapirs, monkeys and crocodiles, plus more than three hundred species of bird. The strict ban on hunting, enforced for over ten years now, makes the Rio Bravo and Gallon Jug (see p.79) area the best place in Belize to actually see these beasts; even pumas and jaguars are frequently spotted. Adjoining the Rio Bravo Conservation Area to the south, the privately owned land of **Gallon Jug** also contains a large area of protected land, in the centre of which is the fabulous Chan Chich Lodge – regarded as one of the best eco-lodges in the world – an incredibly beautiful place to stay.

There's no **public transport** to the Rio Bravo Conservation Area, but if you want to visit or stay at either of the **field stations**, see below.

La Milpa and Hill Bank Field Stations

One of the aims of the Programme for Belize is environmental education and **field stations** have been built at La Milpa and Hill Bank to accommodate both visitors and students – at present these are the only places to stay in the Rio Bravo Conservation Area, though more are planned. Both are quite difficult to get to but, with your own vehicle, could be visited on a day-trip, or you might be able to get a ride in with a warden or one of the other staff; see below for contact details.

Each field station has comfortable (though expensive) **dorms** (US$75 per person), and the facilities utilize the latest "green" technology, including solar power and composting toilets; La Milpa also has beautiful cabañas (US$90 per person; sleep up to six). Prices, though high (discounts for student groups), include three meals and two excursions or lectures a day. To visit or stay at either station contact the appropriate station manager (Ramon Pacheco at La Milpa, Alan Herrera at Hill Bank) through the PFB office, 2 South Park St, Belize City (☎02/75616, fax 75635, email *pfbel@btl.net*) who may be able to arrange transport, or write to PFB, Box 749, Belize City.

La Milpa: the field station and Maya site

Set in a former *milpa* clearing in the higher, northwestern forest, **La Milpa Field Station** has a tranquil, studious atmosphere; deer and ocellated turkeys feed contentedly around the cabins and there are binoculars and telescopes for spotting birds. Guests are mainly students on tropical ecology courses, though anyone can stay. A day-visit to the field station, which includes a guided tour of La Milpa ruins or one of the trails costs US$20, but getting there on public transport is not easy; you'll have to get a bus from Orange Walk to San Felipe, 37km away, and arrange to be picked up there – the PFB office will give details. To get there in your own vehicle, take the road west from Orange Walk via San Felipe to the Mennonite village of Blue Creek, on the Hondo River (a boat here makes the crossing to the Mexican village of La Unión). Beyond Blue Creek the road (paved and in good condition) climbs steeply up the Rio Bravo escarpment, then turns south to the field station and Gallon Jug. Charter flights use the airstrips at Blue Creek and Gallon Jug.

Five kilometres west of the field station is the huge, Classic **Maya city of La Milpa**, the third largest site in Belize. After centuries of expansion, La Milpa was abandoned in the ninth century, though Postclassic groups subsequently occupied the site and the Maya here resisted both the Spanish conquest in the sixteenth century and British mahogany cutters in the nineteenth century. The site is currently being investigated as part of a long-term archeological survey by Boston University; recent finds include major elite burials with many jade grave goods. The **ceremonial centre**, built on top of a limestone ridge, is one of the most impressive anywhere, with at least 24 courtyards and two ball-courts.The **Great Plaza**, flanked by four temple-pyramids (the tallest stands 24m above the plaza floor), is one of the largest public spaces in the Maya world.

Hill Bank Field Station

At the southern end of the New River Lagoon and 70km west of Belize City, **Hill Bank Field Station** is a former logging camp which has been adapted to undertake scientific forestry research and development. The emphasis here is more on extractive forest use, with the aim of revenue generation on a sustainable basis. Selective logging is allowed on carefully monitored plots; chicle, the base ingredient of chewing gum, is harvested from sapodilla trees, and there's a micropropagation lab, growing tropical plants for export without depleting the forest. These and other projects are at the cutting edge of tropical forest management, and there are often students and scientists working here. Some of the Maya sites in the area are currently under investigation by the University of Texas; you can visit them when the archeological teams are working. There's plenty of wildlife around too, particularly birds and crocodiles, and butterflies abound.

There's no **public transport** but with your own transport you can follow the road west from Bermudian Landing (see p.67). It's also possible to approach Hill Bank from Lamanai, by boat along the New River Lagoon.

Gallon Jug and Chan Chich Lodge

Forty kilometres south of the La Milpa field station, the former logging town of **GALLON JUG**, set in neat fenced pastures, is the home of Barry Bowen, reportedly the richest man in Belize. In the 1980s, his speculative land deals led to an international outcry against threatened rainforest clearance. The experience apparently proved cathartic; Bowen is now an ardent conservationist and most of the 125,000 acres here are strictly protected. The focal point is the luxurious, world-class **Chan Chich Lodge** (☎ & fax 02/34419, in US ☎1-800/343-8009, email *info@chanchich.com*; ⑨), with twelve large thatched cabañas set in the plaza of the Classic Maya site of Chan Chich, surrounded by superb forest. The construction of the lodge on this spot (all Maya sites are technically under government control) was controversial at the time, but received Archeology Department approval as it was designed to cause minimal disturbance. Certainly the year-round presence of visitors and staff does prevent looting – a real problem in the past. It is a truly awe-inspiring setting; grass-covered temple walls crowned with jungle tower up from the lodge and the forest explodes with a cacophony of bird calls at dawn. The **guided trails** are incomparable; day or night wildlife sightings are consistently high. You can drive here from Orange Walk (though Blue Creek and La Milpa, see above), but most guests fly in to the airstrip at Gallon Jug; Javier's Flying Service (☎02/45332) has three scheduled flights a week.

Sarteneja and the Shipstern Nature Reserve

Until relatively recently, the largely uninhabited **Sarteneja peninsula**, jutting out towards the Yucatán in the northeast of Belize, could only be reached by boat. The entire peninsula is covered with dense forests, swamps and lagoons that support an amazing array of wildlife and the only village is **Sarteneja**, a lobster-fishing centre that's just beginning to experience tourism. The people here are Spanish-speaking Mestizos with close links to Mexico, though most people will also speak English. Although Sarteneja itself, and especially its shoreline, are pretty enough, it's the **Shipstern Nature Reserve**, 5km before the village, which is the main attraction.

Shipstern Nature Reserve

The **Shipstern Nature Reserve** (daily 8am–5pm; Bz$10 including guided walk), established in 1981, covers an area of eighty square kilometres. The bulk of the reserve is made up of what's technically known as "tropical moist forest", although it contains only a few mature trees as the area was wiped clean by Hurricane Janet in 1955. It also includes some wide belts of savannah – covered in coarse grasses, palms and broad-leaved trees – and a section of the shallow Shipstern Lagoon, dotted with mangrove islands. Taking the superb guided walk along the **Chiclero Trail** from the visitor centre, you'll encounter more named plant species in one hour than on any other trail in Belize.

Shipstern, owned and managed by the Swiss-based International Tropical Conservation Foundation, is a bird-watcher's paradise. The lagoon system supports blue-winged teal, American coot, thirteen species of egret and huge flocks of lesser scaup, while the forest is home to fly-catchers, warblers, keel-billed toucans, collared aracari and at least five species of parrot. In addition there are crocodiles, manatees, coatis, jaguars, peccaries, deer, racoons, pumas and an abundance of insects, particularly butterflies. Though the reserve's butterfly farm did not prove as lucrative as hoped, the wardens still tend the butterflies carefully, releasing them into the forest when mature. Visitors can walk around, observing the insect life-cycle from egg to brilliant butterfly – an amazingly peaceful experience. Within the reserve, camouflaged observation towers enable you to get good **views** of the wildlife without disturbing the animals; you'll need to get one of the wardens to guide you to them.

All **buses** to Sarteneja (see p.81) pass the entrance to the reserve; the headquarters and **visitor centre** are just 100m from the road. You can stay here in neat four-bed dorms (Bz$20 per person) with cooking facilities, and there's a two-roomed house for rent (Bz$80 per day). For information call BAS on ☎02/35004, though there will almost certainly be room if you just turn up.

Sarteneja practicalities

From **SARTENEJA**, guided excursions into the reserve and the surrounding area, either to the many nearby ruins or to seek out wildlife in the lagoons, are easily arranged; ask where you're staying for the best advice. Fernando Alamilla, who runs *Fernando's* (see below) is an excellent fishing guide and can take you across to Bacalar Chico National Park, on Ambergris Caye (see p.98).

Road improvements have made it easier to get to Sarteneja; from Belize City the Perez **bus** leaves the Texaco station on North Front St at 11.30am and 1pm, and Venus at 12.30pm (all times Mon–Sat; Bz$12). They all pass through Orange Walk ninety minutes later, stopping at Zeta's store on Main Street, and the bus crew take a break. It's a further ninety minutes to Sarteneja. Venus also run a daily service from Chetumal to Sarteneja via Orange Walk, leaving at 1.30pm. Buses return to Belize City from Sarteneja at 4am, 5am and 6am. If you're heading for Mexico, you may be able to get a ride in a sailboat or skiff from Sarteneja to Consejo, 13km north of Corozal, and just a few kilometres across the bay from Chetumal; make sure you get your passport stamped (in Consejo or Corozal) before you leave Belize.

There's no shortage of **accommodation** in Sarteneja, or you can stay in the reserve (see p.80). A couple of new hotels have just opened in the village: *Fernando's Seaside Guest House* (☎04/32085; ④), on the seafront, which has spacious, thatched rooms with private bath; and *Sayab Cabañas*, towards the back of the village by the water tower, which has two lovely thatched cabins (with private bath) set in a small garden filled with tropical plants. For a very comfortable room in a private house near the seafront call ☎04/32158 (⑤ including breakfast). The long-established *Diani's Hotel* (☎04/32084; ③), right in the centre of town facing the shore, is inexpensive but rather run-down.

All the places to stay also serve **food**; the thatched *Mira Mar* restaurant on the seafront is also the most obvious bar, and there are several more dotted around the village.

Corozal and around

COROZAL, 45 km north of Orange Walk along the Northern Highway, is Belize's most northerly town, just twenty minutes from the Mexican border. Corozal's location near the mouth of the New River enabled the ancient Maya to prosper here by controlling river and seaborne trade, and two sites – Santa Rita and Cerros – are within easy reach. The present town was founded here in 1849 by refugees from the massacre in Bacalar, Mexico, who were hounded south by the Caste Wars. Today's grid-pattern town is a neat mix of Mexican and Caribbean, its appearance largely due to reconstruction in the wake of Hurricane Janet in 1955. This is a fertile area – the town's name derives from the cohune palm, which the Maya recognized as an indicator of fecundity – and much of the land is planted with sugar cane.

There's little to do in Corozal, but it's an agreeable place to spend the day on the way to or from the border, and is hassle-free, even at night. There's a breezy shoreline park shaded by palm trees, while on the tree-shaded main plaza, the **town hall** is worth a look inside for the vivid depiction of local history in a mural by Manuel Villamar Reyes. In two of the plaza's corners you can see the remains of small forts, built to ward off Indian attacks. On October 12, **Columbus Day** (or PanAmerica Day, as it is now known) – celebrations in Corozal are particularly lively) Mexican fiesta merging with Caribbean carnival.

The **telephone code** for Corozal is ☎04

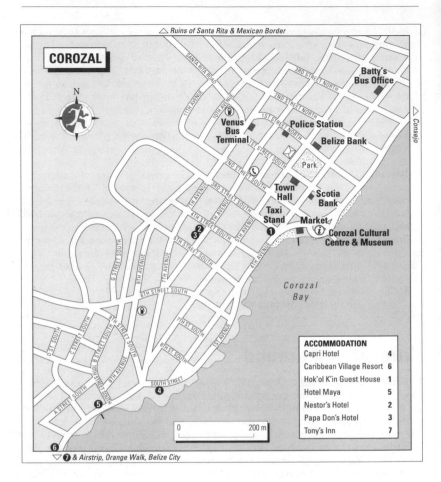

△ *Ruins of Santa Rita & Mexican Border*

COROZAL

N

Batty's Bus Office

Venus Bus Terminal

Police Station

Belize Bank

Park

Town Hall

Scotia Bank

Taxi Stand

Market

Corozal Cultural Centre & Museum

Corozal Bay

△ *Consejo*

ACCOMMODATION	
Capri Hotel	4
Caribbean Village Resort	6
Hok'ol K'in Guest House	1
Hotel Maya	5
Nestor's Hotel	2
Papa Don's Hotel	3
Tony's Inn	7

0	200 m

▽ ❼ & *Airstrip, Orange Walk, Belize City*

Arrival and information

All **buses** between Belize City and Chetumal pass through Corozal. For the Mexican border (20min) they pass through more or less on the hour from 7am to 9pm; for Belize City (3hr) roughly on the half-hour from 5.30am to 7.30pm. The Venus bus depot (☎22132) is near the northern edge of town opposite the Shell station; Batty buses (☎23034) stop at their office on 4th Ave, north of the park. Maya Island Air and Tropic Air operate daily **flights** to Corozal from San Pedro, Ambergris Caye. Jal's travel agency (☎22163) at the south of town, beyond *Tony's Inn*, can organize both domestic and international flights.

For reliable tourist **information**, visit the **Corozal Cultural Centre** (☎23176; Tues–Sat 9am–noon & 1–4.30pm) housed in the restored, bright yellow colonial market building in the waterfront park, just past the new market. Its clock tower is a local landmark and inside there's a museum (Bz$3) with imaginative displays depicting episodes in Corozal's history. The working model of the former logging railway at Gallon Jug (see p.79) is everyone's favourite attraction.

Scotia Bank, on the plaza, is the best place for **cash advances**, and there should be an ATM now. The **post office** is on the west side of the plaza (Mon–Fri 8.30am–noon & 1–4.30pm). For organized **tours** to local nature reserves and archeological sites, contact Henry Menzies at *Caribbean Village* (☎22725); he's also the agent for Belize Transfer Service, and can advise on travel to Mexico. Stephan Moerman (☎22833 or 22539, fax 22278), a French biologist and naturalist, arranges superb guided tours to Cerros (see below) and Bacalar Chico National Park (see p.98).

Accommodation

Corozal has plenty of hotel rooms in all price ranges and you'll always be able to find something suitable. At **Four Miles Lagoon**, a few kilometres from the border, a couple of places offer **camping** on the lakeshore; *Lagoon Camping* has RV sites for Bz$20 and tent sites forBz$10.

Capri, on the seafront at the southern end of 4th Ave (☎22042). Basic rooms, some with private bath. The large, dingy bar is usually quiet, except when there's a dance on. ②.

Caribbean Village Resort, south end of town, across from the sea (☎22045, fax 23414). Good-value, whitewashed, thatched cabins, with hot water, among the palms. Plus an inexpensive restaurant, trailer park (Bz$24) and camping (Bz$10). The owner, Henry Menzies, an expert on local attractions, arranges tours, transfers to Chetumal and airport pickups. Accepts Visa/MC. ③.

Hok'ol K'in Guest House, facing the sea a block south of the market (☎23329, fax 23569, email *maya@btl.net*). A fairly new hotel near the centre of the seafront. Large, tiled rooms with hammocks on the balcony and private bath, and some suites. The ground floor is completely wheelchair-accessible. Owners Marty Conway and Francisco Puck are very helpful, and all the features, including a restaurant, pleasant gardens, and a guest lounge with a book exchange and videos of Belize make this a good-value place to stay. ⑤.

Hotel Maya, south end of town, facing the sea (☎22082, fax 22827). Clean, friendly and well-run, the rooms have been renovated and all have private bathrooms; new rooms have a/c. There's a good restaurant and the owner, Rosita May, is the local agent for Maya Island Air. Accepts Visa/MC. ③–⑤.

Nestor's, 5th Ave South, between 4th and 5th streets (☎22354). Budget hotel, with private showers, though some rooms smell musty. Popular sports bar and restaurant. ③.

Papa Don's, 5th Ave South, next to *Nestor's*. Very cheap, basic, and friendly. ②.

Tony's Inn and Beach Resort, on the seafront, about 1km south of the plaza (☎22055, fax 22829). A touch of well-run luxury in a superb location with secure parking. The spacious rooms (most a/c) with king-size beds overlook landscaped gardens and a pristine beach bar, and there's an excellent restaurant. ⑥.

Eating

Whatever your budget, most of the best meals in Corozal are to be found in the hotels. The popular bar at *Nestor's* serves American and Belizean food, while the *Hotel Maya* serves very good Belizean and Jamaican food in a quieter environment. There's a wonderful restaurant at *Tony's*, and *Haley's* in *Caribbean Village* is renowned locally for its inexpensive Creole food.

Outside of these places the tiny, two-table *Lonchería Barrera*, in the southwest corner of the plaza, serves great, inexpensive Mexican-style dishes, and there are the usual complement of Chinese restaurants. Amazingly, *Le Cafe Kela*, on the seafront just north of the centre, serves authentic French pastries.

Around Corozal: Santa Rita and Cerros

Of the two small Maya sites within reach of Corozal (both daily 8am–4pm; Bz$5), the closest is **Santa Rita** about fifteen minutes' walk northwest of the town. To get there follow the main road in the direction of the border and when it divides take the left-hand fork, which soon brings you to the hospital, the power plant and the raised Maya site. Peter Ponce, the friendly caretaker, will show you around once you've signed in.

Founded around 1500 BC, Santa Rita was in all probability the powerful Maya city known as Chactemal (Chetumal), which dominated the trade of the area. It was still a thriving settlement in 1531 AD, when the conquistador Alonso Davila entered the town, which had been tactically abandoned by the Maya; he was driven out almost immediately by Na Chan Kan, the Maya chief, and his Spanish adviser Gonzalo Guerrero. Pottery found here has connected Santa Rita with other sites in Yucatán, and there were once some superb Mixtec-style murals similar to those found at Tulum, in Quintana Roo. You won't be spellbound by the vastness of the place, though, as only a fraction of it has been unearthed, and it's thought that much of the ancient city is covered by present-day Corozal. The main remaining building is a small pyramid; burials excavated here include that of an elaborately jewelled elderly woman, dated to the Early Classic period, and the tomb of a Classic period warlord, buried with the symbols of his elite status.

The remains of the Preclassic centre of **Cerros**, on the southern shore of Corozal Bay, are best reached by boat in the company of a guide (easy enough to organize in Corozal; see above). In the dry season it's possible to drive to the site through the villages of Progresso and Copper Bank – call the Copper Bank community telephone (☎22950) to check road conditions. Any time of the year mosquitoes can be a problem, so bring repellent. Its strategic position at the mouth of the New River enabled Cerros to dominate the regional water-borne trade, and it was one of the earliest places in the Maya world to adopt the rule of kings. Beginning around 50 BC it grew explosively from a small fishing village to a major city in only two generations. Despite initial success, however, Cerros was abandoned by the Classic period, eclipsed by shifting trade routes. The site includes three large acropolis structures, ball-courts and plazas flanked by pyramids. The largest building is a 22-metre high temple – its intricate stucco masks, representing the rising and setting sun, and Venus as morning star and evening star, are presently covered to prevent erosion, but restoration schemes are planned.

The Mexican border crossing

Heading **into Mexico**, all northbound Batty and Venus buses will take you to either the bus terminal in Chetumal or the nearby market; Batty's has an office in the Chetumal terminal, and as their buses leave in the morning you'll have a head start on travelling through Mexico. The whole journey takes about an hour, including the border crossing. The route takes you to the **Santa Elena border crossing** on the Hondo River, and after you've cleared Belize immigration (paying only the Bz$7.50 PACT exit tax), the bus carries you to the Mexican immigration and customs posts on the northern bank. Border formalities are very straightforward and few Western nationalities need a visa (only France from the EU); simply pick up and fill out your Mexican tourist card. There's no fee to pay entering Mexico. If you want visa advice, check with the Mexican embassy in

Belize City shop

Paslow Building, Belize City

Hut on Caye Caulker

Black howler monkey, Baboon Sanctuary   Jabiru storks, Crooked Tree

Boat trip, Caye Caulker

Half-Moon Caye Natural Monument

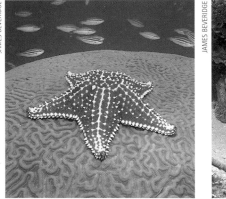

Cushion starfish on brain coral

Gray angelfish

F. TORRANCE, TRIP

Jaguar, Belize Zoo

IAN CUMMING, AXIOM

Fishing at dusk, Caye Caulker

Belize City (see "Listings", p.61). **Moneychangers** on the Belize side will give good rates changing US or Belize dollars for pesos; there aren't any on the Mexican side, though most Mexican banks have ATMs you can use.

travel details

Buses
Bus company addresses and details of services from Belize City are given the box on p.62.

Bermudian Landing to: Belize City (2–3 Mon–Sat; 1hr 15min), via Burrell Boom.
Chetumal to: Belize City (hourly; 3hr 30min, express services 3hr), via Corozal and Orange Walk; Sarteneja (via Orange Walk, Mon–Sat at 1.30pm; 3hr 30min).
Corozal to: Belize City (hourly; 2hr 30min), via Orange Walk (1hr); to Chetumal (hourly; 1hr).

Crooked Tree to: Belize City (4 daily; 1hr 30min).
Orange Walk to: Belize City (hourly; 1hr 30min); to Corozal (hourly 1hr); to Indian Church, for Lamanai (3 weekly on Mon, Wed, ``Fri at 4pm; 2hr).
Sarteneja to: Belize City (Mon–Sat 2–3 daily; 3hr 30min); to Chetumal (Mon–Sat; 1daily).

Planes
Maya Island Air (☎026/2345) and Tropic Air (☎026/2012) each operate three daily flights between Corozal and San Pedro.

CHAPTER THREE

THE NORTHERN CAYES AND ATOLLS

B elize's spectacular **Barrier Reef**, with its dazzling variety of underwater life and string of exquisite islands – known as cayes – is the main attraction for most first-time visitors to the country. The longest barrier reef in the western hemisphere, it begins just south of Cancún and runs the entire length of the Belize coastline at a distance of 15km to 40km from the mainland. One of the richest marine ecosystems on earth, it's a paradise for scuba-divers and snorkellers, the incredible coral formations teeming with hundreds of species of brilliantly coloured fish.

Most of the **cayes** (pronounced "keys") lie in shallow water behind the shelter of the reef, with a limestone ridge forming larger, low-lying islands to the north, and smaller, less frequently visited outcrops – often merely a stand of palms and a strip of sand – clustered toward the southern end of the chain. Though the four hundred cayes themselves form only a tiny proportion of the country's total land area, and only around ten percent have any kind of tourism development, Belize has more territorial water than it does land, and the islands' tourism and lobster-fishing income accounts for a substantial amount of foreign currency earnings.

In recent years the town of **San Pedro**, on **Ambergris Caye**, has undergone a transition from a predominantly fishing economy to one geared to commercial tourism. But there are still some beautiful spots here, notably the protected areas at either end of the caye: **Bacalar Chico National Park** and **Hol Chan Marine Reserve**. South of Ambergris Caye, **Caye Caulker**, which also has a marine reserve, is less – but increasingly – developed, and remains popular with budget travellers. **St George's Caye**, Belize's first capital, occupies a celebrated niche in the nation's history and still has some fine colonial houses as well as a couple of resorts. Many of the other cayes are populated only by fishing communities, whose settlements fluctuate with the season; a few just have a single, exclusive lodge offering sport-fishing and diving to big-spending visitors.

Beyond the chain of islands and the coral reef are two of Belize's three **atolls**: the **Turneffe Islands** and **Lighthouse Reef**. In these breathtakingly beautiful formations the coral reaches the surface, enclosing a shallow lagoon, with some cayes lying right on top of the encircling reef – here you'll find some of the most spectacular **diving** and **snorkelling** sites in the country, if not the world. The Turneffe Islands have a marine research station, on **Calabash Caye**, and a marine reserve is planned, while Lighthouse Reef has the protected **Half Moon Caye** and **Blue Hole Natural Monuments** – the latter an enormous collapsed cave that attracts divers from all over the world. All are regularly visited on day-trips or live-aboard dive boats from San Pedro or Caye Caulker.

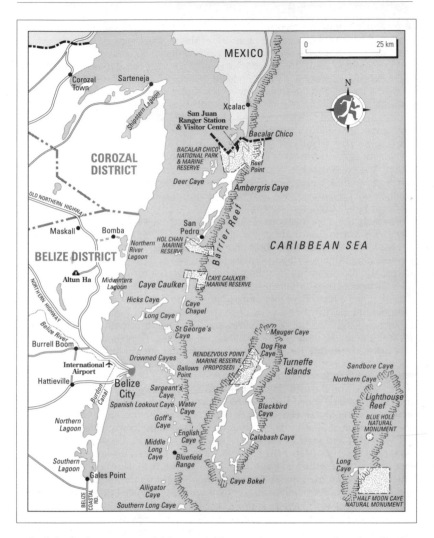

Such is the importance of this astonishing marine ecosystem that virtually the entire barrier reef, the reef surrounding all the atolls and all of Belize's **marine reserves** were declared a **World Heritage Site** in December 1996 – in other words, a place of such significance that its "deterioration or disappearance" would constitute "a harmful impoverishment of the heritage of all nations of the world", to quote UNESCO's World Heritage Convention. The announcement was greeted with tremendous enthusiasm by Belize's dedicated and influential environmental and conservation organizations. Together, the sites are designated the **Belize Barrier Reef Reserve System**.

A brief history of the cayes

The earliest inhabitants of the cayes were **Maya** peoples or their ancestors. By the Classic period (300–900 AD) the Maya had developed an extensive trade network stretching from the Yucatán to Honduras, with settlements and transhipment centres on several of the islands. At least some cities in Belize survived the Maya "collapse" and the trade network existed throughout the Postclassic era – until the arrival of the conquistadors. **Columbus** may have sighted the coast of Belize on his last voyage to the "Indies" in 1502; his journal mentions an encounter with a Maya trading party in an immense dugout canoe off Guanaja, one of the Bay Islands of Honduras (see p.213). Traces of Maya civilization remain on some of the cayes today, especially Ambergris Caye, which boasts the site of **Marco Gonzalez**, near the southern tip, and the remains of a number of ports and trading centres on the northwestern shores. Evidence of coastal trade, such as shell mounds, have also been found on other islands, including Moho Caye off Belize City.

Probably the most infamous residents of the cayes were the **buccaneers**, usually British, who lived here in the sixteenth and seventeenth centuries, taking refuge in the shallow waters after plundering Spanish treasure ships. In time the pirates settled more or less permanently on some of the northern and central cayes. But life under the Jolly Roger became too hot for them in the late 1600s, after Britain agreed to stamp out privateering under the terms of the Madrid Treaties, and a number of them turned instead to logwood cutting. But the wood cutters (the Baymen) still kept their dwellings on the cayes – specifically **St George's Caye** – as the cool breezes and fresh water offered a welcome break from the steaming swamps where the logwood grew. The population of the cayes remained low during the seventeenth and eighteenth centuries, but the settlement on St George's Caye was regarded by the Baymen as their capital until 1779, when a Spanish force destroyed it, imprisoning 140 of the Baymen and 250 of their slaves. The Baymen returned in 1783 and took revenge on the Spanish fleet in 1798 in the celebrated **Battle of St George's Caye** (see p.110). From then on, however, although the elite of the Baymen still kept homes on St George's Caye, the population of the islands began to decline as Belize Town (later City) grew.

Fishermen and turtlers continued to use the cayes as a base for their operations, and refugees fleeing the Caste Wars in the Yucatán towards the end of the last century also settled on the islands in small numbers. During this century the island population has increased steadily, booming with the establishment of the **fishing cooperatives** in the 1960s, which brought improved traps, ice plants and access to the export market. There's now the possibility that the lobster-fishing industry will destroy itself by overfishing.

At around the same time came another boom, as the cayes of Belize, particularly Caye Caulker, became a hang-out on the hippy trail, and then began to attract more lucrative custom. The islanders generally welcomed these new visitors: rooms were rented and hotels built, and a new prosperity began to transform island life. Luxuries not usually associated with small fishing communities in the developing world – colour televisions, telephones, skiffs with large outboard motors – are all evidence of the effects of tourism.

Visiting the cayes

The increasing popularity of Belize as a holiday destination has led to an escalation in land prices, and real estate offices proliferate on San Pedro's main streets, tempting wealthy visitors to invest in a Caribbean island. Luckily, most of the islands are too small and remote to entice the developers. Indeed, getting to many of the cayes and atolls can be a problem, especially if you're limited by time and finances, though access is much easier nowadays. Several organizations have conservation projects on the cayes, requiring self-funded **volunteers** (see p.42), or you could see if a visiting yacht owner needs a crew (they're not all millionaires); alternatively, if you can get together a group of three or four, you might rent a sailboat for a few days – easily done on Caye Caulker – and let a local boatman show you the lesser-known parts of the reef.

Life on the cayes is supremely relaxing, tempting you to take it easy in a hammock, feast on seafood and sip rum punch as the sun sets. The most accessible and least expensive of the islands is **Caye Caulker**, and if you feel the urge to see what's beneath the waves it's easily done from here or from **Ambergris Caye**, to the north. **Divers** can visit sites of almost unbelievable beauty and isolation, either joining a group day-trip or staying at a lodge on the edge of the reef; **dive instruction** is readily available. This kind of fun can be expensive, though. **Snorkelling** is far cheaper, and often just as rewarding. Again, day-trips are on offer on both of the main cayes, visiting three or four different reef sites in a day.

Bird-watching, as anywhere in Belize, is fascinating. Around two hundred species live in or visit the coastal areas and cayes, from ospreys to sandpipers and flamingos to finches. Many otherwise rare birds are relatively common here; for instance, the preservation of the red-footed booby on Half Moon Caye was the main reason for establishing a Natural Monument there in 1982. Catch-and-release **fly-fishing** for bonefish is popular, too, particularly at the Turneffe Island flats; but this is expensive, and you'll probably want to bring your own equipment. Fishing trips for species such as snapper, barracuda and grouper are easily arranged, and a local guide can take you to the best spots. Some snorkelling trips can include a chance of fishing using a handline.

Ambergris Caye and San Pedro

Geographically part of Mexico's Xcalak Peninsula, **Ambergris Caye**, the most northerly and by far the largest of the cayes, is separated from Mexico by the narrow Bacalar Chico channel, dug by the ancient Maya. The island's main attraction and point of arrival is the former fishing village of **SAN PEDRO**, facing the reef just a few kilometres from the southern tip and 58km northeast of Belize City. If you fly into San Pedro, which is the way most visitors arrive, the views are breathtaking: the water appears so clear and shallow as to barely cover the sandy seabed, and the mainland and other islands stand out clearly. But the most memorable sight is the pure white line of the reef crest, dramatically separating the vivid blue of the open sea from the turquoise water on its leeward side – the aircraft fly at so low an altitude, around 100m, that photographs taken from inside the cabin generally turn out well.

As you land at the tiny airport, with the sea to one side and the lagoon to the other, a glimpse at San Pedro shows it taking up the whole width of the island. It's not a large town – you're never more than a stone's throw from the sea – but its population of over four thousand is the highest on any of the cayes. San Pedro is the main destination for over half the visitors to Belize, catering mainly for North American package tours – almost all prices are quoted in US dollars. Some of the

GETTING TO AND FROM AMBERGRIS CAYE

Flying to San Pedro is the easiest and most popular approach: from Belize City Municipal and Belize International airports Maya Island Air (☎02/31140, 2345 in San Pedro) and Tropic Air (☎02/45671, 2012 in San Pedro) between them have flights at least hourly from 7am to 5pm (25min).

Though **boats** from Belize City to San Pedro (1hr 15min; Bz$25 one way) are less frequent than those to Caye Caulker (see box on p.103), there are a few regular fast services. Note that some boats may not run on Sundays, or during the low season, though at least one direct boat will be operating every day of the year. The *Triple J* (☎02/44375) is the best boat on the run and one of the first to leave, at 9am from Courthouse Wharf, returning at 3pm. Another boat, run by the Caye Caulker Water Taxis, leaves from the Marine Terminal by the Swing Bridge at 9am, leaving San Pedro at 2.30pm. In the afternoons the *Thunderbolt* leaves the Swing Bridge at 1pm, returning at 7am, and the *Andrea* leaves Courthouse Wharf at 3pm, returning from San Pedro at 7am.

Travelling **from San Pedro to other cayes**, any of the above scheduled boats also stop at **Caye Caulker** (and there are regular departures from San Pedro to Caye Caulker from 8am to 4.30pm), and they'll also call at **St George's Caye** or **Caye Chapel** if you ask.

Tropic Air and Maya Island Air also fly from **San Pedro to Corozal**, so you could head into Mexico without returning to Belize City.

country's most exclusive hotels, restaurants and bars are here; the few budget places are in the original village of San Pedro, which is also where most of the action takes place, particularly in the evenings.

But despite development, the town just about manages to retain elements of its **Caribbean charm** with two-storey, clapboard buildings still predominating in the centre. However, more lofty concrete structures are an increasingly common feature, and in the built-up area most of the palms have been cut down; more are dying from the "lethal yellowing" disease, sweeping down from the north. Traffic has increased considerably in recent years, creating deep ruts in the sandy streets, which turn into near-impassable mud holes following heavy rain.

One of the most interesting (and hectic) times to be in San Pedro is during the **International Costa Maya Festival**, a week-long celebration featuring cultural and musical presentations from the five Mundo Maya countries (Belize, Mexico, Guatemala, Honduras and El Salvador), held annually in the third week of July. The festival began as a way to drum up visitors during the off-season; it's now so popular you may need to book rooms.

Arrival, information and orientation

Arriving in San Pedro, boats usually dock at the *Coral Beach* or Texaco piers on the front (reef) side of the island. Both are within a block of the centre of town, marked by the seafront **Central Park**. The *Thunderbolt*, however, docks at Cesario's Dock, at the back of the island; from here, head down Black Coral Street to get to the centre. Landing at San Pedro's **airport**, only 500m south of the centre, is almost as convenient. It's at the north end of Coconut Drive – the town's main street running south – and within easy walking distance of any of the hotels in town, though **golf buggies** and **taxis** will be waiting for your custom. If you want to, you can **leave luggage** at the airport while you look for somewhere to stay – see the staff in the Travel and Tour Belize office a few steps north of the airstrip; they can also give good advice and information on hotels (including budget options), or indeed anything else in San Pedro.

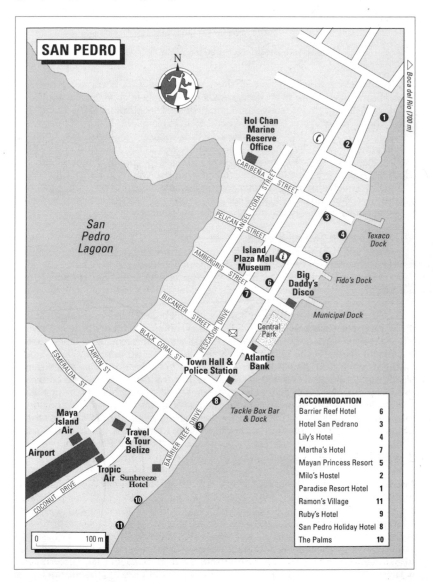

ACCOMMODATION	
Barrier Reef Hotel	6
Hotel San Pedrano	3
Lily's Hotel	4
Martha's Hotel	7
Mayan Princess Resort	5
Milo's Hostel	2
Paradise Resort Hotel	1
Ramon's Village	11
Ruby's Hotel	9
San Pedro Holiday Hotel	8
The Palms	10

Information

San Pedro's official **tourist office** (daily 9am–5pm; ☎2298) shares its location with the new Ambergris Museum (see p.95) in the Island Plaza Mall on Barrier Reef Drive, and any of the travel or tour agencies recommended in Listings (see p.102) can also provide accurate information. It's always worth picking up a copy of the island's free **tourist newspaper**, *The San Pedro Sun*, available from most hotels and restaurants on the caye.

The **telephone area code** for San Pedro is ☎026

Most hotels and gift shops sell the cartoon-style (but accurate) *Savanna's Bohemian Guide*, a **map of Ambergris Caye**. A couple of good, locally published **books** give an insight into the natural and historical background of the island: *The Field Guide to Ambergris Caye*, by Woods et al. explains the history, biology and geology of the caye (Richie Woods, a Belizean marine biologist, can often be found around San Pedro); and, for those interested in the ancient history of the island, there's the excellent *Maya Traders of Ambergris Caye* by Thomas Gudejan. Both are widely available in San Pedro and from bookshops in Belize City.

Finally, as befits Belize's premier tourist destination, Ambergris Caye has one of the best **Web sites** in the country (*www.ambergriscaye.com*) with superbly designed links to most of the businesses on the islands.

Orientation and getting around

The three **main streets** of the town centre run parallel to the beach. Formerly (and more prosaically) called Front, Middle and Back streets, they have now been given names more in keeping with the new upmarket image – Barrier Reef Drive, Pescador Drive and Angel Coral Street. Most locals stick to the old names; in any case it's impossible to get lost.

The town centre is small enough to get around on foot; pleasant enough at any time, it's particularly enjoyable on weekend evenings, when Barrier Reef Drive is closed to vehicles. However, in recent years, the town has expanded rapidly to the north and south, so you might want to **rent a bike**, a **moped** (or a very expensive **golf cart**) from one of the travel agencies to explore the sometimes rough roads further out. Several hotels some distance from the centre have **courtesy bikes** for guests – something you might want to consider when choosing a place to stay. On some occasions you might need a **water taxi**, especially to the northern resorts; you'll often find them by the dock in front of Fido's Courtyard, a group of shops and restaurants on Barrier Reef Drive just north of the park. Armando, with his skiff *Jean Luc*, is very reliable, though at Bz$40 a ride, expensive for less than four people (call ☎014/9448 to check the fare). There's also a **fast ferry** to and from the north – the comfortable *Island Express* (Bz$8 each way), leaving from Fido's every two hours from 7.15am to 11.15pm, returning from 8.15am to 10.15pm.

Accommodation

There are more than fifty **hotels** on Ambergris Caye, most of which, including all the **budget** options, are in San Pedro itself, just a short walk or taxi ride from the airport. **Prices** in general are higher than the rest of Belize but **discounts** on the

---

ACCOMMODATION PRICE CODES

All accommodation listed in this guide has been given a **price code** according to the following scale. The prices refer to the cost of **a double room in high season** (generally December to Easter) in Belize dollars (Bz$), but usually do not include the government hotel tax of seven percent. For more details see p.26.

① under Bz$20	④ Bz$50–70	⑦ Bz$140–190
② Bz$20–30	⑤ Bz$70–100	⑧ Bz$190–240
③ Bz$30–50	⑥ Bz$100–140	⑨ over Bz$240

---

quoted rates are often available, especially in the low season, so it's worth asking for one. Almost everywhere takes credit cards.

You shouldn't have any problem finding somewhere to stay in the high season (December to Easter), with the exception of Christmas and Easter when it's definitely advisable to **book ahead**. At any time, if you arrive without a booking it pays to call around a few of the recommended places first; you're likely to get a better price on your room and the hotel owner can advise you as to whether you need a taxi, and how much it should cost (unlike the rest of Belize, overcharging is rampant here) – they might even pick you up in their golf buggy. As you walk around the island you may see **"room for rent"** signs; these are generally for locals (including expatriates) but worth a try if you plan to stay for a while. There's nowhere that you can **camp** legally, and sleeping rough is not recommended.

Budget to mid-range accommodation

Changes in Latitudes, a kilometre south of town, near the Belize Yacht Club (✆ & fax 2986, email *latitudes@btl.net*). Very friendly, small B&B set in gardens half a block from the sea – guests can use the spacious Yacht Club dock to sunbathe or swim. Immaculately clean rooms, some a/c. Canadian owner Lori Reed is a mine of information, and has a book exchange. Free pickup from the airport and good low-season discounts. Wonderful breakfasts included. ⑤.

Del Rio Cabañas, ten-minutes' walk north of the centre (✆ & fax 2286, in US ✆318/984-9655, email *jewel@globalreach.net*). A range of accommodation run by the very hospitable Linda and Fido Badillo. Las Cabañas are very comfortable wood-and-thatch cabins with fans, facing the sea and surrounded by plants; Chica sleeps 3 (US$60) and has a fridge; Grande, with a kitchen, sleeps 5 (US$100). Rooms in Casa Blanca are modern and have a/c; Los Cuartos are budget rooms with shared bath. Fido offers good-value fishing trips and visits to Altun Ha (see p.68). ④.

Hideaway Lodge, a kilometre or so south of the town, just past the Texaco station (✆2141, fax 2269, email *hideaway@btl.net*). Large, recently renovated, rooms with fan or a/c; especially good value for groups. Relaxing pool area and on-site restaurant serving tasty fish and chips and other European dishes as well as Belizean specialities. Guests can rent bicycles. ⑤.

Laidy's Apartments, along the beach north of the town centre (✆2682). Well-furnished rooms, all with private bath and hot water; good value if you're sharing. ⑤–⑥.

Lily's, in the town centre, south of the main dock (✆2059). Two-storey beachfront hotel; good value considering its sea views. Recently renovated a/c rooms, plus a good restaurant below the hotel. No single rates. ⑤–⑥.

Martha's, Pescador Drive across from *Elvie's Kitchen* (✆2053). Clean, comfortable rooms with fan, bedside lights, and private bathrooms. ④.

Milo's, at the north end of Barrier Reef Drive, on the left just before the *Paradise Hotel* (☎2033, fax 2198). The best-value budget hotel on the caye; basic but clean rooms, some with private bath. Shared bathrooms have hot water. Singles available; quoted prices include tax. No credit cards. ②–④.

Ruby's, Barrier Reef Drive, a very short walk from the airstrip (☎2063, fax 2434, email *rubys@btl.net*). Clean, comfortable, family-run hotel right on the seafront. Rooms get better views and increased rates the higher up you go; all are good value, shared bathrooms especially so. *Ruby's Café*, downstairs, is one of the first to open and the hotel organizes good trips. ③–⑤.

San Pedrano, corner of Barrier Reef Drive and Caribeña St (☎2054, fax 2093). Quiet, clean hotel, in a wooden building, set back slightly from the sea, but with good views and breeze from the verandas. Comfortable rooms with private bath. ④.

More expensive hotels

Barrier Reef Hotel, in the centre of town, opposite the park (☎2075, fax 2719, email *barriereef@btl.net*) Distinctive, white-painted colonial-style building with a pool. The bright, clean rooms all have a/c and there's a good restaurant. ⑦.

Capricorn Resort, on the beach 5km north of town (☎2809, fax 021/2091, email *capricorn@btl.net*). Most people come here for the incredibly good food (see p.100) but there are also three delightful, secluded, wooden cabins with porches, and a beautiful upper-storey suite with a/c, overlooking a pristine beach; all make perfect hideaways. Breakfast is included as is transport by water taxi from town on arrival and departure; bikes available for guests. ⑧.

Caribbean Villas Hotel, 2km south of town (☎2715, fax 2885, email *c-v-hotel@btl.net*). Spacious, very comfortable rooms and well-equipped suites, all with ocean views, set in a garden on the beachfront. Plenty of peace and quiet and relaxation; snooze in a hammock or immerse yourself in the hot tub. An observation tower in the grounds gives views of the lagoon and there's fantastic bird-watching. Free bikes mean you can cycle into town in under ten minutes. The best-value smaller hotel in this range. ⑦–⑨.

Coconuts, on the beach 1500m south of town (☎3500, fax 3501, email *coconuts@btl.net*). A comfortable, modern hotel with clean, well-decorated tiled rooms, all with a/c. Very helpful and informative owners, who provide free bikes for guests and pay the taxi fare when you arrive, so call ahead first. Rates include a good breakfast buffet – good discounts in low season. ⑦–⑧.

Mata Chica Beach Resort, on the beach 7km north of town (☎ & fax 021/3012, email *matachica@btl.net*). The most beautiful and spacious beach cabañas in the country, designed by French/Italian owners Philippe and Nadia and painted in pastel colours that change with the light. Each interior is unique, with murals by French artist Lionel Dumas, and hand-painted tiles in the bathrooms. The reef is just 600m away; guests can sail there aboard the resort's luxurious catamaran. The food is sublime; see *Mambo* p.101. US$165 for a double cabaña. ⑨.

Mayan Princess Resort, Barrier Reef Drive, just north of the centre (☎2778, fax 2784, email *mayanprin@btl.net*). Very comfortable, spacious, well-equipped beachfront suites, each with a large balcony overlooking the sea; the best value suites in town for the price. ⑧.

The Palms, Coconut Drive, just south of the town centre (☎3322, fax 3601, email *palms@btl.net*). Luxury, well-furnished a/c suites overlooking the beachfront in a quiet location, but conveniently near the town. Lots of extras here, including fully-equipped kitchens, daily maid service and a beautiful private pool. Ground-floor rooms are wheelchair accessible. US$158 for a one-bedroom suite. ⑨.

Paradise Resort Hotel, at the north end of Barrier Reef Drive (☎2083 fax 2232, email *paradise@btl.net*). Long-established, very well-run hotel in a great location. Accommodation ranges from thatched double rooms and spacious cabañas, some a/c, to modern villas with kitchenettes sleeping up to six. The shady gardens lead to a beach and private dock, with a dive shop and there's a good restaurant and friendly beach bar. ⑦–⑨.

Playador Hotel, on the beach 1km south of town (☎2870, fax 2871, in Canada ☎604/469-6317, email *playador@btl.net*). Modern, well-furnished, thatched cabañas, rooms and suites (some a/c) in a breezy beachfront location. Good value for groups and offers discounts to

Rough Guide readers. Friendly, comfortable and relaxing, with plenty of space, a pool and dive shop. Also has a good restaurant and a bar with one of the best happy hours on the island. ⑦–⑧.

Ramon's Village, on the beach in front of the airport (☎2071, fax 2214). The largest resort, with every facility, though pricey if you're not on a package. Lovely two-storey, wood-and-thatch cabañas with balcony, most a/c, set among palms on a beautiful white beach with a pool. ⑧.

San Pedro Holiday Hotel, Barrier Reef Drive, on the seafront, just south of the town centre (☎2014, fax 2295, email *holiday@btl.net*). San Pedro's oldest hotel, but with all modern facilities, including a/c. Rooms at the front have refrigerators. There's a very good restaurant and *Celi's Deli* serves good-value snacks. ⑦–⑧.

Victoria House, 3km south of town (☎2067, fax 2429, in US ☎1-800/247-5159, email *victoria@btl.net*). A wide range of amazing accommodation set in a stunning beachfront location and an obvious hit with honeymooners. The luxury villas, cabañas and hotel rooms are set in spacious grounds resembling a botanic garden. Service is excellent and there's a fine restaurant; you get the best overall value on an all-in package. Prices start at US$130 for a double room in high season, and go up to US$545 for a 2-bed villa. ⑨.

Exploring the caye and the reef

Although there are a few places you can visit on land, it's the **water** which is the focus of daytime entertainment on Ambergris Caye, from sunbathing on the docks to windsurfing, sailing, fishing, **diving** and **snorkelling**, and even taking trips on glass-bottomed boats. Many hotels will rent snorkelling equipment and there are several specialist dive shops offering instruction. A word of **warning**: there have been a number of accidents in San Pedro in which speeding boats have hit people swimming off the piers. A line of buoys, not always clearly visible, indicates the "**safe area**", but speedboat drivers can be a bit macho; be careful when choosing where to swim.

Before going snorkelling or diving, whet your appetite for the wonders of the reef with a visit to the excellent **Hol Chan Marine Reserve office and visitor centre** (Mon–Fri 8am–noon & 1–5pm; ☎2247) on Caribeña St. They have photographs, maps and other displays on the marine reserves (see pp.98–9), and the staff will be pleased to answer your questions; you may even be able to get a ride with the ranger up to Bacalar Chico (see below). Equally worthwhile is a visit to the new **Ambergris Museum** in the Island Plaza Mall on Barrier Reef Drive (daily 2–6pm; Bz$5, Sun Bz$2.50), run by the Ambergris Historical Society. Maya pottery comprises some of the oldest exhibits, with colonial weapons and old photographs illustrating the island's history right up to the 1960s.

South of San Pedro, the road continues for several kilometres to the Maya site of **Marco Gonzalez**, though the further you go the swampier and more mosquito-infested the terrain gets. The site is hard to find and there's not a lot to see, but studies have shown that it was once an important trade centre, with close links to Lamanai (see p.75). Archeological teams are still investigating here, so check at the museum to see if work is going on during your visit. At the southernmost tip of the island is the impressive **Hol Chan Marine Reserve**.

A kilometre or so **north of San Pedro**, the **Boca del Rio**, sometimes called "The River" but actually a narrow erosion channel, is crossed during daylight by a tiny ferry (Bz$1 per person) just big enough to take a golf cart (Bz$5); on the other side a rudimentary road (also navigable by golf cart) leads to the northern resorts.

The northernmost section of the caye, now accessible on organized day-trips, boasts the spectacular **Bacalar Chico National Park and Marine Reserve** and several **Maya sites**.

All of the trips described in the text can easily be booked from your hotel or any tour or travel agent.

Diving

For anyone who has never dived in the tropics before, the **reefs near San Pedro** are fine, but experienced divers looking for high-voltage will be disappointed. This is a heavily used area which has long been subjected to intensive fishing, and much of the reef has been plundered by souvenir hunters. To experience the best diving in Belize you need to take a trip out to one of the **atolls** (see box below).

Dive instruction and **local dives** are best done with smaller, independent **operators** rather than the bigger dive shops as both the instruction and guiding will be more tailored to your needs; among the best local operators are Amigos del Mar, at the well-signed dock just north of the centre (☎2706, fax 2648). For the best **advice** on any aspect of diving from San Pedro, or to **book** the dive boats recommended in the box below, contact Chris Allnatt at the Blue Hole Dive Center, on Barrier Reef Drive (☎ & fax 2982), where you can also see photos of the dive boats and watch recent videos taken by divers.

In general, a PADI or NAUI **open water certification**, which takes novices up to the standard of a fully qualified sport diver, costs around US$350; a more basic, introductory **resort course** costs around US$125. For **qualified divers** a two-tank dive costs around US$50, including tanks, weights, air and boat; shop around for the best prices. The best dive shops in San Pedro recommend you make a voluntary contribution of US$1 per tank to help fund the town's **hyperbaric chamber**: this covers you for treatment if you need it, so make sure you fill out the agreement when you sign on to dive.

OFFSHORE AND LIVE-ABOARD DIVE BOATS IN SAN PEDRO

There are two **live-aboard dive boats** based in San Pedro, giving you the opportunity to stay out at the atolls for two to three days. Both fifteen-metre vessels are crewed by professionals, carry safety equipment and sleep five or six, though usually you'll be **camping** on one of the remote cayes of Lighthouse Reef (see p.112); an experience not to be missed. The *Caye Explorer* (☎5019), a charter-only boat, costs US$125 per person per day; the *Offshore Express* (☎2817) has a big sun deck, runs a couple of two-day trips per week, and costs US$250 for five dives. Trips include food. Snorkellers can usually go along as well, paying slightly less than divers. The boats are popular and space is limited, so book well in advance if possible.

For comfortable **day visits** to the Blue Hole and the atolls there's the *Blue Hole Express* (☎2982), a fast twelve-metre boat charging US$165 for divers, US$110 for snorkellers; or the *Miss Gina* (☎2071), a very fast Pro-42 dive boat but slightly more expensive at US$185 for divers, US$125 for snorkellers.

Any of the above boats picks up passengers at Caye Caulker on request, at no extra charge. Several other operators also run day-trips to the Blue Hole, though the boats are generally smaller, which may mean a rougher ride; try Amigos del Mar (see above).

SAFEGUARDING THE BELIZE BARRIER REEF

Coral reefs are among the most complex and fragile ecosystems on earth. Colonies have been growing at a rate of less than 5cm a year for thousands of years; once damaged, the coral is far more susceptible to bacteria, which can quickly lead to large-scale irreversible damage. Remember to follow these **simple rules** while snorkelling, diving or in a boat:

- Never anchor boats on the reef – use the permanently secured buoys.
- Never touch or stand on corals – protective cells are easily stripped away from the living polyps on their surface, destroying them and thereby allowing algae to enter.
- Don't remove shells, sponges or other creatures from the reef, or buy reef products from souvenir shops.
- Avoid disturbing the seabed around corals – quite apart from spoiling visibility, clouds of sand settle over corals, smothering them.
- If you're either a beginner or an out-of-practice diver, practise away from the reef first.
- Don't use suntan lotion in reef areas – the oils remain on the water's surface.
- Check you're not in one of the new marine reserves before fishing.
- Don't feed or interfere with fish or marine life; this can harm not only sea creatures and the food chain, but snorkellers too – large fish may attack, trying to get their share!

If you want to capture the **underwater wildlife** on film but don't have a suitable camera you can rent one from Joe Miller Photography on Pescador Drive (☎2577). Joe is a renowned photographer and offers advanced **instruction**, E-6 **slide processing** and can even undertake emergency repairs. The Blue Hole Dive Center also rents excellent cameras at similar prices.

Snorkelling

Just about every hotel in San Pedro offers **snorkelling** trips, costing around US$15 for three hours, plus about US$5 to rent equipment. If you've never used a snorkel before, practise the technique from a dock first, and get used to seeing shoals of colourful fish. You might also prefer to snorkel in a life-jacket – this will give you greater buoyancy, and help to stop you bumping into the coral. **Snorkelling guides** here (who must also be licensed tour guides) have a great deal of experience with visitors, and they'll show you how to use the equipment before you set off; if they don't seem willing to help novices go with someone else.

Generally, the options available mean you can either head north to the spectacular **Mexico Rocks** or Rocky Point or, more commonly, south to the **Hol Chan Marine Reserve** (see p.98). **Night snorkelling**, a truly amazing experience, is also available, and usually costs a little more than a daytime trip. Several boats take snorkellers out for a **day-trip to Caye Caulker**, employing a mix of motor and sail, and comprising two leisurely snorkelling stops and lunch on the caye, returning to San Pedro around sunset. A day aboard *Rum Punch II* (US$40), a ten-metre sailboat, is supremely relaxing; only equalled by her skipper George's **sunset cruise** (US$15). The 22-metre, motor-powered *Winnie Estelle* has a spacious, shaded deck to spread out on and was formerly used on Chesapeake Bay before being restored and brought to Belize. Her captain, Roberto Smith, operates day-trips to Caye Caulker (US$55); the price includes an open bar and freshly prepared snacks and fruit after the snorkelling stops.

Also to the south, near the Hol Chan reserve, is the extremely popular (but controversial) **shark-ray alley**, where you can swim with **nurse sharks** and **stingrays** in water only 3m deep. Despite their reputations these creatures are fairly inoffensive, and watching them glide effortlessly beneath you is an exhilarating experience. Biologists, however, claim that the practice of feeding the fish to attract them alters their natural behaviour, exposing both the fish and humans to danger – at times the area is so crowded that any hope of communing with nature is completely lost amongst the flailing bodies of the snorkellers.

Other trips and activities

There are plenty of other water-based activities on offer on the caye including **windsurfing** (US$15–50), **para-sailing** (US$40 a flight) and **water-skiing** (US$50 per hour). Many of the larger hotels and resorts rent **hobie-cats** or **kayaks**, or you could check out the equipment and prices at Fido's dock.

In addition to the boat trips to **Caye Caulker** (see above), there are increasingly popular **day-trips** on land from San Pedro to the ruins of **Altun Ha** (see p.68) and even **Lamanai** (see p.75). Rounding the southern tip of the island in a fast skiff, you head for the mainland at the mouth of the **Northern River**, cross the lagoon and travel up the river to the tiny village of **Bomba**. With a good guide this is an excellent way to spot wildlife, including **crocodiles** and **manatees**, and the riverbank trees are often adorned with **orchids**. If you like the wood carvings for sale in the gift shops on the island, stop and examine those offered by the people of Bomba; prices here are lower, and the money goes directly to the carver's family. Two of the best **guides** are Daniel Nuñez (☎2314) and Fido Badillo (☎2286).

The south: Hol Chan Marine Reserve

The **Hol Chan Marine Reserve**, 8km south of San Pedro, at the southern tip of the caye, takes its name from the Maya for "little channel", and it is this break in the reef that forms the focus of the reserve. Established in 1987, its three zones – covering a total of around thirteen square kilometres – preserve a comprehensive cross-section of the marine environment, from **coral reef** through **seagrass beds** to **mangroves**. All three habitats are closely linked: many reef fish feed on the seagrass beds, and the mangroves are a nursery area for the juveniles. As your boat approaches, you'll be met by a warden who explains the rules and collects the entry fee (Bz$5).

The fish are not fed here (as they once were) but they're no longer hunted either, so you'll see plenty of marine life including some very large **snappers**, **groupers** and **barracuda**. Much damage has already been caused by snorkellers standing on the coral or holding onto outcrops for a better look – on all the easily accessible areas of the reef you will see the white, dead patches, especially on the large brain coral heads. **Never touch** the coral – not only will that damage the delicate ecosystem (see box on p.97), but the coral can also sting and cause agonizing burns; even brushing against the razor-sharp ridges on the reef top can cause cuts that are slow to heal.

The north: Bacalar Chico National Park and the Maya sites

A visit to the remote and virtually pristine northern section of Ambergris Caye is an unmissable highlight, not only for the obvious attractions of the **Bacalar**

Chico Marine Reserve and National Park, but also for the chance to see a number of previously inaccessible **Maya sites** on the northern coast. On a **day-trip** from San Pedro you can visit several areas of the reserve and take in two or three of the ten or more Maya sites; the best **guide** to Bacalar Chico is Daniel Nuñez (☎2314).

Travelling by boat through Boca Del Rio and up the west coast, you might briefly stop to observe colonies of seabirds roosting on some small, uninhabited cayes; there are several species of herons and egrets and you might even spot the beautiful and much rarer **roseate spoonbill**, though landing on the islands or disturbing the birds is prohibited. On the way back, you navigate **Bacalar Chico**, the channel dug by the Maya about 1500 years ago to allow a shorter paddling route for their trading canoes beween their cities in Chetumal Bay and the coast of Yucatán. It's so narrow you can practically touch the mangroves on either side as you sit in the boat. At the mouth of the channel the reef is close to the shore; the boat has to cross into the open sea, re-entering the leeward side of the reef as you approach San Pedro, so completing a circumnavigation of the island.

THE NATIONAL PARK AND MARINE RESERVE

Covering the entire northern tip of Ambergris Caye, **Bacalar Chico National Park and Marine Reserve** is the largest protected area in the northern cayes. Its 110 square kilometres extends from the reef, across the seagrass beds to the coastal mangroves and **caye littoral forest**, and over to the salt marsh and lagoon behind. The area of sea within the reserve is designated a Marine Reserve and is protected by Belize's Fisheries Department, while the terrestrial area is a National Park under the protection of Belize's Forestry Department; both are patrolled by rangers based at the headquarters and **visitor centre** at **San Juan**, on the northwest coast, where you register and pay the Bz$5 **park fee**. Near the ranger station a seven-metre-high **observation tower**, built by Operation Raleigh volunteers, allows views over undisturbed forest – it's also used by rangers to control boat traffic in the reserve.

Despite all the development to the south, there's a surprising amount of **wildlife** up here, including crocodiles, deer, peccary and, prowling around the thick forests, several of the wild cats of Belize. Birdlife is abundant and turtles nest on some beaches: contact the Belize Audubon Society (see p.246) or the Hol Chan Reserve office (see p.95) if you want to help patrol the beaches during turtle nesting season.

MAYA SITES

Some of the **Maya sites** in the north of the caye are undergoing archeological investigation and there's a real air of adventure and discovery as you explore the ancient ruins now buried in thick bush and jungle. **Santa Cruz**, about two-thirds of the way up the west coast of Ambergris Caye, is a very large site, known to have been used for the shipment of trade goods in the Postclassic era, though the true function of most of the stone mounds here remains uncertain. Further north, the beach at **San Juan** (see above) was another transhipment centre for the ancient Maya; here you'll be crunching over literally thousands of pieces of Maya pottery. But perhaps the most spectacular site is **Chac Balam**, a ceremonial and administrative centre; getting there entails a walk through mangroves to view deep burial chambers, scattered with thousands more pottery shards.

Eating, drinking and entertainment

There are plenty of places to eat in San Pedro, including some of the best restaurants in the country, and at the very top of the range, the quality of food and wine compares favourably with resorts anywhere in the world. **Prices** are generally higher than elsewhere in Belize, though you'll usually get good service – comparatively rare in much of the country. **Seafood** is prominent at most restaurants, which tend to reflect the tastes of the town's predominantly North American guests; thus you can also rely on plenty of steak, shrimp, chicken, pizza and salads. Many **hotels** have their own dining room, and in many cases also do **beach barbecues**. There are several **Chinese** restaurants, too, the cheaper ones representing the best value on the island. In the evening several **fast food stands** open for business in front of the park on Barrier Reef Drive

Buying your own food isn't particularly cheap here: there's no market and the grocery stores are stocked with imported canned goods. Cooking it might also be a problem (unless of course you're staying in an apartment) as it's not as easy in San Pedro as it is on other islands to improvise your own beach barbecue. The range and quality of groceries is improving all the time, however: Rock's **supermarket** — one on Pescador Drive and one south of town in San Pablo — has the widest selection, while Milo's, at the north end of Barrier Reef Drive, offers the best value. At the luxury end of the scale, there's the Sweet Basil deli, just north of Boca del Rio, with a great selection of imported cheeses, wine and paté. La Popular **bakery**, on Pescador Drive has a wide selection of breads, including Mexican-style *pan dulces*, and there are some **fruit and vegetable stalls** dotted around the centre. Manelly's Ice Cream Parlour, on Pescador, is the best place in town for a sit-down **ice-cream** treat.

Restaurants

Big Daddy's Fast Food, just past the park, in front of *Big Daddy's Disco*. The best and cheapest indoor fast food in town, serving large portions of very good Belizean and Mexican-style dishes at great prices in a new a/c restaurant; open lunchtime until late in the evening.

Capricorn Restaurant, on the beach in the *Capricorn Resort* (see p.94) 5km north of town (☎2809). Chef Clarence is in his element serving wonderful, in fact unbeatable, gourmet food in a beautiful location; try the French crepes, stone-crab cakes or filet mignon/seafood combo. You'll need to book for dinner in high season. You can get back to town from here until at least mid-evening on the *Island Express* ferry; after that you may need a water taxi. Closed Weds.

Celi's Restaurant, in the *Holiday Hotel*. Good seafood and evening barbecues. Closed Wed. *Celi's Deli* does delicious breakfasts and snacks, including the best *tamales* in town.

Duke's, Coconut Drive, across from *Ramon's*. Excellent, family-run restaurant serving great breakfasts, fish, steaks and Mexican-style food at amazing prices (dinner includes a drink and dessert) and surrounded by John Wayne memorabilia. Breakfast and dinner only.

Elvie's Kitchen, on Pescador, across the road from *Martha's* hotel (☎2176). Long an institution in San Pedro, and always serving good burgers and fries, *Elvie's* has now zoomed upmarket, with an expanded menu featuring soups, Caesar salad, steaks, chicken and, of course, lobster and all manner of seafood. The quality is good and the service slick with prices to match; you may need to book for dinner. Gentle live music in the evenings.

Jade Garden, Coconut Drive, south of town. The best Chinese restaurant on the island, and good value too.

Little Italy, next to the *Spindrift Hotel* (☎2866). The finest Italian restaurant in San Pedro; excellent food and service, and a good wine list. Some tables on a patio overlooking the sea;

you may have to book for dinner in high season. Their great-value Mexican-style lunch buffet (11.30am–2pm) has lots of choice.

Mambo, on the beach 7km north of town (✆ 021/3010). The dining room of the *Mata Chica Beach Resort* (see p.94) and Ambergris Caye's top restaurant, with superb food and wine and a classy, romantic atmosphere. Nadia, in charge of the cooking, is Italian and makes her own pasta. The menu changes daily but it's always fabulous; try the exquisite home-made fettuccini or the original paella. *Mambo* frequently features Belize's top musical groups for parties and entertainment. Dinner reservations are essential: guests are picked up from *The Palms* (see p.94) for dinner at 6:30pm; call for lunch.

El Patio, a couple of kilometres south of the centre, next to the Rock's supermarket. Fine dining at very reasonable prices in a lovely courtyard with fountains. Open for all meals.

Rasta Pasta Pizza Amor, in the *Sunbreeze Hotel*, at the south end of Barrier Reef Drive. Another wonderful San Pedro restaurant, serving a range of dishes at reasonable prices, all carefully seasoned with Maralyn and Albert's unique, home-prepared spices and served with quality, home-made wines. A great place for nightlife too.

The Reef, near the north end of Pescador. Really good Belizean food, including delicious seafood, at great prices in a simple restaurant cooled by a battery of fans.

Ruby's Café, Barrier Reef Drive, next to *Ruby's Hotel*. Delicious home-made cakes, pies and sandwiches, and freshly brewed coffee. Open at 6am, so it's a good place to order a packed lunch if you're going on a trip.

Bars and nightlife

Entertainment in San Pedro becomes more sophisticated every year, and the best way to find out what's on (and what's hot) is to ask at your hotel or check the listings in the *San Pedro Sun*; what follows is a brief mention of a few of the highlights. Many of the hotels have fancy bars, several of which offer **happy hours** – usually two for the price of one on local drinks – while back from the main street are a couple of small **cantinas** where you can buy a beer or a bottle of rum and drink with the locals.

Sandals Bar, on Ambergris Street, next to *Martha's Hotel*, is a friendly bar with less outrageous prices than most and a cool sand floor that's a treat for your feet; *ceviche*, a delicious seafood cocktail is served every day, and it's worth checking to see if Mike's doing a barbecue. *Traveller's Cantina*, on Pescador, complete with bat-wing doors, caters to locals and tourists.

Big Daddy's **disco**, in and around a beach bar just past the park, has early evening piano, and a lively reggae band later on. Happy hour here runs from 5 to 9pm and there's a daily beach barbecue. *Genesis Bar*, at the *Sunbreeze Hotel*, run by the same people as *Rasta Pasta*, has a daily happy hour (5–7pm), with free wine tasting, and live reggae and jazz several evenings a week (karaoke on Fridays). For the best beach-side happy hour (5–7pm), head for *Crazy Canuk Bar* at the *Playador Hotel* where you can get in the party mood to the sounds of the resident band *Barefoot Skinny*. The extremely popular *Tarzan's Disco and Nite Club*, opposite the park, has a very lively dance floor, and the *Tackle Box* bar, at the end of the *Coral Beach Hotel* pier, is a good spot to catch a local band.

Listings

Airlines Maya Island Air (✆2345) and Tropic Air (✆2012) each have flights at least every hour to Belize Municipal (and International) airports, calling at Caye Caulker. Any travel agent and most hotels can arrange flights.

Books Many of the larger hotels have gift shops for books on Belize; Sunbreeze has a particularly good selection of other titles as well, and the Book Center on Barrier Reef Drive has a reasonable selection, including guide books and maps; any of these places, or Belizean Arts in Fido's Courtyard, are likely to stock *Rough Guides*.

Banks and Exchange You needn't worry about changing money, as travellers' cheques and US dollars are accepted – even preferred – everywhere. The Atlantic Bank on Barrier Reef Drive (Mon–Fri 8am–2pm, Sat 8.30am–noon) is the best place for cash advances, despite the Bz$10 charge.

Conservation Apart from the Hol Chan office (see p.95) you can contact Green Reef (☎2838, email *greenreef@btl.net*) for information on the marine reserves and ecology of Ambergris Caye. Founded in 1996 to provide environmental education they are about to open a visitor centre in San Pedro, and can provide opportunities for self-funding volunteers in education and biological monitoring.

Laundry Two places in Pescador Drive; washing costs US$3, drying another US$3.

Massage Alexandra Nicholson, owner of Mayan Secrets (☎3370), offers highly recommended professional massage and natural health treatments.

Police Emergency ☎911; police station ☎2022.

Post office on the corner of Buccaneer Street and Barrier Reef Drive, at the side of the Alijua (Mon–Thurs 8am–noon & 1–5pm, Fri 1–4.30pm).

Shopping and souvenirs Belizean Arts in Fido's Courtyard has the island's best selection of paintings by Belizean artists, and a fine range of Central American arts and crafts. Rainforest Rescue, on Barrier Reef Drive, sells beautifully designed, high-quality T-shirts and speciality Belizean foods. At Iguana Jack's, opposite the primary school on Barrier Reef Drive, John Wetserhold creates fascinating ceramic iguanas and lizards. For the best-quality wood carvings and more fine ceramics go to the Best of Belize, near the south end of Pescador Drive.

Travel and tour agencies Your hotel will be able to book any of the tours mentioned in the text; for local trips around the caye and to the mainland Tanisha Tours (☎2314) is the best. For international and regional flights the best place to check is Travel and Tour Belize, on Coconut Drive, near the airport (☎2031, fax 2185), or try Amigo Travel, on Barrier Reef Drive a block before the park (☎2180, fax 2192); both have great expertise in arranging trips throughout Belize and Central America.

Caye Caulker

South of Ambergris Caye and 35km northeast of Belize City, **Caye Caulker**, a little over 7km long, is the most accessible island for the independent traveller, and long a favourite spot for backpackers on the "gringo trail". The island's name derives from that of a wild fruit and a local delicacy, the *hicaco* or coco plum. In 1961 Hurricane Hattie destroyed most of the houses and tore a gash through the island at a point just north of the village. Now widened by mangrove destruction and erosion, "The Split" as it's known, is a popular spot for swimming.

Until recently, tourism existed almost as a sideline to the island's main source of income, **lobster fishing**, which has kept the place going for more than twenty years. Although the lobster catch increased for many years after the setting up of fishing cooperatives, the deployment of more traps over an ever wider area led to the rapid depletion of the **spiny lobster**, once so common they could be scooped onto the beaches with palm fronds. Today their numbers are dangerously low, and specimens smaller than the legal 4oz (115g) are frequently taken and sold to local restaurants. Recent catches were so low that the fishermen were taking the traps in by mid-January, a month earlier than the end of the legal season.

GETTING TO AND FROM CAYE CAULKER

Flights on the San Pedro run stop at the Caye Caulker airstrip, 1.5km south of the village centre; call the airlines' main offices (see box on p.90) for information. On the island the offices are at the airstrip (Maya Island Air ☎2012; Tropic Air ☎2040). However, most visitors to Caye Caulker still arrive by **boat**. There are departures every two hours from 9am to 5pm (45min; Bz$15) from the Marine Terminal in Belize City (☎02/31969). All scheduled boats to San Pedro (see box on p.90) also call at Caye Caulker.

Boats **from Caye Caulker to San Pedro** depart every three hours from 7am to 4pm (check at the Caye Caulker water taxi office; ☎2992) and return roughly every three hours from 8am to 4.30pm. If you're heading for one of the small or uninhabited islands you may have to hire someone to take you there.

Leaving for Belize City, boats depart roughly every two hours from 6.30am to 3.30pm. It's best to check in at the water taxi office and book a place in a boat the day before you leave; the staff will also know the times that the boats on the San Pedro–Belize City run call at Caye Caulker; make sure it's clear which dock the boat is leaving from.

As fishing has declined, the islanders have had to diversify. Fishermen have become hoteliers, and fishing boats now offer snorkelling trips; new hotels and bars are being built, older ones improved, and prices – low for years – have begun to rise. For the moment, however, Caye Caulker remains relaxed and easy-going, managing to avoid most of the commercialism of San Pedro, though with the building of the airstrip and the ever-growing number of hotels and vehicles, it too is beginning to become rather crowded. Recently, the decision was made to allow construction on the larger, previously uninhabited northern part of the island, and some houses have been built on the southern point of this section. The success of a lengthy campaign by many islanders and others in Belize's environmental community, however, has resulted in the protection of the northern tip of the island and a section of the barrier reef as the **Caye Caulker Marine Reserve**, upholding the country's reputation as a leader in the field of natural area conservation.

As yet there is little air conditioning on the island, which is fine most of the time when a cooling breeze blows in from the sea, but it can mean some very sticky moments if the breeze dies. **Sandflies and mosquitoes** can cause almost unbearable irritation on calm days. Sandflies are the worst: inactive in breezy conditions, at other times they make a good insect repellent essential, though even that doesn't seem to last long (some swear by Avon's *Skin-So-Soft*).

The **telephone area code** for Caye Caulker is ☎022

Arrival and information

The **airstrip** is 1km south of the centre. Golf cart taxis can take you to your hotel, though hotels south of the main dock are only a ten-minute walk. **By boat** you'll be dropped off at one of the main piers on the island; either the "front" (east) dock or the "back" (west) dock – easily recognizable as they're longer than the others. Generally Caye Caulker-based boats stop at the Front Dock, and boats continuing

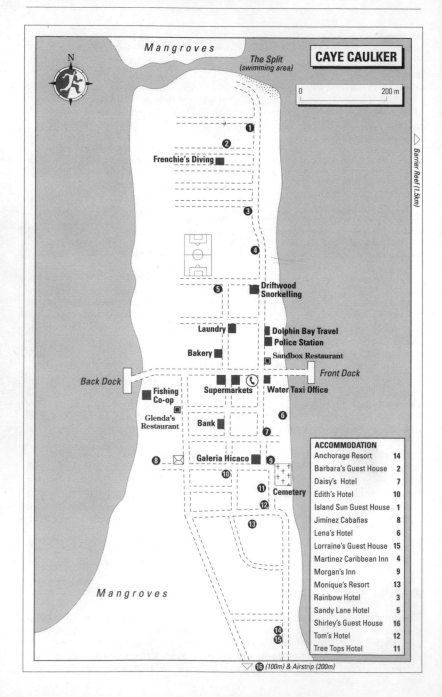

CAYE CAULKER

Mangroves

The Split
(swimming area)

0   200 m

▷ *Barrier Reef (1.5km)*

N

❶
❷
Frenchie's Diving ■

❸

❹

❺   ■ Driftwood
        Snorkelling

Laundry ■   ■ Dolphin Bay Travel
            ■ Police Station
Bakery ■   ◻ Sandbox Restaurant

Back Dock ▭   ▭ *Front Dock*

    ■ ■📞
Fishing ■   Supermarkets   ■ Water Taxi Office
Co-op
  ◻
Glenda's   Bank ■   ❻
Restaurant   ❼

❽ ✉   Galeria Hicaco ■   ❾
      ❿   ✝ ✝
            ⓫ ✝ ✝
               Cemetery
            ⓬

      ⓭

Mangroves

           ⓮
           ⓯

▽ ⓰ *(100m) & Airstrip (200m)*

ACCOMMODATION	
Anchorage Resort	14
Barbara's Guest House	2
Daisy's Hotel	7
Edith's Hotel	10
Island Sun Guest House	1
Jiménez Cabañas	8
Lena's Hotel	6
Lorraine's Guest House	15
Martinez Caribbean Inn	4
Morgan's Inn	9
Monique's Resort	13
Rainbow Hotel	3
Sandy Lane Hotel	5
Shirley's Guest House	16
Tom's Hotel	12
Tree Tops Hotel	11

on to San Pedro call at the Back Dock, though the weather (or just a whim) can change this; it's really only important to know when you're leaving. From either dock you simply walk straight ahead to the **water taxi office**, effectively the centre of the village. They can give **information** and will probably hold your luggage while you look for a place to stay.

As yet, there are no street names on the caye, but the street running along the shore at the front of the island is effectively **"Front Street"**, with just one or two streets running behind it in the centre of the village. Despite the impression given by some signs, a public right of way exists along the shoreline; walking this route allows you to find hotels right on the water. Ilna and Tina Auxillou, who run Caye Caulker's **travel agency**, Dolphin Bay Travel (☎ & fax 2214), have outstanding local knowledge, and can arrange domestic and international flights, tours and trips to other islands. Wendy Auxillou publishes the *Caye Caulker Village Voice*, the island's fortnightly **free newspaper** – it's worth picking up a copy to check the latest listings. For **books** (including *Rough Guides*) and **maps** see *Cindy's Café* (p.109) or Seaing is Belizing (p.107).

There are several **payphones** in the centre and the BTL office is near the water taxi office, on the corner leading to the main dock. The **post office** is on the back street, south of the village centre. The Atlantic Bank (Mon–Fri 8am–noon & 1–2pm) gives Visa **cash advances** (US$5 fee), and an increasing number of businesses accept plastic for payment.

One thing to be aware of in Caye Caulker is the **tap water**; it sometimes smells sulphurous, giving off a rotting odour. This may be the result of natural chemicals in the groundwater, but most places simply use septic tanks for waste disposal, and effluent does seep into the water table. Tap water on the caye should be regarded as **unfit to drink**; make sure your hotel gives you rainwater or bottled water.

Accommodation

Most of the year it's easy enough to find an inexpensive room in one of the small, mostly clapboard **hotels**, but to arrive at Christmas or New Year without a **reservation** could leave you stranded. Even the furthest hotels are no more than ten minutes' walk from the front dock and places are easy to find: the listings below are given roughly in the order you'd come to them walking from the dock. Most places now accept credit cards. There are also a growing number of houses or **apartments for rent**; try M&M Apartments (☎2229) near the football field, or Heredia's Apartments (☎2132). You'll come across other places as you walk around; prices start at about Bz$325 per week.

North from the "front" dock

Sandy Lane Hotel, a block back from the front (☎2217). Small, quiet, and inexpensive with rooms in the original building and newer, more expensive concrete cabins in the grounds. ②–④.

Martinez Caribbean Inn, on the seafront (☎2133). Secure and well run; all rooms with private bath and hot water and some have a/c. The best rooms are at the front, the less expensive ones to the rear. Popular with groups, and great value for three people sharing. *Martinez Restaurant*, just before the *Inn*, also has some budget rooms. ②–③.

Rainbow Hotel (☎2123). Two-storey concrete building with little ambience or privacy: the rooms open onto the path. Clean and secure though, with reliable hot water. ④.

Barbara's Guest House, towards the north end near the Split (☎2025). Friendly, Canadian-run place, with simple, clean rooms, away from the bars and secure for women. No single rates. Guests can use the phone to make collect calls. ②.

Island Sun Guest House, on the seafront, just past *Barbara's* (☎2215). Simple but well-furnished rooms in a great location, with an upstairs deck on which to enjoy breakfast. ③.

South from the "front" dock

Lena's (☎2106). Budget rooms in a wooden building right by the water. Some rooms with private bath. ②.

Daisy's (☎2150). Simple, budget rooms, just back from the sea and run by a friendly family. ②.

Morgan's Inn, opposite Galería Hicaco (where you enquire; ☎2178, fax 2239, email *sbf@btl.net*). Three quiet, roomy cabins set just back from the beach; each sleeps at least three. Perfect for long stays and fine for just a night or two, but no cooking facilities. ③–⑤.

Jimínez Cabañas (☎2175). Five clean, comfortable wood-and-thatch cabins – the best value on the island – surrounded by a delightful garden shaded by coconut trees, run by a friendly family, though not near the shore. Secondhand English-language books for sale. ④.

Edith's, on the corner towards the southern end of the middle street (☎2161). Charging slightly higher prices than it used to, but there's hot water, the rooms (some with private baths) are better furnished than at most budget places, and it's very secure. Bz$2 discount if you book a boat back to Belize City here. ③.

Tree Tops Hotel, just beyond the cemetery (☎2008, fax 2115, email *treetops@btl.net*). Easily the best hotel on the island (indeed the country) at this price, just 50m from the water. Five comfortable rooms, with fridge, cable TV and powerful ceiling fan. Although only one room has private bath, the shared bathroom is immaculate. Owners Terry and Doris Creasey are always extremely helpful, giving reliable tourist information, and will book flights and tours for you. Booking is advisable. ③.

Tom's Hotel (☎2102). A large hotel for Caye Caulker, with twenty bargain rooms, though with cabins in the grounds it's getting quite cramped. Snorkelling equipment for rent, and the owner runs excellent trips to the reef. The older buildings are due to be replaced by an even bigger hotel, so check before you book. ②–④.

Monique's Resort, down the street past *Edith's*, on the left, opposite Celi's store (☎2140). A pair of small cabins with hot water in a peaceful, secure location – very good value for couples, though not that near the shore. ③.

Anchorage Resort, on the shore 300m south of *Tom's* (☎ & fax 2304, email *tourism@cayecaulker.org.bz*). New, two-storey hotel in palm-shaded grounds on the site of the famous old *Anchorage* (the first cabaña resort in Caye Caulker). Lovely, clean, tiled rooms with private bathrooms and balconies overlooking the sea. Great value at the price. ⑤.

Lorraine's Guest House, next to the *Anchorage* (☎2002). Simple but comfortable cabins with hot water, run by a friendly lady. A bargain near the beach. ③.

Shirley's Guest House, facing the sea 200m beyond the *Anchorage*, and the same distance from the airstrip (☎2145). Worth the walk if you want peace and quiet and comfortable, clean rooms in lovely grounds. Slightly more expensive than average, but still good value. ④.

Exploring the reef and the caye

The reef lies only 1.5km from the shore and the white foam of the reef crest is always visible. It's certainly an experience not to be missed: swimming along coral canyons surrounded by an astonishing range of fish, with perhaps even the odd shark or two (almost certainly harmless nurse sharks). Here as everywhere, snorkellers should be aware of the fragility of the reef and be careful not to touch any coral – even sand stirred up by fins can cause damage (see box on p.97).

The northern part of the island is long and narrow, covered in mangroves and thick vegetation that extends right down to the shore: the rare and threatened caye littoral forest habitat. The mangrove shallows swarm with small fish called "sardines" by the fishermen, who use them as bait to catch snapper. At the very northern tip is the **Caye Caulker Marine Reserve**, designated a protected area in 1998 and now visited on boat trips (see below). American **salt-water crocodiles** are sometimes seen here, but you're more likely to find them on the Turneffe Islands or in the more remote coastal areas.

As always your **trip to the reef** will be more enjoyable if you have some idea of what you're seeing. A couple of places offer interpretive **slide shows** of reef and island ecology: at Seaing is Belizing, next to Dolphin Bay Travel, Dorothy Beveridge shows slides covering all aspects of Belize's flora and fauna; in the **gift shop** you can buy slides, film (and get them developed), and books. At the Galería Hicaco, toward the south end of the front street, marine biologist Ellen McRae can explain exactly what it is you're seeing in this amazing underwater world. As a naturalist guide she can also take you for a really well-informed tour of the reef, or an early-morning **Audubon bird walk**, an introduction to the dozens of bird species of the caye – waders from herons to sandpipers, with pelicans, spoonbills and the ever-present frigate birds swooping down with pinpoint accuracy on morsels of fish. A committed environmentalist, Ellen was also the driving force behind the establishment of the Caye Caulker Marine Reserve. The Galería also acts as a centre for environmental information and as the base of the Siwa-Ban Foundation formed to protect the home of the **black catbird**, in the terrestrial section of the Caye Caulker reserve.

Swimming and snorkelling

Swimming isn't really possible from the shore as the water's too shallow. You have to leap off the end of piers or go to "The Split" (see p.102) at the north end of the village. **Trips to the reef** from Caye Caulker are easily arranged and cost around Bz$18–40 per person, depending on where you go. Most last several hours and take in a number of sites; they often used to go to Hol Chan Marine Reserve (see p.98), but now guides take trips to Caye Caulker's own marine reserve. Watch out for the dolphins that often accompany the boats on the way. You can usually rent decent **equipment** (Bz$5–7 for snorkel, mask and fins) from the place where you book your trip; always check it fits well and try to practise from a dock before you go to the reef (for more on this see p.97). A number of offices in the village centre offer snorkelling trips, and there's not a lot to choose between them as much depends on your guide. That said, the best trips and guides are generally offered by Meldie and Barbara of Driftwood Snorkelling, to the north of the main dock (☎2011), which is also the most reliable and has good equipment. Neno and Ramon Rosado, both experienced boat skippers, operate trips from here in the *Red Scorpion*, and Carlos Miller, one of the best tour guides on the caye, can usually be found here.

There are also some recommended **independent guides**, with one of the best trips offered by Ras Creek in his dory *Heritage* (Bz$25). Ras leaves from the main front dock around 11am and takes you out to the reef right in front of the caye. He'll show you nurse sharks and eagle rays in their element as you float above them, with your feet hooked over a pole. Rum punch is provided, and guests help prepare lunch, arriving back as the sun is setting – the perfect end to an utterly relaxing day. Carlos, of Carlos Tours (☎2093) is a very conscientious guide who takes small groups on snorkelling or sailing trips; contact him at *Cindy's Café* (see p.109).

Diving trips and instruction

Frenchie's (☎2234, fax 2074), at the northern end of the village, is the longest-established **dive shop** on the caye and offers safe and very knowledgeable trips, with some great reef diving and visits to Coral Gardens near to the island, as well as night dives and day-trips to Lighthouse Reef and the Blue Hole. A day-trip to the outer atolls, with three dives, costs US$155 and is an unforgettable experience; snorkellers can sometimes go along too. Frenchie can also book you on one of the bigger dive boats from San Pedro (see box on p.96) at no extra charge; you can be picked up from Caye Caulker.

For the best dive **instruction** on the island, up to divemaster level, go to the Caye Caulker School of Scuba (☎2292, fax 2239), just south of *Edith's Hotel*. It's run by Abel and Dawne Novelo and a four-day open water PADI course costs Bz$500; a resort course is Bz$120. You can buy disposable underwater cameras from the dive shops here, but higher-quality photographic equipment is not generally available for rent. If you'd like to learn **underwater photography** get in touch with James Beveridge of Seaing is Belizing (see p.107).

Other activities and trips to other islands

Belize has the largest surviving population of the West Indian manatee, and trips can take you **manatee-watching at Swallow Caye**, south of Caye Caulker, where the gentle animals congregate around a hole in the shallows just offshore; the skipper turns off the motor and poles toward the hole in order not to disturb them. You're almost certainly guaranteed a sighting, often whole family groups. These trips also usually include a visit to **Goff's Caye**, **English Caye** or **Sergeant's Caye** – tiny specks of sand and coral with a few palm trees.

Seaing is Belizing (☎2189) can also offer an **extended sailing trip** to uninhabited reefs and islands; not cheap, but better value here than in Belize City. A four-day trip costs around US$300 for two people. You'll also see signs for **fishing trips** as you walk around. Some of the best are operated by Porfilio Guzman (☎2152) and Roly Rosado (☎2058), who both live near the north end of the village; ask for them by name – any of the locals will direct you. If you want to go around the southern section of the caye on your own you can rent a **kayak** for around Bz$25–40; try *Daisy's* hotel or ask at the Galería Hicaco, where you can also rent a **sailboard** and receive instruction.

Caye Caulker is a good base for **day-trips to the atolls** of the Turneffe Islands and Lighthouse Reef. For snorkellers the best is Jim and Cindy Novelo's expedition to the exquisite **Half Moon Caye** (see p.112), the most easterly of Belize's islands, on the skiff *Sunrise* (Bz$135 including lunch; ☎2195). This all-day trip takes you to places previously accessible only to divers on live-aboard boats. The trip leaves at 6am and you speed across the shallows to the gap in the reef between Caye Caulker and Caye Chapel, heading for the deep blue of the open sea. The route takes you across the northern tip of Turneffe atoll, possibly stopping to snorkel along the eastern edge, before continuing on to Lighthouse Reef. After meeting the red-footed booby birds (and the huge hermit crabs) of Half Moon Caye face to face, it's back in the boat for the unique splendour of the Blue Hole.

Eating, drinking and entertainment

Good cooking, large portions and very reasonable prices are features of all the island's **restaurants**, half of which you'll pass while looking for a room. **Lobster** (in season) is served in every imaginable dish, from curry to chow mein; other **seafood** is generally good value, accompanied by rice or potatoes and sometimes salad. Along the front street are a couple of **fast food** stands, serving *tacos* and *burritos*. There's a good **bakery** on the street leading to the football field and many houses advertise banana bread, coconut cakes and other home-baked goodies. As you walk around you might see children selling bread or pastries from bowls balanced on their heads; it's always worth seeing what snacks are on offer. You can also buy food at several **shops and supermarkets** on the island, which receive regular supplies of bread, milk and vegetables.

Restaurants and cafés

Cindy's Café, on front street, serves mainly breakfasts and snacks – but wonderful ones, with good coffee and fresh fruit juices. Call in for superb home-made bagels, fresh fruit, yoghurt and carrot cake. Cindy is also an expert on Belizean music, and can make tapes of your favourite tracks – she cuts hair too.

Glenda's, at the back of the island, justly famous for delicious cinnamon rolls and fresh orange juice, is a favourite breakfast meeting place.

Marin's Restaurant, towards the south end of middle street, is a very long-established restaurant, serving really good seafood at great prices either indoors or at a table in the shady courtyard.

Martinez Restaurant, on the front, just before *Martinez Inn*. Reasonable Belizean food at very good prices.

Oceanside, next to *Martinez Inn*, and where the frequently notorious *Reef Bar* once was. Has now undergone a welcome transformation, serving tasty, well-presented seafood at good prices.

Rainbow Restaurant, on a deck over the water, opposite the *Rainbow Hotel*. The food's usually good anyway but the location is special.

The Sand Box, by the main front dock. The best restaurant on the island, serving great Italian/American food and local dishes in large portions and fairly swiftly too. Mary Jo and Tom, who designed and built the restaurant, do a great job of running it. Open from 7am for a coffee and roll before the boat. Closed Thurs.

Sobre Las Olas, on the front, beyond the *Rainbow*. Good seafood and steaks in a beach barbecue atmosphere.

Tropical Paradise, at the southern end of front street, serves good-quality Belizean and American-style food at reasonable prices in a comfortable air-conditioned dining room.

Bars and nightlife

Caye Caulker's **social scene** oscillates around the various bars and restaurants, and frequently nowadays there's **live music** to add atmosphere to the evening, especially in the busier places along the front street. Few places are strictly bars, though the three-storey *I&I's*, between the *Tropical Paradise* and *Edith's*, is more bar than restaurant – be careful negotiating the stairs on the way down. Most people are friendly enough, but as the evening wears on and drink takes its toll it can get rowdy. The island is a favourite weekend R & R destination for British soldiers, who are often very young and get drunk quickly, when the macho tendency takes over. Be careful with your money too – Caye Caulker has a criminal element and a drug problem, but only three policemen. Away from the music, evening entertainment mostly consists of relaxing in a restaurant over dinner or a drink.

Shopping and souvenirs

Although **shopping** won't be your main consideration on Caye Caulker, there are a few places where you can buy some unique **gifts**. At *Cindy's Café* (see p.109) you can get locally produced **music**; Wendy Nuñez also sells Belizean music and Garífuna **drums**, as well dazzling hand-painted T-shirts from her house next to Dolphin Bay Travel. Traci's Gifts, next to *Martinez Inn*, has a good selection of original **art** and other good-quality locally-produced gifts at affordable prices, and further north, at Island Designs, Cindy Novelo has the widest range of art, crafts and clothing from throughout Central America.

Other northern cayes and the atolls

Although Caye Caulker and San Pedro are the only villages anywhere on the reef, there are several other islands that can be visited. Caye Caulker is within day-trip distance of some of these (see p.108) and there are a few superbly isolated hotels – called **lodges** – on some reefs and cayes. The attraction of these lodges is the "simple life", usually focusing on diving or fishing; staying at them is generally part of a package that includes transfers from the airport, accommodation, all meals and the sports on offer. Buildings are low-key, wooden and sometimes thatched, and the group you're with will probably be the only people staying there. There are no phones (most are in radio contact with Belize City), electricity comes from a generator, and views of palm trees curving over turquoise water reinforce the sense of isolation.

Caye Chapel

As a diversion during a snorkelling trip you could visit **Caye Chapel**, immediately south of Caye Caulker. Quite different from Caye Caulker, privately owned Caye Chapel has an airstrip, golf course, marina and (usually deserted) hotel. The beaches are cleaned daily and the bar is usually open all day – perfect for a cold beer after a hard day's snorkelling. It was on Caye Chapel that the defeated Spanish fleet paused for a few days after the **Battle of St George's Caye** in 1798, and, according to legend, some of their dead are buried here.

St George's Caye

Tiny **St George's Caye**, around 15km from Belize City, was capital for the Baymen of the eighteenth century and still manages to exude an air of colonial grandeur; its beautifully restored colonial houses face east to catch the breeze and their lush green lawns are enclosed by white picket fences. The sense of history is reinforced by the eighteenth-century cannons mounted in front of some of the finer houses; for another glimpse into the past you could head for the small graveyard of the early settlers on the southern tip of the island. Today, the island is home to the villas of Belize's elite, an adventure training centre for British forces in Belize and a few fishermen, who live toward the northern end in an area known, appropriately enough, as "Fishermen Town".

There's not much here for the casual visitor but some fishing and snorkelling trips do call at St George's Caye. If you do come you may meet Karl and Angelika

Bishof, an Austrian couple who run Bela Carib (☎02/49435), a company that carefully collects and exports tropical fish. The tanks contain a fascinating display of reef creatures and you're welcome to look around; the couple plan to open a **marine aquarium** soon. After your visit take a look at the great T-shirts in their Fishermen Town Gift Shop. The other gift shop on the island, the Unicorn, is run by an American couple, Sally and Neal, from their home. It's the oldest house on the caye, having survived the 1931 hurricane.

Accommodation on the caye is luxurious, expensive and generally sold as a package. *Cottage Colony* (☎02/77051, fax 73253, email *fins@btl.net*; ⑦) is the most affordable place, and has the most beautiful location. Rooms are in extremely comfortable colonial-style, wooden houses with modern facilities set in palm-shaded grounds, and the dining room overlooks the Caribbean. It's a great place for fishing and diving, and perfect for relaxation. *St George's Lodge* (☎02/44190, fax 31460) is an all-inclusive diving resort comprising a main lodge, with a beautiful dining room and six luxury, wood-and-thatch cottages with private verandas. The price (more than US$250 per day for the cottages) includes airport transfer, diving and meals. There's no drinks licence but guests can bring their own.

The Bluefield Range

In the **Bluefield Range**, a group of mangrove cayes 35km southeast of Belize City, you can stay on a remote **fishing camp**. *Ricardo's Beach Huts* (☎02/78469) offer simple, comfortable accommodation (min 2 nights) right on the water, in huts built on stilts. At US$165 per person for three days/two nights it's not cheap, but the price includes transport to and from Belize City, all meals – including, as you might imagine, fresh fish and lobster – and a fishing or snorkelling trip to Rendezvous Caye, right on the reef; *Rough Guide* readers get a discount. Ricardo Castillo is a reliable, expert fishing guide, scrupulously practising conservation of the reef. For more information ask at *Mira Rio* bar, 59 N Front St, Belize City (☎02/44970), where the trips start.

The Turneffe Islands

Though shown on many maps as one large island, the virtually uninhabited **Turneffe Islands** are an oval archipelago 60km long, enclosed by a beautiful coral reef. Situated 40km from Belize City, they consist of low-lying mangrove islands and sandbanks – some quite large – around a shallow lagoon. Currently there is no protected land at Turneffe, but there is a proposal for a new marine reserve at **Rendezvous Point**, on the northwest edge of the atoll. The islands can be visited on day-trips from San Pedro or Caye Caulker.

A few places offer all-inclusive **accommodation**, but the construction of resorts on this remote, fragile island has involved cutting down mangroves and is the cause of much controversy among conservationists. *Turneffe Flats* (PO Box 1676, Belize City), a fishing and diving lodge on the windward, eastern side, charge US$2000 per person for a week's fishing, including the airfare from Miami, New Orleans or Houston. Halfway down the eastern side, *Blackbird Caye Resort* (☎02/33504, fax 30268), is a self-styled "ecotourism development" charging from US$1400 for a week of diving or fishing. Accommodation is in ten wood-and-thatch cabañas; there's no bar, so you'll have to bring your own drinks. Research on bottlenose dolphins, sponsored by Oceanic Society Expeditions, is being carried out here by volunteers. South of Blackbird Caye, **Calabash Caye** is the base for Coral Cay Conservation, where volunteers take part in a research project to complete a systematic investigation of the entire atoll. Participants stay at the University College of Belize marine research centre, sleeping in purpose-built cabins.

The best-value accommodation is offered by *Turneffe Island Lodge* (in Belize ☎ & fax 021/2011, in US ☎1-800/874-0118, email *info@turneffelodge.com*), on **Caye Bokel**, a sandy island at the southern tip of the archipelago. It costs US$1100 per person for a week at the resort; another US$150 or so for diving, more for fishing (both are superb). The cabins have hot and cold water and 24-hour electricity.

Lighthouse Reef, the Blue Hole and Half Moon Caye

About 80km east of Belize City is Belize's outer atoll, **Lighthouse Reef**, made famous by Jacques Cousteau, who visited in the 1970s. The two main attractions are the Blue Hole, which attracted Cousteau's attention, and the Half Moon Caye Natural Monument. The **Blue Hole**, now protected as a Natural Monument, is technically a "karst-eroded sinkhole", a shaft about 300m in diameter and 135m deep, which drops through the bottom of the lagoon and opens out into a complex network of **caves and crevices**, complete with stalactites and stalagmites. It was formed over a million years ago when Lighthouse Reef was a sizeable island – or even part of the mainland. Investigations have shown that caves underlie the entire reef, and that the sea has simply punctured the cavern roof at the site of the Blue Hole. Its great depth gives it a peculiar deep blue colour, and even swimming across is disorienting as there's no sense of anything beneath you. Unsurprisingly, the Blue Hole and Lighthouse Reef are major magnets for **divers**, offering incredible walls and drop-offs. Several **shipwrecks** form artificial reefs; the most prominent is the *Ermlund*, which ran aground in 1971 and looms over the reef just north of Half Moon Caye.

You can visit the atoll as either a day- or overnight trip from San Pedro (p.96) or Caye Caulker (p.108), and *Lighthouse Reef Resort*, on privately owned **Northern Caye**, has luxurious villas and cabañas in splendid isolation. Guests fly in on a fishing or diving package costing around US$1500 a week (☎ & fax 02/31205, in US ☎1-800/423-3114).

The **Half Moon Caye Natural Monument**, the first marine conservation area in Belize, was declared a national park in 1982. Its lighthouse was first built in 1820 and has not always been effective: several wrecks testify to the dangers of the reef. The 45-acre caye is divided into two distinct ecosystems: in the west, guano from thousands of seabirds fertilizes the soil, allowing the growth of dense vegetation, while the eastern half has mostly coconut palms growing in the sand. A total of 98 bird species has been recorded here, including frigate birds, ospreys, mangrove warblers, white-crowned pigeons and – most important of all – a resident population of four thousand **red-footed boobies**, one of only two nesting colonies in the Caribbean. The boobies came by their name because they displayed no fear of humans, enabling sailors to kill them in their thousands, and they still move only reluctantly when visitors stroll through them. Their nesting area is accessible from a platform and the birds are not in the least bothered by your presence. Apart from the birds, the island supports iguanas and lizards, and both loggerhead and hawksbill turtles nest on the beaches, which also attract the biggest hermit and land crabs in Belize.

There's no accommodation on the caye, but **camping** is allowed with the permission of the Belize Audubon Society (see p.246), which manages the reserve; many of the overnight diving expeditions camp here. Visitors must register with the ranger on arrival, and pay the Bz$10 **fee**, which also includes the Blue Hole. The **visitor centre**, built by volunteers from Raleigh, will help you understand the ecology of the caye.

travel details

For a rundown of **flights** and **boats** to the cayes from Belize City and between the cayes themselves, see the boxes on pp.90 and 103.

CHAPTER FOUR

CAYO AND THE WEST

Heading west from Belize City to the Guatemalan border, you travel through a wide range of landscapes, from open grassland and rolling hills to dense tropical forest. It's a journey that takes you from the heat and humidity of the coast to the lush foothills of the Maya Mountains, and into an area increasingly influenced by Spanish-speaking *mestizos*, including large numbers of refugees from other Central American countries.

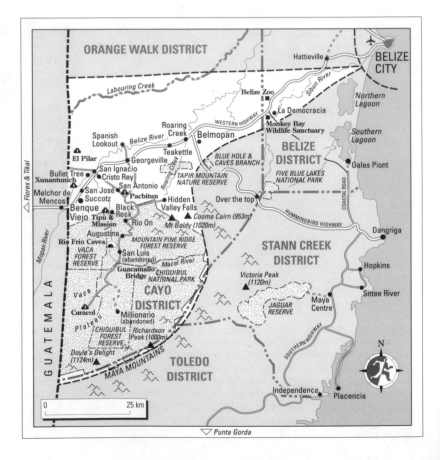

ACCOMMODATION PRICE CODES

All accommodation listed in this guide has been given a **price code** according to the following scale. The prices refer to the cost of **a double room in high season** (generally December to Easter) in Belize dollars (Bz$), but usually do not include the government hotel tax of seven percent. For more details see p.26.

① under Bz$20   ④ Bz$50–70   ⑦ Bz$140–190
② Bz$20–30   ⑤ Bz$70–100   ⑧ Bz$190–240
③ Bz$30–50   ⑥ Bz$100–140   ⑨ over Bz$240

A single road connects Belize City with the Guatemalan border. This is the Western Highway: a fast, paved route that leaves Belize City through mangrove swamps and heads inland across open, sometimes swampy savannah, scattered with pine trees. Before reaching Belmopan the road passes several places of interest: the **Belize Zoo**, well worth a visit if you're interested in the country's natural history, the **Monkey Bay Wildlife Sanctuary and National Park**, and **Guanacaste National Park**, a small reserve designed to protect a section of the original forest along the bank of the Belize River. Beyond this is the capital, **Belmopan**, established in 1970 and surely one of the smallest capital cities in the world.

Heading further west, following the Belize River valley, you start to climb into the foothills of the Maya Mountains, a beautiful area where the air is clear and the land astonishingly fertile. Most of this region, including the entire mountain range, is under official protection in a vast network of national parks, wildlife sanctuaries and forest and archeological reserves – part of Belize's largest continuous area of protected land – stretching from the Caribbean coast to the Guatemalan border. The **Mountain Pine Ridge Forest Reserve**, to the south of the highway, is a pleasantly cool region of hills and pine woods boasting some of the finest lodge accommodation in the country.

San Ignacio, on the Macal River, and only 15km from the Guatemalan border, is the busy main town of Cayo District and the ideal base for exploring the forests, rivers and ruins of western Belize. A canoe or kayak trip along the **Macal River Valley** as the river tumbles from the Maya Mountains into the calmer waters of the tree-lined Macal gorge, is a highlight of any visit to Cayo, and there are jungle cabins to suit all budgets on the riverbanks. The ruins of **Caracol**, the largest Maya site in Belize and a focus for current archeological research, lie deep in the jungle of the Vaca plateau, south of San Ignacio.

Between San Ignacio and the Guatemalan border, the road climbs past the hilltop ruin of **Cahal Pech,** then descends following the valley of the **Mopan River**, where there are more delightful riverside lodges. Belize's westernmost Maya site **El Pilar**, eighteen kilometres northwest of San Ignacio, actually extends into Guatemala, and is the first International Archeological Reserve anywhere in the Maya region. A few kilometres before the frontier itself, at the village of **San Jose Succotz**, an ancient ferry crosses the river, allowing access to another hilltop Maya site, **Xunantunich**, whose highest structures offer stunning views over to Guatemala's department of Petén.

Belize City to Belmopan

Served by frequent buses between Belize City and San Ignacio, the Western Highway leaves the city through the middle of the Lord's Ridge cemetery, then skirts the shoreline, running behind a tangle of mangrove swamps and past **Cucumber Beach Wharf**, a graveyard for the rusting hulks of beached ships. At Mile 5 the road passes the entrance to **Buffer Hole Beach** – no more than a clearing in the mangroves with a pleasant thatched bar overlooking the shore. The water is shallow and silty but clean enough to bathe in. A few kilometres further, you cross the **Sir John Burden Canal**, an inland waterway, now a nature reserve and valuable wildlife corridor, that connects the Belize River with the **Sibun River**. This is the route taken by small boats travelling down to Dangriga and Gales Point (see p.163) via the **Northern and Southern lagoons**. The Sibun River watershed supports abundant birdlife, jaguars, tapirs, howler monkeys and some large crocodiles. A conservation project has been proposed to protect the river – at its mouth are nesting beaches of the endangered **hawksbill turtle**.

After 26km the highway passes through **HATTIEVILLE**, named after the 1961 hurricane that created the refugees who initially populated it. The village started life as a temporary shelter for the homeless, but since then it has become rather more permanent. At Hattieville, there's a turning north to **Burrell Boom** and Bermudian Landing (see p.66), a short cut to the Northern Highway. The curious steep hills to the left on this part of the road are limestone outcrops, quarried for road-building. The highest is **Gracie Rock**, near the Sibun River, the location of fictional "Geronimo" in the film *The Mosquito Coast*. If you want to **stay** in this area and **cruise the Sibun River** and lagoons, take a left turn in Hattieville, down the road to Freetown Sibun. Here *River Haven* (☎02/70529, fax 70530), run by Canadians Ray Parker and Beth McBride, offers the only **houseboats** for rent in Belize. As well as the houseboats, which sleep four (US$790 per weekend, US$1580 per week), there are cabins (US$130) and cabañas (⑦).

The Belize Zoo

Twenty kilometres beyond Hattieville, at Mile 29, the **Belize Zoo** is, for most people, the first point of interest out this way and easily visited on a half-day trip from Belize City. Probably the finest zoo in the Americas south of the US (daily 9am–4.30pm; ☎ & fax 081/3004; Bz$15 for adult foreign visitors, Bz$7.50 for children, Peace Corps, VSO and military personnel) and long recognized as a phenomenal conservation achievement, the zoo originally opened in 1983 after an ambitious wildlife film (*Path of the Raingods*) left Sharon Matola, the film's production assistant, with a collection of semi-tame animals no longer able to fend for themselves in the wild. For locals and visitors alike this means the chance to see the native animals of Belize at close quarters, housed in spacious enclosures which closely resemble their natural habitat.

The zoo is organized around the theme of **"a walk through Belize"**, with a trail that takes you into the pinelands, the forest edge, the rainforest, lagoons and the river forest. The residents include a **Baird's tapir** (known locally as a mountain cow) called April, well known to the schoolchildren of Belize, who visit in their hundreds on her birthday (in April) to feed her a huge vegetable birthday cake; it is hoped that April and her mate Danta will breed. All the Belizean cats are represented and some, including the **jaguars**, have bred successfully. There's also a wide range of birds, including toucans, macaws, parrots, jabiru storks, a spectacled owl and several vultures; other inhabitants include deer, spider and howler monkeys, peccaries, agouti (which sometimes appears on menus as "gibnut"), crocodiles and various snakes.

The zoo is actively involved in conservation education and captive breeding and has achieved international recognition in these fields. One of its greatest successes is the **green iguana** breeding programme, which aims to replenish the numbers taken from the wild for food. Sharon has written several excellent and extremely popular children's books with a strong conservation message. These and other souvenirs are on sale in the **gift shop**. Across the highway from the zoo, **the Tropical Education Center**, as the name suggests, focuses on school and college groups but is well worth a look. There are self-guiding **nature trails**, observation decks, study facilities including a classroom and library, and dorm accommodation. If you're interested in supporting the work of the zoo, or visiting the Tropical Education Center write to PO Box 1787, Belize City.

To **get to the zoo** take any bus between Belize City and Belmopan and ask the driver to drop you; there's a sign on the highway. Zoo staff know the times of buses in either direction. A two-hundred-metre walk brings you to the entrance and the **Gerald Durrell Visitor Centre**, with displays of children's art and exhibits on Belize's ecosystems.

Two kilometres beyond the zoo the **Manatee Road** (or Coastal Road) provides an unpaved short cut (marked by a sign and a couple of bars – the *Midway Resting Place* and *Roadway Inn*) to Gales Point and **Dangriga**. The road is in good condition and served by buses about every two to three hours. A further 2km past the junction and set back 100m from the highway, *Cheers* (☎ & fax 014/9311) is a friendly **bar** run by Canadians Anita, Mike and Chrissy Tupper, where you can get good food at reasonable prices as well as tourist **information**. Should you need to book accommodation somewhere ahead, you can use their cellular phone and fax service. You can go on guided **bird walks** and follow the **orchid trail** in the bush behind the bar.

Monkey Bay Wildlife Sanctuary and onward

Half a kilometre past *Cheers* and 400m off to the left of the highway (signposted at Mile 31 1/2), the **Monkey Bay Wildlife Sanctuary** is a 44-square-kilometre protected area extending to the Sibun River and offering birding and nature **trails** through five distinct vegetation and habitat types. Adjoining the sanctuary across the river is the nine-square-kilometre Monkey Bay National Park. The two protected areas serve as a wildlife corridor spanning the Sibun valley south through karst limestone hills to the Manatee Forest Reserve. Belize Government agencies and NGOs are currently working on an ambitious project to extend this corridor to connect protected areas in northern Belize, across the rapidly developing Western Highway, with those in the south. The "bay" part of the names comes from a sandy beach on the Sibun River that was once inhabited by howler and spider monkeys. The monkeys are now beginning to return after an absence of over twenty years following hurricane disturbance to their habitat.

Monkey Bay is also home to the **Wildlife Care Center** (WCC), a holding facility for confiscated and rescued wild animals, often kept illegally as pets. Established in 1998, the Care Center aims eventually to repatriate those animals which would survive in the wild; raising public awareness of Belize's wildlife protection laws and discouraging the acquisition of wild animals as pets will also be major roles. The WCC is not open to the public but there are training opportunities for foreign students and **conservation volunteers**; you'll need to be self-funded and be able to commit for at least three months. If you're interested, write to the director Robin Brockett, c/o Belize Audubon Society, PO Box 1001, Belize City.

From Monkey Bay, you can take guided **canoe trips** on the Sibun River and to the **crocodile sanctuary** at Cox's Lagoon, north of the highway. Monkey Bay also makes a perfect base to explore little-visited **caves** in the Sibun Hills to the south, all of which have evidence of use by the ancient Maya.

Monkey Bay practicalities

Monkey Bay is easily reached by any **bus** along the highway. The sanctuary headquarters include a **field research station**, which serves as library, museum and classroom. Although the field station specializes in hosting academic programmes in natural history and watershed ecology for students and teachers (it's also the Belize base for Conservation Corridors; see p.246), it's a wonderfully relaxing **place to stay**, either in the bunkhouse (Bz$15) or camping (Bz$10) on raised platforms under thatched roofs (contact the director, Matt Miller, on ☎08/23180, email *mbay@pobox.com*). Monkey Bay is a viable experiment in "off the grid" sustainable living, utilizing solar power, rainwater catchment and biogas fuel for cooking; the **food**, some of it grown in the station's organic gardens, is excellent and plentiful.

Onward: JB's Bar and Banana Bank Lodge

Five hundred metres beyond Monkey Bay, **JB's Bar** is an old favourite with the British Army, whose mementos deck the walls, alongside a word of thanks from Harrison Ford and the crew of *The Mosquito Coast*. In the days when the Western Highway was badly surfaced and bridges would be washed away in heavy rains it was a welcome (and sometimes necessary) rest stop; nowadays it's just another pleasant place to break the journey. The restaurant serves good food and there are comfortable, well-priced **rooms** with electricity, hot water and screened porches, and a house for rent (☎014/0898; ④). There are relaxing views over the peaceful citrus orchards stretching to the Sibun River and the hills beyond, and the owner can arrange **tubing** on the river. *JB's* marks the boundary between the Belize and Cayo Districts, and here the open expanse of pine and savannah begins to give way to rich pastures and citrus groves. The road continues, well-surfaced and fast, to the junction with the Southern Highway.

Twenty-five kilometres beyond *JB's*, and 2km before the turning for Belmopan, opposite the airstrip at Mile 46, a track leads off to the right to **Banana Bank Lodge** (PO Box 48 Belmopan; ☎ 081/2020, fax 2026, email *bbl@pobox.com*; ⑧ including breakfast; no service charge), on the north bank of the Belize River, crossed by foot-passenger boat. This 4000-acre ranch, half of which is still primary forest, is owned by Americans, John and Carolyn Carr. They offer great horse-riding, canoeing, swimming, and there are also dozens of Maya mounds, some quite large. The natural history is astonishing: almost two hundred bird species have been recorded here, and there's a beautiful **lagoon** with resident Morelets crocodiles. There's also a small collection of animals at the ranch, including Tika, a tame jaguar. Carolyn is an accomplished artist and her work is exhibited all over the country; if time permits you can look at her studio. The **accommodation**, with views sweeping down to the Belize River, consists of five wood-and-thatch cabañas and five rooms (some with shared bathroom); all are beautifully furnished in Belizean hardwoods. The food, all home-cooked and mostly home-produced, is superb. **To get there** by car, either follow the track to the riverbank – someone will come down to ferry you across – or take the marked turn-off to the right just beyond **Roaring Creek** village, crossing the Belize River on an old hand-cranked ferry and follow the signs. Without your own vehicle, call the lodge to arrange a pickup in Belmopan.

Guanacaste National Park

Right by the highway, 73km from Belize City at the junction for Belmopan and the Hummingbird Highway, **Guanacaste National Park** (daily 8am–4.30pm; Bz$5 includes a free short tour with ranger) is Belize's smallest national park and the easiest to visit. Here you can wander through a superb area of lush tropical forest at the confluence of Roaring Creek and the Belize River.

Founded in 1973 and officially dedicated as a National Reserve in 1988, the park covers a total area of 52 acres. The main attraction is a huge **guanacaste** or tubroos tree, a forty-metre-high, spreading hardwood that supports some 35 species: hanging from its limbs are a huge range of bromeliads, orchids, ferns, cacti and strangler figs, which blossom spectacularly at the end of the rainy season. The bark, which is particularly hard and partially water-resistant, is traditionally favoured for use as feeding troughs, dugout canoes and mortars for hulling rice. A good-sized guanacaste can produce two or three canoes; this specimen escaped being felled because its trunk split into three near the base. In season the guanacaste produces ear-shaped fruit, used as cattle feed. Sadly, there's only the one mature guanacaste tree, but the rest of the park is just as fascinating and offers a very accessible glimpse of the Belizean forest, as well as some inviting pools for a swim.

Other botanical attractions include young mahogany trees, cohune palms, a cotton tree and quamwood, while the forest floor is a mass of ferns, mosses and vines and wild orchids grow everywhere on trunks and branches. As the park is so close to the road your chances of seeing any four-footed **wildlife** are fairly slim, but armadillos, white-tailed deer, jaguarundi, opossums and agouti have nevertheless been spotted, and recently a small number of howler monkeys have used the park as a feeding ground. Birds abound, with over fifty species, among them blue-crowned motmots, black-faced ant-thrushes, black-headed trogons, red-lored parrots and squirrel cuckoos. Unfortunately mosquitoes are common too, so bring repellent.

Buses will stop right outside the park. Sign in at the **visitor centre** near the entrance, which has maps and information on the park ecology (including a superb exhibit on the life-cycle of the leaf-cutter ants, which you'll see all over Belize), and have a look at the orchid display in the courtyard. Outside, four or five short **trails** take you through the park and along the banks of the Belize River.

Belmopan

From Guanacaste Park the Western Highway pushes on towards San Ignacio and the Guatemalan border, while a paved branch road turns south 2km towards Belize's capital, **BELMOPAN**, beyond which it becomes the Hummingbird Highway, continuing all the way to the coast at Dangriga. For most people, the

BELMOPAN

capital is no more than a break in the bus ride to San Ignacio, though if you're heading to Dangriga or Placencia this is the place to change buses.

Belmopan was founded in 1970 after Hurricane Hattie swept much of Belize City into the sea. The government decided to use the disaster as a chance to move to higher ground and, in a Brasília-style bid to focus development on the interior, chose a site in the geographical heart of the country. The name of the city combines the words Belize and Mopan, the language spoken by the Maya of Cayo. The layout of the main government buildings, designed in the 1960s, is supposedly modelled on a Maya city, with structures grouped around a central plaza; the National Assembly building even incorporates a version of the traditional roof comb. Although these long, grey concrete buildings, set away from the road and surrounded by grass, won their British architect an award, they now have a dismal, shoddy appearance out of line with their importance.

In classic new-town terms Belmopan was meant to symbolize the dawn of a new era, with tree-lined avenues, banks, a couple of embassies and telecommunications worthy of a world centre. Today it has all the essential ingredients bar one – people. Arriving in the market square, the first thing that strikes you is a sense of space. Very few Belizeans other than government officials (who had no option) have moved here. The population was planned at 5000 for the first few years, eventually rising to 30,000. Today, however, it stands rooted at around 6000, as the majority of Belizeans still prefer the congestion of Belize City to the boredom of Belmopan.

Unless you've come to visit a government department, there's no particular reason to stay any longer in Belmopan than it takes your bus to leave. The Archeological Vault once provided the only other real reason (apart from changing buses) for any tourist to visit Belmopan, but that closed a few years ago (a victim of government spending cuts) leaving no permanent venue to display the outstanding range of archeological artefacts found in Belize. However, the theatre opposite the market square sometimes has temporary displays, and a new exhibition area is currently under construction: to find out what's available for viewing call the **Archeology Department** on ☎22106. The **Archives Department** (Mon–Fri 8am–noon & 1–4.30pm, free; ☎22247), 26–28 Unity Blvd, also welcomes visitors and has photographs and documents providing a fascinating glimpse of old Belize.

> The **telephone area code** for Belmopan is ☎010

Practicalities

Buses from Belize City to San Ignacio and Dangriga all pass through Belmopan, and Shaws run a frequent service between Belmopan and San Ignacio, so there's at least one bus an hour in either direction all day; the last bus from Belmopan to Belize City leaves at 6.30pm, to San Ignacio at 10pm and to Dangriga at 6pm. Only Batty has an office.

The buses all pull up in an unpaved square in front of the small **market**, with several food and fruit stands. The nearest **restaurant** is the *Caladium*, beside the Novelos bus terminal (where you can leave luggage); it's good for Belizean dishes. *Mom's Place*, in Harlem Square (the block behind the *Caladium*), is a friendly, inexpensive place where you can always get a vegetarian meal. Nearby, to the left of the market, you'll find the Canadian-run *International Café* (closed Wed & Sat), serving sandwiches, soups, salads and snacks – always with a daily special and vegetarian choices. It's also good for **information** – you can pay to use their phone for local calls, and there's a book exchange.

Just beyond the market are the **banks** (including Barclays, for cash advances), and to the right of the market square is the Ministry of Natural Resources, where you can buy **maps**; the **post office** is just behind here. The **British High Commission** (☎22146) is situated on the North Ring Road, behind the National Assembly building. The BTL **telephone** office is beside the large satellite dish, and the **immigration** office is in the main building beside the theatre.

Hotels in Belmopan cater for the needs and expense accounts of diplomats and aid officials; San Ignacio, less than an hour away, is far more interesting and less expensive. If you do have to stay here, the *El Rey Inn*, 23 Moho St (☎23438; ④), is a pleasant and reasonably inexpensive option. The best place in town is *Bull Frog Inn*, 23 Half Moon Ave (☎22111, fax 23155; ⑥); its comfortable rooms have a/c and TV, and there's a very pleasant restaurant and bar. At time of writing, the *Belmopan Hotel* (☎22327, fax 23066; ⑤), across from Novelos terminal, was undergoing renovation – new beds and carpets may have improved things and it has cable TV and a pool.

Belmopan to San Ignacio

Beyond Belmopan the scenery becomes more rugged, with thickly forested ridges always in view to the south. The Western Highway stays close to the valley of the Belize River, crossing numerous tributary creeks and passing through a series of villages – Roaring Creek, Teakettle, Ontario, Unitedville – and **Santa Elena**, San Ignacio's sister town on the eastern bank of the Macal River. There's been something of an accommodation boom along this route, with a couple of long-established cottage-style **lodges** now joined by several newer enterprises. Alternatively, with your own vehicle you can turn south at Georgeville, 26km from the Belmopan junction, and head along the **Chiquibul Road** in the Mountain Pine Ridge (see p.124); along this unpaved road there are several places to stay and the added attraction of Belize's best **butterfly** farm.

Along the Western Highway

Ten kilometres south of the highway, between Roaring and Barton creeks, **Tapir Mountain Nature Reserve** protects 28 square kilometres of the northern foothills of the Maya Mountains, a rich, well-watered habitat covered in high canopy, tropical moist forest and home to all of Belize's national symbols: Baird's tapir, the keel-billed toucan, the black orchid and the mahogany tree. The reserve, managed by the Belize Audubon Society, is accorded Belize's highest category of protected land. As one criterion of this is to "maintain natural processes in an undisturbed state", Tapir Mountain can only be visited by accredited researchers and is not readily accessible to the public. The designation itself however, does not guarantee protection from hunters, and even from farmers encroaching on the reserve. Call BAS (☎02/35004) for more information.

Although you cannot enter the reserve, you can enjoy spectacular views of it by staying nearby at one of the best new lodges – **Pook's Hill Jungle Lodge** (☎081/2017, fax 08/23361, email *pookshill@btl.net*; ⑧; no service charge) – the turning to which is clearly signposted at Mile 52 at the village of **Teakettle**, 8km west of Belmopan. The nine-kilometre track up to the lodge is bumpy but in good condition. If you're travelling by bus call ahead and one of the owners will pick you up from the junction; the Patnett family, in the yellow house at the junction, will let you use their phone (bring a phonecard).

The lodge is set on terraced hillside in a 300 acre private reserve. **Accommodation** is in nine thatched cabañas, grouped in a small clearing overlooking the thickly forested Roaring River valley and with breathtaking views across the Tapir Mountain Reserve to the Mountain Pine Ridge beyond. Each cabaña has electric light and a private bathroom with hot water provided by burning *cohune* nuts. This spectacular location clearly held attractions for the ancient

Maya too: the lodge sits on a Maya platform and there's a plaza and some small structures behind the cabañas. You don't have to go far to see the **wildlife** either; bird-watching here is in a league of its own and there will almost always be a raptor of some kind, perhaps a bat falcon, hunting or feeding. Every year a pair of spectacled owls raise a brood near the cabins. *Pook's Hill* is also a centre of Belize's green iguana breeding programme. Meals are served in the dining room at the edge of the forest and the **food** is excellent; upstairs a thatched, open-sided deck serves as a bar in the evenings. There's wonderful **nature trails** and superb **horse-riding trails** along farm and forest tracks, and you can hike or ride to more substantial ruins and caves further up the valley. To cool off you can go **tubing** in the river.

Beyond Teakettle, at Mile 54, just over the Warrie Head Creek bridge, is the entrance to **Warrie Head Ranch and Lodge** (☎02/75317, fax 75213; *bzadventure@btl.net*; ⑦), formerly a logging camp and now a working farm offering very comfortable wooden cabins and rooms set back a few hundred metres from the road. The owners have gone to great lengths to provide visitors with a glimpse of Belize's colonial heritage – the rooms have modern facilities but are filled with authentic period furniture, and colonial artefacts abound, including a restored 1904 steam engine once used to haul logs. The outdoor bar, its wooden deck shaded by a beautiful old Bay cedar tree whose branches drip with orchids, is a good place to have a chat with the manager Martin Meadows, a superb naturalist guide, about the next day's trips. The grounds, filled with fruit and native trees, slope down to the creek, where an exquisite series of travertine terraces form turquoise pools – perfect for swimming.

On the bank of Barton Creek to the right of the highway at Mile 60, **Caesar's Place** (☎09/22341, fax 23449, email *blackrock@btl.net*; ⑤) is Caesar and Antonieta Sherrard's café and guest house, with comfortable, attractive rooms, trailer hookups (Bz$15) and space for camping (Bz$7.50). The *Patio Café* is a good place to stop for lunch and serves delicious **home cooking**, with Belizean and American dishes mingling with the flavours of other Central American countries; you can always get a vegetarian meal here too. It's also a good **music** venue, often featuring local band *Mango Jam*. The **gift shop** is one of the best in Belize; Caesar makes great wood carvings using wood properly dried in his solar kiln, and the slate comes from Black Rock. There's also Guatemalan textiles and silver jewellery from Taxco in Mexico. It's a great place to pick up information about Guatemala and Mexico, and Caesar's son Julian can organize canoe or caving trips along the Macal River.

Beyond *Caesar's*, just over the Barton Creek bridge, the two prominent, grass-covered **pyramids** mark the unexcavated Maya site of **Floral Park**; you'll see virtually all there is to see as you pass by in the bus. Six kilometres beyond here, you come to the **Georgeville** junction from where (with your own transport) you can head south along the Chiquibul Road (see p.124). A few kilometres further along the highway, **Central Farm** is Belize's agricultural research centre which often has vacancies for VSO volunteers (see p.42 for details), while just beyond here, on the right, a road leads to **Spanish Lookout**, one of Belize's most successful Mennonite farming communities. At this junction is Holdfast Camp, formerly a British Army base and now Cayo's Matthew Spain charter airstrip – at present there are no scheduled flights to anywhere in Cayo District. The road continues on for another 7km to Santa Elena (see p.125) and San Ignacio.

The Chiquibul Road

At the Georgeville junction, a track leads south to the **Mountain Pine Ridge** (see p.137). This is the **Chiquibul Road** – well used by villagers, foresters and tourists – which reaches deep into the forest, and heads for Caracol (see p.141), crossing the Macal River at the Guacamallo Bridge. You should get off at this junction if you're hitching to **Augustine/Douglas Silva**, headquarters of the Mountain Pine Ridge Forest Reserve, though you really need four-wheel-drive, or a mountain bike, to explore this fascinating and exciting area of hills and jungle properly.

Eleven kilometres along the road, at **Mountain Equestrian Trails** (☎09/23310, fax 23361, in US ☎1-800/838-3918, email *aw2trav2bz@aol.com*; ⑦), you'll find very comfortable accommodation in a tropical forest setting on the edge of the Pine Ridge. The four thatched cabañas, with hot water and lit by oil lamps, are some of the best in Belize, and the tasty meals served in the *Cantina* restaurant feature large portions of Belizean and Mexican-style food. If you want to get even closer to nature *MET* also has an idyllic **tented camp**, *Chiclero Trails*, which is the base for low-impact wildlife safaris that take you deep into the Chiquibul forest. The basic camp price is Bz$120 per person, including three good meals and service charge (and there are excellent packages available) but to get the most out of the experience you should consider a horseback or rafting trip with *MET's* expert guides – Jim Bevis, owner of *MET*, led the first commercial crossing of the Maya Mountain divide. As the name implies, *MET* is primarily oriented towards **horse-riding** vacations and is unquestionably Belize's premier riding centre, with superb riding on nearly 100km of forest trails encompassing various ecosystems.

Jim and Marguerite Bevis, who own *MET*, are also founder members of the **Slate Creek Preserve**, a privately owned tract of over sixteen square kilometres of karst limestone forest bordering the Mountain Pine Ridge Forest Reserve. Local landowners, recognizing the importance of conservation and sustainable development, have cooperated voluntarily to establish the preserve, following the guidelines in UNESCO's Man and the Biosphere Programme. This is just one example of how concern for the environment in Belize has been translated into practical projects benefiting local people.

On the opposite side of the road to *MET*, the **Green Hills Butterfly House** (Christmas to Easter daily 8am–5pm; rest of year appointment only ☎09/23310; Bz$5, minimum 2 people) is Belize's best butterfly exhibit. It's run by Dutch biologists Jan Meerman and Tineke Boomsma. Both are experts in the field – Jan is about to publish his *Field Guide to the Butterflies of Belize and Greater Yucatán*, and Tineke, who specializes in dragonflies and damselflies, has recorded several species new to science (one of which is named after her). The main attraction is the enclosed **flight area**, where scores of gorgeous butterflies flutter around, settling occasionally on the flowers to sip nectar. This is a breeding centre too and (particularly in the early morning) you can watch one of nature's wonders as the caterpillars emerge from their chrysalises. Fascinating as this is, there's lots more to see – to rear butterflies you need to know about their food plants and there's an amazing botanical garden, home to Belize's National Passionflower Collection, a tropical fruit orchard and a renowned collection of epiphytes (air plants).

Santa Elena

Before reaching San Ignacio the Western Highway passes through its sister town of **SANTA ELENA**, on the eastern bank of the Macal River. Though quite a large town, Santa Elena has few of the attractions of San Ignacio, but it is the site of the turn-off to the **Cristo Rey road** (see p.138) towards Augustine/Douglas Silva and the Mountain Pine Ridge. Most visitors choose to stay in San Ignacio but there are a few **hotels** in Santa Elena. By far the best is the *Snooty Fox Guest House* (☎09/22150, fax 3556; ④–⑤), high above the Macal River at 64 George Price Ave, where the spotless rooms are very good value, and there's a sizable apartment too – a comparative rarity in Cayo. The restaurant and bar have great views over the river to San Ignacio. There's secure car parking, good swimming and owner Michael Waight offers the best-value **canoe rental** in the area – just Bz$40 per day, including life-jacket and ice chest. At Santa Elena the Macal River is crossed by the **Hawksworth Bridge**, built in 1949 and still the only road suspension bridge in Belize.

San Ignacio and Cayo District

On the west bank of the Macal River, 35km from Belmopan, **SAN IGNACIO**, is a friendly, relaxed town that draws together much of the best in inland Belize. The main town of Cayo District and the focus of tourism in west-central Belize, it's an ideal base from which to explore the region, offering good food, inexpensive hotels and restaurants, and frequent bus connections. The main rivers tumbling down the western slopes of the Maya Mountains, the **Macal River** and the **Mopan River**, join to form the Belize River just downstream from the town, and the forested hills that begin here roll all the way across Guatemala and south to Toledo District. The evenings are cool and the days fresh – a welcome break from the sweltering heat of the coast – and there's a virtual absence of mosquitoes and other biting insects. The **population** is typically varied: most people are Mestizos – of mixed Spanish and Maya descent – and Spanish is the main language, but you'll also hear plenty of Creole and English and see Creoles, Mopan and Yucatec Maya, Mennonites, Lebanese, Chinese and even Sri Lankans.

Although you can easily use San Ignacio as a base for day-trips, if you'd like to stay in the countryside, numerous guest houses and ranches in the area offer **cottage-style accommodation** and organized trips. On the whole standards are very high and most of them cater mainly to North Americans on packages who come here after a week on the reef, a phenomenon known as a "surf and turf holiday". However, there are some really good-value places in all price ranges; all are covered in the text. Many are booked up the peak season (Christmas to Easter) but, if open, can offer reduced prices in low season. Most offer horse-riding, bird-watching, canoeing, good home cooking and various trips into the surrounding area. All can reached by road and are well signposted from San Ignacio, though to get to a couple of them you'll have to cross the river in a canoe or small boat.

The countryside around Cayo is ideal for exploring on **horseback** which, as with canoeing, can be arranged by the big resorts at a price, though the best deal is offered by Charlie Collins, who runs Easy Rider (☎22203 or 014/8276). Charlie knows the area well, her horses are cared for and she carefully matches riders to the right horse. A **mountain bike** is another great way to explore Cayo and you can take a bike on the bus to San Antonio (for the Pine Ridge); ask at *Eva's* for details. **Caving** is increasingly popular in Cayo; the most experienced caving guide around, Pete Zubrzycki of *PACZ Hotel* (☎09/22110), leads truly amazing trips into the Maya underworld, and can also arrange **rafting** on the Macal River. For the **Maya sites** around San Ignacio, and expertly guided trips to Tikal (see Chapter 5) the most reliable and recommended people are Ramon Silva, who runs International Archaeological Tours, 23 Burns Ave (☎23991, fax 22760), and Tessa Fairweather (☎08/22412), a very experienced private tour guide; Tessa lives in Belmopan but will meet you in San Ignacio.

Some history

The name the Spanish gave to this area was **El Cayo**, the same word they used to describe the offshore islands. (San Ignacio town is usually referred to as **Cayo** by locals, and this is the name you'll often see indicated on buses.) It's an apt description of the area, in a peninsula between two converging rivers, and also a measure of how isolated the early settlers felt, surrounded by the forest. It wasn't just the jungle they had to fear; the forest was also home to a Maya group who valued their independence. **Tipú**, a Maya city that probably stood at Negroman on the Macal River, about 9km south of the present town, was the capital of the province of Dzuluinicob, where for years the Indians resisted attempts to Christianize them. The early wave of conquest, in 1544, made only a little impact here, and the area was a centre of rebellion in the following decades. Two **Spanish friars** arrived in 1618, but a year later the entire population was still practising idolatry. Outraged, the friars smashed the idols and ordered the native priests flogged, but by the end of the year the Maya had once again driven out the Spaniards. Four years later, Maya from Tipú worked as guides in an expedition against the Itzá and in 1641 the friars returned, determined to Christianize the inhabitants. To express their defiance of the Spanish clerics the Maya priests conducted a mock mass, using tortillas as communion wafers and threw out the friars. From then on Tipú remained an outpost of Maya culture, providing refuge to other Maya fleeing Spanish rule, apparently retaining a good measure of independence until 1707, when the population was forcibly removed to Lake Petén Itzá in Guatemala.

Like many places in Belize, San Ignacio probably started its present life as a logging camp. A map drawn up in 1787 simply states that the Indians of this general area were "in friendship with the Baymen". Later it was a centre for the shipment of chicle, the sap of the sapodilla tree and basis of chewing gum. The self-reliant *chicleros*, as the collectors of chicle were called, knew the forest intimately, including the location of most, if not all, Maya ruins. When the demand for Maya artefacts sent black-market prices rocketing later this century, many of them turned to looting.

Until the Western Highway was built in the 1930s (and the road beyond San Ignacio wasn't paved until the 1980s), local transport was by mule or water. It could take ten days of paddling to reach San Ignacio from Belize City, though later small steamers made the trip. Nowadays, river traffic, which had almost died out, is enjoying something of a revival as increasing numbers of tourists take river trips.

The **telephone area code** for San Ignacio and Cayo District is ☎09

San Ignacio and around

San Ignacio's main street is Burns Avenue; along here, or nearby, you'll find almost everything you need, including the best market in Belize. However, the town's best feature is its location and it's an excellent base for day-trips – the river and the surrounding countryside, with hills, farms, streams and forest, are equally inviting, and there are many ways to enjoy them – on foot, by boat or even on horseback.

Arrival and information

Buses stop in the marketplace just behind Burns Avenue. To check times of onward services call Batty on ☎09/22058 or Novelos on ☎09/32054, or ask at the Batty's office in the market area (you can **leave luggage** there too). There's no official tourist office in San Ignacio, but Bob Jones, owner of the long-established *Eva's* bar and restaurant at 22 Burns Ave (☎22267), is renowned for providing first-class **tourist information**. He knows all there is to know about San Ignacio and the surrounding area and whether you're in search of a cheap overnight stop or a country cottage for a week of luxury, he can point you in the right direction. At time of writing *Eva's* was still the only **Internet café** in Belize (email *evas@btl.net*); you can also pick up the local newspaper *The Cayo Trader* here and buy **books** and **maps** at the gift counter.

All the **banks** are on Burns Avenue, though if you need Guatemalan *quetzals* you can save time at the border by using the services of the reliable **money-changers** who'll approach you. The **BTL office** (Mon–Fri 8am–noon & 1–4pm, Sat 8am–noon) is above the St Martin's Credit Union on Far West St; you'll find the **post office** right in the centre, next to Courts furniture store. **Laundry** can be dropped off at *Martha's*, on West Street behind *Eva's*. **Car rental** is available at Western Auto Rental (☎23134). For domestic and international **air tickets** go to Universal Travel, 8 Mossiah St (☎23884, fax 23885).

The Arts and Crafts of Central America, two doors from *Eva's*, sells reasonably priced Guatemalan **gifts**, books (including *Rough Guides*) and maps. Past here, Caesar's Gift Shop sells the same jewellery and wood carvings as at his place on the Western Highway; you can also find out about *Black Rock River Lodge*, in the Macal River valley (see p.135).

Accommodation

The **hotels** in San Ignacio offer the best-value budget accommodation in the country, and you'll almost always find space. For **camping** near town see the *Cosmos* and *Midas* entries.

IN TOWN

Central Hotel, 24 Burns Ave (☎24179). Simple, clean budget hotel with hot water and shared baths. Good local information, and the balcony with hammocks is great for watching the goings-on in the street below. ②.

Cosmos Campground, a fifteen-minute walk from town along the road to Branch Mouth (☎09/22116). Full camping facilities, including decent showers, flush toilets and a kitchen area. As well as tent space (Bz$6), there are eight clean, simple cabins, some with private bath. The site extends right down to the river, and you can rent canoes, bicycles and horses at affordable prices. Ask at the manager's house (signed) on the left just before the camp-ground; he also offers budget rooms and sells delicious fruit juices. ①–②.

Hi-Et Hotel, West St, behind *Eva's* (☎22828). Friendly, family-run budget hotel with one downstairs room and four basic rooms upstairs, each with a tiny balcony, all sharing a cold water bathroom. The least expensive hotel in town, and phenomenally popular; it also has a laundry service and you can order meals. ②.

Martha's Guest House, West St, behind *Eva's* (☎23647). Three comfortable rooms in Martha and John August's home – you can also rent the entire upstairs for a very reasonable

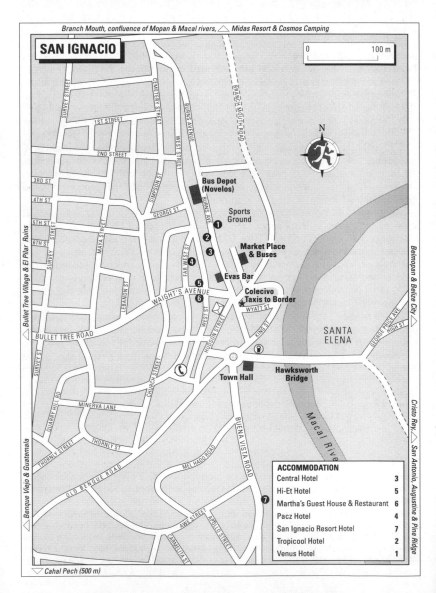

Branch Mouth, confluence of Mopan & Macal rivers, △ Midas Resort & Cosmos Camping

SAN IGNACIO

0   100 m

Bus Depot (Novelos)

Sports Ground

Market Place & Buses

Evas Bar

Colecivo Taxis to Border

SANTA ELENA

Hawksworth Bridge

Town Hall

Macal River

Bullet Tree Village & El Pilar Ruins ◁

Benque Viejo & Guatemala ◁

Belmopan & Belize City ▷

Cristo Rey ◁ San Antonio, Augustine & Pine Ridge ▷

▽ Cahal Pech (500 m)

ACCOMMODATION	
Central Hotel	3
Hi-Et Hotel	5
Martha's Guest House & Restaurant	6
Pacz Hotel	4
San Ignacio Resort Hotel	7
Tropicool Hotel	2
Venus Hotel	1

rate. Guests can use the small kitchen with permission. The homely atmosphere means rooms are much in demand, and you may have to wait to get space, though an extension is planned. The restaurant below is a favourite meeting place, and they have a range of good books on Belize. Also a good drop-off laundry. Accepts Visa. ③.

Midas Resort, Branch Mouth Rd (☎23172, fax 23845). The only resort actually in town, and the best value cabaña place in Cayo. Very comfortable Maya-style thatched cabañas with private bathrooms, set on the riverbank; camping also available. Within walking distance of the town but with the peace and quiet of the countryside. Accepts Visa. ③–④.

PACZ Hotel, 4 Far West St, two blocks behind *Eva's* (☎22110, fax 22972, email *pacz@btl.net*). Five clean, comfortable rooms with hot water in the shared bathrooms; a great bargain, especially for three sharing (no single rates). Pete, the owner, runs adventurous caving and rafting tours, and rents bikes. Reliable information, and a good restaurant below. Accepts Visa. ③.

Tropicool Hotel, Burns Ave, 75m past *Eva's* (☎23052). Bright, clean, budget rooms (the best value in town) with ceiling fans, shared bathrooms with hot water, a sitting room with TV, and a laundry area. ②.

Venus Hotel, 29 Burns Ave (☎23203, fax 22225, email *daniels@btl.net*). Two-storey hotel, the biggest in town, with good rates and the best deal around if you want to stay a week. Rooms vary in quality, so check before you take one; some have a private bath and a few have a/c and TV. The rear balcony has views over the market down to the river. Ask here about *Cahal Pech Village* (see below). Accepts Visa/MC. ②–③.

OUT OF TOWN

The hotels below are all within 3km of San Ignacio, and are listed in the order you approach them on the road to Cahal Pech Maya site (see p.131).

San Ignacio Resort Hotel, 18 Buena Vista St (☎22034, fax 22134, email *sanighot@btl.net*). In a superb location, just ten-minutes' walk uphill from the town centre, with views over the Macal River valley, San Ignacio's premier hotel is renowned locally for hosting Queen Elizabeth on her last visit. Spacious, comfortable rooms (some with balcony and a/c), a dining room terrace overlooking the pool (Bz$5 non-guests) and beautiful gardens. The restaurant (see p.130) is also one of the best in the area and the *Stork Club* bar has a happy hour on Fridays. There's a good tour office for trips to local attractions, and self-guided trails lead down to the river and up to a forested hilltop; ideal for early morning bird-watching. ⑥–⑦.

Piache Hotel, Buena Vista St, across from and just higher up than *San Ignacio Hotel* (☎22032, fax 22685, email *piache@btl.net*). Simple rooms with private bath in a very friendly place with great views, run by Ethel and Godsman Ellis, whose daughter Zoila wrote *On Heroes, Lizards and Passion* (see "Books" p.255) – they're experts on Garifuna history and will organize trips for guests. The hotel has a flower-filled garden, complete with a bar. ③.

Cahal Pech Village, Cahal Pech Hill, just below the Maya site (☎23740, fax 22225, email *daniels@btl.net*). A well-designed and good-value "village" of comfortable wood-and-thatch cabañas on a hillside overlooking San Ignacio. Each cabaña – named after a Belizean Maya site — has electricity and private bath with hot water, and the interiors are decorated with Guatemalan textiles; ouside there's a wooden deck with a hammock. The sixteen-room hotel is equally comfortable. For details ask at *Venus* in town. ⑤.

The Log Cabins, just past Cahal Pech site, on the road to Benque (☎22289, fax 22823). Solidly built, roomy and very comfortable log cabins set in a garden of fruit trees. Guests can order good home-cooked breakfasts and evening meals, and substantial packed lunches for excursions. ⑤.

Windy Hill Resort, just beyond and across from the *Log Cabins*, 3km from town (☎22017, fax 23080, email *windyhill@btl.net*). The first of the "out-of-town" resorts (see pp.134-5, & pp.136-7 for those further out) with 25 very comfortable cabins. Many tours on offer, and nature trails through the grounds. There's also a small pool and a recreation room with cable TV. ⑦.

Eating

Along with its budget hotels, San Ignacio has several good, inexpensive **restaurants**, and there are a number of **fast food stalls** in the market area. If you have anywhere to cook, then the Saturday **market** is worth a visit; it's the best in Belize, with local farmers bringing in fresh-picked produce. It's also a good place to stock up on provisions for trips; see Chris Lowe at the market for his *Fruit-A-Plenty* trail mix, granola bars and home-made peanut butter, also available from local shops. For general groceries, Celina's Store, two blocks from the *Venus Hotel* down Burns Avenue, has the widest selection and the best prices. In the centre of town there are plenty of **fruit stands** laden with bananas, oranges and papayas. You can pick up good fresh **bread** and baked goods from La Popular bakery on West Street, behind *Eva's*, and most afternoons small boys will be around selling tasty, freshly cooked and very inexpensive *empanadas* and *tamales*.

RESTAURANTS

Eva's Bar, 22 Burns Ave. Good, reasonably priced, filling meals, including chilli, chicken, tasty Creole dishes, and some vegetarian options. Usually very busy, it's the information centre of Cayo and a great place to meet fellow travellers and local tour operators. Also has email (*evas@btl.net*) and Internet service, a public phone and a gift shop.

Martha's Kitchen and Pizza Parlour, West St, behind *Eva's*. Under the guest house of the same name and just as well run. Great breakfasts with strong, locally grown coffee, and main dishes of traditional Creole food and pizza. There's always a vegetarian choice and delicious cakes for dessert. Good service too. The patio tables are a popular place to meet for breakfast, and they're candle-lit in the evenings. It's also becoming well known as an information centre and a place to meet your tour guides.

Maxim's, Far West St, behind *Martha's*. One of the best of San Ignacio's numerous Chinese restaurants, serving large portions.

The Running W Restaurant, at the *San Ignacio Hotel*, 18 Buena Vista St. Excellent food in tranquil surroundings, and not at all expensive. Breakfasts are especially good value.

Sandcastle Bar, an open-sided, American-style sports bar on the riverbank, behind the market square. Slightly more expensive than many other places, but worth it for good steak and seafood, and you can get good *nachos* and other bar snacks.

Serendib Restaurant, 27 Burns Ave. Excellent Sri Lankan curries and seafood at very reasonable prices. Good service too.

Drinking and nightlife

Most of the restaurants listed above double as **bars** but if you're looking for something a bit louder, the *Western Bar*, overlooking the market, is a typically Belizean **club**: dark and extremely noisy. The *Blue Angel Disco*, on Hudson Street, now thankfully soundproofed, often has bands at weekends, but has lost its pre-eminent position in the local music scene to the *Cahal Pech Tavern*, a huge thatched structure dominating the hilltop next to *Cahal Pech Village*. It's a regular venue for some of the best bands in Belize – and soundproofed for the benefit of *Village* guests. For a drink in slightly quieter and more comfortable surroundings the *Stork Club* at the *San Ignacio Hotel* is the place to be – though it gets very busy during the Friday evening **happy hour**.

Branch Mouth

Perhaps the easiest introduction to this region is to take the twenty-minute walk to **Branch Mouth**, where the Macal and Mopan rivers merge to form the Belize River. The track leads north from the football field, past rich farmland, with thick vegetation, tropical flowers and butterflies on either side. At the confluence of the rivers is a huge tree, with branches arching over the jade water. A rusting iron mooring ring in the trunk is a reminder of the past importance of river transport; now there are swallows skimming the surface, parrots flying overhead and scores of tiny fish in the water. The scar of raw earth on the opposite bank is evidence of severe flooding in recent years, when the river has risen within metres of the suspension bridge and has even inundated the streets of San Ignacio.

Cahal Pech

Twenty minutes' walk uphill out of town to the southwest, clearly signposted along the Benque road, lie the ruins of **Cahal Pech** (daily 8am–4pm; Bz$5). The name means "place of ticks" in Mopan Maya, but that's certainly not how the elite families who ruled here in Classic times would have known it. Entering the site through the forest you arrive at Plaza B, surrounded by temple platforms and the remains of dwellings; your gaze is soon drawn to **Structure 1**, the Audiencia. If you're used to seeing finely executed, exposed stonework at reconstructed Maya sites then the thick overcoat of lime-mortar on buildings here may come as a bit of a shock. The Classic Maya, however, viewed bare stone facings as ugly and unfinished, and covered all surfaces with a thick coat of plaster or stucco.

Cahal Pech was the royal acropolis-palace of an elite Maya family during the Classic period, and there's evidence of monumental construction from at least as early as the Middle Preclassic, 400 BC, when the city probably dominated the central Belize River valley. Most of what you see dates from the late ninth century AD. There's a **visitor centre** and small **museum** (in theory open daily 8am–4pm; Bz$5, though the visitor centre keeps less regular hours than the site itself). For a cultural experience of an entirely different nature you can stroll across to the adjacent hilltop for a drink at the *Cahal Pech Tavern*.

Barton Creek Cave

Of the many **cave trips** available in Cayo one of the most fascinating is to **Barton Creek Cave**, accessible only by river, and only on a tour (around 4–5hr; Bz$45 per person; minimum three); contact David or Connie at *Martha's Guest House* preferably the day before you'd like to go. David Simpson, your guide, is a multi-lingual Belizean who'll carefully and responsibly show you the astonishing Maya artefacts in the cave. First you drive through the traditional Mennonite settlement of **Upper Barton Creek** to the cave entrance, framed by jungle at the far side of a jade-green pool, where you board the canoe. The river is navigable for about 1600m, and in a couple of places the roof comes so low you have to crouch right down in the canoe, before ending in a gallery blocked by a huge rockfall. The clear, slow-moving river fills most of the cave width, though the roof soars 100m above your head in places, the way ahead illuminated by a 1,000,000 candlepower lamp. Several **Maya burials** line the banks; the most awe-inspiring indicated by a skull set in a natural rock bridge used by the Maya to reach the sacred site. You can climb up to view the remains, some of which are surrounded by pottery vessels, but only from the opposite bank as, like all caves in Belize, Barton Creek Cave is a registered archeological site, and nothing must be touched or removed. If it's been raining a **subterranean waterfall** cascades over the rocks – a truly unforgettable sight. Beyond lie many more miles of passageways, only accessible on a fully equipped expedition.

The Macal River

If the idea of a day or more on the **Macal River** appeals, then any of the resorts can **rent canoes** to paddle on your own (very good value from the *Snooty Fox*, see p.125), but by far the best-value **guided canoe trip** is offered by Tony's River Adventures (☎23292 or contact Tony at *Eva's*). For Bz$25 per person you will be expertly paddled upriver to *Chaa Creek* (see below and p.134) in the morning and float down in the afternoon, and you'll see far more wildlife under his guidance than you could alone. You can also make the trip all the way to Belize City: a week of hard paddling, camping on the riverbank each night. See p.134 for **accommodation** on the Macal River.

The Rainforest Medicine Trail

A canoe trip is the best way to visit the **Rainforest Medicine Trail** (daily 8am–noon & 1–4.30pm; Bz$11.50; ☎09/23870), next to *Chaa Creek Cottages*, taking you through the forest along the Macal riverbank to seek out many of the plants and explain their medicinal properties. There's a large thatched shelter at the entrance with hammocks to rest in and visitors are given a refreshing drink during the explanatory talk before going on the self-guided trail; if you want a **guided tour** it's Bz$17.50 per person and you'll need to book in advance. The trail is dedicated to Don Eligio Panti, a Maya bush doctor (*curandero*) from San Antonio village who passed on his skills to Dr Rosita Arvigo, director and founder of the **Ix Chel Tropical Research Station**, where the trail begins: Don Eligio died in 1996, at the age of 103.

The medical knowledge of the Maya was extensive, and the trail takes in a wide range of traditional healing plants, many of them now used in modern medicine. It's a fascinating experience: there are vines that provide fresh water like a tap; poisonwood, with oozing black sap, its antidote always growing nearby; and the bark of the negrito tree, once sold for its weight in gold in Europe as a cure for dysentery. You'll also see specimens of the tropical hardwoods of the jungle that have been exploited for economic reasons. Today, several plants from the Belize rainforest are being investigated as potential treatments for AIDS; Rosita and the staff at Ix Chel, in collaboration with the New York Botanical Garden, are at the forefront of this research. The more mundane, but very welcome, products of the forest range from herbal teas to blood tonic. Traveller's Tonic, a preventative for diarrhoea, really works, as does Jungle Salve for insect bites, and there are many more cures and tonics available.

Rosita has written about her apprenticeship to the famous *curandero* (see *Sastun*, in "Books", p.258) and is a founder member of the Belize Association of Traditional Healers.

Chaa Creek Natural History Centre

A visit to the marvellous **Chaa Creek Natural History Centre** (daily 8am–5pm; Bz$12), in the grounds of *Chaa Creek Cottages*, next to the Medicine Trail, is the best introduction to Cayo's history, geography and wildlife. If you're spending more than a couple of days in the area try to see this first. With fascinating and accurate displays of the region's flora and fauna, vivid archeological and geological maps, and a scale model of the Macal valley, it's worth a visit in its own right; it also has the **Butterfly Breeding Centre** (included in entry fee) where you can admire the magnificent Blue Morpho. Call to check on the current events programme (☎09/22037).

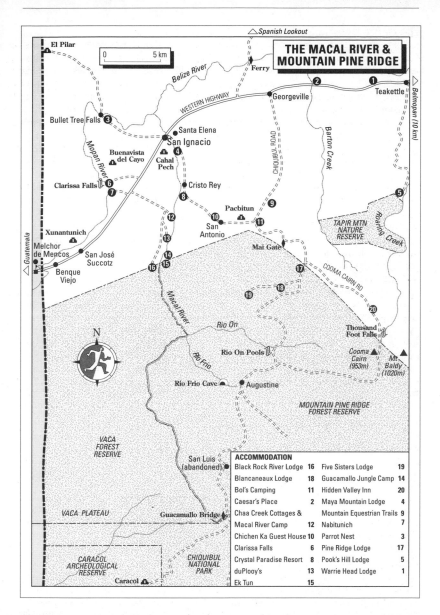

THE MACAL RIVER & MOUNTAIN PINE RIDGE

ACCOMMODATION			
Black Rock River Lodge	16	Five Sisters Lodge	19
Blancaneaux Lodge	18	Guacamallo Jungle Camp	14
Bol's Camping	11	Hidden Valley Inn	20
Caesar's Place	2	Maya Mountain Lodge	4
Chaa Creek Cottages &		Mountain Equestrian Trails	9
Macal River Camp	12	Nabitunich	7
Chichen Ka Guest House	10	Parrot Nest	3
Clarissa Falls	6	Pine Ridge Lodge	17
Crystal Paradise Resort	8	Pook's Hill Lodge	5
duPlooy's	13	Warrie Head Lodge	1
Ek Tun	15		

The Natural History Centre has been instrumental in the successful relocation of **black howler monkeys** from Bermudian Landing (see p.66); the first phase has gone well, with one baby already born to one of the troops, and the second phase, to relocate more troops from the Monkey River area, is currently under way.

The Belize Botanic Gardens

Located at *duPlooy's* (see below), south of *Chaa Creek*, the **Belize Botanic Gardens** (daily 8am–5pm; Bz$10; ☎09/23101) are an ambitious new project established in 1997 on fifty acres of former farmland and forest. The garden is the brainchild of *duPlooy's* owners and avid plant lovers, Ken and Judy duPlooy. There are already around four hundred tree species and 130 orchids, a nursery with over a thousand seedlings, two ponds and several kilometres of interpretive **trails**. The aim is to create a first-class biological educational and study resource for Belizean and overseas researchers, and to conserve many of Belize's native plant species in small areas representative of their natural habitats; they've already gone a long way to achieving this on the ground. The diversity created by these different ecosystems attracts an ever-increasing number of **birds** – and you can be guided around the gardens by **expert naturalist** guide Philip Mai. The garden can be reached by road or river (see below), but it's best to call ahead if you need a guided tour.

Accommodation on the Macal River

Most accommodation along the Macal River (see map on p.133 for locations) is in upmarket **cabaña-style resorts**, beautifully located in the forest above the riverbank, though some do have slightly cheaper options, and most will give discounts to *Rough Guide* readers. There is one budget place, also in a wonderful location. The listings below are in the order that you approach them travelling upriver, though all are accessible by road (for a couple you may also have to cross the river by boat). Any of these places can organize superb **horseback tours** to nearby Maya ruins and some also have **mountain bikes** for rent. If you'd like a relatively easy but picturesque **canoe float** back to town they can take your luggage into town while you drift along enjoying the scenery.

Crystal Paradise Resort, in the village of Cristo Rey, on the east bank of the river (☎ & fax 09/22772). A friendly place with a wide range of accommodation. Owned by the Belizean Tut family, who built the cabañas, rooms and the lovely thatch-roofed dining room. Two delicious meals a day included. Electricity and hot water, and all cabins and some rooms have private baths. There are also some budget rooms, though rates for these don't include meals. The deck outside the dining room overlooks the valley and is a tremendous place for spotting hummingbirds. You can be picked up in San Ignacio if you call before 4.30pm, or get the San Antonio bus along the Cristo Rey road; a taxi costs about Bz$25. ⑤–⑨.

Chaa Creek Cottages, on an unpaved turn-off 10km along the road to Benque (☎09/22037, fax 22501, email *chaacreek@btl.net*). Beautiful, whitewashed wood and stucco cabañas in gorgeous grounds high above the Macal River, with a justly deserved reputation for luxury and ambience. One of the first cottage resorts in Cayo, it's often been featured in TV travel shows, and owners Mick and Lucy Fleming are likeable, modest celebrities. The cottages have tiled floors and bathroom, and range from delightful cabins to a luxury suite with a four-poster bed and jacuzzi; all are lit by oil lamps in the evenings. There's a fine restaurant and bar with spacious outdoor deck. A wonderful trail map guides you through the forest and over the hills to several nearby Maya sites, and the bird list is amazing: around two hundred species have been recorded here. ⑨ but good low season discounts.

Macal River Campsite, on the east bank, just below *Chaa Creek* (☎092/2037, fax 2501). The brainchild of Mick of *Chaa Creek*, with roomy tents under tarps on raised wooden bases. It's camping in comfort, with hot water in clean, tiled bathrooms, and oil lamps in the evening. Big meals are included – though you have to do your own washing up. There's access to all the *Chaa Creek* trails. US$50 per person; good group discounts.

duPlooy's, further along the *Chaa Creek* track (☎09/23101, fax 23301, email *duplooys@pobox.com*). First-rate accommodation, beautifully located in farmland and forest on the west bank of the Macal River, and home to the new Belize Botanic Gardens (see above). Has spacious private bungalows with deck, king-size bed and sofa bed, fridge and coffee-maker (US$150); Jungle Lodge rooms, each with private porch (US$115); and the Pink House (which can be rented by groups), with six rooms, each with a double and single bed (US$40), a kitchen and a large, screened porch. The deck extending from the bar overlooks the river cliffs and provides a walkway into the forest and across to another river overlook that's a superb bird-watching site. Getting here without a vehicle is difficult (taxis are reluctant to risk the stiff climb up the last hill) so there's a shuttle service from the airport (leaves at 1pm); free if you're staying for three nights, Bz$40 if not. ⑤–⑨.

Guacamallo Jungle Camp, on the east bank of the river, and there's no phone; contact David or Connie at *Martha's* in San Ignacio (☎09/23647). Simple cabins high above the river (which you cross in a canoe), located on the edge of a huge and mysterious Maya site; you'll have the pleasure of exploring this on your own. Lots of good food, much of it organically grown near the cabins and a wonderful sense of timelessness as you sit out at night on a Maya mound outside your cabin watching the stars. Bz$45 per person, including transport, dinner and breakfast.

Ek Tun (☎091/2002, in US ☎303/442-6150, email *ektunbz@btl.net*), in a remote location on the east bank of the Macal River, not directly accessible by road. The most luxurious stick-and-thatch cabañas in the country, and there are only two, to preserve the sublime isolation. Each cottage has two bedrooms, one in the loft, hot-water shower and deck overlooking the garden. Gourmet dinner is served under the thatch overlooking the river. Trails lead through the forest and along the river cliffs, dotted with cave entrances, and high above you can see the rare orange-breasted falcon. The 200-acre tract of forest borders the Mountain Pine Ridge Reserve, and there is much evidence of Maya occupation in the area. This is the highest easily navigable point on the Macal River, and you can canoe down to San Ignacio. ⑨.

Black Rock River Lodge, (☎09/22341, fax 23449, email *blackrock@btl.net*); it's possible to drive here, or call at *Caesar's Place* on the Western Highway (see p.123) or the gift shop in San Ignacio (see p.127) to make transport arrangements. Set high above the west bank of the Macal River with stunning views of the jungle-clad limestone cliffs of the upper Macal valley, the solidly built deluxe cabañas have a private hot shower and floors made of smooth stones from the river. Shared bath cabins are also available. Solar power provides electricity. From the open-sided, thatched dining room you can see the river rushing over the black slate which gives its name to the lodge. It's a fairly easy hike from here up to Vaca Falls, or to Vaca or Flour Camp caves, containing some amazing Maya pottery. ⑤–⑥.

The Mopan River

The main tributary creeks of the **Mopan River** rise in the Maya Mountains then flow into Guatemala, running north parallel to the border and re-entering Belize at the village of **Arenal**, 5km south of the border. The river then leaves Belize briefly, rushing under the bridge at the frontier, before the final (and perhaps most picturesque) 25km stretch to its confluence with the Macal River at Branch Mouth (see p.130). There are some attractive and not too serious **white-water rapids** along this stretch, and it's easy enough to arrange kayak or rafting trips on the Mopan; check at any of the resorts listed below (*Clarissa Falls* is best), or with Pete Zubrzycki at *PACZ Hotel* in San Ignacio (☎09/22110).

Five kilometres west of San Ignacio (leaving town along the Bullet Tree road) is the small village **Bullet Tree Falls**, where a bridge crosses the river, and with some very pleasant cabins on the riverbank. As with the Macal River, there are Maya ruins in the vicinity: **El Pilar** and **Buenavista del Cayo** are described on p.136; Xunantunich, the easiest of Belize's major sites to visit, is covered on p.143. For **accommodation** on the Mopan River see pp.136-7.

El Pilar

From Bullet Tree Falls you can visit **El Pilar**, the largest Maya site in the Belize River valley, reached along a rough (motorable) road climbing the escarpment, 14km northwest of the village. There's no public transport to the site but if the archeologists are working there you will probably be able to get a lift, or you could go on horseback or by mountain bike – for all these options check at *Eva's* (see p.130). The site is open daily (no admission charge at present); it covers 40 hectares and includes seventy major structures grouped around 25 plazas.

El Pilar's long sequence of construction began in the Preclassic period, around 450 BC, and continued right through to the Terminal Classic, around 1000 AD, when some of the largest existing temples were completely rebuilt. One reason for such a long period of continuous occupation was almost certainly the presence of numerous springs and creeks in the area – El Pilar is Spanish for "water basin". The most impressive structures – four large pyramids between fifteen and twenty metres high and a ball-court – are grouped around Plaza Copal, from whose west side a flight of steps leads down to a thirty-metre-wide causeway running to **Pilar Poniente** in Guatemala.

The site's position on the frontier might have led to difficulties of access, or even curtailed further study, but the respective governments, urged on by concerned local leaders and the international archeological community, have overcome generations of mutual suspicion to create the **El Pilar Archeological Reserve for Maya Flora and Fauna**, covering an area of nine square kilometres on both sides of the border. One theory under investigation at El Pilar is that the Maya grew a number of different food crops on the same plot, a method known as "forest garden" agriculture, and researchers are attempting to recreate this technique in an experimental and educational exhibit. Several hiking **trails** lead you around the reserve, focusing on both the archeology and natural history of El Pilar, and the site is considered one of the finest bird-watching areas in Cayo. Teo Williams, the caretaker will show you around. His book, *Teo's Way*, is a fascinating account of his life and work; transcribed from taped interviews by Alison Anderson Davies and written largely in Creole, it's on sale at the site.

Buenavista del Cayo

On the east bank of the Mopan River, halfway between San Ignacio and the border, the small Maya site of **Buenavista del Cayo** was once the centre of a wider political region of which Cahal Pech is known to have been a satellite. The ruins are on private land and to visit you need permission from the owner, Pablo Guerra, a shopkeeper in Benque; perhaps the best way to get there is on horseback – Easy Rider (see p.125) runs tours.

The site was excavated between 1984 and 1989 by Jennifer Taschek and Joseph Ball, who discovered a palace, ball-courts, carved stelae, plazas and courtyards. A number of important burial items were also found here, including the famous Jauncy vase, now in Belmopan. There's also evidence that the Maya established workshops to mass-produce pottery on the site. Since excavation, most of the structures have been covered over but there is a charming palace and courtyard in a glade.

Accommodation on the Mopan River

There is less accommodation along the Mopan River than there is along the Macal (see p.134), but what's available is more within the reach of the budget traveller and no less special for it. The resorts below are listed in order of increasing distance from San Ignacio (see map on p.133 for locations).

Parrot Nest, just past Bullet Tree Falls, 5km from San Ignacio (☎09/23702, email *parrot@btl.net*). Five fantastic thatched cabins, one sitting very securely up a tree. Shared bathroom with hot shower. You can rent horses and ride through the forest across the river to visit the ruins of El Pilar, but you'll certainly need a guide. Trucks and cars leave frequently for Bullet Tree from San Ignacio, and it's easy to hitch. ③.

Clarissa Falls, along a signed track to the right off the Benque road, just before the *Chaa Creek* turn (☎09/23916). A very restful place right by a set of rapids and good value if you're on a budget, especially the single rates. There's a wide range of accommodation: simple, clean, stick-and-thatch cabins, some with private bath; a "bunkhouse" cabin with hammocks and shared hot-water showers (Bz$15 per person); space for camping (Bz$7.50 per person) and hookups for RV's. Owner Chena Gálvez serves great home cooking and there's a bar overlooking the falls. Horse-riding, canoeing, rafting and tubing at reasonable rates. ②–⑤.

Nabitunich, down a track just beyond the *Clarissa Falls* turn, off the Benque road (☎09/32309, fax 33096). Mayan for "Stone House", this is the best of the resorts on the Mopan River. Beautiful thatched stone cottages set in 400 acres of forest and farmland, and the gardens have spectacular views of El Castillo at Xunantunich (see p.143). Run by friendly Rudy and Margaret Juan, *Nabitunich* is deservedly popular with bird-watchers. ⑥. Camping (①) also available.

The Mountain Pine Ridge

South of San Ignacio the **Mountain Pine Ridge Forest Reserve** is a spectacular range of rolling hills and jagged peaks formed from some of the oldest rocks in Central America, granite intrusions that have thrust up from below and are part of the bedrock that underlies the entire isthmus. In amongst this there are also some sections of limestone, riddled with superb caves, the most accessible of which are the **Rio Frio Caves** in Augustine/Douglas Silva. For the most part the landscape is semi-open, a mixture of grassland and pine forest in nutrient-poor, sandy soil, although in the warmth of the river valleys the vegetation is thicker gallery forest, giving way to rainforest south of the **Guacamallo Bridge**. Here fertility is ensured by plentiful rainfall, which also renders the smooth, sandy roads in the Pine Ridge difficult to use in the wet season. The rains feed a number of small streams, most of which run off into the Macal and Belize rivers. One of the most scenic is the **Rio On**, rushing over cataracts and forming a gorge – a sight of tremendous natural beauty within view of the picnic shelter. On the northern side of the ridge are the **Thousand-Foot Falls**: actually over 1600ft (490m) and the highest in Central America.

The Pine Ridge is virtually uninhabited but for four or five tourist lodges and one small settlement, **Augustine/Douglas Silva**, site of the forest reserve headquarters. The whole area is perfect for **hiking** and **mountain biking**, but **camping** is allowed only at Augustine/Douglas Silva and at the Mai Gate, beyond San Antonio, and officially you need permission from the Forestry Department in Belmopan (in practice you'll almost certainly be allowed to if you ask nicely when you arrive). It's fairly hard – though rewarding – to explore this part of the country on your own, and unless you have a car, a mountain bike or come on an organized tour, you may have to rely on hitching. To explore the many forestry roads branching off the main reserve road, you need the 1:50,000 topographic maps from the Ministry of Natural Resources in Belmopan (see p.121).

Getting to the reserve

There are two **entrance roads** to the reserve, one from the village of **Georgeville**, on the Western Highway (see p.123), and the other from **Santa Elena**, along the Cristo Rey road and through the village of **San Antonio**, served by four Mesh buses a day from San Ignacio. Keen to encourage responsible tourism, forestry officers are allowing visitors to travel to Augustine/Douglas Silva in the forestry vehicles that generally leave San Ignacio in the early morning; contact the conservation officer in Belmopan (☎08/22079) or San Ignacio (☎092/3280) to see if you can get a ride. If you're up to it, the best way to get around is to rent a **mountain bike** in San Ignacio; the bus to San Antonio takes bikes, or you could put them in the back of a passing pickup truck. It's also possible to **hitch** in and hike around. Any travel agent or resort can arrange **organized tours**: if you're staying at any of the Cayo resorts a full-day tour of the Pine Ridge costs around US$45–50 per person for a group of four, more if you want to go to Caracol(see p.141). If you're **on a budget**, contact Rafael August of Western Adventure Tours through *Martha's*, or Tommy of Tommy's Tours through *Eva's*, who can take you on a superb tour for around half the price. Batty buses (☎02/74924) sometimes organize inexpensive trips to the Pine Ridge at weekends and holidays.

Recent road improvements in the Pine Ridge, particularly on the road to Caracol, make a trip in a **rental jeep** perfectly feasible (most of the year) but always check road conditions first and heed the advice of the forestry officials.

The Cristo Rey road

The **road to Cristo Rey** village begins in Santa Elena, 150m on the right after crossing the Hawksworth Bridge. Two kilometres along this road is the excellent *Maya Mountain Lodge* (☎09/22164, fax 22029, email *mayamt@btl.net*; ⑤–⑥), run by Bart and Suzi Mickler. Set in rich tropical forest, it provides a fascinating introduction to the wildlife of Belize. Accommodation is in colourfully decorated individual cabañas, each with a private bath, electricity and hot water; the larger and slightly cheaper *Parrot's Perch* cabin is ideal for groups. Delicious meals are served in an open-sided dining room, which provides another opportunity for bird-watching; motmots, aracaris and trogons fly just metres away from the table. The lodge sometimes hosts student groups and has a library and lecture area; they especially welcome families and have plenty of activities for kids, including the best illustrated trail guide in Belize. There are great packages available, and if there's space, independent travellers (unless part of a group or in a rented car) can receive a fifty percent discount if carrying this guide.

After another few kilometres you come to **CRISTO REY**, a pretty village of scattered wooden houses on a high bank above the Macal River. Near the beginning of the village Orlando Madrid runs *Sandals Restaurant*, and also has a few simple **cabins** (☎014/7446; ③). Orlando can take you on guided canoe or cave trips and **rents canoes** at good rates.

San Antonio and Pacbitún ruins

In **SAN ANTONIO**, 10km further on from Cristo Rey, the villagers are descendants of Maya (Uxcawal is their name, in their own language) refugees, who fled the Caste Wars in Yucatán in 1847, and most people still speak Yucatec. Their story is told in a fascinating written account of San Antonio's oral history, *After 100 Years*, by Alfonso Antonio Tzul. Nestled in the Macal River valley, surrounded by scattered *milpa* farms, with the forested Maya Mountains in the background, the village is poised to become a base for hiking and horseback tours along old *chiclero* trails. The home of the late Don Eligio Panti, the famous *curandero* who died recently (see p.132), it's a superb place to learn about traditional Maya healing methods, not least by going to see the Garcia sisters, who grew up in the village determined not to let Maya culture be swamped by outside influence. They run the *Chichan Ka Guest House* (☎09/23310, fax 09/22057, email *lucky@btl.net* ③) at the approach to the village, and the bus stops right outside. The guest house has simple but comfortable **rooms** (some with private bath) and panoramic views of the Maya Mountains. It's a very relaxing place to stay; meals are prepared in the traditional way – often using organic produce from the garden – and courses are offered in the gathering and use of medicinal plants. The sisters are also renowned for their slate carvings, and their **gift shop** has become a favourite tour-group stop. Next door is the small **Tanah Museum** (Bz$6), the proceeds from which go towards the establishment of a 500-acre Botanical Garden and Maya Reserve. The Mesh **bus to San Antonio** (Mon–Sat only; 1hr) departs from the market in San Ignacio four times a day between 10.30am and 5pm, returning from San Antonio between 6am and 3pm.

Three kilometres east of San Antonio, on the road to the Pine Ridge, lie the ruins of **Pacbitún**, a major ceremonial centre. One of the oldest known Preclassic sites in Belize (1000 BC), it continued to flourish throughout the Classic period, and Maya farming terraces and farmhouse mounds can be seen in the hills all around. Pacbitún, meaning "stones set in the earth", has at least 24 temple pyramids, a ball-court and several raised causeways, though only Plaza A and the surrounding structures are cleared; this is the highest point in Pacbitún, created when the Maya re-shaped an entire hilltop. The tombs of two elite women yielded the largest haul of Maya musical instruments ever found in one place; drums, flutes, ocarinas (wind instruments) and the first discovery of Maya maracas. Though the site is not always open to casual visitors, José Tzul, who lives on the right just before the entrance, runs Blue Ridge Mountain Rider (☎09/22322) and can arrange horseback tours of the area, taking in Pacbitún (US$50 per day).

The forest reserve

Not far beyond Pacbitún, and 25km before Augustine, the entrance roads meet and begin a steady climb towards the **entrance to the reserve** proper. One kilometre beyond the junction is a **campsite** (①) run by Fidencio and Petronila Bol, a delightful couple, and owners of *Bol's Nature Tours*. Fidencio used to work as a caretaker at several Maya sites, including Pacbitún and Caracol, and Petronila has compiled *A Book of Maya Herbs*. It's a good base, on a ridge with views over to Xunantunich. Fidencio can guide you to several nearby **caves** – the aptly named Museum Cave holds dozens of artefacts, including intact bowls. About 5km uphill from the campsite is the **Mai Gate**, a forestry checkpoint offering information about the reserve as well as toilets and drinking water. Though there are plans to levy an **entrance fee**, for the moment all you have to do is list your name in the visitors' book (to ensure there's no illegal camping).

Once you've entered the reserve, the dense, leafy forest is quickly replaced by pine trees. After 3km a branch road heads off to the left, running for 7km to a point overlooking the **Thousand-Foot Falls**. The setting is spectacular, with rugged, thickly forested slopes across the steep valley – almost a gorge. The long, slender plume of water becomes lost in the valley below, giving rise to the falls' other, more poetic name: Hidden Valley Falls. The waterfall itself is about 1km from the viewpoint, but try to resist the temptation to climb around for a closer look: the slope is a lot steeper than it first appears and, if you do get down, the ascent is very difficult indeed. There's a shelter with toilets at the viewpoint, and since the site is privately owned you'll be approached by Pedro, the caretaker, for the entrance fee (Bz$3). The small gift shop sells cold drinks but no food. The beautiful wooden cabins here belong to the Hidden Valley Institute for Environmental Studies, a research establishment affiliated to the nearby *Hidden Valley Inn*, which you'll have passed on the way in (see "Accommodation" below).

One of the reserve's main attractions has to be the **Rio On Pools**, a gorgeous spot for a swim, 11km further on. Here the river forms pools between huge granite boulders before plunging into a gorge, right beside the main road. Another 8km from here and you reach the reserve headquarters at **AUGUSTINE**. This small settlement, housing forestry workers, has been renamed **DOUGLAS SILVA** (after a local politician), but only some of the signs have been changed. If you're heading for **Caracol**, this is where you can get advice on road conditions from the Forestry Department. You can **stay** at the **campsite** or the **bunkhouse** (①), for which you need camping gear. The building with the thatched tables sells basic supplies and cold beer, but there are no phones.

The **Rio Frio Caves** are a twenty-minute walk from Augustine, following the signposted track from the parking area through the forest to the main cave, beneath a small hill. The Rio Frio flows right through and out of the other side of the hill here and if you enter the foliage-framed cave mouth, you can scramble over limestone terraces the entire way along into the open again. Sandy beaches and rocky cliffs line the river on both sides.

ACCOMMODATION IN THE MOUNTAIN PINE RIDGE

The **resorts** in the Pine Ridge include some of the most exclusive accommodation in the interior of Belize. These lodges, mostly cabins set amongst pines, are surrounded by the undisturbed natural beauty of the forest reserve and have quiet paths to secluded waterfalls; they're ideal places to stay if you're visiting Caracol. The listings below are in the order in which you approach them from the entrance road (see map on p.133 for locations).

Hidden Valley Inn, on the Cooma Cairn road to Thousand-Foot Falls (☎08/23320, fax 23334, in US ☎1-800/334-7942). Twelve roomy, well-designed cottages at the highest elevation of any accommodation in Belize and set in a seventy-square-kilometre private reserve which includes Thousand-Foot Falls. Each cottage has a fireplace stacked with logs to ward off the evening chill. Even the vegetation, pines and tree ferns, appears distinctly untropical, and hiking trails take you to secret waterfalls. Meals are in the spacious main house, with the ambience of a mountain lodge; wood-panelled walls, a crackling log fire and a well-stocked library. The *Inn* has an impressive list of sightings, and you can frequently see the rare orange-breasted falcon. Prices include breakfast, dinner, tax and service charge. ⑨.

Pine Ridge Lodge, on the road to Augustine, just past the Cooma Cairn junction to Thousand-Foot Falls (☎09/23310, fax 22267, in US ☎216/781-6888, email *prlodge@mindspring.com*). Small resort on the banks of Little Vaqueros Creek, with a choice of Maya-style thatched cabins or more modern ones with red-tiled roofs. The grounds and trees are full of orchids and trails lead to pristine waterfalls. The restaurant is a favourite refreshment stop on tours of the Pine Ridge. Breakfast included. ⑦.

Blancaneaux Lodge, 1km beyond Pine Ridge Lodge, then 2km down a track to the right, by the airstrip (☎09/23878, fax 23919, email *blodge@btl.net*). Sumptuous lodge with rooms, cabins and villas overlooking Privassion Creek. Owned by Francis Ford Coppola, it features a few Hollywood excesses, not least the prices, though these are considerably lower during the off season. Villas (up to US$450) have two enormous rooms with varnished hardwood floors, and are decorated with Guatemalan and Mexican textiles, and there's an enormous screened porch with gorgeous views over the creek. Cabañas (US$160) and lodge rooms (US$95 with shared bath) are perhaps more affordable. Meals feature home-grown organic vegetables, pizza and fine Italian wines. ⑦–⑨.

Five Sisters Lodge, at the end of the road past *Blancaneaux* (☎ 091/2005, fax 09/23081, email *fivesislo@btl.net*). Set on the hillside among the granite and pines, this has the best location in the Pine Ridge, and is the pride and joy of owner Carlos Popper. There's eleven comfortable palmetto-and-thatch cabañas, each with hot showers and a deck with hammocks, and less expensive rooms in the main building. The grounds are a profusion of flowers and there's a nature trail through broadleaf forest to Little Vaqueros Falls. Electricity is provided by a small, unobtrusive hydro but the oil lamps are wonderfully romantic. The dining-room deck gives tremendous views of the Five Sisters waterfalls cascading over the granite rocks of Privassion Creek, and there's even a lift to take you to the bottom. Rates include breakfast; other meals are good value if you're on a day-trip. ⑥–⑦.

The ruins of Caracol

Beyond Augustine the main ridges of the Maya Mountains rise up to the south, while to the west is the Vaca plateau, a fantastically isolated wilderness. Here the ruins of **Caracol** (daily 8am–4pm; Bz$10), the largest known Maya site in Belize, were lost in the rainforest for several centuries until their rediscovery by *chicleros* in 1936. They were first systematically explored by A.H. Anderson in 1938: he named the site Caracol – Spanish for "snail" – because of the large numbers of snail shells found there. Other archeologists visited and made excavations in the 1950s, but early reports took a long time to reach the public domain as many documents were destroyed by Hurricane Hattie in 1961. In 1985 the first detailed, full-scale excavation of the site, the "Caracol Project", began under the auspices of Drs Arlen and Diane Chase of the University of Central Florida. Initially expected to take at least ten years, research continues to unearth a tremendous amount of material on the everyday life of all levels of Maya society. Apparently there was a large and wealthy middle class among the Maya of Caracol and dates on stelae and tombs suggest an extremely long occupation. At its greatest extent, around 700 AD during the Late Classic period, Caracol covered 88 square kilometres and had a population estimated to be around 150,000, with over 30,000 structures – a far greater density than at Tikal. What continues to puzzle archeologists is why the Maya built such a large city on a plateau with no permanent water source – and how they managed to maintain it for so long; the Maya-built reservoir is still used when the archeologists are in residence.

It's an amazing experience to be virtually alone in this great abandoned city, the horizon bounded by jungle-covered peaks, through which it's only three hours on foot to Guatemala. Caracol is a **Natural Monument Reserve**, a haven for wildlife as well as archeologists, and you may catch sight of ocellated turkeys feeding in the plazas and tapirs dining at night on the succulent shoots growing on cleared areas. The site is so isolated that in the past it was badly looted; today, a permanent team of caretakers is on guard all year, and the British Army and Belize Defence Force make frequent patrolling visits. During your visit you'll be guided by one of the guards, or, if excavation is in progress, by one of the researchers. Before you set off you should drop into the new **visitor centre**, built by Raleigh volunteers.

THE SITE

Only the city's core, covering 38 square kilometres and containing at least thirty-two large structures and twelve smaller ones around five main plazas is currently open to visitors – though this is more than you can effectively see in a day. The largest pyramid, **Canaa**, is the tallest Maya structure in Belize at 42m (and still one of the tallest buildings in the country), and several others are over 20m high. At the top of this immense restored structure is a small plaza, with three more sizeable pyramids; an altar here has revealed signs of a female ruler. Beneath Canaa a series of looted tombs still have traces of the original painted glyphs on the walls. Archeological research has revealed some superb tombs, with lintels of iron-hard sapodilla wood supporting the entrances and painted texts decorating the walls.

Other glyphs carved on altars tell of war between Caracol and Tikal (see p.154), with power over a huge area alternating between the two great cities. One altar dates Caracol's victory over Tikal at 562 AD – a victory that set the seal on the city's rise to power. Several altars and stelae were deliberately broken by logging tractors in the 1930s, including Altar 23, the largest at Caracol, which clearly depicts two bound captive lords with a row of glyphs above and between them; it has been dated at 810 AD. One of the most awe-inspiring sights in this fantastic city is an immense, 700-year old **ceiba tree** – sacred to the Maya – with enormous buttress roots twice as high as a human being.

The Chiquibul Cave System

Fifteen kilometres beyond Caracol is the vast **Chiquibul Cave System**, the longest cave system in Central America, containing what is reputed to be the largest cave chamber in the western hemisphere. The entire area is dotted with caves and sinkholes, which were certainly known to the ancient Maya and probably used for ceremonies; as yet there has been no cave found in Belize which does not contain Maya artefacts. You need to come on a properly organized expedition if you want to explore. Further south **Puente Natural** is an enormous natural limestone arch, and there's a new research station nearby; if you're lucky you could get a lift in with the researchers.

Succotz and the ruins of Xunantunich

Back on the Western Highway, the village of **SAN JOSÉ SUCCOTZ** lies about 10km west of San Ignacio, right beside the Mopan River, just before Benque Viejo. It's a very traditional village in many ways, inhabited largely by Mopan Maya, who celebrate fiestas here on March 19 and May 3. Under colonial administration the Maya of Succotz sided with the British, a stance that angered other groups, such as the Icaiché (see p.228), who burnt it to the ground in 1867. The villagers here still identify strongly with their Maya culture, and many of the men work as caretakers of other Maya sites in Belize. The Magaña family's art gallery and **gift shop** (signed from the main road) sells superb wood and slate carvings, and there's very basic **accommodation** at the *Xunantunich Hotel* (②) across from the ferry.

Outside fiesta times, Succotz is a quiet village, and the main reason most people visit is to see the Classic period ruins of **Xunantunich** (pronounced Shun-an-tun-ich), "the Stone Maiden", up the hill across the river. Any bus or shared taxi running between San Ignacio and the border will drop you by the venerable, hand-winched **cable ferry** (8am–5pm, lunch break around noon; Mon–Sat free, Sun Bz$3) which carries foot passengers and vehicles across the river. From the riverbank a steep track leads through the forest for a couple of kilometres to the ruins. If you're carrying luggage you can safely leave it in the *Plaza* restaurant (which is also a good source of information), opposite the ferry. You can no longer drive all the way up to the site; vehicles must be left in the new parking area, 250m below the entrance.

Xunantunich

Xunantunich (Mon–Fri 8am–5pm; weekends and holidays 8am–4pm; Bz$10) was explored in the 1890s by Dr Thomas Gann, a British medical officer, and in 1904 Teobalt Maler of the Peabody Museum took photographs and made a plan of the largest structure, A–6, commonly known as El Castillo. Gann returned in 1924, excavated large numbers of burial goods and removed the carved glyphs of Altar 1, the whereabouts of which are now unknown. British archeologist J. Eric S. Thompson excavated a residential group in 1938, unearthing pottery, obsidian, jade, a spindle, seashells, stingray spines and hammers. Recent excavations have found evidence of Xunantunich's role in the power politics of the Classic period – it was probably allied as a subordinate partner, along with Caracol, to the regional superpower Calakmul, against Tikal. By the Terminal Classic, Xunantunich was already in decline, though still apparently populated until around 1000 AD, after the so-called Classic Maya "collapse".

The site is built on top of an artificially flattened hill and includes five plazas, although the remaining structures are grouped around just three of them. The track brings you out into plaza A–2, with large structures on three sides. Plaza A–3, to the right, is almost completely enclosed by a low, acropolis-like building, and plaza A–1, to the left, is dominated by **El Castillo**, the city's largest structure, 40m high, and a prominent symbol of Belize's national identity. As is so often the case, the building is layered, with later versions built on top of earlier ones. It was

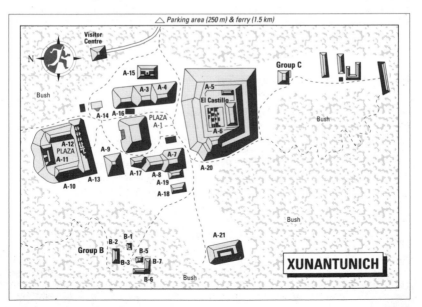

once ringed by a decorative **stucco frieze** carved with abstract designs, human faces and jaguar heads, depicting a king performing rituals associated with assuming authority: this has been extensively restored. The climb up El Castillo is daunting, but the views from the top are superb, with the forest stretching out all around and the rest of the ancient city mapped out beneath you. The Preclassic ruins of **Actuncan** are a couple of kilometres north.

Your first stop should be the marvellous new **visitor centre**; easily the best at any Maya site in Belize. There's a superb scale model of the city and the labels on exhibits will answer most questions. One of the highlights is a fibreglass replica of the famous hieroglyphic frieze, from which you get a much better idea of the significance of the real thing. Nearby, the original small museum has several well-preserved stelae from the site. If you want a **guide** it's worth asking one of the caretakers, Ruben Penados or Ramon Archila, if they have time; they are very knowledgable, having worked on recent excavations and reconstruction.

Benque Viejo and the border

The final town before the Guatemalan border is **BENQUE VIEJO DEL CARMEN**, under half an hour from San Ignacio, where Guatemala and Belize combine in almost equal proportions and Spanish is certainly the dominant language. It's a quiet little place with little to offer the passing traveller, and there's a constant stream of taxis to and from the border post. **Hotels** are basic at best, and you're much better off staying in San Ignacio. If you've time to kill, and are interested in the cultural aspects of *mestizo* traditions, you might want to visit the small El Ba'lum Art Gallery, 43 Churchill St (Mon & Tues 1–4pm, Wed–Sat 9am–noon & 2–4.30pm; Bz$3). There are displays of old photographs and documents, logging and chicle-gathering equipment, paintings and musical instruments. Cubola, Belize's foremost **book and music publishers**, have an interesting gift shop at 35 Elizabeth St (☎09/32241), which sells unusual crafts, including brightly painted models of Belize's colonial-style houses, as well as recordings of the country's top bands. **Crossing the border** is straightforward; full details are given in the box on p.146.

travel details

Belize City to: destinations along the Western Highway and the Guatemalan border (3hr 30min). The Western Highway is served by hourly buses from 5am to 8pm, and most continue over the border to **Melchor de Mencos**: bus companies, main destinations and journey times are covered in the Belize City chapter (see box on p.62), with Batty operating until 10am and Novelos taking over at 11am; each has **express** buses on some journeys.

Benque and the border to: Belize City (buses hourly from 4am to 4pm); in addition, Shaws run a service **between Belmopan, San Ignacio** and **Melchor** (Mon–Fri 7am–5pm), which increases the frequency along this route.

San Antonio to: San Ignacio (Mon–Sat at 6am, 7am, 1pm & 3pm; 1hr).

San Ignacio to: Belize City (Batty and Novelos run regular services, including expresses; hourly until 5pm; 3hr); **Belmopan** (Batty, Novelos and Shaws buses; hourly; 50min); **San Antonio** (Mon–Sat 4 daily from 10.30am–5pm; 1hr); **to the border** (Batty, Novelos and Shaws; frequent services and every 30min during peak times 7.30am–4pm; 30min), most continue to the market in **Melchor de Mencos**. Buses for the border pass through San José (20min) and Benque Viejo (25min), though if you're headed this way it's often easier and quicker to take a shared **taxi** for Bz$4 per person.

CHAPTER FIVE

TIKAL AND FLORES

For increasing numbers of visitors to Belize, the chance to make side-trips across the western border into **Guatemala**, to see the famous **Maya sites** and spectacular **nature reserves**, is one not to be missed; it's also relatively easily done, either on organized tours or independently. Here, in the vast northern department of **Petén**, there are literally hundreds of ruins – many of them completely buried in the jungle – but few provide the same combination of intrigue and accessibility as **Tikal**, which is arguably the most magnificent of all Maya sites and situated only two hours from the border. The monumental temple-pyramids tower above the Tikal rainforest, testament to the fact that Petén was the heartland of the ancient Maya civilization during the Preclassic and Classic periods (around 300 BC–900 AD), and that it was here, during the latter, that Maya culture reached the height of its architectural achievement. Set on an island in Lake Petén Itzá, the charmingly picturesque town of **Flores** is the departmental capital, while nearby, on the mainland, the growing town of **Santa Elena** is the transport hub of the department.

There are a couple of other Maya sites worth stopping off for en route to Tikal: **Yaxhá**, the third largest site in Petén, and **Topoxté** both occupy beautiful, lakeside settings around 30km from the bustling yet nondescript border town of **Melchor de Mencos**. If you're travelling to Tikal by bus from the Belize border you'll need to change at the village of **Puente Ixlú**, from where it's only a couple of kilometres to the peaceful village of **El Remate** – a good base if you plan to spend more than a day exploring the area. Those with the time for a more extended trip could make for the village and ruins of Uaxactún, to the north of Tikal, which also serve as a jumping-off place for expeditions to more remote sites in the north.

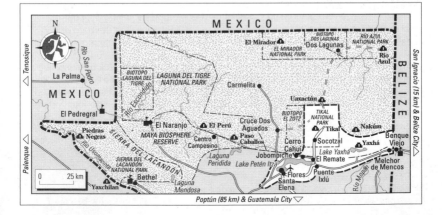

ACCOMMODATION PRICE CODES

The accommodation in this chapter has been given a **price code** according to the scale below, which represents the cost of **a double room in high season**. The scale is in US$, due to the fluctuation in exchange rate of the *quetzal* (see box below).

① Under US$10	④ US$25–35	⑦ US$70–95
② US$10–15	⑤ US$35–50	⑧ US$95–120
③ US$15–25	⑥ US$50–70	

But archeology isn't the only thing to tempt you over the border. Petén is a huge, rolling expanse of tropical forest, swamps, lakes and dry savannahs, stretching into the Lacandón forest of southern Mexico. Tikal itself lies at the centre of a large national park, which forms part of the **Maya Biosphere Reserve**,

---

GUATEMALA PRACTICALITIES: CROSSING THE BORDER AND MOVING ON

BASICS

Buses from Belize City to the border pass through San Ignacio (see p.63) hourly and usually continue to the marketplace bus station in the town of Melchor de Mencos, 2km beyond the border (see below for details of moving on from the border). Alternatively you could **fly**: Tropic Air and Maya Island Air have daily services from Belize International to Flores/Santa Elena at 8am and 2.30pm (US$80 one way), returning at 9.30am & 4pm. Aerovias flies the same route at least three times a week.

Guatemala is a **Spanish**-speaking country and (except if you're on a fully guided tour) you'd be wise to acquire at least some knowledge of the language; overcharging foreigners is routine and the better you are at getting by the less likely you are to be ripped off. The unit of **currency** is the *quetzal* (Q) and the current **exchange rate** is around Q5.50–6 to the US$. You can easily **exchange cash** (US or Belize dollars) or cash travellers' cheques at the border. If you're not going to Flores (where there are ATMs) make sure you have enough cash (*quetzales* or dollars) to last your trip; only the more expensive hotels will take **credit cards**, though you can usually get someone to accept or to cash US$ traveller's cheques. **Prices** for transport, accommodation, food and almost everything else are much cheaper than in Belize – by as much as forty or fifty percent in most cases. El Remate (on the road to Tikal) and Flores have some of the best **budget accommodation** in the country; in either you can get a decent double room for under US$10.

Finally, in Guatemala you'll need to take even greater **safety** precautions than you do in Belize. Gangs of **armed robbers** target tourists along this route and the Guatemalan authorities do little to ensure tourists' safety, though police patrols along the road are stepped up after an incident. You'll be at greater risk travelling in a tourist minibus than on the public bus; some tour companies hire an armed guard to accompany their groups. In any circumstances the border crossing (and indeed travel to Tikal) is best attempted **in daylight**. The journey time is short enough to allow you to have breakfast in San Ignacio and get to your destination by early afternoon at the latest.

BORDER PRACTICALITIES

Both the Belizean and Guatemalan **border posts** are on the eastern bank of the Mopan River, 15km west of San Ignacio. The border post will probably be your first covering 16,000 square kilometres of northern Petén: in theory the largest tropical forest reserve in Central America and extraordinarily rich in **wildlife**, particularly birds, though you're also guaranteed to see **howler** or **spider monkeys**. One of the best places to get an understanding of the forest (apart from Tikal itself) is to visit the **Cerro Cahuí reserve** near El Remate.

Tours to Tikal, by air or overland, are offered by many of the lodges in Cayo (see Chapter 4) and by travel agencies throughout Belize. However, it's also very easy (and a good deal less expensive) to do it on your own so, unless time is extremely short, don't be talked into taking a one-day tour: apart from needing the extra time to do the ruins themselves justice, you'll miss the highlights of dawn and dusk at the site, when the forest canopy bursts into a frenzy of sound and activity. **Accommodation** is easy enough to find, not only in Tikal itself, but in Yaxhá, El Remate and Flores. The **airport** (served by domestic and international flights) and the **bus terminals** for all services in Petén and to Guatemala City are in Santa Elena; if you're heading anywhere else in the country or indeed crossing to Mexico you'll have to pass through here first.

experience of being overcharged in Guatemala: although **visas** are not needed by most nationalities, you'll usually be asked to pay inflated **entry fees** – about Q10 (about US$1.50). Make sure you get enough time to cover your visit and ask for the maximum if you're travelling onwards – though the most you're likely to get is thirty days. Although there's a **bank** just beyond immigration which gives reasonable rates (Mon–Fri 8.30am–2pm; no ATM or cash advances), it's quicker and easier to use the **moneychangers** who'll pester you on either side of the border; bargain with a couple and you'll get a fair rate. You can also change money at good rates (and with more privacy) in the supermarket next to the *Hotel Frontera Palace* (see below). There's no official **tourist information** office at the border (Inguat, the Guatemalan Tourist Commission, has an office in Flores and a booth at the airport), but you can get reliable information about the route to Tikal from the *Hotel Frontera Palace*.

If you need **to stay at the border**, the best option is the *Hotel Frontera Palace* (☎ & fax 926-5196; ③), just past Guatemalan immigration, on the riverbank before the bridge. It has pleasant thatched cabins (with hot water) and a restaurant. Owner Marco Gross knows Petén extremely well and can organize trips to any of the Maya sites; find out about Yaxhá (see p.148) here. There are also several cheap hotels in the centre of town.

MOVING ON FROM THE BORDER
Buses to Flores (2hr 30min) for the **Puente Ixlú junction** (see below) will usually be waiting at the border; if not you can go to the market in Melchor to find one – a shared taxi from the border will cost a couple of *quetzales* or it's a fifteen-minute walk up the hill to the right. The official bus **fare** to Flores is Q10; even if you're only going as far as Puente Ixlú (1hr 45min) you'll still be asked for at least this by the Pinita bus employees, so get a Rosita bus if there's a choice. Buses depart from the border at 8am and 10am; thereafter every 2–3hrs until 5pm (see box on p.160 for return details). At the border you'll also be approached by **taxi** and **minibus** drivers; they'll charge about US$10 per person to Flores or Tikal – after some bargaining – and leave whenever they have a load. The best minibus deal is offered by Manuel Sandoval, who runs Transportes Memita; he aims to have a regular departure from the border to Tikal, leaving at 9am and charging US$18 return.

Melchor de Mencos to El Remate

The sixty kilometres from the **Belize border to the Puente Ixlú junction** takes you through rolling countryside and farmland, past a series of small villages, populated mainly by fairly recent settlers to Petén, and past the Maya sites of **Yaxhá** and **Topoxté**. Although unpaved, the road is in good condition, and runs roughly parallel to a chain of lakes – the largest of which is **Lake Petén Itzá** – used in Maya times as the main route across the region. Near the shore of Lake Petén Itzá the unpaved road meets the paved Flores–Tikal road at the village of **Puente Ixlú**, from where you can continue west to Flores, or north, through **El Remate**, for Tikal.

Yaxhá and Topoxté

Thirty kilometres from Melchor the road passes about 8km to the south of **lakes Yaxhá and Sacnab**, beautiful bodies of water ringed by dense rainforest. Lake Yaxhá is home to two Maya ruins well worth a visit: **Yaxhá**, on a hill overlooking the northern shore, and **Topoxté**, on an island near the southern shore. The turn-off is clearly signposted and the bus driver will stop if you ask. If you haven't arranged accommodation at *El Sombrero* (see below) then you'll probably be faced with a sweltering two-hour walk to get there, though there is some traffic to and from the village of La Máquina, 2km before the lakes. Just before you reach the lakes you pass a **control post** where you may be asked to sign in. From here it's 3km to the site: head along the road beween the lakes then turn left (signed) for Yaxhá.

Yaxhá, covering several square kilometres of a ridge overlooking the lake, is primarily a Classic period city. Although some restoration has been completed, don't expect the manicured splendour of Tikal. What you can count on here, though, is real atmosphere as you try to discover the many features still half hidden by the forest. The site is open daily (free at the time of writing); if you're not on a guided trip then one of the guardians will show you around for a small fee. The ruins are spread out over nine plazas and around five hundred structures have been mapped so far, including several huge pyramids and large acropolis complexes. The tallest and most impressive pyramid, Structure 216, 250m northeast of the entrance, rises in tiers to a height of over 30m; the recent restoration enables you to climb to the top for spectacular views over the forest and lake.

Topoxté, a much smaller site on the easternmost of three small islands, is best reached by boat from *El Sombrero*. There is a 4km trail to a spot opposite the islands but you still have to get over to them – and large crocodiles inhabit the lake. The structures you see are not on the scale of those at Yaxhá, and date mainly from the Late Postclassic, though the site has been occupied since Preclassic times. Work is in progress to restore some structures.

If you want to **stay** nearby, the wonderful, solar-powered *Campamento El Sombrero* (☎926-5299, fax 926-5198, ④); or check at the *Hotel Frontera Palace* at the border, see box on p.147), 300m from the road on the south side of the lake, has rooms in wooden jungle lodges and space for **camping**. There's another *campamento*, run by locals on behalf of Inguat, on the far side of the lake, below Yaxhá, where you can pitch a tent or sling a hammock beneath a thatched shelter for free.

Puente Ixlú and El Remate

Beyond the Yaxhá junction the road continues for around another 30km to the tiny village of **PUENTE IXLÚ**, at the junction with the Flores–Tikal road; coming from the Belize border you'll need to get off here if you want to go to Tikal. Inside the thatched **information** hut you'll find a large map of the area, showing the little-restored **ruins of Ixlú**, 200m down a signed track from the road, on the shore of **Lake Zac Petén**.

EL REMATE, 2km north along the shore of Lake Petén Itzá from Puente Ixlú, is a quiet, friendly village and, if you intend to spend more than a day at Tikal, a convenient place to base yourself; the accommodation here is cheaper and better value than at the site itself and all minibuses to and from Tikal pass through the village. At the time of writing there was no permanent electricity supply and no telephones in El Remate, but the villagers may have both by the time you read this. Further west along the lakeshore, the road passes the **Biotopo Cerro Cahuí** – a 6.5 square kilometre wildlife conservation area with lakeshore, ponds and Maya ruins in undisturbed tropical forest – en route to the village of Jobompiche.

Accommodation in El Remate

In the absence of exact addresses, the **accommodation** below is listed in the order in which you approach it from the village of Puente Ixlú: minibuses will stop outside any, but you'll have to pay extra for the last place. Beyond *La Casa de Don David*, the route follows the road round the northern shore of the lake to the village of Jobompiche.

El Mirador del Duende, on the right of the road, high above the lake and reached by a stairway cut into the cliff. An incredible collection of whitewashed, stucco cabañas that look like igloos decorated with Maya glyphs. Manuel Soto, the owner, is an expert on jungle lore, and leads hikes to all of Petén's archeological sites. The restaurant serves vegetarian food and offers great views over the lake, especially at sunset. ①.

La Mansión del Pajaro Serpiente, just beyond *El Mirador del Duende* (☎ & fax 926-0065). Set in a tropical garden, the stone-built, thatched, two-storey cabañas provide the most comfortable accommodation in the area. Each has a living room, bedroom, immaculate bathroom and superb lake views. When available, the smaller cabañas, usually used by tour guides or drivers, are just as comfortable and around half the price. ④–⑥.

La Casa de Don David, at the junction with the road to the *biotopo* Cerro Cahuí, 300m beyond *La Mansión*. Probably the most atmospheric place in El Remate: comfortable wooden bungalows and rooms, most with private bathroom; hot water and some lighting is supplied by solar power. Owners David and Rosa Kuhn offer great hospitality and wonderful home cooking. David is a mine of information about Petén and will pick you up from Puente Ixlú if you ask (send a message with one of the village children on a bike). ②.

Casa Mobego, 500m past Don David's, down the road from El Remate to Cerro Cahuí, on the right. A good budget deal and right by the lake: the simple, well-constructed stick and thatch cabañas have great lake views and there's a good, inexpensive restaurant. ①.

El Gringo Perdido, 3km down the road to Cerro Cahuí. A long-established place in a supremely tranquil lakeshore and forest setting, offering rooms with a mosquito-netted bunk-bed and bath, as well as some basic cabañas, camping, and a fine restaurant. Rooms ④, cabañas ②, camping ①.

Tikal

Immediately north of El Remate the road climbs a limestone escarpment, and though most peoples' minds are fixed on the mighty ruins of **Tikal**, only 30km ahead, a quick glance behind will reward you with superb views of the lake. The landscape becomes more undulating and the settlements begin to thin out as you approach the entrance (about halfway to the site itself) to **Tikal National Park**, a protected area of some 370 square kilometres. At the barrier, you pay a Q50 **entrance fee** (in theory payable every day you stay at the site, but not strictly enforced). If you arrive after dusk you will automatically be issued with a ticket for the next day. Beyond the barrier lies the forest, its damp air filled with the screeches of birds and noises of insects.

The sheer scale of Tikal as it rises above the forest canopy is overwhelming, and the atmosphere spellbinding. Dominating the ruins are the five enormous **temples**: steep-sided pyramids that rise up to 60m from the forest floor, and around which lie literally thousands of other structures, many still hidden beneath mounds of earth. The ruins are open from 6am to 6pm; extensions to 8pm can be obtained from the *inspectoría* (7am–noon & 2–5pm), a small white hut to the left of the entrance to the ruins.

Getting there

Coming by bus **from the Belize border** you need to change at Puente Ixlú (see p.149) look for the *Zac Petén* restaurant on the left. Local buses to Socotzal, a village along the road to Tikal, and to Jobompiche, will take you to **El Remate**, from where any passing minibus will take you to Tikal for around Q10. **From Santa Elena**, the daily Pinita bus to Tikal leaves from the marketplace at 1pm, passing through El Remate about an hour later and continuing to Tikal (Q7; 2hr from El Remate) and Uaxactún, 24km north of Tikal. For El Remate, local buses leave from the market every couple of hours from 6am. **From Flores** (see p.156) any hotel or travel agent will arrange transport in one of the fleet of minibuses leaving hourly from 4am to early afternoon; tickets cost Q30 return. Linea Dorada has a luxury bus to Tikal at 7am. El Remate is also served by minibuses that go direct to Tikal **from the airport**, connecting with flights from Belize City. **Car rental** is also available from the airport or from Santa Elena (see "Listings" p.159).

Leaving Tikal is simple: minibuses run back to El Remate or Flores (all day when full; Q10–15) and, if you're heading in the other direction, the daily bus from Santa Elena to Uaxactún (where there are a couple of hotels) passes through the site at about 3pm; returning from Uaxctún to Santa Elena at 6am, passing Tikal around 7am.

Visiting the site: information, accommodation and facilities

At the entrance to the ruins is a **visitor centre** with the standard overpriced café and gift shop. The highlight here though is the **scale model of Tikal** and the **lithic museum** (daily 9am–4pm; entry included in site ticket), containing a selection of the finest stelae and carvings from the site. Also at the entrance is a **post office** and a few shops. The best guide to the site is William R. Coe's *Tikal, A Handbook to the Ancient Maya Ruins*, while *The Birds of Tikal* is useful for identifying some of the hundreds of species you might come across as you wander round.

Should you want to stay, there are three **hotels** (all with restaurants) at the entrance, but they're fairly expensive and not especially good value, though you can often get discounts out of season. The *Jaguar Inn* (☎926-0002) has rooms (⑤) or camping (①; rents tents or hammocks), the *Tikal Inn* (☎ & fax 926-0065; ⑤) has thatched bungalows, pleasant rooms and a pool, but, for those with more money to spend, the *Jungle Lodge* is the largest and most luxurious option, with a pool, bungalow accommodation (⑥) and some "budget" rooms (③), although the latter are often full (reservations can be made from a travel agent in Belize). Finally, for a $6 fee you can **camp** or sling a **hammock** under one of the thatched shelters in the cleared space used as a campsite across from the entrance. Hammocks and mosquito nets can be rented either on the spot or from the *Comedor Imperio Maya* at the entrance. There's a shower block at the entrance to the campsite, but the water supply is sporadic and electricity is only available from 6pm to 9.30pm.

There are three simple **comedores** at the entrance; all offer a limited menu of traditional Guatemalan specialities – eggs, beans and grilled meat and chicken, and a few "tourist" dishes. For longer (and pricier) menus, try the hotel restaurants. During the day cold drinks (*refrescos*) are sold from numerous spots around the ruins, though it's always a good idea to bring some water.

The Sylvanus G. Morely Museum

At the entrance, between the *Jungle Lodge* and *Jaguar Inn* hotels, is the one-room **Sylvanus G. Morely Museum** (Mon–Fri 9am–5pm, Sat & Sun 9am–4pm; $2), named after the great Maya scholar who recorded many of the inscriptions at Tikal. It houses some of the stelae found here, including the remains of **Stela 29**, one of the oldest pieces of carving found at Tikal (dating from 292 AD), and many artefacts, including tools, jewellery, pottery, obsidian and jade. There's a spectacular **reconstruction of Ah Cacaw's tomb**, one of the richest ever found in the Maya world, containing 180 worked jade items in the form of bracelets, anklets, necklaces and earplugs, and delicately incised bones, including the famous carving depicting deities paddling canoes bearing the dead to the underworld. Also on display are beautiful polychrome ceramics from the burial.

Some history: the rise and fall of Tikal

According to archeological evidence, the first occupants of Tikal arrived around 700 BC, though there's nothing to suggest that it was a particularly large settlement at this time. The earliest definite evidence of buildings dates from 500 BC, and by about 200 BC ceremonial structures had emerged, including the first version of the **North Acropolis**. Two hundred years later the **Great Plaza** had begun to take shape and Tikal was already established as a major site with a large permanent population. For the next two centuries art and architecture became increasingly ornate and sophisticated, though Tikal remained a secondary centre, dominated by **El Mirador**, a massive city about 65km to the north.

The closing years of the **Preclassic** (250–300 AD) saw trade routes disrupted and alliance patterns altered, culminating in the decline and abandonment of El Mirador. In the resulting power vacuum the two sites of **Tikal** and **Uaxactún** emerged as substantial centres of trade, science and religion. Less than a day's

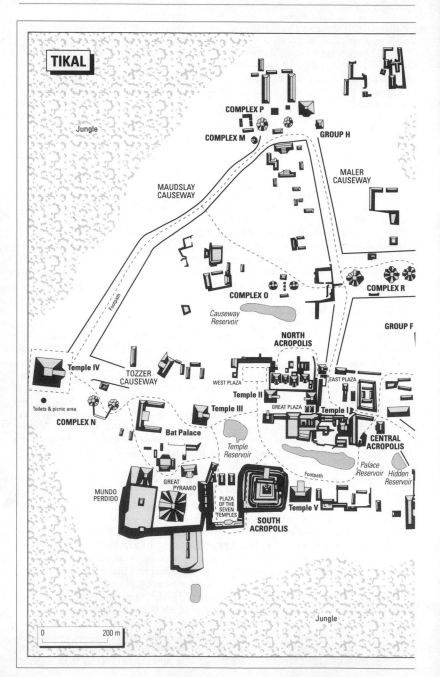

TIKAL

Jungle

COMPLEX P

COMPLEX M

GROUP H

MAUDSLAY
CAUSEWAY

MALER
CAUSEWAY

Footpath

COMPLEX O

COMPLEX R

Causeway
Reservoir

GROUP F

Temple IV

NORTH
ACROPOLIS

TOZZER
CAUSEWAY

WEST PLAZA

EAST PLAZA

Toilets & picnic area

Temple II

Temple III

GREAT PLAZA

Temple I

COMPLEX N

Bat Palace

CENTRAL
ACROPOLIS

Temple
Reservoir

Palace
Reservoir

Hidden
Reservoir

Footpath

MUNDO
PERDIDO

GREAT
PYRAMID

PLAZA
OF THE
SEVEN
TEMPLES

Temple V

SOUTH
ACROPOLIS

Jungle

0   200 m

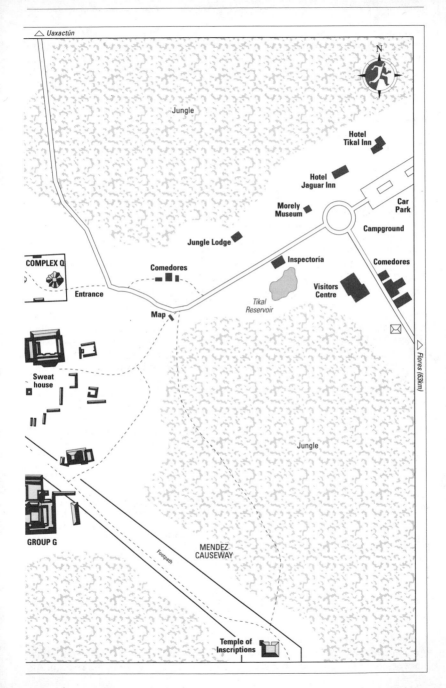

walk apart, the growing cities engaged in a heated competition which could have only one winner. Matters finally came to a head in 378 AD, when, under the inspired leadership of Great Jaguar Paw, Tikal's warriors overran Uaxactún, enabling Tikal's rulers to dominate central Petén for much of the next five hundred years.

This extended period of prosperity saw the city's population grow to somewhere between 50,000 and 100,000, expanding to cover an area of around thirty square kilometres. Crucial to this success were Tikal's alliances with the powerful cities of Kaminaljuyú (near present-day Guatemala City) and Teotihuacán (to the north of modern Mexico City); stelae and paintings from the period show that Tikal's elite adopted Teotihuacán styles of clothing, pottery and weaponry. In the middle of the sixth century, however, Tikal suffered a huge setback. Already weakened by upheavals in Mexico, where Teotihuacán was in decline, the city now faced a major challenge from the east, where the city of **Caracol** (p.141) was emerging as a . major regional power. Caracol's ambitious leader, **Lord Water**, launched his first attack on Tikal in April 556 AD, but failed to take the city; a year later he was back, this time managing to assume control and subdue Tikal's powerful elite. For the next 140 years Tikal was overshadowed by the new power of Caracol.

By the middle of the seventh century, however, Caracol's stranglehold had begun to relax and Tikal embarked upon a dramatic renaissance under the formidable leadership of **Ah Cacaw**, Lord Chocolate. During his dynamic reign the main ceremonial areas were reclaimed from the desecration suffered at the hands of Caracol, and Tikal regained its position among the most important of Petén cities. Ah Cacaw's leadership gave birth to a revitalized and powerful ruling dynasty; in the hundred years following his death, Tikal's five main temples were built, and Ah Cacaw's son, **Yax Kin Caan Chac** (who ascended the throne in 734 AD) had his father's body entombed in the magnificent **Temple I**. Temples and monuments were still under construction at Tikal as late as 889 AD.

What brought about Tikal's final **downfall** remains a mystery, but what is certain is that around 900 AD almost the entire lowland Maya civilization collapsed, and that by the end of the tenth century Tikal had been abandoned. Afterwards, the site was used from time to time by other groups, who worshipped here and repositioned many of the stelae, but it was never occupied again.

The site

The size of the ruins at Tikal can at first seem daunting. But even if you only make it to the main plaza, and spend an hour relaxing on top of a temple, you won't be disappointed. The **central area**, with its five main temples, forms by far the most impressive section; if you start to explore beyond this you can wander seemingly forever into the maze of smaller structures and outlying complexes. Outside the main area are countless smaller **unrestored structures**, and though they pale beside the scale and magnificence of the main temples, if you're armed with a good map (the best is in Coe's guide to the ruins, available from the gift shop), it can be exciting to explore some of these rarely visited sections. Tikal is certain to exhaust you before you exhaust it.

From the entrance to the Great Plaza
As you walk into the ruins, the first structures that you come to are the rather unevocatively named **Complex Q** and **Complex R**. Dating from the reign of Ah

Cacaw, these are two of the seven sets of twin pyramids built to mark the passing of each *katun* (a period of twenty 360-day years). Only one of the pyramids (in Complex Q) is restored, with the stelae and altars re-erected in front of it. The carvings on the copy of **Stela 22** (the original is in the visitor centre), in the small enclosure set to one side, record the ascension to the throne in 768 AD of Tikal's last known ruler, **Chitam**, portrayed in full regalia, complete with enormous sweeping headdress and staff of authority.

Following the path as it bears around to the left, you approach the back of Temple I, from where it's a few short steps to the **Great Plaza**, the heart of the ancient city. Surrounded by four massive structures, this was the focus of ceremonial activity at Tikal for around a thousand years. The recently restored **Temple I**, towering 44m above the plaza, is the hallmark of Tikal; its other name – the Jaguar Temple – derives from the jaguar carved in its door lintel, though this is now in a museum in Basel. The temple was built as a burial monument to contain the magnificent **tomb of Ah Cacaw** (see opposite), one of Tikal's most powerful rulers, who ascended the throne in 682 AD. Within the tomb (a reconstruction of which is in the Morely museum, see p.151) at the temple's core, the skeleton was found facing north, surrounded by an assortment of jade, pearls, seashells and stingray spines; the latter were a traditional symbol of human sacrifice. Some magnificent pottery was also discovered here, depicting a journey to the underworld made in a canoe rowed by mythical animal figures. The steep pyramid is topped by a three-room building and a hollow roof comb that was originally brightly painted. Unfortunately the stairway on Temple I is roped off, though it may be reopened in the future.

Standing opposite, like a squat version of Temple I, **Temple II** stands 38m high, although when its roof comb was intact it would have been the same height as Temple I. It's a fairly easy climb to the top, and the view, almost level with the forest canopy, is incredible, with the great plaza spread out below. As an added bonus, you'll almost certainly see toucans in the nearby branches.

The North Acropolis, the Central Acropolis and Temple V

The **North Acropolis**, which fills the whole north side of the plaza, is one of the most complex structures in the entire Maya world. In traditional Maya style it was built and rebuilt on top of itself; beneath the twelve temples that can be seen today are the remains of about a hundred other structures, some of which, including two four-metre-high **masks**, have been uncovered by archeologists. One of the masks, facing the plaza and protected by a thatched roof, is clearly visible; the other can be reached by following the dark passageway to the side – you'll need a torch. In front of the North Acropolis are two lines of **stelae** carved with images of Tikal's ruling elite, with circular altars at their bases. These and many stelae throughout the site bear the marks of **ritual defacement**, carried out when one ruler replaced another to erase any latent powers that the image may have retained.

On the other side of the plaza, the **Central Acropolis** is a maze of tiny interconnecting rooms and stairways built around six smallish courtyards. The buildings here are usually referred to as palaces rather than temples, although their precise use remains a mystery. The large two-storey building in Court 2 is known as **Maler's Palace**, named after the archeologist Teobert Maler who made it his home during expeditions in 1895 and 1904. Further behind the Central Acropolis, **Temple V**, thought to be a mortuary shrine to an unknown ruler, is 58m high and supports a single tiny room. The temple is currently undergoing a huge restoration project, partly financed by Spain; work is expected to be completed by the year 2000 when the view from the top should be superb, offering a great profile of Temple I and the whole of the Great Plaza.

From the West Plaza to Temple IV

The **West Plaza**, behind Temple II, is dominated by a large Late Classic temple on the north side, and scattered with various altars and stelae. From here the **Tozzer Causeway** – one of the raised routes that connected the main parts of the city – leads west to **Temple III**, covered in jungle vegetation. Around the back of the temple is a huge palace complex, of which only the **Bat Palace** has been restored, while further down the causeway, on the left-hand side, is **Complex N**, another set of twin pyramids. In the northern enclosure of the complex, the superbly carved **Stela 16** shows the ruler Ah Cacaw.

Looming at the end of the Tozzer Causeway, the massive **Temple IV**, at 64m, is the tallest of all the Tikal structures. Built in 741 AD, it is thought by some archeologists to be the resting place of the ruler **Caan Chac**, whose image was depicted on wooden lintels built into the top of the temple. To reach the top you have to scramble up ladders, over roots and rocks, and finally up a metal ladder around the side of the pyramid. Slow and exhausting as this is, it's always worth it, offering one of the finest views of the whole site. All around you the green carpet of the canopy stretches out to the horizon, interrupted only by the great roof combs of the other temples. At any time this view is enthralling – at sunset or sunrise it's unbeatable.

The Plaza of the Seven Temples and the Mundo Perdido

The other main buildings in the centre of Tikal lie to the south of the Central Acropolis. Here, reached by a trail from Temple III, you'll find the **Plaza of the Seven Temples**, which forms part of a complex dating back to before Christ. There's an unusual triple ball-court on the north side of the plaza, and to the east, the unexcavated South Acropolis. Finally, to the west of here is the **Mundo Perdido**, or Lost World, another magical and very distinct section of the site with its own atmosphere and architecture. The main feature, the **Great Pyramid**, is a 32-metre-high structure whose surface conceals four earlier versions, the first dating from 700 BC. From the top of the pyramid you get awesome views towards Temple IV and the Great Plaza and it's another excellent place to watch the dramatic sunrise or sunset.

Flores and Santa Elena

Although it's the capital of Petén, **FLORES** is an easy-going, sedate place with an old-fashioned atmosphere – quite different from the rough, bustling commercialism of other towns in Petén. A cluster of cobbled streets and ageing houses built around a twin-domed church, it sits beautifully on a small island in Lake Petén Itzá, connected to the mainland by a causeway; even if you're heading back to Belize, it's worth making the small detour on the way back from Tikal.

The **lake** is a natural choice for settlement and its shores were heavily populated in Maya times. **Tayasal**, capital of the Itzá, on the island that was to become modern Flores, was the last independent Maya town to be succumb to Spanish rule – conquered and destroyed in 1697. For the entire colonial period (and indeed up to the 1960s) Flores languished in virtual isolation, having more contact with neighbouring Belize than the capital. The modern emphasis lies across the water in the ugly, sprawling twin towns of **Santa Elena** and **San Benito**: Santa Elena, opposite Flores at the other end of the causeway, strung out between

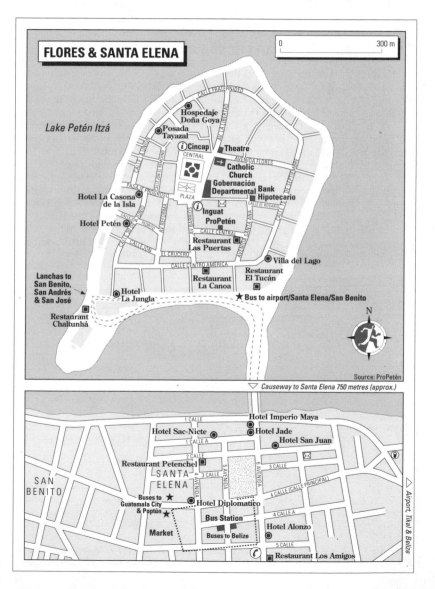

FLORES & SANTA ELENA

0   300 m

Lake Petén Itzá

CALLE FRATERNIDAD

Hospedaje
Doña Goya
Posada
Tayazal
(i) Cincap
CENTRAL
Theatre
AVENIDA FLORES
Catholic
Church
Gobernación
Departmental
Bank
Hipotecario
Hotel La Casona
de la Isla
PLAZA
(i) Inguat
ProPetén
Hotel Petén
CALLE CENTRAL
Restaurant
Las Puertas
EL CRUCERO
CALLE CENTRO AMERICA
Villa del Lago
Restaurant
El Tucán
Lanchas to
San Benito,
San Andrés
& San José
Restaurant
La Canoa
Hotel
La Jungla
★ Bus to airport/Santa Elena/San Benito
Restaurant
Chaltunhá

N

Source: ProPetén

▽ Causeway to Santa Elena 750 metres (approx.)

SAN
BENITO

1 CALLE
Hotel Imperio Maya
Hotel Sac-Nicte
Hotel Jade
1 CALLE A
Hotel San Juan
2 CALLE
Restaurant Petenchel
3 CALLE
SANTA
ELENA
Buses to
Guatemala City
& Poptún
Hotel Diplomatico
Bus Station
Market
Buses to Belize
Hotel Alonzo
5 CALLE
Restaurant Los Amigos

△ Airport, Tikal & Belize

the airport and the market, has banks, hotels and buses; you won't need to venture into the chaotic mire of San Benito.

Today, despite the steady flow of tourists passing through for Tikal (the capital's main business), Flores retains a genteel air, with residents greeting one another courteously as they meet in the streets, and it offers pleasant surroundings in which to stay, eat and drink. And if you're not going to the Guatemalan highlands but want to buy *típica* clothing and **gifts**, you'll find shops here have better prices than at Tikal.

Arrival, information and accommodation

Arriving by bus or minibus from Belize or Tikal, you'll be dropped on or near Calle Principal (4 Calle) in Santa Elena, just a few blocks from the causeway to Flores. The **airport** is 3km east of the causeway; **local buses** (*urbanos*) make the trip into town for Q1, but as this entails a time-consuming change halfway, it's easier to take a taxi ($2). *Urbanos* run across the causeway into Flores about every ten minutes; they'll stop anywhere along the route. *Urbanos* to the airport leave from the Flores end of the causeway about every twenty minutes.

Inguat has an **information booth** at the airport, and another office on the central plaza in Flores (Mon–Fri 8am–4pm; ☎926-0669), whose staff, while helpful, will probably direct you across the plaza to **CINCAP** (Centro de Información sobre la Naturaleza, Cultura y Artesanías de Petén; Tues–Sat 9am–1pm & 2–8pm, Sun 2–6pm), to examine their more detailed maps, books and leaflets about northern Petén. If you're planning a trip to the more remote parts of the Maya Biosphere Reserve check with **ProPetén** on C Central (Mon–Fri 8am–5pm) for current information on routes and guides.

Accommodation

Flores/Santa Elena has undergone an accommodation boom in recent years and the sheer number of new **hotels** keeps prices very competitive. There are several good budget places in Flores itself, so you won't really need to stay in Santa Elena unless you have a really early bus to catch – and even then you can arrange a taxi. All the top-range hotels listed below take **credit cards**.

FLORES

Hotel la Casona de la Isla (☎926-0692, fax 926-0593). Attractive, modern rooms with private bath and a/c. Also has a swimming pool and spectacular sunset views from the terrace restaurant/bar. ⑤.

Hospedaje Doña Goya (no ☎). Friendly, family-run budget guest house, offering clean, well-lit rooms, some with private bath and balcony, and the best prices on the island for single rooms. ①.

Hotel La Jungla (☎926-0634). The best value in this price range, with gleaming tiled floors and private baths with hot water. Also has a good restaurant. ②.

Hotel Petén (☎926-0593; fax 926-0692). Friendly, small, modern hotel, run by the ever-helpful Pedro Castellanos. Though the rooms are a shade overpriced they all come with fans, private bath and lake views. ④.

Posada Tayazal (☎ & fax 926-0568). Good budget hotel, with decent rooms, some with private baths; best budget option if *Doña Goya* is full. ①.

Villa del Lago (☎ 926-0629). Modern, two-storey building with pretty, comfortable rooms. The small breakfast terrace at the rear is a great place to enjoy the sunrise. ②.

SANTA ELENA

Hotel Alonzo, 6 Ave 4–99 (☎926-0105). Reasonable budget rooms, some with balconies and a few with private bathrooms (the communal bathroom is distinctly grubby). Also a restaurant and a public telephone. ①.

Hotel Imperio Maya, 6 Ave & 1 C. Cleanish, street-level rooms with fan, right by the causeway to Flores. ①.

Hotel Jade, 6 Ave. A shambolic, backpackers' stronghold near the causeway, but with the cheapest beds in town. ①.

Hotel Sac-Nicte, 1 C A 4–45 (☎ & fax 926-0092). Clean rooms with fans and private shower; those on the second floor have views of the lake. ②.

Hotel San Juan, 2 C (☎ & fax 926-0042). Doubles as the Pinita bus terminal and organizes trips to Tikal, but it's not particularly good value, and is distinctly unfriendly. Most guests are captives straight off the Pinita bus; head elsewhere if you can. ①–②.

Eating and drinking

Good, cheap places **to eat** are in short supply in Santa Elena and Flores, although a few places do cater specifically to tourists. The ones below represent just a small selection of the longer-established places.

Flores

La Canoa, C Centro America. Popular, good-value place, serving pasta, great soups and some vegetarian and Guatemalan food, as well as excellent breakfasts.

Chaltunhá, opposite *Hotel Santana*, right on the water. Great spot for lunch, snacks and sandwiches, and not too expensive.

Las Puertas, signposted off C Santa Ana. Paint-splattered walls, live music and some very good pasta and healthy breakfasts. Worth it for the atmosphere.

El Tucán, a few metres east of the causeway, on the waterfront. Excellent fish, enormous chef's salads, very good Mexican food and the best waterside terrace in Flores.

Santa Elena

Restaurant los Amigos, 6 Ave, opposite Telgua. Santa Elena's best restaurant, with a fairly extensive menu that also caters for vegetarians.

Restaurant Leo Fu Lo, next door to the *Hotel Jade*. Delicious, but expensive Chinese food.

Restaurant Petenchel, 2 C, beyond *Hotel San Juan*, past the park. Simple, good food: the nicest place to eat around the main street. You can leave your luggage here while checking on buses or looking for a room.

Listings

Banks Banks in Flores will only change travellers' cheques; for cash exchange and advances you'll need to go to one of the banks along Calle Principal in Santa Elena. The best place to change cash is Banoro (Mon–Sat 8.30am–8pm); for credit/debit card cash advances use Banco Industrial (24-hour ATM), for Visa, and Banco G&T for Mastercard (less good ATM).

Car rental Budget, Hertz, San Juan and Koka operate from the airport, and there are some offices in Santa Elena; rates start around US$65 per day.

Communications You can phone and send faxes from the Telgua office, on 5 C in Santa Elena, but you're better off using one of the many private telephone and fax services: in Santa Elena try the *Hotel Alonzo*; in Flores there's Cahuí, 30 de Junio (daily 7am–7pm; ☎ & fax 926-0494), which is also a good place to leave messages and pick up information, or Martsam Travel (see "Travel agent" below), a few doors away – both usually have someone who speaks a little English. There are two places in Flores from where you can send email: *C@fénet* on Ave Barrios (daily 9am–9pm), and Arpa on C Centro America. Make sure you actually see the messages sent, as there have been instances of email not getting through.

Laundry Lavandería Amelia, behind CINCAP in Flores, or Petenchel on C Centro America (both Q18 to wash and dry).

Post office In Flores, the post office is two doors away from the Inguat office; in Santa Elena it's two blocks east of the *Hotel San Juan* (both Mon–Fri 8am–4.30pm).

Doctor Centro Medico Maya, 4 Ave near 3 Calle in Santa Elena, down the street by the *Hotel Diplomatico* (☎926-0180), is helpful and professional, though no English is spoken.

Travel agent The most helpful is Martsam Travel (☎ & fax 926-0493, email *martsam@guate.net*) at the western end of C Centro America in Flores; they sell flights, tours and tickets to Belize.

MOVING ON FROM FLORES

Buses to **Melchor de Mencos** (for the Belize border; 3hr) leave from the marketplace in Santa Elena: Pinita at 5am, 8am, and 11am; Rosita at 5am, 7am, 9.30am, 11am, 2pm, 3pm and 6pm. Linea Dorada, C Principal in Santa Elena (☎926-0070) runs a daily luxury bus **to Belize City** at 5am (5hr; US$20), which continues on to the Mexican border at Chetumal (8hr; US$30) and connects with another service up the coast to **Cancún**.

All the Guatemala City **bus companies** have offices on C Principal in Santa Elena, and there are more than twenty departures daily to the capital. Linea Dorada (daily 7.30pm) is the best.

Tickets for **flights** to Belize City (at least 2 morning and 2 afternoon daily) and Guatemala City (at least 8 daily) can be bought at the airport or at any travel agent in Santa Elena and Flores. Other flights include Aviateca to Cancún (daily at 5pm) and Aerocaribe to Cancún via Chetumal (Mon–Fri at 5.30pm).

CHAPTER SIX

THE SOUTH

To the south of Belmopan Belize is at its wildest. Here the central area is dominated by the Maya Mountains, which slope down towards the coast through a series of forested ridges and valleys carved by sparkling rivers. As you head further south the climate becomes more humid, promoting the growth of dense **rainforest**, rich in wildlife. The forests here have evolved to cope with periodic hurricanes sweeping in from the Caribbean and have in the

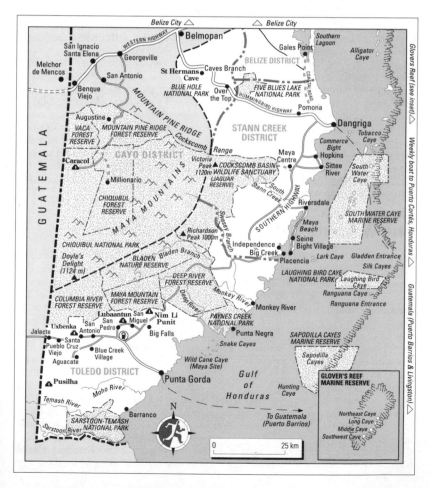

past been selectively logged for mahogany. Among the broadleaf forests there are also large stands of Caribbean pine, looking strangely out of place in the tropics. The **coastal strip** south of Belize City is a band of savannah, swamp and lagoon, while beyond Dangriga the shoreline is composed of sandy bays, peninsulas and mangrove lagoons. In the far south the estuaries of the slow-moving Temash and Sarstoon rivers, lined with the tallest **mangrove forest** in Belize, form the country's southernmost national park, adjoining protected land in Guatemala.

Population density in this part of Belize is low, with most of the towns and villages located on the coast. **Dangriga**, the largest settlement, is home of the **Garífuna** people – descended from Carib Indians and shipwrecked, enslaved Africans (see box on pp.170–1) – and allows access to a number of idyllic cayes, such as Tobacco Caye and South Water Caye, sitting right on top of the barrier reef and the focus of a large new **Marine Reserve**. The villages of **Gales Point**, on Southern Lagoon, north of Dangriga, and **Hopkins**, on the coast to the south, are worth visiting to experience their tranquil way of life. Further south, the **Placencia peninsula** has become established as the focus of coastal tourism in southern Belize; from here you can visit the **Laughing Bird Caye National Park** and the stunning **Silk Cayes** lying beyond, just inside the reef.

Inland, the Maya Mountains remain unpenetrated by roads, forming a solid barrier to land travel except on foot or horseback. The Belize government, showing supreme foresight, has placed practically all of the mountain massif under some form of legal protection, whether as national park, nature reserve, wildlife sanctuary or forest reserve. The most accessible area of this rainforest, though still little visited by tourists, is the **Cockscomb Basin Wildlife Sanctuary**, a reserve designed to protect the sizeable jaguar population and a good base for exploring the forest. You'll come across plenty of tracks – but don't count on seeing a jaguar. The Southern Highway comes to an end in **Punta Gorda**, a final outpost, from where you can head south to Guatemala or visit Maya villages and ruins in the southern foothills of the Maya Mountains.

The Manatee Road and Gales Point

To head south from Belize City you first need to go west; either to Belmopan for the Hummingbird Highway (see p.164), or to the start of the **Manatee (or Coastal) Road shortcut to Dangriga**. The unpaved Manatee Road heads southeast from Mile 30 on the Western Highway, skirting the village of **La Democracia** and reaching the Hummingbird Highway at Melinda, 15km from Dangriga. The road is usually in good condition and is served by five buses a day (Z-Line and Ritchie's) on the Belize City/Dangriga route. Along the way the scenery is typical of southern Belize: citrus plantations, pine ridges and steep limestone hills covered in broadleaf forest. There is also a route south **by boat** which takes you along some amazing **inland waterways**, travelling upstream on the Haulover Creek, then along the Burdon Canal, across the Sibun River and through **Northern and Southern Lagoons**, though since the completion of the road few villagers use this route. It is, however, used by some tour groups and if you get a chance to travel this way to Gales Point you should take it.

Much of this rich wetland area is protected as part of the **Burdon Canal Nature Reserve**, and the lagoons are such an essential breeding ground for rare wildlife, including jabiru storks, turtles, manatee and crocodiles, that the government has established the **Manatee Special Development Area** to encourage sensitive conservation-oriented development. The area is bounded on the west by the limestone Peccary Hills, riddled with caves, and the shores of the lagoons are cloaked with mangroves.

Gales Point

If you want to explore this little-visited area, the tranquil Creole village of **GALES POINT**, straggling along a narrow peninsula jutting into the Southern Lagoon, is the ideal place to begin. Buses along the Manatee Road pass the junction to Gales Point, 4km from the village itself; some buses go all the way into the village, others are usually met by a van to take passengers in – check first if you don't fancy the walk. As the peninsula is only about 20m wide this side road is the only "street" and you'll see several signs pointing to houses offering simple bed and breakfast **accommodation** (③); to book ahead call the community telephone on ☎021/2031. *Gentle's Cool Spot*, a small bar and restaurant at the point where the buses turn around also has a few simple, clean rooms (②), and recently a couple of basic **campsites** have opened – *Metho's Camping* has space in a sandy spot for Bz$5 per person. The most luxurious accommodation is *Manatee Lodge* (☎08/23320, fax 23334, in US ☎1-800/334-7942; ⑨, includes dinner, breakfast, service charge and tax), a two-storey, colonial-style building set in lush lawns lined with coconut trees in a beautiful location right at the tip of the peninsula. The rooms (all non-smoking) are spacious and comfortable and the meals are superb. On the upper floor a wooden deck offers great views at sunrise and sunset. Guests have use of canoes and small sailboats to enjoy the lagoon.

Scenery and wildlife are the big attractions here: the lagoon system is the largest manatee breeding ground in the entire Caribbean basin, and Belize's main nesting beaches of the endangered **hawksbill turtle** lie either side of the mouth of the Manatee River. The villagers have formed the Gales Post Progressive Cooperative to protect their wildlife and encourage tourists to visit. With help from international conservation organizations and volunteers they guard the turtle nesting beaches and have installed signs and buoys warning boatmen to slow down to avoid harming the manatees. Renting a dory (traditionally a dugout canoe) for about Bz$10–15 per day allows you to explore the waterways, or you can take a trip with Moses Andrewin, an expert local **guide**. Gales Point is also a centre of **traditional drum-making**; you can learn to make and play drums at Emett Young's Creole Drum School. Emett often performs elsewhere so it's best to check ahead (call the community phone) to see if he's at home. You'll also learn a lot about local history and culture – made even more enjoyable while sipping the home-produced cashew wine in the evenings.

The Hummingbird Highway

After recent re-surfacing work, the **Hummingbird Highway**, heading southeast from Belmopan to Dangriga, is one of the best roads in Belize. Before the road was built in 1954 travel to Dangriga and points south was by sea. The scenery is magnificent as the road heads steadily over the hills through lush forest with the eastern slopes of the **Maya Mountains**, coated in greenery, rising to the right. Until recently, much of this forest was untouched, but here and there Salvadoran or Guatemalan refugees have hacked down a swathe of jungle to plant maize and beans, and you're rarely out of sight of citrus plantations. The hills form part of a ridge of limestone mountains, riddled with underground rivers and caves. About 19km out of Belmopan the road crosses the **Caves Branch River**, a tributary of the Sibun River. The upper reaches of this and other nearby valleys hold some of Belize's finest **caves**. Further on, just past the highest point on the road is the stunningly beautiful **Five Blues Lake National Park**; beyond here the road follows the Stann Creek valley, lined with citrus groves, virtually all the way to Dangriga.

St Herman's Cave and the Blue Hole National Park

Just beyond the Caves Branch River, by the roadside on the right, is **St Herman's Cave** (daily 8am–4pm; Bz$8, valid also for the Blue Hole), one of the most accessible caves in Belize. Any bus between Belmopan and Dangriga will drop you at the cave or the Blue Hole, making an easy day-trip (the wardens know the times of onward buses), but to really appreciate the mysteries of caving in Belize you need to stay nearby, preferably at the *Caves Branch Jungle Lodge* (see below).

You pay the entrance fee at the new **visitor centre**, then follow the marked trail for ten minutes to the cave entrance, squashed beneath a dripping rock face. To enter, down steps that were originally cut by the Maya, you'll need a flashlight. Inside, you clamber over the rocks and splash through the river for about twenty minutes, admiring the stunning formations, before the cave appears to end. To continue beyond, and emerge from one of the other entrances, you need to go on a tour – one of the best is organized by Pete Zubrzycki of *PACZ Hotel* in San Ignacio (see p.129). A new **interpretive trail**, with a spectacular observation platform, leads over the cave for 4km to a **campsite**; for details enquire at the visitor centre or at the BAS, who manage the park (☎02/34988).

Another signed trail leads 3km from the cave, over the ridge, to the **Blue Hole National Park**, which you can also reach by continuing along the highway for 2km. The Blue Hole is actually a short but deep stretch of underground river – *cenote* in Mayan – whose course is revealed by the collapse of a karst cavern, flowing on the surface for about 50m before disappearing beneath another rock face. Its cool, fresh turquoise waters, surrounded by dense forest and overhung with vines, mosses and ferns are perfect for a refreshing dip.

THE CAVES BRANCH JUNGLE LODGE
The best place **to stay** near the Blue Hole (and indeed along the whole Hummingbird Highway) is *Caves Branch Jungle Lodge* (☎ & fax 08/22800, email

caves@pobox.com), halfway between St Herman's Cave and the Blue Hole and about 1km from the road; it's easily accessible and signed from the highway. The lodge is set in a huge area of superb, high canopy forest on the banks of the beautiful Caves Branch River and offers a range of comfortable, rustic accommodation to suit all budgets. The highlights are the spacious, screened cabaña suites, with a king-size bed, private bathroom with hot shower and a living room with wicker furniture (⑧); there are great private cabañas too (⑥). For budget travellers even the bunkhouse (Bz\$30 per person) has flush toilets and showers, and finally there's camping and hammock space (Bz\$10); all prices include tax , and there's no service charge. Delicious and filling meals, served buffet-style, are eaten together in a simple dining room. Try to plan at least two nights here; even if you don't take any of the trips on offer, one day just won't seem long enough.

Caves Branch is run by Canadian Ian Anderson, who, together with the expert local guides, leads truly amazing **guided tours** through some of the area's most spectacular **caves** and along crystal-clear rivers running through the limestone hills. All the caves contain Maya artefacts – ceramics, carvings and the like – with abundant evidence of Classic period ceremonies. Some caves are dry, and you must take great care not to touch the glittering crystal formations as you climb over rocks and around stalagmites. **Rafting trips** on the Sibun River, both by day and night, takes you silently through the forest, or you can float on **inner tubes** 9km along a subterranean river, your headlamp piercing the intense darkness. The guides here are experts in natural history, and also lead more challenging **overnight ruins and wildlife treks** in the forest, including a four-day "Jungle Quest" survival course. The cave and river trips are not cheap (on average about US\$65 per person) but well worth it, as the guest book entries testify.

Over the Top and Five Blues Lake National Park

Beyond the Blue Hole the Hummingbird Highway is well paved, undulating smoothly through the increasingly hilly landscape, eventually crossing a low pass. This is the highest point on the road, and the downhill slope is appropriately, if unimaginatively, called **Over the Top**. On the way down, the road passes through **St Margaret's Village**, where a women's cooperative arranges bed and breakfast **accommodation** in private houses (☎081/2005; ③).

A few kilometres past the village, the *Over the Top Restaurant* stands on a hill at Mile 32, overlooking the junction of the track to **Five Blues Lake National Park**, seventeen square kilometres of luxuriantly forested karst scenery, centred around a beautiful lake. Named for its constantly changing colours, the lake is another *cenote* or "blue hole", caused by a cavern's collapse. Register at the office by the road junction, where you can arrange a guide; if this is closed ask at *Over the Top*, who will also let you leave luggage. It's about an hour's walk to the lake and the road is passable in a good vehicle. Trails enable you to explore the practically deserted park, and boats can be rented on the lake.

Two kilometres along the track to Five Blues Lake, a branch to the right fords a river and continues another 3km through orange groves and forest to *Tamandua* (☎ & fax 06/23536 – call ahead to check if it's open), an organic fruit farm in a small valley surrounded by towering, jungle-draped limestone cliffs. It's an amazingly peaceful **place to stay** – bounded on three sides by the park, with plenty of opportunity to encounter wildlife. The thatched, A-frame cabins (⑦), perched above a creek (used for bathing), are great value; there's also a bunkhouse (②) with a kitchen, and you can camp (①).

Continuing south for 3km on the Hummingbird Highway from Over the Top there's more accommodation at *Palacio's Mountain Retreat*; buses stop right outside. Retired policeman Augustus Palacio has built ten cabañas (⑤, including breakfast), overlooking a river; it's great for swimming and there's a ten-metre waterfall just upstream. There are also three rooms in the main house (④).

On towards Dangriga

Palacio's Mountain Retreat marks the start of the **Stann Creek valley**, the centre of the Belizean citrus fruit industry. Bananas were the first crop to be grown here, and by 1891 half a million stems were being exported through Stann Creek (now Dangriga) every year. However, this banana boom came to an abrupt end in 1906, when disease destroyed the crop, and afterwards the government set out to foster the growth of **citrus fruits**. Between 1908 and 1937 the valley was even served by a small railway – many of the highway bridges were originally rail bridges – and by 1945 the citrus industry was well established.

Today it accounts for about thirteen percent of the country's exports and, despite widely fluctuating prices, is heralded as one of the nation's great success stories – although for the largely Guatemalan labour force, housed in rows of scruffy huts, conditions are little better than on the oppressive coffee *fincas* at home. The presence of tropical parasites, such as the leaf-eating ant, has forced the planters to resort to powerful insecticides, including DDT. Two giant pulping plants beside the road produce concentrate for export.

The last stretch of the Hummingbird Highway is flat and relatively uninteresting. Ten kilometres before Dangriga, the filling station is a useful place to refuel without going into town; just beyond is the junction with the **Southern Highway** to Punta Gorda.

Dangriga

DANGRIGA, formerly called Stann Creek, is the district capital and the largest town in southern Belize. It's also the cultural centre of the **Garífuna**, a people of mixed indigenous Caribbean and African descent, who overall form about eleven percent of the country's population. Since the early 1980s Garífuna culture has undergone a tremendous revival; as a part of this movement the town was renamed Dangriga, a Garífuna word meaning "sweet waters" — applied to the North Stann Creek flowing through the centre.

The most important day in the Garífuna calendar is November 19, **Garífuna Settlement Day**, when Dangriga is packed solid with expatriate Belizeans returning to their roots and the town erupts into wild celebration. The party begins the evening before, and the drumming and *punta* dancing pulsate all night long. In the morning there's a re-enactment of the arrival from Honduras, with people landing on the beach in dugout canoes decorated with palm leaves. Christmas and New Year are also celebrated in unique Garífuna style. At this time you might see the *wanaragu* or *Jonkunu* (John Canoe) dance, where **masked and costumed dancers** represent figures consisting of elements of eighteenth-century naval officers and Amerindian tribal chiefs wearing feathered headdresses and carrying shell rattles on their knees. Dangriga is also home to some of the country's most popular artists, including painter Benjamin Nicolas, painter and guitarist Pen Cayetano, drum-maker Austin Rodríguez and the Warribagaga Dancers and

Turtle Shell Band; the artists have small galleries here, and you may catch a live dance performance. Fine **crafts** are produced as well; distinctive brown and white basketware, woven palm-leaf hats and baskets and dolls in Garífuna costume.

During quieter times the atmosphere is enjoyably laid back, though there's little to do during the day. As the south of the country becomes more accessible, however, Dangriga is becoming increasingly useful as a base for visiting south-central Belize, the cayes offshore and the mountains, ruins and jaguar reserve inland.

Arrival, orientation and information

In addition to buses heading just **for Dangriga**, all buses between Belize City and Punta Gorda call here (see pp.62–3 for details of bus companies and services in Belize City). Generally there will be a service every hour or so from 8am to 5pm;

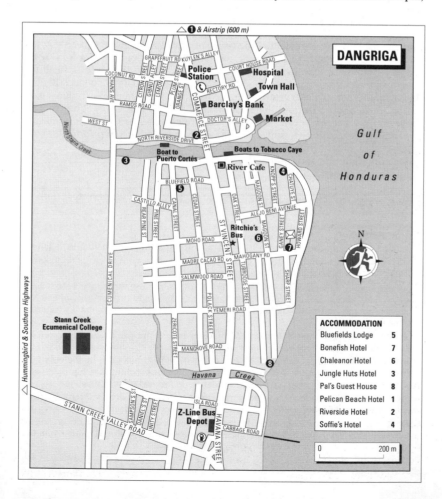

DANGRIGA

Gulf of Honduras

ACCOMMODATION	
Bluefields Lodge	5
Bonefish Hotel	7
Chaleanor Hotel	6
Jungle Huts Hotel	3
Pal's Guest House	8
Pelican Beach Hotel	1
Riverside Hotel	2
Soffie's Hotel	4

0   200 m

a few of these (at present three Z-Line departures and two Ritchie's buses) will use the Manatee (or Coastal) Road (see p.162). If you're heading south **from Belmopan** the first bus to leave is the James Bus, at 9am. **Arriving**, buses enter Dangriga at the south end of town: Z-Line have a modern terminal about 1km south of the centre, while Ritchie's office is a few blocks further north; you can leave luggage at either. Many buses will in fact continue to the centre and a **shuttle bus** plies the main street. Dangriga's **airstrip**, by the shore, just north of the *Pelican Beach Hotel* is served by flights on Tropic Air (☎02/45671) and Maya Island Air (☎22659), every couple of hours to and from Belize City, and south to Placencia and Punta Gorda.

The centre of town is marked by the **road bridge** over the South Stann Creek, with the main thoroughfare leading north as Commerce Street and south as St Vincent Street. Almost everything you're likely to need, including **hotels, restaurants, banks** and **boat transport**, is on or near this road. **The post office** is on Caney Street, in the southern half of town, a block back from the sea.

There's no official tourist office in Dangriga, but for reliable **tourist information** and friendly service call in at the office of Aquamarine Adventures (☎ & fax 23262), in *Soffie's Hotel*, 1 Chatuye St, on the south bank of the river. Run by an English/Belizean couple Derek and Debbie Jones, this is the place to head for information on anything in the Dangriga area, from dive boats to Tobacco Reef to staying in the Jaguar Reserve, to domestic flights – they can even arrange a tour of the *Marie Sharp's* factory, home of Belize's famous hot sauce. They're also about to open Belize's second **Internet café** (*djones@btl.net*), and the walls are filled with details of tours to suit all budgets. You can use the **payphone** (for coin or card calls) and the gift shop sells *Rough Guides*.

For both domestic and **international flights** check at Treasured Travels, 64 Commerce Street (☎22578).

The **telephone area code** for Dangriga is ☎05

Accommodation

Dangriga has experienced something of a hotel-building boom in the last few years, resulting in an ample choice of places to stay and – with some real bargains on offer – no need to stay in a cheap dive.

Bluefield Lodge, 6 Bluefield Rd (☎22742). Very clean, secure and well run, it's everything a budget hotel should be but rarely is. Manager Louise Belisle is very welcoming and has good-value rooms with really comfortable beds, some with private bath and TV. Reliable information too. ③.

Bonefish, 15 Mahogany St (☎22165, fax 22296). Good hotel with cable TV, hot water, carpets and a/c, and some very good-value rooms with fan. Specializes in fishing trips. ④–⑥.

Chaleanor Hotel, 35 Magoon St (☎22587, fax 23038). Newish hotel run by the very hospitable Chadwick and Eleanor Usher, with very clean, spacious rooms, all with private bath. You can enjoy your meals from the rooftop restaurant. Very good value at this price. ④.

Jungle Huts, on the riverbank upstream from the town centre bridge (☎23166). Pleasant thatched cabañas and hotel rooms with private bath and hot water, some with TV. ④.

Pal's Guest House, 868 Magoon St, by the bridge over Havana Creek (☎ & fax 22095). Good-value accommodation in two buildings: budget rooms (some shared bath) are in the older part; newer beachfront rooms all have private baths and TV. ②–⑤.

Pelican Beach Resort, on the beach north of the town, next to the airstrip (☎22024, fax 22570, email *pelicanbeach@alt.net*). Rooms at the front are in a wooden colonial-style building; there's a concrete building behind. The most expensive hotel in town, and frankly the best beachfront rooms, while beautiful, are overpriced; even at the back, upstairs rooms cost more than downstairs ones. Prices do come down out of season and it's worth asking for a discount. It's a popular hotel for tour groups, and owners Therese and Tony Rath are prominent in Belize's conservation organizations. The dining room features a large marine aquarium. ⑥–⑨.

Riverside Hotel, right beside the bridge (☎22168). Clean rooms (some with bath) in a good location with a vantage point over the river. Prices are per person; a good deal for singles. ②.

Soffie's, 1 Chatuye St, south bank of the river, heading towards the sea (☎22789, fax 23262, email *djones@btl.net*). A range of rooms and all good value, most with private bath and a balcony with fine sea and river views; some suites and some budget rooms too. Great place for information; see opposite. ②–⑤.

Eating, drinking and nightlife

If you're going to try **Garífuna food** in Belize, Dangriga is the place to do it. There are a few **food stalls** around the Z-Line station, and some are fine, but the best place for Garífuna cooking is *Pola's Kitchen*, 25 Tubroose St, at the south end of town. The walls are decorated with Garífuna artefacts and it has a no-smoking policy that is probably unique in Belize. Dishes such as *hudut* (also called *fufu*) feature plantain cooked in coconut sauce, and there's *sere*, a delicious fish and vegetable stew, also flavoured with coconut. The restaurant at the *Pelican Beach* is the top place in town – resident chef Bill is skilled in preparing all of Belize's cultural specialities. The *River Café*, on the south bank of the river, just over the bridge, is a good restaurant catering for local boatmen and visitors waiting for boats to Tobacco Caye. It serves Creole food, including great breakfasts and is another good place to pick up information on the surrounding area. *King Burger* (not what you might think) under the *Riverside Hotel* serves good rice, chicken, burgers, fruit juices, fish and conch soup (a Belizean delicacy), and the restaurant at *Soffie's* is good value. Of the several Chinese restaurants on the main street, the *Starlight* is the best value.

For picnic supplies you could try the **market** on the north bank of the river, by the sea, but it's very small – for other groceries it's best to head for the *Southern Pride* supermarket, by Barclays Bank. Opposite the bank, the Dangriga **bakery** has good bread and buns.

There's no shortage of **bars** in Dangriga, though some, particularly those calling themselves clubs, like the *Kennedy Club,* the *Culture Club* and the *Harlem Club,* are particularly dubious-looking, both inside and out. In the centre of town, near the bridge, the *Riviera Nite Club* is Dangriga's newest and most sophisticated nightspot. Along the beach to the north of the centre, the *Round House* is a good place to meet the locals and dance on the sand.

Offshore: Tobacco Range Cayes and Columbus Reef

The **Tobacco Range** is a group of mangrove cayes (a couple of which have accommodation) just behind the beautiful **Tobacco Reef**, about 16km east of Dangriga. The largest caye in the range, **Man-O'-War Caye**, is a **bird sanctuary** named after the frigate birds or man o'-war birds you'll see hanging on the breeze with outstretched wings. In the breeding season the males develop an immense, bright red balloon on their throats and the island is full of nesting birds; watching the birds from a boat is fine but you can't land on the island. **Mayan**

Island, just north of Man-O'-War Caye, offers good-value, new **accommodation** in spacious, wooden cabañas, each with a double bedroom, a living room with a veranda facing the reef and a private bathroom with hot water (⑦, includes all meals, no service charge). The boat transfer from Dangriga is extra, about Bz$35 per person, depending on the group size. There's also a dive centre. Contact Aquamarine Adventures in Dangriga (see p.168).

A HISTORY OF GARÍFUNA

The Garífuna trace their history back to the island of **St Vincent,** one of the Windward Islands in the eastern Caribbean. At the time of Columbus' landing in the Americas the islands of the Lesser Antilles had recently been settled by people from the South American mainland, who had subdued the previous inhabitants, the Arawaks. These new people called themselves *Kalipuna,* or *Kwaib,* from which the names *Garífuna,* meaning cassava-eating people, and *Carib* probably evolved; St Vincent was Yurimein. The natives the Europeans encountered were descendants of Carib men and Arawak women. A few thousand descendants of the original Caribs still live in Dominica and St Vincent.

In the early seventeenth century Britain, France and the Netherlands vied for control of the islands, fighting each other and the Caribs. The admixture of African blood came in 1635 when two Spanish ships, carrying slaves from Nigeria to their colonies in America, were wrecked off St Vincent and the survivors took refuge on the island. At first there was conflict between the Caribs and the Africans, but the Caribs had been weakened by wars and disease and eventually the predominant race was Black, with some Carib blood, becoming known by the English as the **Black Caribs** – in their own language they were *Garinagu,* or *Garífuna.* For most of the seventeenth and eighteenth centuries St Vincent was nominally under British control but in practice it belonged to the Garífuna, and in 1660 with the Treaty of Basse Terre the islands of Dominica and St Vincent were granted in "perpetual possession" to the Caribs.

In 1763 however, Britain attempted to gain full control of St Vincent, but was driven off by the Caribs, with French assistance. Another attempt twenty years later was more successful, and in 1783 the British imposed a treaty on the Garífuna, allowing them over half of the island: the treaty was never accepted, however, and the Garífuna continued to defy British rule, resulting in frequent battles in which the French consistently lent the Garífuna support. The last serious attempt by the Garífuna to establish their independence took place in 1795, when both sides suffered horrendous casualties. The Garífuna lost their leader, Chief Joseph Chatoyer, and on June 10, 1796, after a year of bitter fighting, the French and Garífuna surrendered to the British.

The colonial authorities could not allow a free Black society to survive amongst slave-owning European settlers, so it was decided to deport the Garífuna population. They were hunted down, their homes (and in the process some of their culture) destroyed, and hundreds died of starvation and disease. The survivors, 4300 Black Caribs and 100 Yellow Caribs, as they were designated by the British, were transported to the nearby island of Balliceaux; within six months over half of them had died, many of yellow fever. In March 1797, the remaining survivors were loaded aboard ships and sent to **Roatán,** one of the Bay Islands, off the coast of Honduras (see p.203). One of the ships was captured by the Spanish and taken to Trujillo, on the mainland, and barely 2000 Garífuna lived to make the landing on Roatán, where the British abandoned them.

At the southern tip of Tobacco Reef sits the slightly larger **South Water Caye**, while to the northeast, **Columbus Reef** is another superb section of the barrier reef with some small cayes scattered along its length, including the tiny Tobacco Caye perched on its southern tip. Each caye has a number of delightful places to stay – sunsets out here can be breathtakingly beautiful, outlining the distant Maya Mountains with a purple and orange aura.

Perhaps in response to pleas for help from the Garífuna, who continued to die on Roatán, the Spanish Commandante of Trujillo arrived and took possession of the island, shipping the 1700 survivors to Trujillo where they were in demand as labourers. The Spanish had never made a success of agriculture here and the arrival of the Garífuna, who were proficient at growing crops, benefited the colony considerably. The boys were conscripted and the Garífuna men gained a reputation as soldiers and mercenaries. Soon they began to move to other areas along the coast, and in 1802, 150 of them were brought as wood-cutting labourers to work in Stann Creek and Punta Gorda. Their intimate knowledge of the rivers and coast also made them expert smugglers, evading the Spanish laws that forbade trade with the British in Belize. Their military skills were even more useful and by 1819 a Garífuna colonel was commander of the garrison at San Felipe in Guatemala, while in 1820 two Garífuna soldiers received (posthumous) awards from the king of Spain for their bravery in the defence of Trujillo.

In the early **nineteenth century** small numbers of Garífuna moved up the coast to Belize, and although in 1811 Superintendent Barrow of Belize ordered their expulsion, it had little effect. When European settlers arrived in Stann Creek in 1823 the Garífuna were already there and were hired to clear land. The largest single migration to Belize took place in 1832 when vast numbers, under the leadership of Alejo Benji, fled from Honduras (by then part of the Central American Republic) after they had supported the wrong side in a failed revolution to overthrow the Republican government. It is this arrival which is today celebrated as Garífuna Settlement Day, though it seems likely many arrived both before and after.

In 1825 the first Methodist missionaries arrived in Belize, and by 1828 they had begun to visit Stann Creek, or "Carib Town" as the settlers knew it. They were outraged to discover a bizarre mix of Catholicism, ancestor worship and polygamy, in which the main form of worship was "devil dancing", but they had little success in their struggle to Christianize the Garífuna beyond the adoption of various new rituals such as baptism.

By the start of this century, the Garífuna were well established in the Stann Creek area, with the women employed in bagging and stacking *cohune* nuts and the men working in agriculture. Throughout the nineteenth and twentieth centuries the Garífuna travelled widely in search of work. To start with they confined themselves to Central America (where they can still be found all along the Caribbean coast from Belize to Nicaragua), but in World War II Garífuna men supplied crews for both British and US merchant ships. Since then trips to the US have become an important part of the local economy, and there are small Garífuna communities in New York, New Orleans, Los Angeles and even in London.

Belize has a National Garífuna Council, and its scholars are attempting to create a written language. The council has already published *The People's Garífuna Dictionary* and school textbooks are available. *The First Primer on a People Called Garífuna* by Myrtle Palacio is in English and available in Belize. There's an excellent US-based Garífuna **Website** (*www.garifuna-world.com*) listing cultural events and current developments in the entire Garífuna community.

MOVING ON FROM DANGRIGA

Returning to Belize City, Z-Line buses (☎22732) leave at 5am, 6am, 8am, 9am, 10am, 10.15am, 1.30pm and 4pm. Ritchie's (☎ 23132) leave at 5.30am and 8.30, both using the Coastal Road. If you're continuing south bear in mind that buses to **Punta Gorda** don't necessarily originate here; the first Z-Line bus leaves at noon, then 4pm and 7pm, and there's also one James bus around noon. Try to buy a ticket in advance, which should guarantee a seat; the journey takes five hours over dirt roads. All buses to Punta Gorda stop at **Independence** (2hr) – also known as **Mango Creek** – where you can pick up boats to Placencia, and there's also a Z-Line bus daily at 2.30pm.

There are always at least three daily services from Dangriga to **Placencia** (2hr), but departure times are continually changing as the two rivals, Ritchie's and Z-Line, battle it out: currently they depart daily at 11.30am, 12.30pm and 4.30pm; at least one calls at **Hopkins** (40min) and **Sittee River** – usually the 11.30am Ritchie's service.

For Puerto Cortes in Honduras a fast **skiff** leaves each Saturday at 9am (US$50; around 3hr) from the north bank of the river, two blocks up from the bridge; be there an hour before departure with your passport so that the skipper, Carlos Reyes (☎05/23227), can take care of the formalities.

Tobacco Caye

Tobacco Caye, ideally situated right on the reef, is the easiest caye to reach in this area and has the most accommodation. **Boats** leave every day from near the bridge, but currently there are no regular departures; check details at *Soffie's* or the *River Café* in Dangriga, where you can meet the boat skippers. The most prompt and reliable service is operated by Captain Buck, though any of the hotel owners on the island will take you, and maybe arrange a package deal. It's a forty-minute trip and the one-way fare is Bz$30.

The cayes of Columbus reef were originally visited by turtle fishermen; Tobacco Caye was later farmed by the first Puritan settlers, taking its name from the main crop. The island is tiny, just five acres in area. If you stand in the centre you're only a couple of minutes from the shore in any direction, with the unbroken reef stretching north for miles. The island's **dive shop**, *Second Nature Divers* (☎05/37038) is excellent and offers good-value PADI courses, equipment rental and trips to the atolls. A single-tank local dive (plus equipment) costsBz$50; a dive course is Bz$450.

ACCOMMODATION

Accommodation here is simple but comfortable, and generally good value; you'll be staying either in wooden buildings on the sand or cabins right over the sea. In most cases the price includes all meals, but here more than anywhere it's essential to check what you're paying for – and whether the price is quoted in US or Belize dollars. Any of the places listed can arrange scuba-diving, fishing and snorkelling trips.

Gaviota Coral Reef Resort (☎05/22294 or 014/9763, fax 23477). Cabins on the sand and over the water, and budget rooms in the main building (upstairs rooms are more expensive), all with shared bath and all very clean. There's electric light from a solar panel on a timer and good snorkel equipment for rent. Wonderful food and rates include meals. Owners Bert and Marie Swasey can arrange cheaper transport for guests. ⑤–⑥.

Island Camps Caye Resort (☎ 02/72109 or ☎014/7160, fax 02/70350). Seven small double cabins and three great larger cabins, one with private bath. Simple living quarters but the food is excellent and a solar panel provides light in the evening. Earthwatch volunteers are based here for part of the year, studying reef ecology. Meals around Bz$30 per day. ⑤–⑦.

Lana's on the Reef (☎05/22571 or 014/7451) Simple rooms in a lovely wooden house, shared bathroom. Great, even gourmet food – the best on the island – and good coffee, in a romantic atmosphere. Rates include meals. ⑦.

Ocean's Edge Lodge (☎014/9633). Four wooden cabins connected by a walkway in a perfect location overlooking the reef; all have private bath and hot water. The layout inside (and out) makes you feel like you're in a comfortably furnished ship's cabin. Rates include meals. ⑤.

Reef's End Lodge (☎05/22419, fax 22828). Stay right on the shore in a cabin room or in one of a pair of private cabañas, all with private bath. The restaurant is built over the sea on the tip of the reef, and the bar is a fantastic place to enjoy the sunset. Rates include meals. ⑤–⑦.

South Water Caye

Eight kilometres south of Tobacco Caye and about three times the size, **South Water Caye** is arguably one of the most utterly beautiful – and exclusive – islands in Belize. Like Tobacco Caye it sits right on the reef and offers fantastic, very accessible snorkelling and scuba-diving in crystal-clear water. The island takes its name from a well in the centre of the island, which made it a fresh-water stop for passing fishermen – the well still exists today. South Water Caye is now the focus of a large new **marine reserve**, which is also a World Heritage Site, and the southern end of the island is part of a small nature reserve. Turtles sometimes nest in the sand here, and the reef curves around offshore protecting the pristine beach.

Most resorts have their own very good **dive shop** and there's also the Living Reef Dive Centre (☎05/22214), which offers PADI dive courses and trips to Glover's Reef, where there's a resort on Long Caye (p.178). The island's **accommodation** is upmarket and expensive and has to be booked in advance; rates given are either for groups or for an all-inclusive package. Overnight rates are available, but this may entail paying at least US$125 one way for a skiff from Dangriga. The tiny island off the south end of the caye is **Carrie Bow Caye**, where the Smithsonian Institute has a research station; you can sometimes visit but there's no tourist accommodation.

PACKAGE ACCOMMODATION
Blue Marlin Lodge (☎05/22243, fax 22296, in US ☎1-800/798-1558, email *marlin@btl.net*). The most luxurious accommodation on the island, set in a wide expanse of raked, white sand under the coconut trees. Three dome-shaped, white-washed, carpeted a/c cabins, with beautiful bathrooms; comfortable wooden a/c cabins with a deck over the sea; and wood-panelled rooms in a typical wooden "caye house". The thatched dining room, which extends over the sea, serves delicious meals. *Blue Marlin* specializes in diving holidays: instruction from the resident dive-master, Martin Green, leading to PADI certification, is available and there's a fleet of dive boats. Prices are US$1450 for a week's package including transfers from the international airport, meals and diving.

Leslie Cottages (☎05/22119, fax 23152, in US: International Zoological Expeditions (IZE), 210 Washington St, Sherborn, MA 01770; ☎508/655-1461, fax 655-4445, email *ize2belize@aol.com*) offers accommodation in wooden cottages and rooms in a tropical field research station, and is ideal for a quiet holiday; overnight rates work out around ⑦, excluding meals. Complete packages for four including transportation, accommodation, meals and maid service cost US$600 per person.

The remainder of the accommodation on the caye is owned and operated by the *Pelican Beach Resort* in Dangriga (☎22024, fax 22570, email *pelicanbeach@alt.net*), with a range of idyllic options in a stunning location at the south end of the island; rates include meals. As the island is a marine reserve every attempt is made to minimize the environmental impact: electricity is provided by solar cells; ice is bought over from the mainland for cooling drinks; and the bathrooms have (odourless) composting toilets. **Osprey's Nest** (US$171 double, ⑨) is a three-bedroom house with large verandas, built on stilts over the white sand and shaded by palms; **Heron's Hideaway** (US$171 double, ⑨) is a secluded little house built in the mangroves, overlooking the reef in the corner of the island. **Pelican's Pouch** (US$151 double, ⑨), a former convent, is a two-storey, wooden colonial building with five rooms upstairs, each with a veranda front and back overlooking the sea. **The Pelican's University** on the west side of the island, designed to house groups, often students, is a two-storey building with five bunk-bedded rooms, a large kitchen and recreation area; definitely a fine place to study. It costs US$60 per person per day for groups up to 22, including meals.

The Southern Highway to the Jaguar Reserve

To the south of Dangriga the country becomes more mountainous, with settlements mainly restricted to the coastal lowlands. The only road heading in this direction is the **Southern Highway**, running from Dangriga to Punta Gorda. Unpaved with the exception of the far southern section, the road surface is nevertheless frequently graded and strong bridges have been built, high above the river levels, so it should be passable except during the very worst rainstorms. For its entire length the highway is set back from the coast, running beneath the peaks of the Maya Mountains, often passing through pine forest and vast citrus and banana plantations. Several branch roads lead off to settlements, such as **Hopkins**, a Garífuna village on the coast, and the nearby Creole village of **Sittee River**, where you can catch the boat to the idyllic cayes of **Glover's Reef**. From the village of **Maya Centre**, 36km south of Dangriga, a road leads west into the Cockscomb Basin Wildlife Sanctuary, generally referred to as the **Jaguar Reserve**.

Hopkins

Stretching for more than 3km along a shallow, gently curving bay, and thickly shaded by palm trees, **HOPKINS** is home to around a thousand Garífuna people, who, until recently, made their living from small-scale farming and fishing, often paddling dugout canoes to pull up fish traps, or using baited handlines. Their houses, traditionally small wood and thatch structures, have now mostly been replaced by less visually appealing but more secure concrete buildings.

Named after a Roman Catholic bishop who drowned in 1923, the village was first settled in 1942, after a hurricane had levelled its predecessor – the community of Newtown, a few kilometres to the north. The population is proud of its traditions, and Garífuna Settlement Day on November 19 is celebrated enthusiastically with singing, dancing and above all the beating of drums – an integral part of the Garífuna culture. Only recently having become part of the tourist circuit, Hopkins still sees few visitors, and as a stranger you'll be made to feel welcome by the exuberant friendliness of the villagers, particularly the children.

It's a pleasant place to spend a few days relaxing, with food and accommodation in all price ranges, and you can rent kayaks, windsurf boards and bicycles. Unfortunately, the water immediately offshore is silty and the beach is sometimes littered, but it's possible (though not always easy) to organize trips to the reef and cayes further out; the view back towards the village from the sea, with the high ridges of the Maya Mountains in the background, is breathtaking.

Arrival and orientation

The **bus** service to Hopkins is a little unpredictable, but there's at least one daily run to and from the village; currently the 11.30am Ritchie's service from Dangriga to Placencia calls in en route. In the other direction, buses from Placencia to Dangriga call in at about 7am; check at your hotel for the current situation. There are also plenty of trucks between Dangriga and Hopkins, making **hitching** a fairly reliable option. You might also want to ask around where the **boats** tie up by the bridge in Dangriga and see whether anyone from Hopkins is in town – they may be willing to give you a lift and this is definitely the best way to arrive.

As there are no street names in Hopkins, the best way to locate anything is to describe its position in relation to the point where the road from the Southern Highway enters the village, dividing it roughly into northern and southern halves. The main road heading south through the village is paved, though the asphalt gives way to sand at the southern end; this road continues 5km to Sittee River (see p.176), though in the rainy season it's often inundated.

The central road junction is increasingly becoming the village **information centre** – boards and signs point the way to hotels and restaurants and there's a little shop too. At the time of writing only a few places have private telephones but you can make calls on the two **community telephones**: ☎05/22033 in the Nuñez store at the roadside in the south of the village; ☎05/22803 in the BTL office. Hopkins is changing fast and there are certain to be more places and services than are currently listed here.

Accommodation

There's plenty of **accommodation** in the village. Some places now have private phones, so you can book ahead if you want, though this is rarely necessary.

Hopkins Inn, south of the centre, on the beach (☎05/37013, email *hopkinsinn@btl.net*). Friendly place with three immaculate white-washed cabins with hot showers, fridge and coffee-maker. Owners Rita and Greg Duke can arrange trips on their Hobie-cat. Continental breakfast included. ⑤.

Jaguar Reef Lodge, on the beach, 1km or so beyond the south end of the village (☎ & fax 021/2041, in US ☎1-800/289-5756; email *jaguarreef@btl.net*). Luxury resort with large, thatched cabañas in beautifully landscaped grounds and in a superb location. It's often used by top nature tour companies. The restaurant, under a huge thatched roof overlooking the beach, is excellent and so is the service. The resort organizes first-class trips to the reef and inland to the Maya ruins of Mayflower, currently being excavated by Tulane University. Kayaks and bikes are available free for guests, and there's a dive shop with instruction. US$150 double; rates are reduced considerably in summer, and there's no service charge. ⑨.

Lebeha, at the north end of the village – *lebeha* means "the end". Inexpensive rooms in a brightly painted, thatched house surrounded by plants. Also has space for hammocks and camping. There's good food, including vegetarian dishes, and fresh bread. ②.

Parasol, on the beach at the north end (☎05/37009 or 014/7071). Two lovely, simple beach-front cabins with private bathroom and deck in grounds surrounded by a white picket fence. There's also a popular bar and restaurant and *palapa* (thatched) tables on the beach. Boat for trips. ⑤.

Ransome's Seaside Cabaña (☎05/22889 in Dangriga). Wonderful two-bedroom, fully-furnished cabin set in a tropical garden south of the centre. Owner Barry Swan has kayaks and bicycles for rent. Meals can be ordered. ⑤.

Sandy Beach Lodge, on the beach at the south end (☎05/37006). Six simple, spacious, good-value rooms in wood-and-thatch cabins (most with private bath), run by Belize's only women's cooperative. Meals, served at set times, feature seafood cooked in Creole and Garífuna style. There's also a house for rent at Bz$80 per day. ③.

Swinging Armadillos, on the beach 150m north of the centre (☎05/37016). Two small and comfortable rooms perched over the sea just beyond the small bar and restaurant of the same name (see below). Friendly owner Mike Flores has a boat and a truck for trips and also rents bikes. ③.

Eating and drinking

A few simple **restaurants** and **bars** have opened up in Hopkins in recent years, though by now there are sure to more than those listed here. *Over the Waves*, on the beach in the village centre, is recommended; if you ask you'll be allowed to leave luggage here while you look for a room. *Swinging Armadillos*, 120m to the north, is a great little restaurant billed as a "hammock lounge" by owner Mike Flores. Swing in the shade and enjoy the sea breeze while sipping a cold drink.

For **live music**, look out for the Hopkins Ayumahani Band, who play at the *Laru Beya* bar, on the beach where the road from the highway enters the village.

Sittee River

A few kilometres south of the Hopkins turn-off is the junction of the road to **SIT-TEE RIVER**, a pleasant place in its own right, but most useful as a jumping-off point for Glover's Reef (see opposite). The 8km dirt road from the Southern Highway roughly follows the north bank of the river, as does the village itself, and on the way in you'll see signs to the ruins of the nineteenth-century **Serdon Sugar Mill**, now preserved as a local park and a good spot for bird-watching. The road from Hopkins (see p.174) has been improved, though it's still a little rough in places. Sittee River is served by the same buses as Hopkins on the Dangriga/Placencia route.

Sittee River and its banks offer great opportunities for spotting wildlife; apart from the dozens of bird species there are freshwater turtles and crocodiles. Most visitors here are on their way to *Glover's Atoll Resort*, and there are a few **places to stay**: be warned that sandflies in Sittee River can be atrocious and the screens or mosquito nets provided are essential. The great-value *Toucan Sittee* (☎05/37039), signed at the entrance to the village from the Hopkins road, is by far the best accommodation option, set in a beautiful riverbank location and graced by toucans most mornings. It's owned by the extremely hospitable Neville and Yoli Collins, who provide some of the best budget accommodation in the country, in solidly built, well-furnished wooden cabins, with electric light and hot showers. Rooms start at ③, and there're also a couple of apartments with fridges (⑤), and very comfortable dorm beds (Bz$15), or you can camp (Bz$7). The food is really good, with lots of fresh fruit (including sixteen varieties of mango) and vegetables, and they rent **canoes** and **bikes**. In the village there's the rather basic

Glover's Guest House (③), and *Isolene's*, on the riverbank, also offers rooms (③) and has a good restaurant serving simple meals.

A few kilometres further down the river at **Possum Point** there's a **campsite** that's part of an ecological field station with an offshore reef ecology centre on **Wee Wee Caye**, a tiny mangrove island 15km off the coast. The campsite is mainly used by students but to enquire call ☎05/22888.

If you need to stock up on **supplies** for your trip to Glover's Reef there's Hill Top Farm for vegetables and Reynold's Store for most other basic goods.

Glover's Reef

The southernmost of Belize's three coral atolls, **Glover's Reef** lies between 40 and 50km off Dangriga. Named after British pirate John Glover, the reef is roughly oval in shape, about 35km north to south, and its only cayes are in the southeastern section. Physically, it's the best developed atoll in the Caribbean, rising from ocean depths of over 600m, with the reef wall beginning at 10m. It offers some of the best **wall diving** in the world, and inside the beautiful aquamarine lagoon are hundreds of **patch reefs** – a snorkelling wonderland. It's also the most biologically diverse atoll in the Caribbean, home to rare seabirds such as the white-capped noddy; all the cayes have nesting ospreys, and Belize's marine turtles nest on the beaches. There are also vitally important grouper spawning grounds on the northeast of the atoll, and immense **whale sharks** – the largest fish in the world – pass through on their southward autumn migration.

These unique features helped to bring about the decision in 1993 to declare the whole atoll a protected area – **Glover's Reef Marine Reserve**. This special status was further enhanced by its designation as a World Heritage Site in 1996. The atoll is divided into management zones and no fishing is allowed from any of the cayes. All of the cayes here offer some **accommodation**, mostly in purpose-built camps and cabins for **sea kayaking** groups, though there is one upmarket diving lodge. However, apart from its biological attributes, another feature that makes Glover's Reef so unusual among the remote atolls is that one of the cayes has accommodation within the reach of budget travellers – *Glover's Atoll Resort* on Northeast Caye (see below).

The cayes

Covered in thick coconut and broadleaf forest, and with evidence of Maya fishing camps, **Northeast Caye** is home to *Glover's Atoll Resort* (☎05/23048 or 014/8351, email *jungled@btl.net*). The resort has ten simple, self-catering **beach cabins** (U\$149 per person per week, including transport from Sittee River) and space for **camping** (U\$80 per week). Some of the cabins are wooden, some are stick and thatch cabañas, and all overlook the sea and the reef. Drinking water (stored rainwater) is provided and you shower in water drawn from a shallow well. Unless you're in a pre-booked group (in which case you can organize to be catered for), you'll have to bring your own food and make your own meals; cooking is done on a kerosene stove, or on the barbecue pit nearby. Some fish and basic supplies are available and one evening each week features a pot-luck supper. Activities (paid for separately) include sea kayaking, fishing, snorkelling, scuba-diving with PADI or NAUI certification, and sailing to all the other cayes on the *Pelican*. The resort's motor/sail boat, *Christmas Bird*, picks up guests in Sittee River each Sunday morning, and leaves the caye the following Saturday; the trip takes up to four hours, longer if under sail.

   Long Caye, just across the channel from Northeast Caye, is the base for the sea-kayak expeditions run by Slickrock Adventures (see "Basics", p.6); accommodation is mostly in wooden cabins on stilts. There's also some accommodation used by IZE and Living Reef Dive Centre expeditions (see p.173 for contact details). Four kilometres to the southwest, **Middle Caye** is in the wilderness zone of the reserve, and has a marine research and monitoring station run by the Wildlife Conservation Society; you can visit with permission, and there are some interesting displays on the ecology of the atoll. **Southwest Caye**, 5km beyond Middle Caye, is the base for the sea-kayak groups of *Island Expeditions* (p.5 in "Basics"), where guests stay in spacious, comfortable white tents. The caye has been sliced in two by a hurricane and on the other part, divided by a narrow channel, is *Manta Reef Resort* (☎02/32767, in the US ☎1-800/326-1724). Diving and fishing packages cost around U$1400 per week.

The Cockscomb Basin Wildlife Sanctuary and Maya Centre

Back on the mainland, the jagged peaks of the **Maya Mountains** rise to the west of the Southern Highway, their lower slopes covered in dense rainforest. The tallest summits are those of the Cockscomb range, which includes Victoria Peak, at 1120m the second highest mountain in Belize and a dramatic sight on a clear day. In 1888 the Goldsworthy Expedition made the first recorded successful attempt on the summit of Victoria Peak, though it's certain that the ancient Maya were first to make it to the top. Beneath the sharp ridges is a sweeping bowl, part of which was declared a **jaguar reserve** in 1986; it has since been expanded to cover an area of over four hundred square kilometres – the **Cockscomb Basin Wildlife Sanctuary**.

   The area was inhabited in Maya times, and the ruins of **Kuchil Balam**, a Classic period ceremonial centre, still lie hidden in the forest. It was also exploited by the mahogany loggers; the names of their abandoned camps, such as Leave If You Can and Go to Hell, illustrate how they felt about life in the forest. In more recent times the residents of Quam Bank, a logging camp and Maya village moved out of the Cockscomb when the reserve was established, relocating to the present village of **MAYA CENTRE** on the Southern Highway.

   Technically, this is a **tropical moist forest**, with an annual rainfall of up to 300cm that feeds a complex network of wonderfully clear streams and rivers, most of which eventually run into the Swasey River and the South Stann Creek; the sanctuary also performs a vital role in watershed protection. The forest is home to a sizeable percentage of **Belize's plant and animal species**. Among the mammals are tapir, otter, coati, deer, anteater, armadillo and, of course, jaguar, as well as all other cat species. Over 290 species of bird have also been recorded, including the endangered scarlet macaw, the great curassow, the keel-billed toucan and the king vulture. It is particularly important as a refuge for the largest raptors, including the solitary eagle and the white hawk eagle. And there's an abundance of reptiles and amphibians, including the red-eyed tree frog, the boa constrictor and the deadly fer-de-lance snake (known as tommy-goff in Belize). The forest itself is made up of a fantastic range of plant species, including orchids, giant tree ferns, air plants (epiphytes) and trees such as *banak, cohune*, mahogany and ceiba.

The sanctuary is managed by the Belize Audubon Society, with some financial assistance from WWF and WCS, and from Jaguar cars. There is an opportunity for a limited amount of **voluntary work** in the reserve, maintaining trails, working on displays in the visitor centre, or even tracking howler monkeys; contact BAS in Belize City (see p.246).

Maya Centre practicalities

All buses heading south from Dangriga pass **MAYA CENTRE** village, from where a rough ten-kilometre track leads to the sanctuary headquarters. You need to sign in and pay the reserve entrance fee (Bz$10) at the thatched **craft centre** (selling good, well-priced slate carvings and embroidery) at the road junction in Maya Centre. Just beyond, the small **shop** sells basic supplies and cold drinks, including beer, and there's a small restaurant behind. The shop is run by Julio Saqui, a skilled guide who operates Julio's Cultural and Jungle Tours (☎051/2020) – the best way to organize a guide if you're thinking of attempting the hike to Victoria Peak, or indeed anywhere in the Cockscomb. The people of Maya Centre know the reserve intimately, and are by far the **best guides** around. Although many tour operators will tell you that you can't get into the Jaguar Reserve without going on a tour, you can easily walk in from Maya Centre – it takes a couple of hours or so along the gentle uphill slope, and you can leave any excess luggage with Julio. If you've come without transport and don't fancy the walk you can **ride in** with Julio's brother, Ernesto, the former director of the reserve, in his pickup for Bz$25. Heading through towering forest and fording a couple of fresh, clear streams, the track crosses the Cabbage Hall Gap before reaching the Cockscomb visitor centre (see below).

If you need somewhere to **stay in Maya centre**, Ernesto and his wife Aurora run *Nu'uk Che'il* (Mayan for "in the middle of the forest") *Cottages* (☎051/2021; ③): simple but delightful thatched cabañas, with shared bathroom and hot water. The **restaurant**, serving Maya and Belizean food, is a great place to get a filling meal on your way to or from the reserve. Aurora is one of the Garcia sisters (see p.139), and has developed a medicinal trail (Bz$4) in the forest next to the cottages and makes **traditional herbal medicines**, for sale in the H'men Herbal Centre. The Saquis and other families in Maya Centre are a few of the totally genuine proponents of the concept of "eco-tourism", and staying here is a perfect way to learn about the life of the forest and experience Maya culture. You can also spot lots of wildlife along the adjacent Cabbage Haul Creek – it's particularly good for birds.

The Jaguar Reserve

At the sanctuary headquarters, in a cleared grassy area surrounded by beautiful tropical foliage, there's an excellent **visitor centre**, with a model of the Cockscomb Basin, displays on the area's ecology, and maps and trail guides; you can also pick up a copy of *Cockscomb Basin Wildlife Sanctuary*, a superb and detailed guide to the history, flora and fauna of the reserve. If you want to stay in the reserve, there's comfortable dorm **accommodation** in two styles; the old huts for Bz$12, and a newer, purpose-built dorm (Bz$20 per person) behind the main buildings. There are also comfortable rooms (④), and even a house for rent; the latter is designed for study and tour groups, and there's a classroom and kitchen. The **campground** (Bz$5) is a little further on. If you're not on a group tour you'll have to bring your own food and cook it on a gas stove.

Although the basin could be home to as many as fifty of Belize's six-hundred-strong **jaguar population**, your chances of seeing one are very slim. However, it's an ideal environment for plant-spotting, for serious bird-watching or for seeking out other ever-evasive wildlife, and the trail system in the Cockscomb is the best developed in any of Belize's protected areas. There are several well-maintained shortish trails leading through the forest to the bank of South Stann Creek, or to exquisite waterfalls framed by jungle which you can follow with a self-guiding leaflet, giving you a taste of the forest's diversity. **Inner tubes** are available from the ranger's office; walk upstream and float down for an amazingly tranquil view of the forest. The **Ben's Bluff Trail** is a strenuous but worthwhile 4km hike from the riverside to the top of a forested ridge – where there's a great view of the entire Cockscomb Basin – with a chance to cool off in a delightful rocky pool on the way back. If you're suitably prepared you can climb Victoria Peak – a two-day hike each way – with backcountry **campsites** prepared by Raleigh volunteers.

Sapodilla Lagoon Wildlife Refuge and Black Cat Lodge

Continuing on the Southern Highway for 3km past Maya Centre you'll reach the turn-off for the privately owned **Sapodilla Lagoon Wildlife Refuge** (signed on the left-hand side of the road; buses will stop here), where you'll probably have a better chance of actually spotting a **jaguar** or a nesting jabiru stork than anywhere else in the country. The refuge, owned by American Larry Staley, stretches along both sides of the highway, from the eastern foothills of the Maya Mountains to the coast at Sapodilla Lagoon, bounded in part by the Sittee River, and includes a range of habitats. Larry has built trails and observation platforms and converted the main house into *Black Cat Lodge*, which his girlfriend Anna runs like a very relaxed youth **hostel**. It's a 25-minute walk in from the road, and accommodation is in bunk beds and hammocks, with shared bathroom. The price (Bz$40 per person) includes three meals (food is supplied, guests cook for themselves, bring your own drinks), horse-riding and use of the canoe. **Camping** is free, and you pay only for food. There's no need to book; just show up, even at night, though you can write to Larry, c/o Sittee River Village.

The Placencia peninsula

Sixteen kilometres south of Maya Centre a good dirt road heads east from the Southern Highway through pine forest and banana plantations for 13km, reaching the sea at the tiny settlement of **Riversdale**. This marks the start of the **PLACENCIA PENINSULA**, a narrow, sandy finger of land separating the Caribbean and Placencia Lagoon and curving down 26km to **Placencia**, a small, laid-back fishing village, light years from the hassle of Belize City, and now catering to an increasing number of tourists.

As you travel south down the peninsula you'll pass a dozen or so (mostly upscale) resorts and hotels, most of them owned and operated by expatriate North Americans. Accommodation is usually in cabins with private bathrooms and electricity. Meals, if not included in the tariff, come to around U$30 per day, and hotel tax and a ten percent service charge may be added to bills. In addition to the pleasures of a Caribbean beach just a few steps away, most of the resorts also have access to Placencia Lagoon, and can arrange diving trips and tours

Temple of the Wooden Lintel, Caracol   Hidden Valley Falls, Cayo

Mountain Pine Ridge

Keel-billed toucan

A. BRODEN, ISLAND EXPEDITIONS

Kayaking, Glover's Reef

JAMES BEVERIDGE

Flint artefacts, Lamanai museum

R. POWERS, TRIP

ELLEN MCRAE

Great egret in coconut palm

Fisher boys, Roatán, Honduras

Mopan mask maker, Maya Centre

Woman grinding corn, Orange Walk

Temple complex, Tikal

Looking south over Glover's Reef

Hunting Caye, South Belize

inland to the Jaguar Reserve and several Maya ruins. At the time of writing a couple of resorts were under construction in Riversdale, but for the moment the first of the peninsula's resorts are in **MAYA BEACH**, a beautiful stretch of coast with wide, white sand beaches halfway to Placencia. Below here the previously little-visited Garífuna village of **Seine Bight** now has several places to stay, though the majority of the peninsula's budget accommodation is in Placencia village itself. The whole route is served by several daily buses from Dangriga.

The **telephone area code** for Placencia is ☎06

Maya Beach resorts

The resorts here are listed in the order you approach them from the north, and all are right by the road.

Xcape Resort (☎014/7361, email *xcape@btl.net*). Good-sized wooden cabins on the beach, with fans and private bathrooms. The resort is run by the Curry family from Texas and the restaurant serves Belizean and Tex-Mex food at reasonable prices, with a daily special. Fishing trips arranged and Mickey can repair tackle. ⑤.

Green Parrot Beach Houses, next to *Xcape* (☎ & fax 224880, email *greenparrot@btl.net*). Spacious wooden houses (sleep up to five) raised on stilts. Owned by Canadians Ray Twanow and Colleen Fleury, these are good value for families or a small group: each house has a living room, a loft bedroom with a queen-size and a single bed, a superb kitchen and a deck with hammocks. There's also an excellent restaurant and the rates include continental breakfast and transport from Placencia airstrip. Guests can use the email service. ⑧.

Singing Sands Inn, just south of the *Green Parrot* (☎ & fax 22243, email *ssi@btl.net*). Six lovely wood and thatch cabins and a good restaurant and bar. There's a good pool for dive training and the coral outcrops here are great for snorkelling. ⑦.

Seine Bight to Placencia

Three kilometres beyond Maya Beach the Garífuna village of **SEINE BIGHT** now has several (mostly overpriced) resorts and hotels, some of which look out of place alongside the dilapidated shacks in the village. One of the best places is the *Hotel Seine Bight* (☎23536, fax 23537, email *mikepam@btl.net*; ⑦), run by English couple Mike and Pamela Hazeltine. The hotel has well-designed, wooden thatched cabañas and suites (some two storey) decorated with Garífuna artefacts and set around a pool on the beach; each has a private bathroom and deck. The popular, intimate restaurant has a full-service international menu and live music in the evenings; you may have to book for dinner in high season (the price includes a taxi from Placencia if you need one). The daily lunch buffet is always good value. The only other reasonably priced accommodation is *Aunt Chigi's Place* (③), a distinctive collection of brightly painted green and yellow buildings set back from the road near the school.

Seine Bight, reputed to have been founded by privateers in 1629, was possibly given its present name by French fishermen deported from Newfoundland after Britain gained control of Canada. The present inhabitants, numbering about 700, are descendants of the Garífuna settlers who arrived in Seine Bight around 1869. The village is certainly worth a visit even if you're not staying; you can play pool in the *Sunshine Bar* and listen to Garífuna music in the *Kulcha Shak* (which also has basic but overpriced rooms). At the south end of the village you can visit *Lola's Art*

Gallery and Laguñedu Cafe, where Lola Delgado displays her superb (and afford-able) oil and acrylic paintings of village life – in great demand to decorate the rooms of the resorts. Lola's husband Edward is also an artist, producing fine wood carvings. Lola is a great cook and serves superb Creole or Garífuna dinners fol-lowed by drumming, singing and dancing. It's a good evening but you'll need to check when she's cooking – there's no phone, so you may have to call in first.

Resorts from Seine Bight to Placencia

Beyond Seine Bight another series of resorts offers upscale **accommodation**; the list below is in the order you approach them from the north. Even though they're pricey, most places will give *Rough Guide* readers worthwhile discounts.

Luba Hati, 1km south of Seine Bight (☎23402, fax23403, email *lubahati@btl.net*). The name is Garífuna for "House of the Moon", and the rooms, featuring original tiles and artwork and designed with Italian flair, are named after the word for moon in several languages. Run by Franco and Mariuccia, who offer some of the best food and hospitality in Belize, the terraces on two levels are a perfect place to savour the evening breezes – and the moonlight. Price includes continental breakfast and transfer from the airstrip. ⑨.

Serenity Resort, 2km south of Seine Bight (☎23232, fax 23231, email *serenity@btl.net*). Twelve large, comfortable, sky-blue cabins with patio, and a ten-bedroom hotel with a con-ference centre, often used by church and study groups. Has an excellent restaurant and there are great views from the roof. ⑦.

Rum Point Inn, just north of the airstrip, 4km from Placencia (☎23239, fax 23240, in US ☎1-800/747-1381, email *rupel@btl.net*). Expert naturalists Corral and George Beaver offer the most sumptuous (and expensive) rooms on the peninsula. The unique, giant mushroom-shaped whitewashed cabins, with windows cut into the roof and plants growing inside, are spacious, cool and very comfortable, and there are some new suites. There's also a pool, to help with dive instruction, and the *Auriga II*, with a highly professional crew, is one of the best dive boats in the country. With emphasis on archeology, science and natural history, the library is the best of any hotel in the country, and the restaurant is first-class (non-residents must book). US$225 double, including all meals, high season. ⑨.

Kitty's Place, just south of the airstrip (☎23227, fax 23226, email *kittys@btl.net*). Conveniently near the village and one of the nicest options in this area, with a variety of accommodation including apartments, beach cabañas, garden rooms, a studio and rooms in a couple of colonial-style houses on the beach,. Every room is really comfortable, the atmos-phere is sublime, and the grounds and views are unbeatable. The restaurant serves delicious Belizean and international food and breakfast is included in the room price. *Kitty's* offers trips out to French Louie Caye (see p.187). ⑧–⑨.

Turtle Inn, 1km north of the village (☎23244, fax 23245, email *turtleinn@btl.net*). Seven wood-and-thatch cabañas on a gorgeous, palm-lined beach. Skip White, the American owner, has built a superb, relaxed resort for diving, fishing and jungle tours. No added service charge; tips are optional. Guests can use sea kayaks and bicycles. Rates include breakfast. ⑧.

Placencia

Perched on the tip of the peninsula, shaded by palm trees and cooled by the sea breeze, **PLACENCIA** is a welcome stop after the bus ride from Belize City or Dangriga. It is also one of the few places in mainland Belize with proper beaches, and this, together with the abundant, inexpensive accommodation makes it a great place to relax. Unfortunately its remote location and distance from the reef put many of the tours out of the reach of travellers on a low budget, though more options are becoming available.

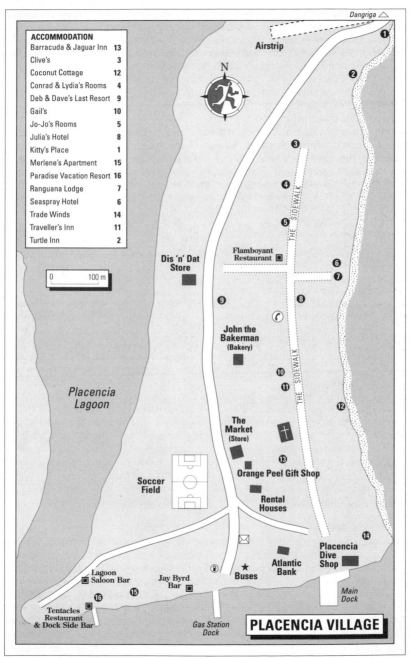

PLACENCIA VILLAGE

ACCOMMODATION

Barracuda & Jaguar Inn	13
Clive's	3
Coconut Cottage	12
Conrad & Lydia's Rooms	4
Deb & Dave's Last Resort	9
Gail's	10
Jo-Jo's Rooms	5
Julia's Hotel	8
Kitty's Place	1
Merlene's Apartment	15
Paradise Vacation Resort	16
Ranguana Lodge	7
Seaspray Hotel	6
Trade Winds	14
Traveller's Inn	11
Turtle Inn	2

0   100 m

Placencia Lagoon

Dangriga

Airstrip

N

THE SIDEWALK

Dis 'n' Dat Store

Flamboyant Restaurant

John the Bakerman (Bakery)

The Market (Store)

Orange Peel Gift Shop

Rental Houses

Soccer Field

Placencia Dive Shop

Atlantic Bank

Buses

Lagoon Saloon Bar

Jay Byrd Bar

Tentacles Restaurant & Dock Side Bar

Gas Station Dock

Main Dock

The easiest way to reach Placencia is on one of the regular Maya Island or Tropic Air **flights** from the international or municipal airports (about 45min). Much cheaper are the direct **buses from Dangriga**, which leave between 11.30am and 4.30pm. You can also hop over easily on the regular **boat service** from **Independence/Mango Creek**, the small town just across the lagoon, where residents come to buy supplies and the older children go to school. For full transport details in Independence, see p.189.

Arrival and orientation

Buses from Dangriga end up at the beachfront gas station, right at the end of the peninsula (they return between 5am and 7am – check at your hotel for exact times, or the *Seaspray*, where they sell tickets). If you're **flying** in there's usually a taxi (Bz$20, and you can share the cost) waiting to take you to the village; if not it's only a three-minute walk to *Kitty's* where you can call Brad's Taxi (☎014/7307). Boats from Independence (see p.189) usually arrive at the main dock, by the gas station. If you're looking for **budget rooms** you should get off the bus when you see the sign for the *Seaspray Hotel*, about halfway through the village, on the left-hand side of the road. Head for **the sidewalk**, a concrete walkway that winds through the palms like an elongated garden path, and you'll be at the centre of a cluster of hotels and restaurants.

Information

There's no official **tourist office** but locals, most of whom (or their family) will have some interest in a tourist business, are glad to answer questions; the Orange Peel Gift Shop, across from the soccer field, supplies hand-drawn **maps** of the village and peninsula. A few good sources of information are the tour office next to the gas station (with a reliable **public telephone** outside), the *Jay Byrd Bar*, just past the gas station and Wende Bryan at the *Barracuda and Jaguar Inn*, who's head of the local BTIA.

The **post office**, without a permanent home, is currently across from Olga's Store, near the gas station, and the new **BTL office** is by the sidewalk in the centre of the village. The Atlantic **bank**, across from the main dock by the gas station, is open at least three mornings a week, and there's a branch of Barclays in Independence (open Friday mornings only); both can give **cash advances**. If your hotel doesn't do **laundry**, try Willie's Laundry, at the north end of the village. Finally there's a basic **medical centre** in the village, with a nurse, but usually no doctor – if you need one you'll probably have to go across to Mango Creek.

Accommodation

In Placencia village proper there's a wide choice of **accommodation**, and you should have no problem finding a room provided you don't arrive at Christmas, New Year or Easter without a booking. Possibilities begin at the sidewalk, and as you wend your way down it seems as though every family is offering **rooms**. If you want a **house to rent** the best-value place is offered by Ted Berlin (☎23172), who, in addition to being a qualified acupuncturist, has a couple of simple but charming places to rent for around Bz$150 per week. He'll let them out by the day if available (③) – note that they do get booked up quickly.

BUDGET ACCOMMODATION

Clive's, at the northern end of the sidewalk. The cheapest option, with simple cabins and plenty of space for camping. ①–②.

Conrad and Lydia's Rooms, near the north end of the sidewalk (☎23117). Very good value, clean, secure rooms run by a friendly family, who'll cook breakfast on request. They also have a house to rent. ③.

Deb & Dave's Last Resort, on the road, the bus will stop outside (☎23207, fax 23334, email *debanddave@btl.net*). The nicest budget place in the village: lovely, very comfortable wooden rooms with a shared, clean bathroom with hot water. You can rent bikes and **kayaks** here and Dave is a superb tour guide. ③.

Gail's, to the right of the sidewalk, near the centre – look for the sign. Two simple but roomy cabins; each can sleep three. ②.

Jo-Jo's Rooms, by the sidewalk, north of the centre (☎23168). A couple of bargain cabins, run by a friendly Canadian expatriate. ②.

Julia's Hotel, in the centre of the village, just south of the *Seaspray* (☎23185). Small hotel, with clean, simple rooms on the beach, between the sidewalk and the sea. There's a porch, though not much sea view. ②.

Paradise Vacation Resort, follow the path to the right from the end of the sidewalk, at the main dock (☎23179; fax 23256). Two-storey hotel where most of the rooms have private bath and hot water. Large deck upstairs where you can enjoy the breeze. Very good value. ③.

Seaspray Hotel, on the beach in the centre of the village (☎ & fax 23148, email *seaspray@btl.net*). A popular, well-run hotel with a range of accommodation, all with bath, hot water and all recently renovated. Owners Jodie and Norman Leslie have reliable information and sell tickets for Ritchie's bus. ④–⑤.

Traveller's Inn, signed from the sidewalk, just south of the centre (☎23190). Five basic rooms – the cheapest in the village – with shared bath, and some in a separate building with private bath. Run by a friendly couple. ②.

MID-RANGE AND ABOVE

Barracuda and Jaguar Inn, signed just past the market, towards the south end of the village (☎23330, fax 23250). Two varnished wooden cabins with two double beds and coffee-maker, and a large deck with lounge chairs and a hammock, set in luxuriant tropical gardens (a pool is planned). Run by Canadian Wende Bryan, it's Placencia's best value in this range and the bar is a great place to exchange information and arrange trips. Rates (discounts if you show the *Rough Guide*) include breakfast. ⑤.

Coconut Cottage, on the beach, just south of the centre (☎ & fax 23234). Two gorgeous, well-decorated and immaculately clean cabins in a quiet location, equipped with fridge, coffee-maker and hot-water shower, run by American Kay Westby; need to book in high season. ⑤.

Merlene's Apartment, west from the south dock, turn right at the gas station (☎23264). The best studio apartment in the village, with a double and a single bed and a kitchen with a huge fridge and stove. A balcony runs along the front and you can watch the sunrise over Placencia Caye. The restaurant serves the best home cooking in Placencia; rates include breakfast. ⑥.

Ranguana Lodge, on the beach in the centre of the village (☎ & fax 23112). Very friendly and well run, with beautiful white cabañas featuring hardwood interiors. All have hot water, fridge and coffee-maker, plus balcony and hammocks. Three are on the beach; the two others have sea views. This is the place to book for Ranguana Caye (see p.188). ⑥.

Trade Winds, on the south point (☎23122, fax 23201). Five cabins with fridge, coffee-maker, hot water and deck, and five newer rooms, all on a spacious plot that gets the sea breezes. Run by Janice Leslie, Placencia's former postmistress and a mine of local knowledge. ④ & ⑥.

Eating, drinking and nightlife

There are plenty of good **restaurants** in Placencia, though even more than else-where in Belize, places change management fast, so it's always worth asking a resident's advice first. There are also a number of good restaurants at the resorts along the peninsula, and it may be worth sharing a cab to try somewhere differ-ent. Most places close early; you'll certainly have a better choice if you're at the table by 8pm.

Fresh **bread** is available from John The Bakerman, just north of the market, and from a number of local women who bake Creole bread and buns. The large shop known as The Market is the main place for produce or any other shopping: get there early as fresh goods are soon sold out. Olga's Store, near the gas sta-tion, probably has the best range of supplies in the village, and there are sever-al other small grocery stores. A large, American-run store, Dis' n' Dat, at the roadside in the centre of the village, sells a wide range of non-perishable foods.

Chili's, at the south point, near the main dock. A bargain food counter in what Bill, the owner calls, a "chicken shed"; try the enormous vegetarian burrito. Best at lunchtime.

Daisy's Ice Cream Parlour, set back from the sidewalk, just south of the *Seaspray*. Long-established and deservedly popular place for ice cream, cakes and snacks, and now serving complete meals.

Merlene's Restaurant, just past *Brenda's* (☎23264). Great for breakfast (usually the first to open), serving good coffee and fantastic home-made bread and cakes. Lunch and dinner are equally good, especially for fish, but it's tiny so you may have to book.

Omar's Fast Foods, on the sidewalk, just south of the centre. Really inexpensive, and some-times even fast, but the quality can vary. Great, filling burritos.

La Petite Maison, just south of The Market (☎23172). Classic French cuisine superbly served in a romantic, candlelit atmosphere. The set menu changes daily and you get a won-derful five-course dinner. At Bz$46 it's pricey by Placencia standards but worth it for a spe-cial occasion. Bud and Barbara Edrick, from New York, are only in Placencia during the win-ter, and since they only serve eight dinners it's best if you reserve a table, preferably the day before. Open Tues–Sat.

Pickled Parrot Bar & Grill, at the *Barracuda and Jaguar Inn*. Very friendly place under a big thatched roof, this is consistently the best restaurant in the village, serving fresh seafood, great pizza, pastas and salads. The bar has wonderful tropical blender drinks.

Tentacles, built over the water at the south end of the village. Superb location to enjoy the sunset. Steaks, pasta and seafood, but variable service and quality, so check first.

Nightlife

The **evenings** in Placencia are as relaxed as the days and there are plenty of **bars**, ideal for drinking rum and watching the sun set; an increasing number have **live music** to enhance the party mood. One of the best beachfront locations is the *Cozy Corner* (formerly a disco of the same name), with a deck and tables under the palms, while nearby, on the sidewalk, the *Sunrise* has a band at weekends. Turn right at the sign by the soccer field for *Lagoon Saloon*, run by long-time Placencia residents Mike and Bonnie Cline and a favourite meeting place at the south end of the village; it closes early though, so is best for an early evening drink.

Around Placencia, offshore and inland

In general, trips from Placencia can be tailor-made to your preference and per-haps your pocket, and you can arrange anything from an afternoon on the water to a week of camping, fishing, snorkelling and sailing. The main **reef** lies about 30km offshore; this distance means that snorkelling and diving trips are more expensive here than at many other places in Belize. Here are the exquisitely beautiful **Silk Cayes**, where the Barrier Reef begins to break into several smaller reefs and cayes, and also many smaller islands and coral heads closer to the shore. Among them are the **Bugle Cayes** and **Lark Caye**, while many trips take in uninhabited **Laughing Bird Caye**, a recently expanded National Park. Several other cayes have resort **accommodation**.

Diving on any of these places is excellent, with fringing and patch reefs, and there's such a wide choice that during a month-long stay you need never go to the same site twice. Booking your scuba-diving through a dive shop (rather than an independent guide) is usually the least expensive option. Placencia Dive Shop at the southern end of the sidewalk (☎23313) has friendly, safety-conscious service, excellent guides and the best dockside facilities; it's also good value at US$60 for a two-tank dive. Also worth trying, especially for PADI courses, is Aquatic Adventures, on the dock at the end of the village (☎23182).

Placencia lagoon is ideal for exploring in a **canoe** (Bz$20 per day), available from Dave Dial at the gas station, who also rents a small **sailboat** (Bz$50); you may even spot manatee, though it's more likely to be a series of ripples as the shy giant swims powerfully for cover. **Kayaks** and **bikes** (Bz$30 per day each) can be rented from Sundowner Tours, in the post office, or from Dave Vernon at *Deb & Dave's*. The best **fishing guides** in the village are Martin Westby of Gone Fishing (☎23330), with an office at the *Barracuda and Jaguar Inn*, and Bernard Leslie who runs Ocean Motion (☎23162), from a small office near the southern end of the sidewalk. It's also worth **heading inland** from Placencia – up the thickly forested banks of the **Monkey River** or to the Jaguar Reserve (see p.179).

French Louis Caye

Kitty Fox and her partner Ran (from *Kitty's Place*; see p.182) offer a great sea-kayaking trip to **French Louis Caye**, a tiny island fringed with mangroves 10km offshore. You paddle the kayak, camp on the caye overnight (using your own equipment, or sleeping in a hammock in the two-storey wooden house if no one else is using it) and food is provided; all for US$50 per person, including snorkelling gear. If you want exclusive use of the caye it costs US$150 for two people, including transport and snorkelling equipment; you can cook at the wooden house or Kitty can organize someone. Mosquitoes are not a problem as there's no open fresh water. All around is great snorkelling, with numerous hard and soft corals, sea anemones and huge schools of tiny fish among the mangrove roots, and you can visit at least half a dozen uninhabited cayes nearby. French Louis Caye even has a resident pair of ospreys, who nest in a mature white mangrove and successfully rear chicks every year.

Wippari Caye

Lying 14km from the mainland, **Wippari Caye** (30min by boat) is one of the nearer cayes to Placencia; it's also one of the most affordable, especially if you like **fishing**. Accommodation here is in wooden cabins (Bz$70 per person) or a dorm room (Bz$45); the rates include meals but not transport (around Bz$40). There's also a self-catering house for rent: contact George Cabral, who lives next to the *Sunrise Bar* in Placencia (☎23130). Prices tend to fluctuate considerably, so check first what's included. The island is the heart of the **bonefish fishing** area, and there are sea kayaks for guests.

Little Water Caye

Thirty kilometres east of Placencia, just beyond Laughing Bird Caye National Park, **Little Water Caye** is a beautiful, palm-studded island renowned for the clarity of the water and the quality of the fly-fishing in the lagoon shallows. In this idyllic, remote location, *Little Water Caye Resort* (☎ & fax 061/2019 or 014/7727, email *seidel-hartung@t-online.de*), run by Andreas Weustefeld, originally from Germany, has three spacious wooden cabins right at the water's edge. A stay here is part of a package; around US$750 for one week (shorter stays available), including transfers from Placencia, all meals and full snorkelling equipment; diving can also be arranged.

Ranguana Caye

Ranguana Caye, 35km southeast of Placencia, is a jewel of an island just 120m long by 20m wide. The sand is softer here, the palm trees taller and more stately than in Placencia, and the sunsets glorious, silhouetting mountain ranges in Honduras and the Maya Mountains in Belize. The *Ranguana Reef Resort* (contact *Ranguana Lodge* in Placencia; see p.185) offers accommodation in beautiful wooden cabins (⑤) facing into the almost constant breeze. Camping is also available (②). The showers and toilets are immaculate and there's even hot water and electricity. Ranguana Caye is surrounded by patch reefs; for divers the shelf and drop-off down to 800m begin 750m offshore. Transport to the caye is not included in the price; a boat for up to four people costs US$85 each way.

The Monkey River

One of the best day-trips from Placencia takes you by boat 20km southwest to the almost pristine **Monkey River**, teeming with fish, birdlife and, naturally enough, howler monkeys. Dave Dial of Monkey River Magic (☎23208, fax 23291) runs the best **tours**, his wildlife expertise complemented by the experienced local guides from Monkey River village. He also has some good packages with accommodation available for guests on his tours. Tours from Placencia set off by 7am (US$40, including a continental breakfast), leaving from the dock by the gas station. A thirty-minute dash through the waves is followed by a leisurely glide up the river and a walk along forest trails. Lunch is usually taken on a sandbank on the river or you can get a meal in *Alice's Restaurant* in **MONKEY RIVER TOWN** (in reality a small village), where there's also time to enjoy a drink in the *Driftwood Bar*, at the river mouth, on the widest beach in Belize. If you want **to stay**, try *Enna's Hotel* (④), which has decent basic rooms and 24-hour electricity, though it's a bit overpriced; there are probably other places by now. For local information call Monkey River community telephone on ☎06/22014, and for a guide call Eloy Cuevas (☎06/22014), or ask at *Enna's* for Evaristo Muschamp.

As the south of Belize becomes more accessible, the Monkey River area is becoming increasingly important for tourism; the 22km dirt road connecting the village to the Southern Highway is being improved and you may well be able to drive there now. On the coast just north of the mouth of the Monkey

---

INDEPENDENCE TRAVEL CONNECTIONS

Just across the lagoon from Placencia, **Independence**, though of little intrinsic interest, is a useful travel hub and is served by all **buses** between Dangriga and Punta Gorda. Buses leave Dangriga daily at about 2.30pm (2hr) or you can take any service to or from Punta Gorda. There's a regular **boat to Placencia** – the *Hokey Pokey* (☎22376; 35min; Bz$15) – which leaves at 8.30am and 2.30pm, returning from Placencia at 10am and 4pm; the boatman usually meets the arriving buses. Otherwise, if you wait around for a while, you may be able to get a lift on a boat with a Placencia local. The fare depends on what you're willing to pay – reckon on around Bz$15. A charter costs at least Bz$30.

Heading north from Independence, Z-Line buses leave for **Dangriga** (2hr) at 8am, noon and 3pm, and south to **Punta Gorda** (3hr) at 2pm, 6pm and 9pm. The James bus also passes through once daily, heading south about 2.30pm. Z-Line buses take a rest/meal stop at the *Cafe Hello* in Independence; the James bus stops at *Marita's* (the better restaurant), across the way on Hercules Avenue.

Although some maps show Mango Creek and Independence as two places, the creek just lends its name to one end of town; Independence begins at the road junction. With all these transport connections you should be able to avoid getting stuck **overnight** here. If you do, the *Hello Hotel* (☎06/22428; ⑤), mainly used by business people, has some a/c rooms; you could also try the clean, simple *Ursula's Guest House* (②) on Gran Main Street. The Barclays **bank** (Fri am only) gives cash advances.

River, a couple of new places (only accessible by boat) offer **accommodation**. *Bob's Paradise*, 2km north of the river (☎014/8206, in US ☎954/429-8763, email *bobsparadise@webtv.net*; ⑧, including breakfast), has three good wooden cabins with comfortable beds, fridge and hot shower, near the water's edge. There's a pleasant thatched bar and restaurant but the rooms are overpriced unless you're dedicated to fishing – which is very good. Just south of here, *The Monkey House* (☎014/8912; ⑥) is a better option for non-fishermen. Run by American couple Sam and Martha Scott, it also has three very pleasant wooden cabins with private bathrooms, each with a screened porch and furniture made in their own workshop; the dining room is just yards from the sea and the food is great.

The far south: Toledo District

South of the Placencia and Independence junctions, the Southern Highway leaves the banana plants and the grim settlements squashed beside the plantation roads, twisting at first through pine forests, and crossing numerous creeks and rivers. There are only a few villages along the way, and new citrus plantations are always in view, the neat ranks of trees marching over the hills. The mountains to the west are all part of the country's system of forest reserves, national parks and nature reserves, though conflicts over the status of some protected areas are emerging as Toledo District (whose residents often feel they live in Belize's "forgotten district") becomes more developed. Wildlife is abundant but the reserves are often inaccessible, though on the northern border of Toledo, at **Red Bank**, you can see one of the largest concentrations of **scarlet macaws** in Central America.

Although the Maya of Belize are a fairly small minority within the country as a whole, in Toledo the two main groups – Mopan and Kekchí – make up about half the population. For the most part they live in simple villages, very similar in appearance to their Guatemalan counterparts; the verdant, mountainous landscape of the far south resembles that of Guatemala's Alta Verapaz and southern Petén, where the ancestors of many of Belize's Maya came from. The biggest of the Maya villages are **San Antonio** and **San Pedro Columbia**, reached by a good side road heading west from the highway. These villages have hotels; you can visit many other villages and stay in simple guest houses.

There's plenty of evidence that the ancient Maya lived here too, with ruins scattered in the hills around the villages. The best-known site is **Lubaantun**, where the famous Crystal Skull was "discovered", but **Nim Li Punit**, with some impressive stelae, is an easy visit from the highway. The Southern Highway ends in **Punta Gorda**, the southernmost town in Belize and the only town in Toledo. It's the base for visits to both the inland villages and the southernmost cayes, and is connected to **Puerto Barrios** in Guatemala by several daily skiffs.

Red Bank

Fourteen kilometres south of the junction to Riversdale and Placencia a side road heads 6km west to the small Maya village of **Red Bank**, the focus of a campaign to preserve the habitat of the largest-known concentration of **scarlet macaws** in Belize – if not Central America. These spectacular members of the parrot family have generally been considered uncommon in Belize; knowledge of the flock – which could number over two hundred birds – only came to light when word reached conservation organizations in Belize City that villagers (who had no idea of the macaws' protected and endangered status) were hunting them for food. The Programme for Belize and the Belize Audubon Society immediately devised proposals to establish a tourism project in the hope that income from visitors would bring economic benefits to the people of Red Bank. So far, a four-roomed cabin (③) with a deck overlooking a pretty creek, has been built near the village, in sight of the macaws feeding on the fruit trees in the surrounding hills. Villagers are also being trained to guide visitors and there are **trails** to waterfalls and caves. There's currently no regular transport to Red Bank, but trucks leave daily from and to Independence. For details on staying or visiting contact the PFB or the BAS in Belize City (see pp.41–2), or telephone Geronimo Sho on the Red Bank **community telephone** (☎06/22233).

South to Punta Gorda: Nim Li Punit and Big Falls

About 73km from the Placencia junction, near the Maya village of **Indian Creek**, are the ruins of **Nim Li Punit**, a Late Classic period Maya site possibly allied to nearby Lubaantun. The site is only 1km west of the highway and the track is signposted. Although it's an easy visit from the road, few people bother to stop – a pity since it's home to the largest and one of the best-preserved stelae in Belize. Any passing bus will stop – even if the driver doesn't know the site, he'll know Whitney's store and gas station, just below the turn-off for the ruins; someone in the store will look after your luggage while you visit the site. On the way in you pass the village **Arts and Crafts Centre**, often untended due to lack of custom.

The ruins, discovered in 1976, lie on a ridge with views over the maize fields of the village to the entire southern coastal plain beyond – a scene largely unchanged since ancient times. A total of 25 stelae were found here, eight of them carved; **Stela 14**, at almost 10m high, is the tallest in Belize, and one of the tallest anywhere in the Maya world. Unfortunately, the site was badly looted soon after its discovery and in 1997 several of the stelae were again badly damaged – this time by fire and machete. You enter through a plaza with walls and buildings of cut stones, a characteristic of sites in southern Belize, and pass through the ball-court to the South Group, which holds most of the carved stelae. Although Stela 14 lies on the ground – in fact it was never erected – it's still an impressive sight, with panels of glyphs above and a richly attired ruler below: it's his elaborate headgear that gives Nim Li Punit its name, being Kekchí for "big hat". **Stela 15**, dated to 721 AD and the earliest stela here, is smaller yet even more impressive. Carvings on this great sandstone slab depict a larger-than-life figure in the act of dropping an offering – perhaps *copal* incense or kernels of corn – into an elabo-rately carved burning brazier supported on the back of a monster. To his right, a much smaller figure also makes an offering into the brazier, while on his left side a column of very clear glyphs separates the main figure from an attendant, or guard; all three figures are almost entirely surrounded by panels of glyphs. At the moment there's no entry fee to the site, but there are plans to charge one; ask caretaker Placido Ash to show you around.

Big Falls

Ten kilometres further south, the road to **Silver Creek** branches off to the right, and with your own transport you can use this route to visit the Maya villages and the ruins of Lubaantun (see p.199). Just beyond the junction, near the village of **BIG FALLS**, is the only **hot spring** in Belize, a luxurious spot for a warm bath. The spring is on a farm owned by Peter Aleman, who also runs a small shop and guest house (③). You can camp for a few dollars but you'll have to ask permission first. Don't expect to have the place all to yourself at weekends, however, as the pools are a popular picnic spot. There's a major bridge over the Rio Grande here and just over the bridge, on the hot springs creek just before it joins the main river, some villagers have built a group of thatched **cabañas** (③) – look for the sign *Xaiha* (hot water) on the right. The river is beautiful and you can bathe in the falls and rent **canoes** to paddle upstream. The paving of the Southern Highway had reached Big Falls in 1998, and it's likely to have been followed by a telephone service. However, at the time of writing there was no phone and no reli-able way to contact the village, so you'll either have to take a chance and just get off the bus – it's only a short walk – or check at *Nature's Way* in Punta Gorda (see p.194). The junction from the Southern Highway to San Antonio and the Maya vil-lages is 7km south of Big Falls – marked by a gas station at a place called "The Dump"; beyond here the road is smooth and fast all the way into Punta Gorda, 35km to the south.

Punta Gorda

The Southern Highway eventually comes to an end in **PUNTA GORDA** (com-monly known as PG), the heart of the isolated Toledo District – an area that has until recently been hard to reach and largely overlooked by planners and devel-opers. However, the first section of the highway north from Punta Gorda is now paved and the few visitors who make it out here are rewarded by spending a few days at the Maya villages inland (see p.197), where you can experience a way of life far removed from the rest of Belize. Offshore, the **Sapodilla Cayes** form the focus of Belize's newest **marine reserve**. Punta Gorda's position on low sea cliffs allows cooling breezes to reduce the worst of the heat but there's no denying that this is the wettest part of Belize. The trees are heavy with mosses and bromeliads, their lush growth encouraged by heavy rains which can last for days.

To the north of Punta Gorda are the remains of the Toledo settlement, which was founded in 1867 by Confederate emigrants from the US. Many of the original settlers soon drifted home, discouraged by the torrential downpours and the

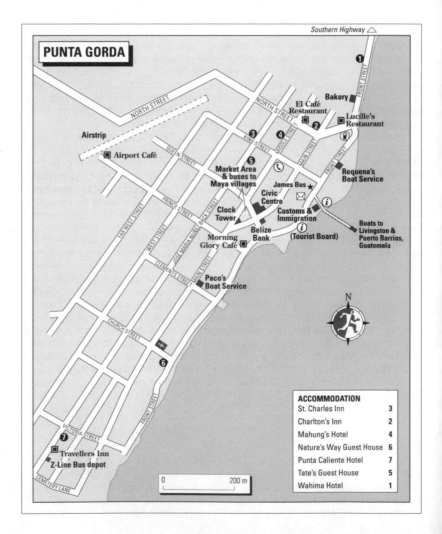

PUNTA GORDA

Southern Highway

NORTH STREET
NORTH STREET
FRONT STREET
❶
Bakery
El Café
Restaurant
Lucille's
Restaurant
❷
❾
KING STREET
Airstrip
❸
❹
MIDDLE STREET
MAIN STREET
FRONT STREET
QUEEN STREET
Airport Café
❺
Requena's
Boat Service
Market Area
& buses to
Maya villages
James Bus
Civic
Centre
PRINCE STREET
Customs &
Immigration
Clock
Tower
FAR WEST STREET
WEST STREET
JOSE MARIA NUÑEZ
BACK STREET
Belize
Bank
Morning
Glory Café
(Tourist Board)
Boats to
Livingston &
Puerto Barrios,
Guatemala
CLEMENTS STREET
MAIN STREET
Paco's
Boat Service
N
CHURCH STREET
FRONT STREET
❻
VICTORIA STREET
❼
Travellers Inn
Z-Line Bus depot
CEMETERY LANE

0   200 m

ACCOMMODATION	
St. Charles Inn	3
Charlton's Inn	2
Mahung's Hotel	4
Nature's Way Guest House	6
Punta Caliente Hotel	7
Tate's Guest House	5
Wahima Hotel	1

rigours of frontier life, but their numbers were boosted by Methodists from Mississippi. The Methodists were deeply committed to the settlement and, despite a cholera epidemic in 1868, managed to clear 160 acres. By 1870 sugar was the main product, with twelve separate estates running their own mills. The settlement reached its peak in 1890, after which it was threatened by falling sugar prices. Most farmers moved into alcohol production, but for the Methodists this was out of the question, and they preferred to feed their molasses to their cattle. By 1910 their community was destitute, although it was largely as a result of their struggle that Toledo was permanently settled.

Today's town has a population of around four thousand – a mixture of Mestizos, Garífuna, Maya and Creoles, with a few Lebanese and Chinese as well. It's the focal point for a large number of villages and farming settlements and the busiest day is Saturday, when people from the surrounding villages come in to trade. Despite the recent minor building boom, Punta Gorda remains a small, unhurried, friendly town and you won't encounter any hassle.

The **telephone area code** for Punta Gorda is ☎07

Arrival and information

Buses from Belize City, via Dangriga, take around eight or nine hours to reach Punta Gorda; Z-Line go all the way through the town to their depot at the end of José María Nuñez Street (☎22165), while James buses stop at their office near the main dock (☎22049). **Skiffs to and from Puerto Barrios** in Guatemala use the main dock by the immigration office, roughly in the centre on the seafront. The airstrip, served by five or six daily **flights** from Belize City, is only five blocks west of the centre. For details of moving on from PG, see the box on p.195.

Despite having relatively few visitors Punta Gorda is practically awash with **information centres**. The privately run Toledo Visitors Information Center (TVIC; ☎22470), by the ferry dock, offers homestay accommodation in the Maya villages; it's run by with Alfredo and Yvonne Villoria, who have a guest house in San Pedro Columbia. The Belize Tourist Board has a very informative office on Front Street (Tues–Sat 9am–noon & 1–4.30pm, Sun 9am–noon; ☎22531); the staff will know the times of all the buses to the Maya villages.

The group of government buildings opposite the main dock houses the **post office** and a **public phone**; the BTL office is a block further on. The only **bank** is the Belize Bank (Mon–Fri 8am–1pm, Fri also 3–4pm), at the top corner of the main square, across from the Civic Center. There will usually be a **moneychanger** outside the immigration office when the international boats are coming and going; it's best to get rid of your Belize dollars before you leave.

Accommodation

During the last couple of years there has been a spate of **hotel** building in the village, in the expectation of a rapid rise in the number of visitors enjoying the area's many attractions. While numbers have increased, however, few people spend long here, and there are plenty of bargains.

Charlton's Inn, 9 Main St (☎22197, fax 22471). This two-storey concrete building has rooms (some a/c) with private bath, hot water and TV; there's also cold water to drink. The *Inn* has safe parking and owner Duwane Wagner can arrange car hire and sell domestic air tickets. ②–④.

Mahung's, corner of North and Main streets (☎22044). Reasonable, inexpensive rooms with hot water; some private baths, a/c and TV. Bicycle rental available. ③.

Nature's Way Guest House, 65 Front St (☎22119, email *thfec@btl.net*). The best budget place in Punta Gorda; renowned as a meeting place and information point. Private rooms and clean, comfortable dorm accommodation (Bz$16), overlooking the sea. Good meals served in the wholefood restaurant. Owner William "Chet" Schmidt, a committed environmentalist, has been in PG for thirty years and is a driving force behind the Toledo Ecotourism Association, housed in an office in front of the hotel. Chet can arrange trips to the villages and rents kayaks and canoes. ③.

Punta Caliente, 108 José María Nuñez St (☎22561), next to the Z-Line terminal. Clean, comfortable rooms with private bath, ceiling fan, and cable TV. Owner Alex Arzú is a historian of the Garífuna, and the restaurant – one of the best in town – is virtually a small museum of Garífuna culture. ③.

St Charles Inn, 23 King St (☎22149). Clean and quiet, with carpeted rooms with TV. At the top end of the scale for Punta Gorda, and recommended. ④.

Tate's Guest House, 34 José María Nuñez St, two blocks west of the town centre (☎22196). A quiet, friendly, family-run hotel with some a/c rooms. ③–④.

Wahima, 11 Front St (☎22542). Inexpensive, basic and friendly hotel, right on the seafront; on the bus route, so you can be dropped off at the door. Some rooms have a/c, fridge and TV. A small restaurant/bar next door provides local colour. ②–④.

Eating, drinking and nightlife

Restaurants in Punta Gorda are basic but the situation is improving; there are several newer places where the quality is better, and it's certainly easy to get a filling meal at a reasonable price. Some of the best food is served in tiny family restaurants, often with no formal name, while the *Punta Caliente Hotel* has one of the best restaurants in town, with Creole and Garífuna dishes, and a daily special. The *Morning Glory Café* (closed Mon) on Front Street serves seafood, burgers and snacks in clean, bright surroundings, and you can get the good old Creole staples of rice and beans in the pleasant surroundings of *Lucille's*, by the Texaco station further north along Front Street. Just beyond here *Mangrove* is a bright, new place serving seafood, burgers, steaks, and vegetarian options. *El Café*, behind *Charlton's Inn*, does the best coffee in town and opens for breakfast at 6am. Finally, the *Airport Café* (at the airstrip) is surprisingly good. There's a good **bakery** on Front Street, past the Texaco station, and you can get excellent bread and buns at the little shop just past the *Morning Glory Café*.

The best place to enjoy an early evening drink is *Waluco's*, though it's 2km from the centre; follow Front Street north over the metal bridge. It's popular with expats (there's a surprising number in PG), there's a deck to enjoy the breeze and the beers are at normal prices. Otherwise **nightlife** is either a quiet drink with a meal or a visit to one of several **bars and clubs,** such as the *Starlight* on Main Street. If you're desperate for loud **music,** there's the *Massive Rock Disco* opposite the bus depot.

Staying around Punta Gorda: Toledo's ecotourism projects

Ecotourism is a buzzword throughout Belize, and several projects in Toledo are poised to reap the benefits. Their aim is to achieve a balance between the need for economic development and the need to preserve the rich natural and cultural heritage of the area. It is hoped that small numbers of "low impact" visitors will provide additional income to villages without destroying the communities' traditional way of life. One interesting project is the cultivation of cacao beans, to produce

chocolate; almost all of the crop around here is used to make the delicious *Maya Gold* organic chocolate sold in the UK. The ancient Maya used cacao beans as money; Belize was a great centre of production and the beans were traded over great distances. You'll often see cacao beans drying on special concrete pads as you travel through the villages.

Many Maya villages in Toledo are sited in **Indian Reservations**, designated as such in colonial times to protect the Maya subsistence lands. Title, however, remained with the government (which leases logging concessions), not the Maya who actually occupied the reserves. Recent developments in forestry policy have alarmed community leaders, who fear that so-called "conversion forestry", where all trees over a certain size on the reservations are allowed to be cut down for timber production, will cause further severe erosion and silt up previously clear streams used for drinking. The **Toledo Ecotourism Association**, 65 Front St, Punta Gorda (☎22680, fax 22119) aims to combat the destruction of the forest where the participants make their livelihood by offering visitors a **Guest House and Eco Trail Program**. Thirteen villages in southern Toledo are involved in the project; each has an eight-bed guest house (Bz$18 per person) and meals are taken at different houses to allow distribution of the income. Each village has its own attraction, be it a cave, waterfall, river or ruin, and there are guided walks or horse rides (around Bz$7 per hour; 4hr minimum); there may also be canoes to rent. The villagers have an extensive cultural knowledge of the medicinal uses of plants and the ancient Maya myths and this can be an excellent way to find out about Maya culture and experience village life without feeling like an intruder. The programme has also raised the consciousness of the villagers themselves as they learn to use both the concept of ecotourism and the political process to protect their forest; its efforts were rewarded in 1997 with a tourism industry prize

---

MOVING ON FROM PUNTA GORDA

Z-Line (☎22165) **buses** leave for Belize City (8–9hr) at 5am, 9am and noon; the James (☎22049) bus departs at either 4.30am, 6am or 11am, depending on the day of the week. Buses for the **Maya villages** leave between noon and 1pm (on the days they run) from the streets next to the Civic Center; the tourist office will have full details. Most bus companies are literally one-man operations and Sunday is their day off. **San Antonio** is the biggest village and has two buses, Chun's and Prim's – at least one of them will continue to **Jalacté** on the Guatemalan border (not a legal crossing for visitors). There are departures at noon (Mon, Wed, Fri & Sat) for **San Pedro Columbia** (for Lubaantun) and you can usually get here any day with rides in pickup trucks. Most other villages have just one bus, which travels at least on **market days** (Wed & Sat) and sometimes other days as well. Returning from the villages all buses leave early – around 3.30–5.30am.

To **Puerto Barrios** in Guatemala there are several regular daily **skiffs** (Bz$20 or Bz$25; 1hr in good weather). It's preferable (though not essential) to buy your ticket the day before you travel, so the skipper can get the paperwork ready. The best boats are Paco's (leaves at 8.30am; ☎22246), Requena's (leaves at 9am; ☎22070), and Carlos Carcamo's (leaves at 4pm). You will have to pay the PACT exit fee (Bz$7.50). Some boats will call at **Lívingston** if there's suffcient demand. Returning, boats leave Barrios at 8am or 10am, 1pm & 2pm.

For **flights** check the airlines' offices at the airstrip: Maya Island (☎22856); Tropic (☎2208).

for "Socially Responsible Ecotourism". The guest houses detailed in the text on pp.198–9 are part of the programme.

As an alternative to the guest house programme the TVIC (☎22470) promotes the "**host family network**", in which visitors stay in a village with a Mopan or Kekchí Maya family, participate in village work – grinding corn, chopping firewood, cooking tortillas and the like – and sleep in a hammock. In either programme you'll find few modern conveniences like electricity and flush toilets (though most villages have community telephones, operating on a solar panel), but if you go with an open mind you'll have a fascinating and rewarding experience and the villagers will be happy to teach you some Maya words.

Out to sea: the cayes and the coast

The cayes and reefs off Punta Gorda mark the southern end of Belize's Barrier Reef. The main reef has already started to break up here, leaving several clusters of islands, each surrounded by a small independent reef. Though visited by specialist sea-kayaking tours, the whole area gets relatively little attention from international tourism and is very interesting to explore. At the moment there are few tour operators in Punta Gorda who can reliably run trips to the reef, but if you check with the information centres on p.193, or with Chet at *Nature's Way*, you can find out the latest news.

The closest cayes to Punta Gorda are the **Snake Cayes**, hundreds of tiny islands in the mouth of a large bay, where the shoreline is a complex maze of mangrove swamps; the area is proposed as a marine reserve, partly to protect the many **manatees** living in this shallow water habitat. On Wild Cane Caye archeologists, with the assistance of Earthwatch volunteers, have found evidence of a Maya coastal trade centre. Further out, in the Gulf of Honduras, are the **Sapodilla Cayes**, the largest of which, **Hunting Caye**, has an immigration post to deal with visitors. Other cayes in this group, notably **Lime Caye**, **Franks Caye** and **Nicolas Caye** have some tourism development planned, and will consequently face increasing visitor pressure in the near future. The designation of the Sapodilla Cayes as a marine reserve means that these cayes now receive some protection, though the presence of day-trippers from Guatemala and Honduras can mean a difficult job for the already thinly stretched conservation agencies. The reserve's management plan is still under development; Will Maheia, one of PG's hard-working environmentalists and director of the Toledo Institute for Development and Education, is devising a plan to train net fishermen to become fly-fishing guides. TIDE is involved with many other practical projects; if you're interested in **volunteering** contact Will at PO Box 150, Punta Gorda (☎22274).

From Punta Gorda you can see range upon range of mountains in Guatemala and Honduras, but the Belizean **coastline south** of here is flat and sparsely populated. Tidal rivers meander across a coastal plain covered with thick tropical rainforest that receives over 350mm of rain a year, forming a unique ecosystem in Belize. The Temash River is lined with the tallest mangrove forest in the country, the black mangroves towering over 30m above the riverbanks, while in the far south, the Sarstoon River, navigable by small boats, forms the border with Guatemala; the land between these rivers is now the **Sarstoon-Temash National Park**. These rivers are sometimes paddled on tours run by sea-kayaking companies (see "Basics", pp.5–6), this time using inflatable river kayaks.

The only village on the coast down here is **BARRANCO** (community phone (☎07/22138), a small, traditional Garífuna settlement of two hundred people, which you can visit through the village guest house programme (see p.195). A rough seasonal road connects the village with the Southern Highway, but most people rely on traditional dories, now motor-powered, to get to Punta Gorda.

Towards the mountains: Maya villages and ruins

Heading inland from Punta Gorda towards the foothills of the Maya Mountains, you meet yet another uniquely Belizean culture. Here **Mopan Maya** are mixed with **Kekchí** speakers from the Verapaz highlands of Guatemala. For the most part each group keeps to its own villages, language and traditions, although both

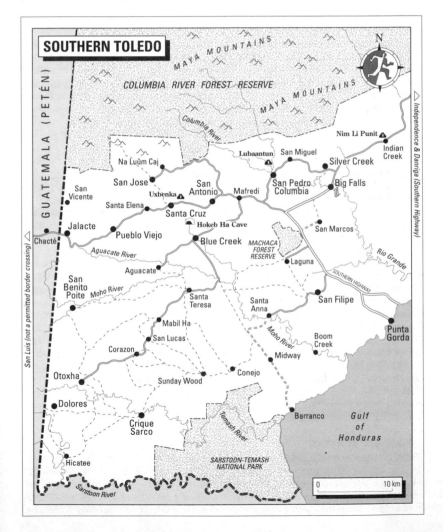

are partially integrated into modern Belizean life and many speak English. Guatemalan families have been arriving here for the last hundred years or so escaping repression and a shortage of land at home, and founding new villages deep in the forest. Several families a year still cross the border to settle in land-rich Belize, along routes that have been used for generations. The villages are connected by road and all have a basic bus service from Punta Gorda (see box on p.195), although moving around isn't that easy and in many places you'll have to rely on hitching, despite the fact that there isn't much traffic. A good option is to rent a bike from *Mahung's* (see p.194). The people here are of course used to walking, and the villages are also connected by an intricate network of footpaths.

San Antonio and Uxbenka

The Mopan Maya village of **SAN ANTONIO**, perched on a small hilltop, is the easiest settlement to reach, as it's served by daily buses from Punta Gorda. It also has the benefit of *Bol's Hill Top Hotel* (community phone ☎07/22124; ③), which has simple **rooms** with electric light and superb views. There are a couple of shops in the village, and you can get **meals** at Theodora's or Clara's houses, behind *Bol's*. The area is rich in wildlife, surrounded by jungle-clad hills and swift-flowing rivers. Further south and west are the villages of the Kekchí Maya, fairly recent immigrants who still retain strong cultural links with Guatemala.

The founders of San Antonio were from the Guatemalan town of San Luis just across the border, and they maintain many age-old traditions. Among other things the Indians of San Luis brought with them their patron saint – opposite *Bol's Hotel* is the beautiful **stone-built church** of San Luis Rey, currently looked after by an American Jesuit order. The church is the third to stand on the site (two previous versions were destroyed by fire) and its most remarkable feature is a set of superb stained-glass windows depicting the twelve apostles and other saints donated by the people of St Louis, Missouri. The villagers also adhere to their own pre-Columbian traditions and fiestas; the main one takes place on June 13, and features marimba music, masked dances and much heavy drinking.

Seven kilometres west from San Antonio, 1km before the village of **Santa Cruz**, are the ruins of **Uxbenka**, a fairly small Maya site, superbly positioned on an exposed hilltop, with great views towards the coast. Uxbenka's existence only became known to archeologists in 1984 after reports of looting in the area: there's now a site caretaker, who lives in Santa Cruz. As you climb the hill before the village you'll be able to make out the shape of two tree-covered mounds to your left. Though the site has not been fully excavated, you can still make out a couple of pyramids and a plaza, and there are several badly eroded stelae, protected by thatched shelters. There's a **guest house** at the entrance to the village, and several buses a week; some continue to **Jalacté** on the border. All around are **trails** through the forest to rivers and waterfalls, and you can walk over to **San José** (with a guest house and on a bus route; community phone ☎07/22972) in about three hours.

Blue Creek and Pusilha

At Mafredi, about 4km before San Antonio, a branch road (served by buses from PG) heads off south and west to **BLUE CREEK**, where the main attraction is the village's namesake – a beautiful stretch of water that runs through magnificent rainforest. The junction is marked by *Roy's Cool Spot*, where you can get a meal and a drink. Four kilometres down the road to Blue Creek you can **stay** in the simple bamboo and wood cabins of *Roots and Herbs* (③), where Pablo and Sonia Bouchub can teach you about the medicinal plants of Toledo. The food is excellent and Pablo is a great **guide**; the bird-watching is fantastic and he knows routes to ruins, lagoons and caves.

Another 3km brings you to Blue Creek itself, and whether you're walking or driving you won't miss the river, as the road crosses it in the middle of the village; the **guest house** is across the bridge and to the left. To get to the best **swimming** spot, walk upriver along the right-hand bank (facing upstream), and in about ten minutes you'll come to a lovely turquoise pool and the wooden cabins of *Blue Creek Rainforest Lodge*, set among the trees (⑧, including meals). The lodge is under the same ownership as *Leslie Cottages* on South Water Caye (see p.173), where you should call to book ahead. The **aerial walkway** here, 25m above the river and extending into the forest on the opposite bank, is unique in Belize. It was built to study the ecology of the forest canopy but visitors can use it by arrangement; you're strapped into a harness before climbing ladders fixed to a large tree on the riverbank. Back at ground level, the **source of Blue Creek**, where the water gushes from beneath a mossy rock face, is about another fifteen minutes' walk upriver. Alongside is the entrance to the **Hokeb Ha cave**, which is fairly easy to explore. The entire area is made up of limestone bedrock honeycombed with caves, many of which were sacred to the Maya, and doubtless there are still plenty of others waiting to be rediscovered. If you want to experience the cave in solitude don't come on a Sunday: it's starting to get crowded. Sylvano is the best guide in Blue Creek and can take you to Maya altars deep in the Blue Creek cave, accessible only by boat.

About 7km west of Blue Creek is the Kekchí village of **Aguacate**, beyond where the road climbs a ridge leading to the valley of the Moho River, near the border with Guatemala. Further up the valley are the ruins of **Pusilha**, a large Maya ceremonial centre. The city is built alongside the river on a small hilltop and although many of the buildings are quite extensive, none is very tall, reaching a maximum height of just 5 or 6m. The site has yielded an astonishing number of carved monuments and stelae, including zoomorphs in a style similar to those at Quiriguá in Guatemala, leading archeologists to suggest that at some stage Pusilha may have been under Quiriguá's control. The site's most unusual feature is the remains of a stone bridge. The ruins are accessible by boat, on foot or on horseback, which could make the whole business rather expensive.

San Pedro Columbia and Lubaantun

To visit the ruins of Lubaantun (daily 8am–4pm; Bz$8) from San Antonio, get a lift along the road to the Southern Highway and turn left at the track leading **to SAN PEDRO COLUMBIA**, a Kekchí village. The bus to San Antonio drops you at the entrance road, about 4km from the village – there's sometimes a truck waiting to ferry passengers over the final section of the journey, and the village also has its own bus service. To get to the site head through the village and cross the bridge over the Columbia River, just beyond which you'll see the track to the ruins, a few hundred metres on the left. If you ask around in the village one of the older boys will gladly show you the way; the ruins are about a twenty-minute walk.

Lubaantun, which means "Place of the Fallen Stones" in modern Mayan – not its original name – is a major Late Classic ceremonial centre which at one time covered a large area. The site is on a high ridge and from the top of the tallest building you can (just) see the Caribbean, over 30km away. Maya architects shaped and filled the hillside, with retaining walls as much as 10m high. Some restoration has now begun and the pyramids are quite impressive, as is the surrounding forest.

It now seems that the site was only occupied briefly, from 700 to 890 AD, very near the end of the Classic period. There are five main plazas with eleven major structures and three ball-courts. The architecture is unusual in a number of ways: there are no stelae or sculpted monuments other than ball-court markers, and the whole site is essentially a single acropolis, constructed on a series of low ridges. Another unusual feature is the absence of mortar; the stone blocks are carved with particular precision and fitted together, Inca-style, with nothing to bind them. The plainness and monumentality of Lubaantun's architecture is again similar to the later buildings at Quiriguá in Guatemala, and there may have been some connection between the two sites.

Lubaantun was brought to the attention of the colonial authorities in 1903 and the governor sent Thomas Gann to investigate. A survey in 1915 revealed many structures, and three ball-court markers were removed and taken to the Peabody Museum. The British Museum expedition of 1926 was joined in 1927 by J. Eric S. Thompson, who was to become the most renowned Maya expert of his time. No further excavations took place for over forty years until Norman Hammond mapped the site in 1970, producing a reconstruction of life in Lubaantun which showed the inhabitants' links with communities on the coast and inland. Lubaantun's wealth was created by the production of cacao beans, used as money by the civilizations of Mesoamerica.

THE CRYSTAL SKULL OF LUBAANTUN

Perhaps Lubaantun's most enigmatic find came in 1926, when the famous **Crystal Skull** was unearthed here. The skull, made from pure rock crystal, was found beneath an altar by Anna Mitchell-Hedges, the adopted daughter of the British Museum expedition's leader, F.A. Mitchell-Hedges. By a stroke of luck the find happened to coincide with her seventeenth birthday, and the skull was then given to the local Maya, who in turn presented it to Anna's father as a token of their gratitude for the help he had given them. It is possible that the "discovery" was a birthday gift for Anna, placed there by her father who had acquired it on his previous travels, although she strenuously denies the allegation. Anna Mitchell-Hedges still owns the skull; she recalls how she spotted sunlight glinting off it during the excavation of a rubble-filled shaft and promises to reveal more in the course of time.

While mystery and controversy still surround the original skull, London's British Museum has another crystal skull which – according to Dr G. M. Morant, an anthropologist who examined both skulls in 1936 – is a copy of the one found at Lubaantun. He also concluded that both of the life-size crystal skulls are modelled on the same original human head but could give no answer as to their true age and origin. The skull was formerly on display in the Museum of Mankind, but when this closed the British Museum decided not to exhibit it, as its origin could not be proved. While on display in the Museum of Mankind, its label was suitably vague: "Possibly from Mexico, age uncertain . . . resembles in style the Mixtec carving of fifteenth-century Mexico, though some lines on the teeth appear to be cut with a jeweller's wheel. If so it may have been made after the Spanish Conquest." There is a similar, smaller crystal skull in the Musée de l'Homme in Paris, and others exist too; all attract great interest from "New Age" mystics, who believe that crystal has supernatural properties.

PRACTICALITIES

Several places in and around San Pedro (community phone ☎07/22303) offer **accommodation**. Alfredo and Yvonne Villoria have a bright, clean **bed and breakfast** room on their sustainable technology farm, *Dem Dats Doin'* (☎07/22470; ③), on the right a kilometre before the village. The couple aim to be as self-sufficient as possible, growing an astonishing range of organic fruits and vegetables, and generating methane gas from the farm animal wastes. Check at the TVIC by the dock in Punta Gorda. There's a **guest house** in the village and a small hotel is under construction. Through the village and 3km beyond the turn off to the ruins (follow the signs), a steeply undulating road leads to *Fallen Stones Butterfly Ranch* (☎07/22167; ⑧ including breakfast), which has comfortable wooden cabins on a hilltop with superb views over the Columbia River Forest Reserve to the Maya Mountains beyond. The cabins all have a private showers with hot water and electricity, and the dining room juts over a ridge, offering good food and even more gorgeous views at dawn and dusk. The **butterflies** are reared in what amounts to a tiny (and charming) industrial process; every step, from the mating and egg-laying, through the stages of caterpillar development, to the critical packing of the chrysalis for shipping, is governed by meticulous timing – all carefully supervised by the "ranch" workers, who look after their insect babies with tender loving care.

travel details

The Southern Highway doesn't have as many buses running along it as the Northern and Western highways, and bus schedules are not as reliabl. However, as road improvements take effect journey times will shorten and timetable reliability will improve. The main routes are listed below; other buses to the smaller villages are covered in the text.

Bus company offices and departure frequencies from Belize City to Dangriga, Placencia and Punta Gorda are covered in the box on p.62.

Buses

Dangriga to: Belize City (10 daily; 2–3hr); **Hopkins** and **Sittee River** (1–2 daily; 40min); **Placencia** (2–3 daily; 2hr); **Punta Gorda** (5 daily; 5hr). All buses between Dangriga and Punta Gorda stop at **Independence**/Mango Creek.

Hopkins and Sittee River to Dangriga (daily around 7am).

Placencia to Dangriga (2–3 daily; 2hr); all connect with departures to Belize City.

Punta Gorda to: Dangriga (5 daily; 5hr); to **Belize City** (5 daily; 8–9hr)

Flights

Maya Island Air (☎31362) and Tropic Air (☎02/45671) each have at least four daily flights from **Belize City to Dangriga** (25min); most continue to **Placencia** (a further 20min) and **Punta Gorda** (20min beyond Placencia).

International Boats

Dangriga to **Puerto Cortés**, Honduras (weekly skiff, on Sat; 3hr)

Punta Gorda to **Puerto Barrios**, Guatemala (at least 3 daily; 1hr)

CHAPTER SEVEN

THE BAY ISLANDS (ISLAS DE LA BAHÍA)

S trung in a gentle curve less than 60km off the north coast of Honduras, the stunning **Bay Islands** with their clear, calm waters and abundant marine life, are the country's major tourist attraction and an ideal foray from Belize onto Honduran soil. Resting along the world's second largest barrier reef, the islands are the ideal destination for cheap diving, sailing and fishing, while less active types can sling a hammock on one of the many palm-fringed, sandy beaches and snooze in the shade, watching the magnificent sunsets. Composed of three main islands and some 65 smaller cayes, this sweeping 125km island chain lies on the Bonacca Ridge, an underwater extension of the the mainland Sierra de Omoa mountain range. **Roatán** is the largest and most developed of the group; **Guanaja**, to the east, is a more exclusive resort destination, and **Utila**, the closest to the mainland, attracts budget travellers from all over the world. All three islands offer superb diving and snorkelling opportunites.

Even old hands get excited about the waters here, where lizard fish and toadfish dart by, scarcely distinguishable from the coral; eagle rays glide through the water like huge birds flying through the air; tetchy damselfish get in your face if

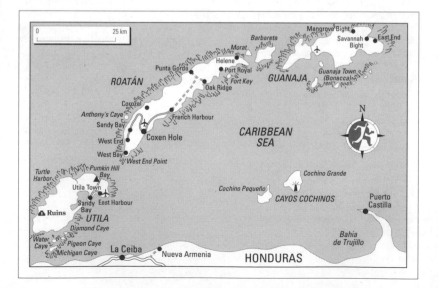

ACCOMMODATION PRICE CODES

The accommodation in this chapter has been given a **price code** according to the following scale. The prices refer to the cost of **a double room in high season** (generally December to Easter) in US dollars.

① Under US$5	④ US$15–25	⑦ US$60–80
② US$5–10	⑤ US$25–40	⑧ US$80–100
③ US$10–15	⑥ US$45–60	⑨ over US$100

you invade their territory, and parrotfish chomp steadily away on the coral. Meanwhile, barracuda and nurse sharks circle the waters, checking you out from a distance. In addition, the world's largest fish, the whale shark, which can reach up to 16m long, is a regular visitor to the channel between Utila and Roatán in October and November; dive shops on both islands run trips to look for the marine giant.

The best time to visit the islands is from March to September, when the water visibility is good, and the weather is clear and sunny with little rain; October and November are very wet, with lighter rains occurring from December to February. Daytime temperatures range between 25 and 29°C all year, but the islands benefit from almost constant cooling east-southeasterly trade winds. Watch out for **mosquitoes** and **sandflies**, which are endemic on all the islands: lavish coatings of baby oil help to repel the latter, which are at their worst on Guanaja.

A brief history

The **Paya Indians** were the most likely first inhabitants of the Bay Islands, leaving behind ruins and fractions of ceramics. On June 11, 1502, during his fourth journey to the Americas, **Columbus** landed on Guanaja, naming it "Isla de los Pinosi" (Pine Island), and the islands were half-heartedly colonized by the Spanish soon after. The swampy shores and shallow reef, impassable for big vessels, made serious settlement impossible, but in the seventeenth and eighteenth centuries provided perfect cover for **pirates** and buccaneers. The notorious pirate Captain Henry Morgan is said to be buried somewhere on Utila; his treasure from the raid on Panamá in 1671 remains undiscovered beneath Roatán.

In 1797, around three thousand Garífuna were forcibly transported by the British from the island of St Vincent to Roatán. The Spanish soon persuaded the majority of these to move to Trujillo on the mainland, leaving only a small settlement, which still exists today, at Punta Gorda on the north coast. After 1821 an influx of white Cayman islanders arrived, and were joined by a wave of freed slaves, following the abolition of slavery in 1830. These new immigrants settled first on Utila, then on Roatán, and eventually on Sheen and Hog Cayes, now Bonacca Town, and built the distinctive houses that stand on stilts, out of the range of disease-carrying insects. From 1852, the islands were governed by the British, who, much to the dismay of the locals, turned them over to Honduras because of pressure from North America, who feared British expansion. However, the islands remained culturally separate from the mainland, holding onto their language – **English** – and unique traditions. Even today, although Spanish is spoken in the schools and government offices, and is spreading further as growing numbers of mainlanders come in search of work, the language on the street is English, with a unique Creole-like accent.

ECO-FRIENDLY MEASURES ON THE BAY ISLANDS

Though foreign travellers delight in the fact that they can live very cheaply on the Honduras Bay Islands, life for the locals is not quite so sweet. With an economy in steady decline, the increasing shift towards tourism has resulted in some serious growing pains. Numbers of **lobster**, traditionally one of the best sources of income, are depleting rapidly, and an average fisherman may use up to eight tanks in one day diving deeper and deeper to find them, risking potentially fatal decompression sickness. One way for visitors to help is not to accept lobster under the legal size of 4oz in restaurants and stores. **Water shortages** are also a problem, and tourists use on average three times as much water as locals: try not to run taps or flush toilets needlessly. To cut down on **waste products**, you could bring a water purifier instead of repeatedly buying plastic jugs, and re-use plastic bags. You can also help by supporting locally owned businesses and taking special care not to leave litter.

As in most of Central America, **religion** plays a significant role on the islands, with a large Catholic population as well as a considerable number of Seventh Day Adventists.

Although fishing and working away on cargo ships and oil rigs remain important sources of income for the islanders, the local economy is increasingly coming to rely on **tourism**. Since the early 1990s, there has been a huge growth in the number of visitors to the islands, which shows no signs of abating. Whilst the tourists have undoubtedly brought economic benefits, questions are now being raised about the environmental impact and the long-term wisdom of selling off the the islanders' heritage.

Getting to the islands

The growth in tourism to the islands over the past few years means that all three are served by regular air and boat connections. Most flights and the scheduled ferry service leave from the coastal city of **La Ceiba** (see opposite) from where there are also occasional unscheduled boats. The only direct route to the Bay Islands from Belize is **by air**; Caribbean Air flies from Belize City to Roatán once a week. Alternatively, you can go by **boat from Dangriga** to Puerto Cortes, Honduras (3 weekly; 3hr), and then continue by bus to San Pedro Sula (1hr), and on to La Ceiba, 32km from Utila. The Cotraibal bus from San Pedro to Trujillo leaves at 9am, noon and 3pm from 1a Av, 7–8 C SO, stopping at La Ceiba (3hr) on the way.

If you need **to stay** the night in San Pedro, the good-value *Hotel Terraza,* 6a Ave, 4–5 C SO (☎503108; ③), is close to the bus terminal, with private bathrooms, hot water and TV; alternatively, there's the *Hotel San Pedro*, 3a C, 1–2 Ave SO (☎531513; ②), with a variety of rooms ranging from basic to comfortable. However, if you have the option, you should press on to **La Ceiba**, which is much nicer and has a well-deserved reputation as party city of Honduras. The *Hotel Iberia,* Ave San Isidro (☎430401; ③) is a good bet and has rooms with air conditioning, bath and TV, some with balconies overlooking the street. For restaurants, bars and clubs, head for 1a Calle which runs along the seafront, and is the heart of the city's Zona Viva.

Flights and boats from La Ceiba

Daily **flights** to the islands leave from **Golosón International Airport**, 11km west of La Ceiba on the road to Tela. Outside peak holiday season, you can buy tickets to Roatán by simply turning up at the airport, though you'll need to buy tickets to the other islands in advance. Isleña and Sosa have offices on the central plaza in La Ceiba, while the other airline companies' offices are at the airport. Note that flights are sometimes cancelled with little or no notice, and delays are commonplace. Flight schedules are also liable to last-minute change, so always doublecheck times.

Boats to the islands (Roatán and Utila only) leave from the **Muralla de Cabotaje** municipal dock, about 5km to the east of the city. The *MV Tropical* has regular, scheduled services to Roatán (2hr) and Utila (1hr); fares to both are around $10 one-way.

Monday: La Ceiba–Roatán 5am; Roatán–La Ceiba 7.30am; La Ceiba–Utila 10am; Utila–La Ceiba 11.30am; and La Ceiba–Roatán 3.30pm.

Tuesday–Friday: Roatán–La Ceiba 7am; La Ceiba–Utila 10am; Utila–La Ceiba 11.30pm; and La Ceiba–Roatán 3.30pm.

Saturday: Roatán–La Ceiba 7am; La Ceiba–Roatán 11am; and Roatán–La Ceiba 2pm.

Sunday: La Ceiba–Roatán 7am; and Roatán–La Ceiba 3.30pm.

In addition, the *MV Starfish* cargo supply boat leaves Utila for La Ceiba every Monday at around 5am, returning on Tuesday at around 11am; tickets can be bought at the dock ($8 one-way). You'll also find no shortage of unscheduled boats to take you to Roatán, Utila or Guanaja; ask around at the docks for details.

Utila

The smallest of the islands and closest to the mainland, **Utila** is famed for its multitude of **scuba-diving** facilities at some of the cheapest rates in the world. And even if you don't want to don tanks, the superb waters around the island offer great swimming and snorkelling possibilities. Utila is still the cheapest of the islands, with the cost of living only slightly higher than on the mainland, although prices are gradually rising. Life is laid-back and people are on the whole friendly, although opportunistic crime is on the increase. As elsewhere, respect local customs in dress and don't walk around in your bathing suit. Note also that drinking from glass bottles on the street is prohibited.

Arrival, orientation and information

The vast majority of Utila's small population is concentrated in the east of the island around a large, curved harbour. If you arrive by air, you'll land at the **airstrip** in a region known as **The Point**, at the eastern end of the harbour. West of here, the main settlement, **East Harbour**, is where you'll dock if you arrive by boat; further west lies the region known as **Sandy Bay**. The island's main road, a twenty-minute walk end to end, runs along the seafront from the airstrip to Sandy Bay; the second road, **Cola de Mico Road**, heads inland from the dock, then turns into a dirt track winding north across the island.

Wherever you arrive, you'll be met by representatives from the dive schools with **maps** and information on special offers. Many schools offer free accommodation during their courses, but it's worth checking out the various options before signing up. For more objective **information**, the Utila branch of BICA (Bay Islands' Conservation Association) has a visitor and information office on the main street between the airstrip and the dock, though its opening hours are erratic (usually Mon–Fri 9am–noon and a couple of hours in the afternoon). You could also pick up a copy of the monthly *Utila Times* from its office next to *Rubi's Inn*, which provides useful information about local events.

Accommodation

Utila has more than 25 affordable guest houses and hotels, and a profusion of rooms for rent, but they fill up fast especially at Christmas and Easter. Everywhere is within walking distance of the dock and airstrip, and the accommodation listed here is in the order that you come to it, walking west along the road from the airstrip. There are few places to **camp** except on the cayes.

Despite interminable plans to install 24-hour **power**, the main generator for the island usually turns off at midnight and restarts at 5am, cutting out sporadically during the day. Many places have their own generators, however, so check before paying for a room.

ON THE ROAD FROM THE AIRSTRIP TO THE DOCK

Sharkey's Cabins, behind *Sharkey's Reef Restaurant*, close to the airstrip (☎425 3212). Set in a peaceful garden, the rooms are a/c and have private bathrooms: there's a terrace with great views over the lagoon. ④.

Trudy's (☎425 3103). A very popular place, with large, clean rooms, and you can swim from the dock at the back. ③.

Cooper's Inn (☎425 3184). One of the best budget places on the island, with clean, basic rooms and friendly management. ①.

Rubi's Inn, two minutes' walk from the dock (☎425 3240). Very clean, with airy rooms and views over the water; kitchen facilities are available. ②.

COLA DE MICO ROAD

Blueberry Hill, just beyond Thompson's bakery, on the opposite side of the road (☎425 3141). Characterful cabins with basic cooking facilities: run by friendly owners. ①.

Mango Inn, five minutes' walk up the road (☎425 3335). A beautiful, well-run place built in local style and set in shady gardens. It has a range of rooms, from a/c, thatched bungalows for two, to pleasant dorms ($3 per person). Also has a book exchange and laundry service, and the attached *Mango Café* is a lively spot serving good food. ②.

SANDY BAY

Utila Lodge, behind Hondutel (☎425 3143). Also a dive resort, the *Lodge* is the best hotel in town and offers daily rates as well as weekly packages for divers and non-divers. It has its own dock and can arrange fishing trips. ⑦.

Hotel Utila, two minutes' walk beyond the dock (☎425 3140). All the rooms in this large, modern building, come with private baths and TV, and some have a/c. ③.

Seaside Inn, opposite Gunter's Dive shop (☎425 3150). A reasonable place, though it fills up quickly: the newer rooms have private baths. ①.

Margaritaville Beach Hotel, ten minutes' walk west of the dock (☎425 3266). A new place with large, airy rooms, and a peaceful seafront location: all rooms have private baths. ②.

Diving

Diving is the main activity on Utila. Coral is still abundant, especially the regal pillar coral and sponges, and you'll see lots of marine life, too – look out for the huge parrotfish, the (non-threatening) nurse sharks, and the sea turtles and rays. The most dramatic diving is off the northern coast. At night the water lights up with phosphorescence; shake your hand in the water to see tiny particles glow green.

Prices are pretty standard across all the dive schools. Currently, a three- to five-day PADI course costs around $140 in high season (Dec–April) and $125 in low season (May–Nov). **Safety** is a more pertinent issue: when choosing a school, you should make sure you get along with and understand the instructors (many of whom speak a number of languages), check all the equipment and ensure that all the boats have working oxygen and a first-aid kit. Anyone with asthma or ear problems will not be allowed to dive. BICA sells diving **insurance** for $2 a day, a worthwhile investment, and has also been installing buoys on the dive sites to prevent boats anchoring on the reef; check that your school uses these when mooring. **Recommended schools** include the Utila Dive Centre (UDI), on the road between the dock and the airport; Gunter's Dive Shop, two minutes' walk west of the dock, which also rents out sea kayaks; Alton's, two minutes' walk west of the airstrip; and Underwater Vision, opposite *Trudy's*. Salty Dog's, a minute's walk west of the dock, has **underwater photography** equipment for rent, and many of the dive shops also rent out **snorkelling** equipment for around $10 a day.

Swimming, snorkelling and walks

The best swimming near town is at the **Blue Bayou**, a thirty-minute walk from town, where you can bathe in chest-deep water and snorkel further out. Hammocks are slung in the shade of coconut trees and there's a food stand selling burgers and beers; snorkelling gear is also available for rent. East of town, **Airport Beach,** at the end of the airstrip, offers good snorkelling just offshore, as does the little reef beyond the **lighthouse**. The path from the end of the airstrip up the east coast of the island leads to a couple of small coves – the second is good for swimming and sunbathing, though the heaps of garbage dilute the pleasure somewhat. Five minutes beyond the coves, you'll come to the **Ironshores**, a mile-long stretch of low volcanic cliffs with lava tunnels cutting down to the water.

Another pleasant walk (about 5km) is along the Cola de Mico Road across the island to **Pumpkin Hill** and beach, about an hour's walk from East Harbour. Here, the 82m hill gives good views across the island while down on the beach lava rocks cascade into the sea, forming underwater caves. There's good snorkelling here when the water is calm, though it's not safe to go into the caves.

The Cayes

Utila Cayes – eleven tiny outcrops strung along the southwestern edge of the island – were designated a wildlife refuge in 1992. **Suc Suc** (or Jewel) **Caye** and **Pigeon Caye**, connected by a narrow causeway, are both inhabited, and the pace of life here is slower even than in Utila. Small launches regularly shuttle between Suc Suc and Utila (75¢), or can be rented to take you across for a day's snorkelling, if you have your own equipment. *Vicky's Rooms* on Suc Suc (③) offers basic **accommodation**, and there are a couple of reasonable restaurants and a good fish market.

Boats from Utila (prices are negotiable, and depend on the number of passengers) will take you to **Water Caye**, an idyllic stretch of white sand, coconut palms and a small coral reef, even more idyllic for the absence of sandflies. Camping is allowed (bring all your food, equipment for a camp fire and water), and a caretaker turns up every day to collect $1 for use of the island (hammocks are an extra $1 to rent). Full moon parties take place here every month.

Eating

Lobster and fish are staples on the islands, as are the Honduran dishes of rice, beans and chicken. In recent years, however, pasta, pizza and pancakes have also become widely available. For cheap snacks, head for the evening stalls near the dock, which do a thriving trade in *baleadas* (tortillas filled with beans, cheese and onions). Note that most of the restaurants stop serving at around 10pm.

Bundu Café, on the main street, east of the dock. Serves European-style breakfasts and lunches, and shows English-language films at night. Food served Mon–Wed, Fri & Sat 9am–3pm.

Golden Rose, just past the "7–11" in Sandy Bay. Dive instructors and locals rate this as the island's best restaurant for its tasty local dishes.

Jade Seahorse, on Cola de Mico Road. Serves great breakfasts and *licuados*, and good seafood.

Mango Café, in the *Mango Inn*. A popular place with an interesting selection of tasty European food and a lively bar. Closed Mon.

Mermaid's Corner, at *Rubi's Inn*. Thre's a great atmosphere in this popular pasta and pizza restaurant, though service can be very slow.

Sharkey's Reef Restaurant, at *Sharkey's Cabins*. The nearest Utila gets to gourmet cuisine, specializing in delicious fish and vegetarian dishes. Prices are high (around US$9 for a meal and drinks), but worth it for the wonderful California-style and Caribbean food. Only serves dinner; closed Mon & Tues.

Thompson's Bakery, Cola de Mico Road. A popular place to hang out, read, drink coffee and meet other travellers, while sampling the good-value breakfasts, or range of daily baked goods. The book exchange here is crammed with paperback romances. Open 6am–noon.

Utila's Cuisine, close to the dock. An unpretentious local place where you can feast on cheap chicken and meat dishes.

Utila Reef, on the airstrip road, close to Trudy's. Tasty local and international dishes are served on an upstairs terrace overlooking the water. The daily specials, such as lobster and rice salad, are particularly good.

Nightlife

The *Seabreaker* bar, opposite *Rubi's Inn*, on the waterfront, has a party every Tuesday, Thursday and Saturday night, with a cocktail hour, happy hour and music until 11pm. On Saturday nights, the party continues until 3am at *07*, just west of *Rubi's Inn*, with a disco playing mainly reggae and a little techno. The *Casino*, by the dock, attracts a more local crowd with reggae and a dash of salsa and merengue. During the rest of the week, the *Mango Café* is a popular spot for cheap beer and a quiet drink, while the *Bucket of Blood*, on Cola de Mico Road, has regular happy hours and late-night drinking. If you fancy a game of billiards, the national sport in Honduras, head for the pool hall (open till 11pm) behind the *Bucket of Blood*.

Listings

Banks Banco Atlántida and Bancahsa, both close to the dock, exchange money and offer advances on Visa cards (Mon–Fri 8–11.30am & 1.30–4pm, Sat 8–11.30am).

Bicycles can be rented for around $2 a day from the house next to Henderson's Grocery store, just west of the dock, and from other venues around town – look for the handwritten signs.

Book exchange The *Bundu Café,* on the main street, east of the dock, has a book exchange.

Doctor The Medical Clinic is just beyond the immigration office (Mon–Fri 8–11.30am).

Immigration office is next to Hondutel in Sandy Bay (Mon–Fri 9am–noon & 2–4.30pm).

Port office In the large building in the main dock (Mon–Fri 8.30am–noon & 2–5pm, Sat 8.30am–noon).

Post office In the large building in the main dock (Mon–Fri 9am–noon & 2–4.30pm, Sat 9–11.30am).

Telephones Hondutel is next to the immigration office (Mon–Fri 7am–noon & 2–5pm).

Travel agents Tropical Travel and Utila Tour Travel Centre, both east of the dock on the airstrip road, can book and confirm flights to La Ceiba, and elsewhere in Central America.

Roatán

Some 50km from La Ceiba, **Roatán** is the largest of the Bay Islands, more than 40km long and about 3km wide. Accommodation is geared towards wealthy holidaymakers staying in luxury all-inclusive resorts and doing anything from scuba-diving to nature hiking in the hardwood forests. **Coxen Hole**, the capital of the Bay Islands, is the commercial centre, while **West End** and **West Bay**, with their idyllic beaches, are the place to head for absolute relaxation.

Arrival and getting around

Regular flights from La Ceiba, San Pedro Sula and occasionally further afield land at the **airport**, on the road to French harbour, 3km from Coxen Hole – the main town on the south side of the island. Collective taxis to Coxen Hole cost L.20 ($1.50); alternatively, you could walk to the road and wait for one of the public minibuses which head to town every thirty minutes or so (L.10; 80¢). There're an information desk, a hotel reservation desk, car rental agencies and a bank at the airport. The **ferry dock** is in the centre of Coxen Hole.

A paved road runs west–east along the island connecting the major communities. **Minibuses** leave regularly from Main Street in Coxen Hole, heading west to Sandy Bay and West End (every 30min until late afternoon) and east to Brick Bay, French Harbour, Oak Ridge and Punta Gorda (every hour or so until late afternoon); fares are L.7–15 (50¢–$1). However, if you really want to explore, you'll need to **rent a car** or **motorbike**. In addition to the agencies at the airport, Sandy Bay Rent a Car has offices at Sandy Bay and West End, where you can rent jeeps for $45 per day, and motorbikes for $25 a day.

Coxen Hole

Coxen Hole (aka Roatán Town) itself is dusty and run-down and most visitors come here only to change money or shop. All of the town's practical facilities and most shops are on a hundred-metre stretch of Main Street, near where the buses stop. For tourist **information**, pick up a copy of the *Coconut Telegraph*, a magazine about the island and its events from the Cooper Building. The headquarters of BICA (Mon–Fri 9am–noon & 2–5pm) also has information on places of interest on the island as well as its flora and fauna. For **changing travellers' cheques**, dollars and cash advances on Visa cards try Bancahsa, or Credomatic. The **immigration office** and the **post office** are both near the small square on Main Street, while **Hondutel** (for telephones) is behind Bancahsa. HB Warren is the largest **supermarket** on the island and there's a small, not too impressive general **market**, just behind Main Street.

Unless you have a very early flight you're unlikely to want **to stay** here, but if you need to, the *Hotel Cayview*, on Main Street (☎445 1222; ⑤), has comfortable rooms with air-conditioning and private baths, and the *Hotel El Paso*, on Main Street (☎451059; ②) has clean rooms, but communal bathrooms. There are a number of cheap *comedores*, serving standard Honduran **food**, while the friendly *Pava Pizza* on Main Street sells decent pizzas, as well as sandwiches and snacks. *Que Pasa Cafe*, in Librería Casi Todo 11, on Ticket Street, serves European-style breakfasts and snacks.

Sandy Bay

Midway between Coxen Hole and West End, **SANDY BAY** is an unassuming community with a couple of interesting attractions. The **Institute for Marine Sciences** (Sun–Tues & Thurs–Sat 9am–5pm; $4), based at *Antony's Key Resort* (see below) has exhibitions on the marine life and geology of the islands and a museum with useful information on local history and archeology. You can also watch daily bottle-nosed dolphin shows (Mon, Tues, Thurs & Fri 10am & 4pm, Sat & Sun 10am, 1pm & 4pm; $4), and dive or snorkel with the dolphins ($100 and $75 respectively; must be booked in advance). Across the road from the institute, several short nature trails weave through the jungle at the **Cambola Botanical Gardens** (daily 8am–5pm; $3), a riot of beautiful flowers, lush ferns and tropical trees. Twenty minutes' walk from the gardens up Monte Carambola you come to the **Iguana Wall**, a section of cliff that's a breeding ground for iguanas and parrots. From the top of the mountain you can see across to Utila on clear days.

There are a few places **to stay** in Sandy Bay, all of which are clearly signposted off the main road, or the dirt track that cuts off it to the sea. The cheapest option is the non-smoking *Beth's Place* (☎445 1266; ②), with clean rooms, and communal bathrooms and kitchen; snorkelling equipment is also available for rent. Slightly more upmarket is the *Oceanside Inn* (⑥), with large rooms and a good restaurant. More upmarket still is *Antony's Key Resort* (☎445 1003, fax 445 1140; only offers weekly packages), one of the smartest places on the island, with cabins set among the trees and on a small caye. All-inclusive dive packages start at $600 per person per week. The nicest place **to eat** is the popular bar and restaurant, *Rick's American Café*, set on the hillside above the road. It serves US-style burgers, seafood and snacks, and is open for dinner all week and brunch on Sundays.

West End

With its calm waters and incredible soft white beaches, **West End**, 14km from Coxen Hole, makes the most of its ideal setting, gearing itself mainly towards travellers who can afford to pay that bit more for a little slice of heaven. Set in the southwest corner of the island, round a shallow bay, the village has retained a laid-back charm, and the gathering pace of tourist development has done little to dent the friendliness of the villagers.

The paved road from Coxen Hole finishes at the northern end of the community, by **Half Moon Bay**, one of the village's best beaches. A sandy track runs alongside the water's edge, ending at a small bridge at the far end of the village, beyond which lies another good beach. At the end of the paved road, the Coconut Tree store sells a good selection of groceries. The best place for **renting** bicycles, motorbikes, inflatable boats, snorkelling gear and other water equipment is the little stall under the trees just past the Librería. Joanna's Gift Shop, about five minutes' walk from the Librería, sells handicrafts and swimwear.

ACCOMMODATION

Accommodation is listed in the order that you'll come to it, as you arrive in the village. During low season (May–Nov) it's worth negotiating a discount, particularly for longer stays.

Coconut Tree Cabins, on the paved road at the entrance to the village (☎445 1648). Comfortable, spacious cabins all with covered porches, fridges and hot water. ⑥.

Chilie's, turn right at the end of the paved road, and walk for about 100m. A new, English-owned place with dorm beds and private rooms in a two-storey house. At the back is a kitchen for guests' use; you can camp in the large garden. ②.

Half Moon Bay Cabins, at the northern edge of Half Moon Bay; follow the track for about 300m past *Chilie's* (☎445 1075). Upmarket place with a lively restaurant and bar. Secluded cabins scattered around wooded grounds, close to the water's edge; all have fan or a/c. ⑥.

Dolphin Resort, turn left onto the dirt track, and it's about 200m down on the left. Small, clean rooms in a brick building, all with a/c, private baths and hot water. ④.

Pinnochio's, continue 200m past the *Dolphin Resort*, then turn left at the signed turn for Stanley's Island restaurant (fax 445 1841). This new wooden building, set on a hillside above the village, has clean, airy rooms with bath and hot water. The owners are very friendly and there's a good restaurant downstairs. ④.

Jimmy's Lodge, at the southern end of the village, ten minutes' walk from the paved road. Extremely basic backpackers' institution, with mattresses on the floor in a large dorm and a hose shower; under $3 per person. Hammocks can also be slung, if there's room, and the beach location is great.

EATING AND DRINKING

There is a more than adequate range of **places to eat** in West End, with fish featuring heavily on many menus, although pasta and pizza are increasingly popular. **Drinking** can drain your pocket fast in West End. It's best to seek out the half-price **happy hours** at many of the restaurants and bars; starting at around 4.30pm, many of them last until 10pm. The *Blue Mango Bar*, on the seafront 200m beyond Librería Casi Todo, has a nightly happy hour from 5pm to 7pm. The *Cool Lizard* on the beach just past *Jimmy's Lodge* is another fine spot for the sunset-watching.

Cannibal Café, in front of the *Dolphin Resort*. One of the cheapest places to eat, though serves mostly snacks. The *baleadas* and *quesadillas* (large tortillas filled with cheese) are good value and come in huge portions.

WATERSPORTS IN AND AROUND WEST END

Diving courses for all levels are on offer in West End. Most places charge similar prices, with a standard four-day open-water course costing around $200. Some schools include basic accommodation in the price. See p.207 for details of insurance and safety precautions when choosing a dive school. Tyll's Dive and West End Divers, next to each other on the main drag about 100m south of the paved road, are two of the more popular shops with good safety records.

The reef lying just offshore provides some suberb **snorkelling**, with the best spots being at the mouth of Half Moon Bay and just offshore from *Jimmy's Lodge* (see above). You can also rent out **sea kayaks** from Sea Blades, at the Librería Casi Todo: expect to pay around $12 for a half day, and $20 for a full day. Belvedere's, on the waterfront about 30m south of Librería Casi Todo, runs popular, hour-long **glass-bottomed boat** tours for $8, while Flame & Smoke, on the beach beyond *Jimmy's Lodge* charters boats for half- or full-day **fishing trips**.

Pinocchio's. Serves an eclectic range of meat, fish and pasta dishes at reasonable prices. The chicken and vegetable risotto for $5 is particularly tasty. Closed Wed.

Rudy's Coffee Stop, just before Joanna's Gift Shop on the paved road. Serves great breakfasts of banana pancakes, omelettes, fresh coffee and juices. Closed Sun.

Salt and Pepper, above the Coconut Tree Store. A wide-ranging gourmet menu, which includes French, Italian, Indian and Mexican dishes. Expect to pay upwards of $10 a head, with wine, but the relaxed atmosphere and excellent cooking make it worth the money.

Seaview Restaurant, halfway along the main drag. A popular joint, with a nicely laid-out eating area. The large, well-prepared pizzas are good value, through service can be appallingly slow.

Stanley's Island Restaurant, up the hill behind *Pinocchio's*. A locally owned restaurant serving good food at reasonable prices. The *tapado* (fish stew) and coconut bread are particularly delicious.

West Bay

Two kilometres southwest of West End, towards the tip of Roatán, **West Bay** is a stunning, white sand beach, fringed by coconut palms and leading into crystal-clear water. The tranquillity of the place has been only mildly disrupted by the rash of cabañas and restaurants that have appeared in recent years, and, provided you avoid the sandflies by sunbathing on the jettys, you'll be as near to paradise as you can get. There's great snorkelling at the southern end of the beach where the reef meets the shore. It's a pleasant forty-five-minute stroll south along the beach and over a few rock outcrops from West End to West Bay; alternatively, you can take one of the small launches that leave *Foster's Restaurant* regularly – the last one returns at 9pm. A dirt road also runs here: from West End, head up the road to Coxen Hole and take the first turning on the right. If you want to stay, the *Bananarama Dive School* (no phone; ⑤) and *Cabaña Roatána* (☎445 1271; ⑥) are both halfway along the beach and rent out pleasant cabins.

East of Coxen Hole

From Coxen Hole, the paved road runs northeast past the small secluded cove of **Brick Bay** to **FRENCH HARBOUR**, a busy fishing port and the island's second largest town. More attractive than Coxen Hole and less run-down, it's a lively place to stay for a couple of days, and all the accommodation is right in the centre. *Harbour View Hotel* (☎455 5390; ④) has reasonable rooms with bath and hot water, whilst the more upmarket *Buccaneer Hotel* (☎455 5032; ⑦) has a pool, a large wooden deck overlooking the water and a disco at weekends. The best place to eat is *Gio's*, by the Credomatic building on the waterfront, where you can dine on excellent but pricey seafood; for more local fare, try *Pat's Place*, 50m further on.

From French Harbour the road cuts inland along a central ridge to give superb views of both the north and south coasts of the island. After about 14km it reaches **OAK RIDGE**, a quaint fishing port with wooden houses strung along its harbour. There are some nice unspoilt beaches to the east of town, accessible by launches from the main dock. The best place to stay is the clean and pleasant *Hotel San José* (☎435 2328; ④), on a small caye a short distance across the water from the dock. Launches run from the main dock to the caye on demand (50¢). Some 5km from Oak Ridge, on the northern coast of the island, **PUNTA GORDA** is the oldest Garífuna community in Honduras and the oldest settlement on Roatán. If you want to stay, *Ben's Dive Resort*, on the waterfront (☎451916; ⑤), has comfortable cabins, while *Los Cincos Hermanos*, in the centre, has basic, clean rooms (②).

Guanaja

The easternmost Bay Island, **Guanaja** is the most beautiful, undeveloped and expensive of them all and had been designated a Marine National Park. It actually consists of two islands, separated by a narrow canal, with the main settlement, **Bonacca** or **Guanaja Town**, sitting on a small caye a few hundred metres offshore from the larger island. It's here that you'll find the island's shops and main residential area, as well as the bulk of the reasonably priced accommodation. All the houses in Bonacca are built on stilts above the water – vestiges of early settlement by the Cayman islanders – and the only way to get around is by water taxi, which adds both to the atmosphere and to the cost of living. The only villages of any substance on the island are **Savanah Bight** (on the east coast) and **Mangrove Bight** (on the north coast).

Arrival and information

Guanaja **airstrip**, is on the main island, next to the canal. Aside from a couple of dirt tracks there are no roads, and the main form of transport is small launches. Boats from the main dock in Bonacca meet all flights, and there are collective services from the airstrip to Savanah Bight at 7am and 11am. Rides can be hitched on private boats to Mangrove Bight for a nominal fee. If you arrive **by boat**, you'll come in at the main dock in Bonacca. The Capitania de Puerto, on the main pier, has **information** on unscheduled boat services to the other islands and points on the Honduran mainland.

Bonacca itself is built on wooden causeways over the canals, many of which have now been filled in. The main causeway, running for about 500m east–west along the caye with a maze of small passages branching off it, is where you'll find all the shops, **banks** and businesses. You can change dollars and travellers' cheques at Banco Atlántida, to the left of the dock, and Bancahsa, to the right of the dock (both Mon–Fri 9am–noon); Bancahsa also gives cash advances on Visa cards.

Accommodation

Most of the hotels on Guanaja are luxury all-inclusive dive resorts offering weekly packages, which need to be booked in advance. In contrast, Bonacca has a small number of reasonably priced hotels, and a private house, just before the *Hotel Alexander*, which **rents out rooms** for under $10 per person.

BONACCA

Hotel Alexander, at the eastern end of the main causeway, to the right of the dock (☎453 4326). The best location in Bonacca, whose large, comfortable rooms have private bathrooms and balconies overlooking the water. ⑥.

Hotel Miller, halfway along the main causeway (☎453 4327). The building is slightly run-down, but the rooms are in reasonable condition. Most have hot water and, for a little extra, a/c. ③.

Hotel Rosario, opposite the *Hotel Miller* (☎453 4240). A modern building, with comfortable rooms, all with private bath, a/c and TV. ⑤.

BIG ISLAND

Unless otherwise stated, all prices are per person for a week-long package.

Bahía Resort, on the south side of the island across from Bonacca (☎453 4212). One of the smaller resorts, with accommodation in comfortable bungalows and a pool. Packages start at $800.

Bayman Bay Club, on the north side of the island (☎453 4179). Has well-furnished cabins set on a wooded hillside above the beach. Packages including dives and all meals cost $700–750.

Hillton Hotel, by the airstrip (☎453 4299). The clean rooms all have private baths and TV. Though its location is not as scenic as some of the other resorts, it is the cheapest option on the main island, and lets rooms by the night. ⑤.

The Island House Resort, on the north side of the island (☎453 4196). A very pleasant resort, close to several expanses of beautiful beach. Packages start at $590.

Posada del Sol, on the south side of the island (☎453 4186). The cabins are scattered around sixty acres of ground, and the amenities here include pool, tennis courts, sea kayaks and snorkelling equipment. Packages start from $340 for three nights.

SMALL ISLAND

West Peak Inn, towards the western tip of the Small Island (fax 453 4219, email *david@vena.com*). A relaxed place with comfortable cabins close to good, deserted beaches and a trail up to the 94m-high West Peak. Prices include all meals. ⑥.

Around the island

The larger island boasts the highest point of the entire Bay Islands, **Michael's Peak** (412m), covered with Caribbean pine forest and hardwoods. More than 50km long, and about 6km wide, it's a stunning, untouched place, with lovely waterfalls and incredible views of sea and jungle. A superb trail leads from Mangrove Bight up to Michael's Peak and down to Sandy Bay (on the south coast), affording stunning views of the island and surrounding reef; fit walkers can do the trail in a day, though you can camp on the summit, provided you bring your own provisions.

Diving is excellent all around the big island and particularly on the southern shore but it can be difficult if you don't go through a resort package; if you want to do it independently, Dive Freedom, in the Coral Café building on the main causeway in Bonacca, rents out equipment and runs courses. The small rocky headland of **Michael's Rock**, west of the Island House, is surrounded by stretches of beautiful white beach, with good snorkelling close to the shore. **Fishing** and **snorkelling** can be fixed with local boatmen who charge $10–15 to take you out on the water. In many areas, however, the reef is close enough to swim to if you have your own snorkel gear.

Eating and drinking

There are several **restaurants** in Bonacca, most of which stay open till around 9pm and close on Sundays. None are particularly cheap, however, as most of the supplies have to be shipped in from the mainland, and the real gourmet eating experiences are reserved for the package resorts on the big island. In Bonacca itself, try *Bonacca's Garden*, halfway along the main causeway, or the restaurant at the *Hotel Alexander*, both of which serve reasonably priced local dishes. The *Up and Down Restaurant*, close to *Bonacca's Garden*, serves good pizza and pasta, while the *Coral Café* is a popular spot to hang out, though the drinks are better than the food.

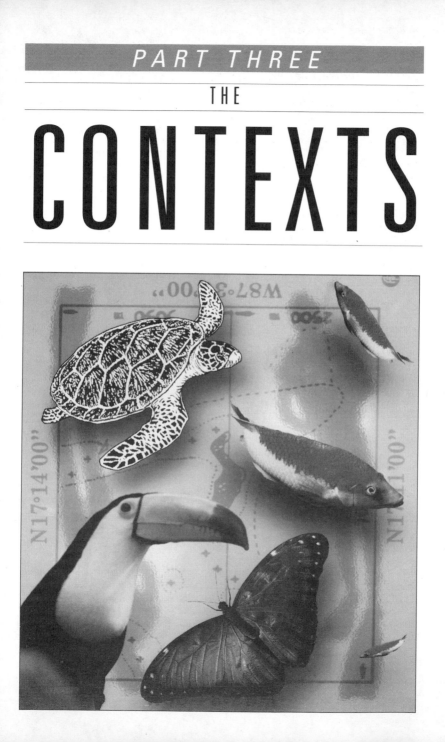

HISTORY

Belize is the youngest nation in Central America, only gaining full independence from Britain in 1981, and its history has been markedly different from the surrounding Latin American republics since at least the mid-seventeenth century. Although the whole region, including Belize, was (to a greater or lesser degree) colonized by Spain in the sixteenth century, it was the colonial entanglement with Britain that gave Belize its present cultural, social and political structures.

Prior to the arrival of Europeans the area now called Belize was part of a vast region known to archeologists as **Mesoamerica**, stretching from north-central Mexico to El Salvador and Honduras. Within this imprecisely defined geographical area the individual cultures shared several common characteristics, including a complex, accurate calendar, hieroglyphic writing, a similar cosmology and religion and a highly organized, stratified society. They may also have shared a common origin, in the Olmec civilization, which arose in southern Mexico around 3000 years ago. This definition is designed to exclude the native tribes of North America (whose culture remained largely nomadic) and to group together the pre-Columbian civilizations of their southern neighbours. By far the most important of these as far as Belize is concerned are the **Maya**, whose culture began to emerge here as early as 2000 BC and whose cities were at the height of their power between 250 and 900 AD.

PREHISTORY

Delving further back into the past, archeologists are on uncertain ground, piecing together a rough idea on the basis of scattered archeological remains and a handful of written texts. Prior to the advent of Maya civilization very little is known about the area, and the early Maya remain fairly mysterious. Set out here is a brief overview of many separate theories, none of which can claim to dominate the academic debate. Over the last few years the situation has, if anything, become even more confused, as excavations of important new sites (especially in Belize) throw up information that casts doubt on many accepted notions. At any moment our whole understanding could be overturned by new discoveries, and there is certainly still a great deal to learn.

Archeological opinions differ as to when the first people arrived in the Americas, but the most widely accepted theory is that Stone Age hunters crossed the Bering land bridge from Asia in several waves, beginning probably around 25,000 years ago and travelling via an ice-free corridor at a time when sea levels were lowered by advancing glaciers. These early hunters rapidly spread southwards, developing the **Clovis** culture (named after characteristic stone projectile points first identified in Clovis, New Mexico) at least 11,000 years ago; worked stone flakes from this era have been found at Richmond Hill, a site in Orange Walk District. The Clovis people subsisted primarily on hunting the abundant large mammals, including mammoths, mastodons, deer and horses. By 9000 years ago, however, the northern ice sheets were in full retreat, and the big game disappeared during the long period of hot, dry weather that followed.

The scarcity of game, combined with climatic change and altered vegetation patterns, forced the hunters to adopt a different way of life, turning to more intensive use of plant foods. During this period (known as the **Archaic** period) the food plants vital to the subsequent development of agriculture, such as peppers, squash, beans and, most important of all, maize, were domesticated. Analysis of pollen grains from that time, found in lake deposits in Petén, Guatemala, reveal that the region (and presumably adjacent Belize too) was an area of savannahs and broad-leaved woodland; the tropical forests did not appear until the Classic period, by which time the Maya could more easily control its profuse growth.

This transition into more settled, primarily agricultural, societies enabled the development of an identifiable culture, becoming broadly known as **Proto-Maya**. There is archeological evidence of Archaic sequences in Belize dating from 7500 BC until later than 2000 BC, though few visible remains from that period can be seen today. An early language, Proto-Maya, was in use in the western highlands of Guatemala, and probably in other places too, including Chiapas in Mexico.

THE EARLY MAYA IN BELIZE

Somewhere between 2000 and 1500 BC we move into the **Preclassic** (also known as the Formative) period (2000 BC–250 AD). These periods are terms used by archeologists to describe the earliest developments in the history of the culture we recognize as distinctly Maya; each main period is itself usually subdivided into Early, Middle and Late. The boundaries of the different periods are not marked by exact dates, and should be understood as cultural and technological milestones, when particular architectural, administrative and artistic advances were in widespread use: current excavations appear to be pushing back the date when the earliest breakthroughs were made.

The **Early Preclassic** (roughly 2000 BC–1000 BC) marks the beginning of recognizable patterns of agriculture, notably the annual cutting and burning of forest by people living in settled villages in order to plant maize. Crops would have provided part (and increasingly the main part) of their food needs, supplemented by hunting, fishing and foraging for wild plants. There's currently no evidence of structures larger than dwellings for this period, but ceramics were produced; pottery found at Cuello, near Orange Walk, dates from around 1000 BC and is among the earliest ceramics in the Maya lowlands.

Elsewhere in Mesoamerica big changes were taking place that were to have a far-reaching impact throughout the region. The first great culture to emerge was the Olmec civilization, originating around 3000 BC in the coastal plain of Veracruz, in Mexico. The Olmecs, often regarded as the true ancestors of Maya culture, developed a complex polytheistic religion, an early writing system and a calendar known as the "Long Count", later adopted by the Maya.

By the **Middle Preclassic** (1000 BC–300 BC) there was a substantial increase in population – evidence of numerous settlements can be found right across the Maya area, from southern Guatemala to northern Yucatán, including almost all of Belize, in particular the main river valleys. Similar styles of red and orange monochrome pottery of the Mamóm style, and stone metates for grinding corn, have been found in all the settlements. It is thought that some kind of Maya language was spoken throughout the area, and that a common belief system, practised from a very early date, may have provided the stimulus and social cohesion to build bigger towns. At the same time, as in all early agricultural communities, food surpluses would have eventually freed some to become seers, priests and astronomers. By 750 BC Nakbé, in northern Petén, was a large city, perhaps the first one in the Maya world, evidence that the Maya had progressed far beyond a simple peasant society.

Further advances in architecture and what amounted to an explosion of Maya culture and population came in the **Late Preclassic** (300 BC–250 AD), when the **Chicanel culture** dominated the northern and central areas of the Maya world. The famous Maya corbeled arch (which was not a true arch, with a keystone, but consisted of two sides, each with stones overlapping until they eventually met, and thus could only span a relatively narrow gap) was developed in this period, and the whole range of buildings became more ambitious. Large pyramids with elaborate temples were built at Tikal, El Mirador and Río Azul in Petén. In northern Belize, Cuello, Nohmul, Lamanai and Cerros were the great centres, all featuring major feats of public architecture, some of which can still be seen today. Lamanai and Cerros controlled Preclassic trade routes, and probably continued to do so right through the Classic and into the Postclassic period. The Belize River valley was fully settled, with local centres such as Cahal Pech, Pacbitún and El Pilar expanding and consolidating their power.

The question of what sparked this phase of rapid development is a subject of much debate, though most archeologists agree that the catalyst was the Olmec culture. The Maya adopted and adapted these outside influences, and developed complex administrative mechanisms to feed and control the growing population. As in any advancing society, a hierarchical ruling structure evolved. In the Maya world ultimate military and spiritual power was vested in kings, who established ruling dynasties and communicated with the gods by spilling their own blood at propitious festivals.

THE CLASSIC PERIOD

The development that separates the Late Preclassic from the **Early Classic** period (250 AD–600 AD) is the introduction of the Long Count calendar and a recognizable form of writing. This appears to have taken place before the fourth century AD and marks the beginning of the greatest phase of Maya achievement.

Developments in the Maya area were still powerfully influenced by events to the north. The cultural influence of the Olmecs was replaced by that of **Teotihuacán**, which dominated Central Mexico during the early Classic period. Armed merchants spread the power of Teotihuacán as far as Yucatán, Petén and Belize, bringing new styles of ceramics and alternative religious beliefs: complete military invasion and subjugation, however, was a fairly unlikely scenario. Whatever happened around 400 AD, the overwhelming power of Teotihuacán radically altered life in Maya lands. In Petén, Tikal's rise to power must have been helped by close links with Teotihuacán, and both cities prospered greatly: Tikal has a stela (a freestanding carved monument) depicting a lord of Tikal on one side and a warrior from Teotihuacán on the other.

All of the cities we now see as ruined or restored sites were built during the Classic period, almost always over earlier structures. Elaborately carved stelae, bearing dates and emblem-glyphs, tell of actual rulers and of historical events in their lives – battles, marriages, dynastic succession and so on. The deciphering of these dates has provided confirmation (or otherwise) of archeological evidence and offered a major insight into the Maya elite. Broadly speaking, the Maya region was made up of independent city-states, bound together by a coherent religion and culture and supporting a sophisticated trade network. The cities jostled for power and influence, a struggle that occasionally erupted into intense warfare. Exactly how the various centres related to one

another is unclear, but it appears that three or four main centres dominated the Maya area through an uncertain process of alliances, though no city held sway throughout the entire region. Calakmul, in Campeche, Mexico, and Tikal were the nearest of these "superstates" to Belize, but in 562 AD Caracol, in southern Cayo district, defeated Tikal, as shown by a Caracol ball-court marker. Detailed carvings on wooden lintels and stone monuments at the site depict elaborately costumed lords trampling on bound captives. It's unclear whether this victory of a previously subordinate city over the dominant regional power was the cause of the major upheaval that followed, but dramatic change was to come.

The collapse of Teotihuacán in the seventh century caused shock waves throughout the civilizations of Mesoamerica as advances were temporarily halted by what is known as the **Middle Classic Hiatus**. No stelae were erected in the Maya cities and many existing monuments were damaged and defaced. In all likelihood the dominant Maya centres suffered revolts, and warfare raged as rival lords strove to win political power. However, as the new kings established dynasties, now free of Teotihuacán's military or political control, the Maya cities flourished as never before. Architecture, astronomy and art reached degrees of sophistication unequalled by any other pre-Columbian society. Many Maya centres were much larger than contemporary Western European cities, then in their "Dark Ages": Caracol had an estimated 150,000 people.

The prosperity and grandeur of the **Late Classic** (600–850 AD) reached all across the Maya lands: from Bonampak and Palenque in the west, to Calakmul and Uxmal in the north, Altun Ha and Cerros in the east, and Copán and Quiriguá in the south, as well as hundreds of smaller centres. Masterpieces of painted pottery and carved jade (their most precious material) were created, often to be used as funerary offerings. Shell, bone and, rarely, marble were also exquisitely carved; temples were painted in brilliant colours, inside and out. Most of the pigments have faded long ago, but vestiges remain, enabling experts to reconstruct vivid images of the appearance of the ancient cities.

THE TERMINAL CLASSIC AND POSTCLASSIC

Though when the end came for each Classic Maya centre it was abrupt, it took a century or so (**Terminal Classic**; 850–c.1000 AD) for the Classic Maya civilization to be extinguished in Belize. By 750 AD political and social changes began to be felt; alliances and trade links broke down, wars increased and stelae were carved less frequently. Cities gradually became depopulated and new construction ceased over much of Belize after about 830 AD. Bonampak, in Chiapas, was abandoned before its famous murals could be completed, while many of the great sites along the River Usumacinta (now part of the border between Guatemala and Mexico) were occupied by militaristic outsiders.

The reason for the decline is not (and may never be) known, though it was probably a result of several factors. The growth and demands of the unproductive elite may have led to a peasant revolt, while the increase in population put great strains on food production, possibly exhausting the fertility of the soil, and epidemics may have combined to cause the abandonment of city life. At the end of the Classic period there appears to have been strife and disorder throughout Mesoamerica. By the tenth century, the Maya had abandoned their central cities and those Maya that remained were reduced to a fairly primitive state.

But not all Maya cities were entirely deserted: those in northern Belize, in particular, survived and indeed prospered, with Lamanai and other cities in the area remaining occupied throughout the **Postclassic** period (c.900 –1540 AD). The Yucatán peninsula, which appears to have escaped the worst of the depopulation, came under the influence (possibly by outright conquest) of the militaristic Toltecs, who came from central Mexico in 987 AD, creating a hybrid of Classic Maya culture.

From around 900 AD to the time of the Spanish Conquest the Yucatán peninsula and northern Belize consisted of over a dozen rival provinces, bound up in a cycle of competition and conflict. Northern Belize was part of the Maya province of **Chactemal** (later known as Chetumal), covering an area from around Maskall to Laguna Bacalar in Quintana Roo, and with Santa Rita, near Corozal, as its possible capital. Chetumal was a wealthy province,

producing cacao and honey; trade, alliances and wars kept it in contact with surrounding Maya states up to and beyond the Spanish conquest of Aztec Mexico. Further south the forests were thicker and the ridges of the Maya Mountains intruded across the land. To the Maya of Chetumal this area was known as Dzuluinicob – "land of foreigners", whose capital was Tipú, probably located at Negroman, on the Macal River south of San Ignacio. The Maya here controlled the upper Belize River valley and put up strenuous resistance to attempts by the Spanish to subdue and convert them.

THE FIRST EUROPEANS

The general assumption that Belize was practically deserted by the time Europeans arrived is now widely discredited. The native population in 1500 is estimated to have been around 200,000 – almost as high as it is today – and the Maya towns and provinces were still vigorously independent as the Spanish found to their cost on several occasions.

The first **Europeans** to set eyes on the mainland of Belize were the Spanish sailors Pinzón and de Solis in the early sixteenth century, but they didn't attempt a landing. The first, accidental, contact occurred in 1511, when a small group of shipwrecked Spanish sailors managed to reach land on the southern coast of Yucatán: five were immediately sacrificed, the others became slaves. At least one of the slaves must have escaped and regained contact with his fellow countrymen, because when **Cortés** reached Cozumel in 1519 he knew of the existence of two other enslaved survivors of the shipwreck, and sent gifts to their masters for their release. Geronimo de Aguilar immediately joined Cortés, but the other survivor, Gonzalo Guerrero, refused: Guerrero had married the daughter of Na Chan Kan, the chief of Chetumal, and preferred life among his former captors. Because of his knowledge of Spanish tactics he became a crucial military adviser to the Maya in their subsequent resistance to Spanish domination: the archeologist Eric Thompson calls him the first European to make Belize his home.

In the early years of the conquest few reports were made of contact with the Maya in Belize, probably because the Spanish had no stories of gold or treasure – their overriding obsession. In 1525 Cortés himself almost certainly passed through southern Belize on his epic march from

Veracruz in Mexico to punish a rebellious subordinate in San Gil de Buena Vista, near the mouth of the Río Dulce on the Bay of Honduras. The course of his march took Cortés and his retinue of 140 Spanish soldiers and 3000 Indians across the unknown territory of the Maya heartland, which still contained many thriving towns and cities. At Tayasal on Lake Petén Itzá, he was welcomed by Can Ek, chief of the Itzá who had heard of Cortés' cruelty in conquering Mexico and decided not to oppose him. The expedition continued southwards, to the valley of the Sarstoon River, the present boundary with Guatemala. After reaching and pacifying the rebels Cortés sailed north to Mexico, without apparently realizing that Yucatán was not an island.

ATTEMPTED CONQUEST

For the Spanish it proved relatively simple to capture and eventually kill the "living god" leaders of such militaristic, unified and highly organized empires as the Aztecs and Incas. However, at the time of the conquest, the Maya of present-day Yucatán and Belize were not united into a single political entity and the rulers of the Maya provinces were accustomed to dealing with enemies either by fighting or forming temporary alliances to retain their independence – one reason why the Spanish found this region so difficult to subdue.

In 1528 **Francisco de Montejo**, granted permission by the Spanish Crown to colonize the islands of Cozumel and Yucatán, established a settlement called Salamanca, on the mainland coast south of Cozumel. At the same time his lieutenant, **Alonso Dávila**, led an overland expedition south. Neither was particularly successful: both groups encountered hostile Maya, and Dávila was forced to turn away from Chetumal by Maya under the command of Gonzalo Guerrero. A second attempt by Dávila to found a town at Chetumal, in 1531, was marginally more successful but nevertheless short-lived. This time (on the advice of Guerrero, who realized they could not defeat the Spanish outright) the Maya had abandoned the town; it was then occupied by Dávila and renamed **Villa Real** – the first attempt by Spain to conquer and settle the area which later became Belize. Once established, however, Dávila and his troops were continually harassed by the Maya and were driven out eighteen months later,

fleeing south along the coast of Belize, eventually reaching Omoa in Honduras. For some years after Montejo and Dávila's unsuccessful attempts to conquer Chetumal, the Maya in Belize remained largely free from Spanish interference. Chetumal regained its important trading links and was also a powerful military ally, sending fifty war canoes to Omoa in 1542 to assist the local chief fighting the Spanish.

Montejo's vision of ruling a vast province of the Spanish empire comprising the whole of Yucatán, Belize and Honduras was not to be fulfilled. His son, Montejo the Younger, completed the conquest of Yucatán, establishing his capital at **Mérida** in 1542: Montejo himself was occupied in settling Honduras. In theory the area of the Montejos' colonial administration initially stretched from Honduras to Yucatán, and would have included Belize, but in practice the interior was never completely pacified nor were administrative boundaries clearly defined.

Late in 1543, however, **Gaspar Pacheco**, his son Melchor and his nephew Alonso began another chapter in the sickeningly familiar tale of Spanish atrocities, advancing on Chetumal, destroying crops and food stores and ruthlessly slaughtering the inhabitants. In a letter to Spain, cleric Fray Lorenz de Bienvenida wrote: "Nero was not more cruel [than Alonso Pacheco]. He passed through and reached a province called Chetumal, which was at peace. . . . This captain with his own hands committed outrages: he killed many with the garrotte, saying 'This is a good rod with which to punish these people'."

By 1544 the Pachecos had subdued Maya resistance sufficiently to found a town on Lake Bacalar, and claim *encomienda* (tribute) from villages around Chetumal. It is likely that the Pachecos also conquered parts of Dzuluinicob to the south, though for a time Tipú was the centre of an alliance between the two adjacent Maya provinces, showing that there was still armed resistance to Spanish domination.

During the second half of the sixteenth century missions were established, including one at Lamanai in 1570, and the Spanish, with difficulty, strengthened their hold over northern Belize. The Maya resentment that was always present beneath the surface, however, boiled over into total rebellion in 1638, forcing Spain to abandon the area of Chetumal and Tipú completely and more or less permanently.

In the mid-seventeenth century the nearest permanent Spanish settlements to Belize were Salamanca de Bacalar in southern Yucatán and Lake Izabal in Guatemala. Records are scarce, but it is likely that the Maya of Belize were under some form of Spanish influence even if they were not under Spanish rule. Perhaps the determination of Maya resistance deterred Spain from attempting to fully colonize the area; perhaps the Maya fled to inaccessible forests in an attempt to retain their independence. Repeated **expeditions** were mounted by Spanish friars and colonial leaders during the seventeenth century in an attempt to bring the heathen Maya of Tipú into the fold of the Catholic Church, though these were never more than partially successful.

In 1695 a Spanish mission met leaders of the Itzá to discuss the **surrender of the Itzá**. The negotiations were fruitless and in 1697 Spanish troops attacked Tayasal, the Itzá capital on Lake Petén Itzá (the site of modern Flores), bringing Maya independence in Petén to an end – at least in theory. At Tipú the struggle was to continue with simmering resentment until 1707, when the population was forcibly removed to Lake Petén Itzá. This cruel act effectively ended Spanish attempts to settle the west of Belize, as it would be impossible to establish a successful colony without people to work for the Spanish landowners.

In the late seventeenth century Bacalar was abandoned after years of **Maya and pirate attacks**. Spain's forces were simply too stretched to cope with securing the vast (and relatively gold-free) territory from Campeche on the Gulf of Mexico to Nicaragua. English, and later British, trade and territorial ambitions now focused on America and the Caribbean, resulting in almost continuous conflict with Spain. The capture of Jamaica in 1655, after 150 years of Spanish rule gave England a base in the Caribbean from which it could harass Spanish shipping and support the growth of its own colonies.

THE ARRIVAL OF THE BRITISH

The failure of the Spanish authorities to clearly delineate the southern boundary of Yucatán subsequently allowed **buccaneers** or pirates (primarily British) preying on the Spanish treasure fleets to find refuge along the coast of Belize, and ultimately led to Guatemala's claim to British Honduras and refusal to recongnize Belize's independence. Had Spain effectively occupied the area between Yucatán and Honduras it is unlikely that British influence – and a British colony – would have been allowed to become established. When Spain attempted to take action on various occasions to expel the British pirates and woodcutters there was confusion over which Spanish captain-general maintained jurisdiction in the area. Consequently the pirates were able to flee before the Spanish arrived and could return in the absence of any permanent Spanish outposts on the coast.

British incursions along the Bay of Honduras were first made by buccaneers, resting and seeking refuge after raids on Spanish ships and settlements. Some of the great Elizabethan sailors, such as Raleigh, Hawkins and Drake may have landed on the coast of Belize, though there are no records to prove this. Indeed records of any kind concerning settlements or even temporary camps until the 1700s are scarce: while the dates of the establishment of other British colonies in the Caribbean are known, there was no attempt on the part of the British government to colonize Belize itself.

Other European powers, notably **France** and **the Netherlands**, were also keen to establish a foothold in the Caribbean. Companies were set up to equip privateers, who were really government-sanctioned pirate ships, to raid the Spanish treasure fleets. Treasure wasn't always easy to come by and sometimes they would plunder the piles of **logwood**, cut and awaiting shipment to Spain. The wood itself, hard and extremely heavy, was worth £90–110 a ton, and the trade was controlled by Spain. Back in Europe logwood was used in the expanding textile industry to dye woollens black, red and grey. Naturally such an abundance of convertible wealth attracted the attention of the buccaneers, once they learned of its importance. By the mid-seventeenth century (possibly as early as 1638) British buccaneers had settled on the coasts of Campeche and the Spanish Caribbean.

The various treaties signed between Britain and Spain from the late seventeenth to mid-eighteenth centuries, initially designed to outlaw the buccaneers, eventually allowed the British to establish logwood camps along the rivers in northern Belize. However, this was never intended to legitimize permanent British settlement of a territory which Spain clearly regarded as its imperial domain. Thus, the British settlements in Belize periodically came under attack whenever Spain sought to defend its interests. But the attention of the European powers rarely rested long upon the humid and insect-ridden swamps where the logwood cutters, who were becoming known as **Baymen**, worked and lived. The British government, while wishing to profit from the trade in logwood, preferred to avoid the question of whether or not the Baymen were British subjects. For the most part they were left to their own devices.

Life in the logwood camps was uncomfortable, to say the least. Though the wood was mainly cut in the dry season, it was too heavy to float and the men had to build rafts to float it down to the river mouth in the rainy season, where it was stored awaiting shipment. The Baymen lived in rough huts thatched with palmetto leaves (known as "Bay leaf" and still seen today, mainly in tourist cabañas), surviving on provisions brought by ships from Jamaica. These ships also brought rum, which the Baymen drank with relish whenever it was available. An English merchant (writing in 1726) reports: "Rum Punch is their Drink, which they'll sometimes sit for several Days at . . . for while the Liquor is moving they don't care to leave it."

Though many of the woodcutters had "voluntarily" given up buccaneering, raiding of Spanish ships still occurred in the later years of the seventeenth century, only to be punished by Spain whenever it had the will and opportunity. One such reprisal against British woodcutters in the Bay of Campeche left the survivors imprisoned in Mexico and led to Belize becoming the main centre for logwood cutting.

As the gangs of woodcutters advanced further into the forests in search of **mahogany** (which had overtaken logwood as the principal export by the 1760s and was increasingly valuable for furniture-making) they came into contact with the Maya of the interior. Although the Baymen had no wish to colonize or convert the Maya they did capture some for slaves, and records show that the early buccaneers took Maya captives to trade in the slave markets of Jamaica. By the mid-eighteenth century the Maya had been so weakened by disease and depopulation that they could offer only limited resistance to British incursions into their territory.

Spanish attacks on the settlements in Belize occurred throughout the eighteenth century, with the Baymen being driven out on several occasions. Increasingly though, Britain – at war with Spain from 1739 to 1748 (the War of Jenkins' Ear) and France from 1743 to 1748 (the War of the Austrian Succession) – began to admit a measure of responsibility for the protection of the settlers. For the British there was little to lose.

In 1746, in response to requests from Belize, the governor of Jamaica sent troops to aid the Baymen, but this assistance didn't stop the Spanish laying waste to the settlement in 1747 and again in 1754. The **Paris Peace Treaty** of 1763 was the first (of many) to allow the British to cut logwood, but since it did not define boundaries the governor of Yucatán sent troops from Bacalar to ensure that the cutters confined themselves to the Belize River. In 1765 Admiral Burnaby, the commander-in-chief at Jamaica, visited Belize to ensure that the provisions of the treaty, vague though they were, were upheld. As so often in the reports of naval officers concerning the condition of the settlers, he found them "in a state of Anarchy and Confusion". The admiral, recognizing that the Baymen would benefit from some form of British laws and regulations, drew up a simple set of laws concerning the maintenance of justice in a remote and uncouth area where the British government did not care to become too closely involved. These rules, known as **Burnaby's Code**, gave authority to a bench of magistrates, supported by a jury, to hold quarterly courts with the power to impose fines. The Baymen attached an importance to the Code (though they apparently rarely obeyed it) beyond that which Burnaby had intended, and even voted to increase its scope a year later.

A century of antagonism, boundary disputes and mutual suspicion between the Spanish colonial authorities and the woodcutting (ex-buccaneering) Baymen meant that relations were never secure: the Spanish feared raids on their treasure ships, and the Baymen feared being driven out of what was ostensibly Spanish imperial territory. Spanish reprisals and animosity to Britain had fostered in the settlers a spirit of defiance and self-reliance, and the realization that British rule was preferable to Spanish, as long as they could choose which of its institutions to accept.

The Baymen's tenure in Belize was still very uncertain, however. In 1779 Spain (then allied with France on the side of the American colonies fighting for independence from Britain) sent a fleet from Bacalar to Belize and captured all the inhabitants of St George's Caye – the capital of the Baymen – imprisoning them in Mérida and Havana. The Versailles Peace Treaty (1783) did little to resolve the question of the Bay settlement, but a convention signed three years later allowed timber to be cut as far south as the Sibun River. The clause that rankled with the independent-minded settlers most was that no system of government could be established without approval from Madrid. True to their "turbulent and unsettled disposition", the Baymen ignored the strictures of the convention, cutting wood where they pleased and being generally unruly. After 1791 the settlement was without even the little-regarded authority of a superintendent appointed by the governor of Jamaica.

THE BATTLE OF ST GEORGE'S CAYE

The final showdown between the waning Spanish empire and the Bay settlers (supported this time by a British warship and troops), the **Battle of St George's Caye**, came as a result of the outbreak of war between Britain and Spain in 1796. Don Arturo O'Neil, an Irishman and the governor of Yucatán assembled ships and troops, determined to drive out the British settlers and this time to occupy Belize. The Baymen appealed to Lord Balcarres, the governor of Jamaica, for help, and a **Lieutenant-Colonel Barrow** was despatched to Belize as superintendent, to command the settlers in the event of hostilities. At a vital **Public Meeting** held on June 1, 1797, the Baymen decided by 65 votes to 51 to defend the settlement rather than evacuate. A few companies of troops were sent from Jamaica and slaves were released from woodcutting to be armed and trained. The sloop **HMS Merlin**, under the command of Captain John Moss, was stationed in the Bay, local vessels were armed, gun rafts built and an attack was expected at any time. Throughout the next year the mood of the defenders vacillated between aggression and despair. Under the supervision of Colonel Barrow the men of Belize, now under martial law, prepared for war – albeit grudgingly in some cases. The Baymen (and their slaves) would have to defend themselves with the scant resources at their disposal.

The **Spanish fleet**, reported to consist of 32 vessels, including sixteen heavily armed men-of-war and 2000 troops, arrived just north of St George's Caye in early September 1798. On September 3 and 4, several of the Spanish warships attempted to force a passage over Montego Caye Shoals, between Long Caye and St George's Caye, but were repulsed by the Baymen's sloops. Stakes put down by the Spanish to mark the channels through the shoals were removed by the defenders, who knew these waters well. Colonel Barrow and Captain Moss correctly guessed that the Spanish would now try to seize St George's Caye. The *Merlin* and part of the Baymen's tiny fleet sailed there on the evening of September 5, securing it just as twelve of the heaviest Spanish warships were attempting to do the same.

The next few days must have passed anxiously for both sides: the Spanish with their massive firepower severely restricted by the shallow water; and the Baymen with their small but highly manoeuvrable fleet awaiting the impending attack – with the Baymen's slaves apparently at least as eager to fight the Spanish as were their masters. On the morning of **September 10, 1798**, fourteen of the largest Spanish ships sailed to within a mile and a half of St George's Caye, keeping to the deep water to the east, and began firing. Captain Moss of the *Merlin* held his fire – the Spanish broadsides were falling short. At 1.30pm he gave the order to open fire. Guns blazing, the *Merlin* and the Baymen's fleet swept forward, wreaking havoc among the heavy and crowded Spanish ships. The Spanish fleet, already weakened by desertions and yellow fever, suffered heavy losses and fled in disorder to Caye Chapel. There they remained for five days, burying their dead on the island. On the morning of September 16 the defeated fleet sailed for Bacalar, still harassed by the Baymen.

Though a victory was won against overwhelming odds, the Battle of St George's Caye was not by itself decisive. No one in Belize could be sure that the Spanish would not once again attempt to remove the Baymen by force. The legal status was as before: a settlement where the inhabitants could cut timber but which did not constitute a territory of the British empire. Sovereign rights remained, nominally at least, with Spain.

However, in purely practical terms the power of the Spanish empire was waning while the British empire was consolidating and expanding. But in Belize the slaves were still slaves though they had fought valiantly alongside the Baymen: their owners expected them to go back to cutting mahogany. Emancipation came no earlier than elsewhere in the British empire. Indeed controversy still exists within Belize over the fact that the battle was fought between two European powers to establish rule over a colony. It created the conditions for Belize to become an integral part of the British empire and enabled the slave owners to claim that the slaves were willing to fight on behalf of their masters. Whatever its legacy, the 1798 expedition was the last time that Spain attempted to gain control over Belize; Britain gradually assumed a greater role in the government of the settlement.

SETTLERS AND SLAVES

A report by a Spanish missionary in 1724 mentions the ownership of **slaves** by English settlers, and it's possible that slaves were brought in (from Jamaica and Bermuda) before that time. The British population of the settlements in the Bay of Honduras during the century and a half following the arrival of the first buccaneers had never been more than a few hundred, their livelihoods dependent on the attitude of the authorities in the adjacent Spanish colonies. In order to gain concessions from Spain favourable to the Belize settlement, Britain had agreed to relinquish claims to the Mosquito Shore (a British protectorate along the coasts of Honduras and Nicaragua) in the **Convention of 1786**. Many of the aggrieved inhabitants displaced by the convention settled in Belize, and by 1790 the population had reached over 2900, of whom over 2100 were slaves.

Over the years the view that slavery in Belize was somehow less harsh has emerged. It's a misconception that may have arisen because of the differences between plantation slavery as practised in the West Indies and the southern United States, and the mainly forest labour that slaves in Belize were required to perform. The misconception has evolved into a myth, skilfully manipulated by apologists for colonialism, who maintain that during the pivotal Battle of St George's Caye slaves voluntarily fought "shoulder to shoulder" with their White masters, and

thus preferred slavery over the freedom offered by the Spanish authorities to any slave who escaped to Spanish territory. Although some slaves did fight alongside their masters in 1798, they also continued to escape: in 1813 fifteen slaves belonging to Thomas Paslow, one of the heroes of the battle, escaped "because of ill-treatment and starvation"; their desperation evidence enough to refute the myth. Records of **slave revolts** from 1745 to 1820 are further indication that relations between master and slaves were not as amicable as some would like to believe.

The Whites in the settlement, always vastly outnumbered by their slaves, feared rebellion at least as much as they feared attack by the Spanish. The biggest (and arguably most successful) revolt occurred in 1773 when six White men were murdered and at least eleven slaves escaped across the Hondo River, where they received asylum from the Spanish authorities. This was not a display of altruism on the part of the Spanish, since encouraging slaves to flee the British settlement was calculated to weaken its economy.

The nature of slavery in Belize was very different from that on the sugar plantations in the West Indies. The cutting of mahogany involved small gangs working in the forest on their own or on a fairly harmonious level with an overseer. The slaves were armed, with firearms in some cases, to hunt for food and for protection against Maya. Skills developed in searching for the trees, cutting them down and transporting them to the coast gave the slaves involved a position of trust that their masters depended on for the continuation of their own way of life. Manumission, whereby a slave might purchase freedom or be freed as a bequest in a will, or simply a gift, was much more frequent in Belize than in the Caribbean islands, perhaps as an indication of the greater informality of Belizean society. However, treatment could still be harsh and little protection was offered by the law. Owners could inflict up to 39 lashes or imprison their slaves, and if a slave was hanged for rebellion the owner could be compensated for the loss of property.

Ironically, it was the Abolition Act of 1807 – which made it illegal for British subjects to continue with the African slave trade but not to transport slaves from one British colony to another – that gave the settlers in Belize recognition as **British subjects**. If Belize was not a colony (which it clearly was not) then slaves could not be transported between Jamaica and the settlement. Superintendent Arthur, the British government's representative and upholder of the law in Belize, decided that the settlers in Belize were British subjects and therefore forbidden to engage in the slave trade. The **Abolition Act of 1833** ended slavery throughout the British empire, and contained a special clause to include Belize. The passing of the Act, however, did not end slavery immediately: "freed" slaves were to be called "apprentices", required to work for their masters for forty hours per week with no pay before being allowed to work for payment. This abuse continued until 1838, when the former slaves were fully and legally free. Despite the inherent immorality in the institution of slavery the Act provided for compensation to be paid to the owners for the loss of property, rather than to the former slaves for the suffering they had undergone for so long – and, at £53 per slave, the compensation paid was higher than in any British colony.

THE SETTLEMENT BECOMES A COLONY

The consolidation of British logging interests in the eighteenth century and the grudging, tentative steps towards recognition from Spain, led to a form of **British colonial government** gradually becoming established in the Belize settlement. The **Public Meeting**, with its origins in the early 1700s, was the settlers' initial response to the need for some rudimentary form of government. At first informal, the meetings slowly assumed greater importance, and by the 1730s were electing magistrates, with powers to hold courts and impose fines, though in the democratic spirit of the time only property-owning White men could vote. Free Coloured men were allowed to vote at the Public Meeting after 1808, though their franchise was limited by burdening them with higher property requirements than that of Whites. Burnaby's Code in 1765 reinforced and enlarged the jurisdiction of the magistrates, and allowed the laws passed at the Meeting to be enforced by the captain of a British naval ship, though reports by visiting naval officers almost invariably commented on the lamentable inability of the settlers to keep their own laws.

These early examples of Britain's acceptance of some form of responsibility to the settlers led

to the appointment in 1784 of the first **Superintendent**, Captain Despard, who took up his post in 1786. The office of superintendent, always held by an army officer, appears to have been a difficult one. They often faced an unsupportive Public Meeting, which wanted to run the settlement without "interference" from London. Gradually though, the powers of the superintendent grew, while those of the magistrates lessened. The election of magistrates ceased altogether in 1832, after which they were appointed by the superintendent. The office of superintendent was moving towards the role (though not the title) of a lieutenant-governor of a colony, and in 1854 an elected **Legislative Assembly** was formed, establishing the beginnings of colonial-rule parliamentary democracy. The assembly began petitioning for recognition as a colony, arguing that the settlement was in fact, if not in law, already a British colony. Earl Grey, at the Colonial Office, supported the assembly and Palmerston, the British prime minister, agreed. On May 12, 1862, the Belize settlements, with the boundaries that still exist today, became the **Colony of British Honduras**.

Partly as a result of arguments about raising finance, the Legislative Assembly dissolved itself in 1870 and was replaced by a Legislative Council. This enabled the British government to establish a Crown Colony form of government in 1871, in line with colonial policy throughout the West Indies. Now under the control of a governor, appointed by the Colonial Office, the self-determination of the settlers was effectively reduced.

MEXICAN AND GUATEMALAN CLAIMS

After the Battle of St George's Caye in 1798 Spain continued to maintain its claim to Belize, and the **Treaty of Amiens** in 1802, required Britain to hand back to Spain the territory captured during the war. Spain took this to include Belize, though the Baymen had no intention of leaving. But in the face of gathering difficulties throughout the Spanish empire, and Britain's willingness to assist the settlers in the defence of Belize, Spain's claim became increasingly insupportable.

Although **Mexico's independence**, achieved in 1821 and followed two years later by the colonies in Central America, marked the end of the Spanish empire on the mainland of the Americas, it didn't signal the end of external claims to Belizean territory. The years between the collapse of the Spanish empire and the close of the nineteenth century were filled with claim and counter-claim and with treaties made and broken – a situation not entirely resolved today.

Mexico's claim to at least the northern part of British Honduras as an extension of Yucatán was unacceptable to the British government, and eventually, after numerous diplomatic exchanges, an **Anglo-Mexican Treaty** was ratified in 1897. However, Mexico stated that should Guatemala successfully revive any of its claims to British Honduras then Mexico would press a claim to the area north of the Sibun River.

Guatemala's claim has been the source of more belligerent disagreement with Britain, and there's no doubt that the British government shares much of the blame for the confusion. In treaty after treaty Britain regarded Belize as a territory under Spanish sovereignty, and long after Spain's expulsion from the area, Britain maintained the fiction of Spanish sovereignty, which only complicated relations with the independent Guatemala. The Guatemalan claim to the territory of Belize rested upon the acceptance in international law of *uti possidetis* – the right of a colony which successfully gains independence from a colonial authority to inherit the rights and territory of that authority at the time of independence. For this to be valid, however, (even if Britain accepted the premise of *uti possidetis* – which was doubtful) the entire territory of Belize would have had to have been under Spanish control in 1821. Since this was clearly not the case the British position was that Guatemala's claim was therefore invalid.

In a vain attempt to reach a settlement Britain and Guatemala signed the **Anglo-Guatemalan Treaty** in 1859: the interpretation of this treaty and its various clauses has been the source of controversy and dispute ever since. The treaty, which in the British view settled the boundaries of Guatemala and Belize in their existing positions, was interpreted by Guatemala as a disguised treaty of cession of the territory outlined – if the crucial and controversial Article 7 of the treaty was not implemented – and not a confirmation of the boundaries. Under the provisions of Article 7, Britain agreed to fund and build a road from

Guatemala City to the Atlantic coast and in return Guatemala would drop its claim to Belize. If the road was not built then the territory would revert to Guatemala. Although a route was surveyed in 1859, Britain considered the estimated cost of £100,000 to construct the road too high a price to pay to secure the territory of Belize, and for this and other reasons the road was never built. The disputes were no nearer resolution when the settlement became the colony of British Honduras in 1862. The provisions of this article continued to be a cause of rancour and disagreement between the two countries for decades, and despite conventions and negotiations no agreement was reached. Finally, in 1940, Guatemala repudiated the treaty on the grounds that the provisions of Article 7 were not fulfilled, and the new constitution of 1945 declared Belize – Belice in Spanish – to be the 23rd department of Guatemala. In 1948 Guatemala made the first of several threats to invade Belize to "recover" the territory: Britain responded by sending cruisers and troops, the first of many military deployments required to counter this threat over the next four decades. With hindsight, £100,000 in 1859 would have been a comparative bargain.

THE CASTE WARS OF YUCATÁN

The terrible, bloody **Caste Wars** of Yucatán began with a riot by Maya troops at Valladolid in 1847. They sacked the town, killing Whites and spreading terror throughout the peninsula, and came within a hair's breadth of capturing Mérida, and throwing off White rule completely. From 1848, as Mexico sent troops to put down the rebellion, thousands of Maya and *mestizo* **refugees** fled to Belize, increasing the population of Orange Walk and Corozal and clearing the land for agriculture. The superintendent in Belize encouraged them to stay as they brought sugar cane and much-needed farming skills.

The rebellious Cruzob Maya (taking their name from a sacred "talking cross") occupied a huge, virtually independent territory in the east of the Yucatán peninsula. They established their capital at Chan Santa Cruz, well to the north of Belize, giving them their alternative name – the **Santa Cruz Maya**. At this time, the border between Belize and Mexico was not clearly defined and the Belize woodcutters came into conflict with the Santa Cruz Maya, who attacked the mahogany camps and took prisoners for ransom. The alarm spread throughout Belize and eventually a compromise was reached, whereby the settlers would pay a ransom to secure the prisoners' release, and would furthermore pay royalties to the Santa Cruz for the rights to cut wood in the Maya territory. In fact British merchants in Belize profited from the war by selling the Santa Cruz Maya arms, provoking strong protests from Mexico.

The story is further complicated by suspicion between the Santa Cruz and another Maya group, the **Icaiché**, who were not in rebellion and consequently were not trusted by the Santa Cruz. In 1851 the Icaiché were attacked by the Santa Cruz Maya, leading the Mexican government to propose an alliance between themselves and the Icaiché against the Santa Cruz. The Icaiché leaders requested British help in their negotiations, and since the woodcutters wanted to enter Icaiché lands to log mahogany, the Belize timber companies were also signatories to the treaty. In the **treaty of 1853** the Icaiché were granted virtual autonomy in the lands they occupied in return for recognizing the authority of Mexico, and the British were allowed to cut wood under licence in the Icaiché lands, in what was to become the northwest of Belize. The British woodcutters viewed the agreement as a means to expand their territory at the expense of both the Icaiché and a weakened Mexico.

It was now the turn of the Icaiché to demand rent from the British loggers; again this was only paid after **Maya attacks** on the camps. The continuing British arms trade with the Santa Cruz Maya incensed the Icaiché, and the flames were fanned further when they were attacked by the Santa Cruz. After years of broken agreements and betrayal the Icaiché, supported by Mexico and led by **Marcos Canul**, attacked mahogany camps on the Rio Bravo and the New River in 1866, capturing dozens of prisoners and spreading panic throughout the colony. The lieutenant governor declared martial law and sent for reinforcements from Jamaica. Raids and counter-raids continued for years, as the Maya sacked villages in Belize and colonial troops destroyed Maya villages and crops in reprisal. Canul briefly occupied Corozal in 1870, and even his death following a battle at Orange Walk in 1872 did not put an end to the raids. Corozal became a fortified military base,

and, although the attacks diminished, the danger of Maya attacks wasn't over until 1882 when the Icaiché leader, Santiago Pech, met the governor in Belize City to recognize British jurisdiction in the northwest.

THE TWENTIETH CENTURY: TOWARDS INDEPENDENCE

By 1900, free for the moment from worries about external threats, Belize was an integral, though minor, colony of the British empire. The population in the census of 1901 was 37,500, of whom 28,500 were born in the colony.

Comfortable complacency set in and the predominantly White property owners could foresee no change to their rule. The workers in the forests and on the estates were mainly Black, the descendants of former slaves, known as "Creoles". Wages were low and the colonial government and employers maintained strict controls over workers, with the power to imprison labourers for missing a day's work and stifling any labour organizations.

Belizeans rushed to defend the "Mother Country" in **World War I** but the Black troops from Belize were not permitted to fight a White enemy and were placed in labour battalions in British-held Mesopotamia. On their return in 1919, humiliated and disillusioned, their bitterness exploded into violence and the troops were joined by thousands of Belize City's population (including the police) in looting and rioting; an event which marked the onset of Black consciousness and the beginnings of the independence movement. The ideas of Marcus Garvey, a phenomenally industrious and charismatic Jamaican Black leader, and founder of the Universal Negro Improvement Association (UNIA), were already known in Belize – the colonial government's ban on *Negro World*, the UNIA's magazine, contributed to the severity of the 1919 riot – and in 1920 a branch of the UNIA opened in Belize City. Garvey believed that the "Negro needs a nation and a country of his own" – a sentiment which found increasing support among all sectors of Black society in Belize. Garvey himself visited Belize in 1921.

The status of workers had improved little over the last century and the Depression years of the 1930s brought extreme hardship, the disastrous hurricane of 1931 compounding the misery. The disaster prompted workers to organize in 1934 after an unemployment relief programme initiated by the governor was a dismal failure. Antonio Soberanis emerged as a leader, founding the Labourers and Unemployed Association (LUA), and holding regular meetings in the "Battlefield" – a public square outside the colonial administration buildings in Belize City. Soberanis was arrested in October 1934 while arranging bail for pickets at a sawmill who had been arrested. He was released a month later, and the meetings resumed. The colonial government responded by passing restrictive laws, banning marches and increasing the powers of the governor to deal with disturbances.

World War II gave a boost to forestry and the opportunity for Belizeans to work abroad, though conditions for the returning soldiers and workers were no better than they had been following World War I. Even in 1946 political power lay with the tiny wealthy elite who controlled the Executive Council and with the governor, a Foreign Office appointee. The devaluation of the British Honduras dollar at the end of 1949 caused greater hardship. A cautious report on constitutional reform in 1951 led to a **new constitution**, and in 1954 a **general election** was held in which all literate adults over the age of 21 could vote. These elections were won with an overwhelming majority by the **Peoples' United Party** (PUP), led by George Price, and ushered in a semblance of ministerial government, though control of financial measures was retained by the governor. Belize became an internally **self-governing colony** in 1964, a step intended to lead to full independence after a relatively short time, as was the policy throughout the Caribbean. Until then, however, the British government, through the governor, remained responsible for defence, foreign affairs and internal security. The National Assembly became a bicameral system with an appointed Senate and an entirely elected House of Representatives.

The delay in achieving independence was caused largely by the **dispute with Guatemala** as to its still unresolved claim to Belize. At least twice, in 1972 and 1977, Guatemala moved troops to the border and threatened to invade, but prompt British reinforcements were an effective dissuasion. The situation remained tense but international opinion gradually moved in favour of Belizean independence.

INDEPENDENCE AND THE BORDER DISPUTE

The most important demonstration of worldwide endorsement of Belize's right to self-determination was the **UN resolution** passed in 1980, which demanded secure independence, with all territory intact, before the next session. Further negotiations with Guatemala began but complete agreement could not be reached: Guatemala still insisted on some territorial concessions. On March 11, 1981, Britain, Guatemala and Belize released the "Heads of Agreement", a document which, they hoped, would eventually result in a peaceful solution to the dispute. Accordingly, on September 21, 1981, Belize became an independent country within the British Commonwealth, with Queen Elizabeth II as head of state. In a unique decision British troops were to remain in Belize, to ensure the territorial integrity of the new nation.

The new government of Belize, formed by the PUP with George Price as premier, continued in power until 1984, when the United Democratic Party (UDP), led by **Manuel Esquivel**, won Belize's first general election after independence. The new government encouraged private enterprise and foreign investment, and began a programme of neo-liberal economic reforms which meant privatizing much of the public sector. The next general election, in 1989, returned the PUP to power.

In 1988 Guatemala and Belize established a joint commission to work towards a "just and honourable" solution to the **border dispute**, and by August 1990 it was agreed in principle that Guatemala would accept the existing border with Belize. The only sticking point preventing full recognition by Guatemala was a geographical anomaly in the extreme south, where the territorial waters of Belize and Honduras formed a common boundary, making it theoretically possible for Guatemalan ships to be excluded from their own Caribbean ports. The PUP government's response was to draft the **Maritime Areas Bill** in August 1991, which would allow Guatemala access to the high seas by restricting Belize's territorial waters between the Sarstoon River and Ranguana Caye, 100km to the northeast. This measure proved acceptable to Guatemala's President Serrano, and on September 11, with just ten days to go before the celebrations for

Belize's tenth anniversary of independence, Guatemala and Belize established full diplomatic relations for the first time.

The air of euphoria soured somewhat during 1992 as opposition to Serrano's controversial recognition of Belize became more vocal and was ultimately challenged in Guatemala's Constitutional Court. Eventually the court decided that the president had not actually violated the constitution, and in November 1992 Congress (albeit with thirteen abstentions) conditionally approved Serrano's actions. The Guatemalan president's remaining time in office was short, however: in May 1993 he attempted to rule without Congress, and by June was overthown and in exile. Belize's premier, George Price, hoped to gain from the confusion this caused and, with the opposition UDP deeply divided, called a snap general election in July 1993. To his astonishment the gamble failed, and Manuel Esquivel's UDP was allowed a second term of office.

The territorial dispute remains a stumbling block in relations between the two countries with Guatemala's President Arzú restating the claim to Belize soon after his election in 1996. Despite this, the outlook is probably brighter than at any time in history; Arzú claims to be committed to resolving the dispute through negotiation and the countries continue to exchange ambassadors.

MODERN BELIZE

Belize's democratic credentials are beyond dispute: at each general election since independence the voters have kicked out the incumbent government and replaced it with the opposition. Under pressure from the World Bank to reduce government spending and widen the revenue base, the Esquivel government slashed thousands of public sector jobs and imposed a highly unpopular VAT: acts that led directly to the UDP's resounding defeat in the **August 1998 General Election**, in which even the prime minister lost his seat. With campaign pledges to repeal the "killer" VAT, the PUP, under the leadership of **Said Musa**, captured 25 out of 29 seats in the National Assembly in an unprecedented landslide, though it's extremely unlikely that the new government can keep such rash promises.

Despite a booming tourist industry that brings in almost $100 million a year, agriculture remains the mainstay of Belize's **economy**, accounting for 25 percent of GNP: around $135 million per year. Sugar is the most important agro-export, followed by bananas and citrus products. Figures are obviously not available for Belize's income from the lucrative drug transhipment business, but this illicit economy is as least as large as the official one.

Per capita income is high for Central America, at over US$2500, boosted by the remittances many Belizeans receive from relatives abroad, mainly in the US. This apparent advantage is offset by the fact that many of the brightest and most highly trained citizens leave Belize, fitting in well in English-speaking North America.

Though traditional links with Britain and the Commonwealth countries in the West Indies remain strong, Belize is being inexorably drawn into the proposals for a **Free Trade Area of the Americas**. The initial step, the imminent signing of a Free Trade Agreement with Mexico (though this may now be a little further off with the recent change of government) is viewed with alarm by many Belizean workers who fear that an end to all tariffs will further depress agricultural prices and drive the small manufacturing base into bankruptcy. Even worse in many peoples' eyes, these proposals signal an end to the fixed rate of exchange with the US$, leading to potentially catastrophic devaluation of the Belize dollar. And, regardless of the populist rhetoric of the PUP, Belize is firmly linked to the US-dominated international financial structures, and will have to face increasing challenges from global competition in the early years of the next century.

CHRONOLOGY OF THE MAYA

25,000 BC	**Paleo-Indian** First waves of nomadic hunters from Siberia.
10,000 BC	**Clovis culture** Worked stone tools found at many sites in North and Central America.
7500 BC	**Archaic period** Beginnings of settled agricultural communities throughout Mesoamerica; maize and other food crops cultivated.
4500 BC	**Proto-Maya period** First Maya-speaking groups settle in western Guatemala; Proto-Maya speakers probably spread throughout extent of Maya area.
2000 BC	**Preclassic or Formative period** Divided into: Early: 2000–1000 BC; Middle: 1000–300 BC; Late: 300 BC–250 AD The Maya began building centres which developed into the great cities of the Classic period. Trade increased and contact with the **Olmec** on the Gulf coast of Mexico brought many cultural developments, including the calendar and new gods. **Kaminaljuyú** dominates highland Guatemala, **El Mirador** is the most important city in Petén, and by 1000 BC Lamanai was a large city.
250 AD	**Classic period** Divided into: Early: 250–600 AD; Late: 600–850 AD; Terminal: 850–c.1000 AD During this period Maya culture reaches its height. Introduction of the Long Count **calendar**, used to mark dates of important events on stelae and monuments. The central lowlands are thickly populated, with almost all of the sites now known flourishing. The great monumental architecture associated with the Maya mainly dates from the Classic period. **Caracol** is the largest Classic Maya city in Belize.
850 AD	**Terminal Classic period** Decline (some say collapse) of Classic Maya civilization for reasons which remain unclear. Population decline and abandonment of many Maya cities, though some in Belize – notably **Lamanai** – survive throughout the Terminal Classic period.
987 AD	Yucatán sites show strong evidence of **Toltec culture**, possibly a result of invasion. Toltec culture grafted onto the region's Maya culture, possibly also extending into Belize.
1000 AD	**Early Postclassic period** Re-focus of populations. Some centres, such as Xunantunich, which survived the Terminal Classic, are now abandoned but many centres in Belize continue to thrive. Toltec domination of the Guatemalan highlands.
c. 1250	Rivalry and trade among the city-states of Petén, Yucatán and Belize. New, competitive, power structures formed by centres along the trade routes. **Tayasal** (Flores) rises to dominance in Petén. Cities in the river valleys of Belize grow rich controlling trade routes.
1511	First **Spanish contact with Maya** in Yucatán; Spanish sailors are captured.
1521	Aztec capital Tenochtitlán falls to Spanish troops commanded by **Cortés**.
1531	**Alonso Dávila** makes first attempt to capture and settle at Chetumal.
1543/4	Gaspar and Melchor **Pacheco** brutally conquer southern Yucatán and northern Belize.
1570	**Spanish mission** established at Lamanai; eight others built in northern Belize.

CHRONOLOGY OF BELIZE

1618	Spanish priests Fuensalida and Orbita visit Tipú, where they punish the Maya for worshipping "idols"; the Maya burn the church in defiance.
1630–40	Led by Tipú, the **Maya revolt against Spanish rule**. First pirate attacks on Bacalar, just north of Hondo River.
1640s	First **buccaneer** (pirate) settlements at mouth of Belize River.
1670	**Treaty of Madrid**, under which European powers begin to restrict piracy. Buccaneers start to cut logwood in the swamps of Belize. Spain claims sovereignty over Belize (but never effectively colonizes the area).
1716 onward	First **Spanish attacks** on British woodcutters (Baymen) in Belize. These attacks continue until 1798; at times the whole population of the settlement is driven off or captured, but the Baymen always return. African slaves brought from Jamaica to cut wood.
1763	**Treaty of Paris** allows British to cut and export wood in Belize; Spanish continue to maintain sovereignty but Britain increasingly prepared to defend settlers' rights.
1786	**Convention of London** allows Baymen to cut wood, but not to establish plantations, fortifications or government. First **British Superintendent** in Belize.
1798	**Battle of St George's Caye**: settlers and slaves under the command of British army and with support from the Royal Navy defeat a Spanish invasion fleet.
1821–24	Mexico and the Central American republics gain **independence** from Spain. Both Mexico and Guatemala claim sovereignty over Belize.
1832	Main date of arrival of **Garífuna** from Honduras, though some were already in Belize.
1838	Emancipation of slaves (four years later than in Britain).
1847–1900	**Caste Wars in Yucatán** Maya refugees flee to northern Belize; other groups of Maya raid towns and settlements in Belize until 1880.
1859	**Anglo-Guatemala Treaty** and other agreements aim to end dispute over sovereignty of Belize, but no real conclusion reached.
1862	Belize becomes part of the British empire as the colony of **British Honduras**.
1871	Status of British Honduras changed to **Crown Colony**.
1919	Belizean troops riot on return from World War I. Start of **nationalist sentiment** which begins calls for independence.
1931	**Hurricane** devastates Belize City and the entire coast.
1945	New Guatemalan constitution defines "Belice" as a department of Guatemala.
1950	PUP formed.
1954	New constitution introduces universal adult suffrage. PUP wins the **general election**.
1964	Belize gains **full internal self-government**. Independence delayed by Guatemala's claim to Belize. Guatemala threatens to invade in 1972 and 1977.
1979	First of 40,000 **refugees** from Guatemala and El Salvador arrive in Belize.
1981	Belize gains **independence** on September 21. **George Price** of PUP is prime minister.
1984	First general election after independence. UDP wins; **Manuel Esquivel** becomes prime minister.
1989	PUP wins general election; George Price is again prime minister.
1991–3	Guatemala's President Serrano agrees to recognize Belize. Diplomatic relations are established but no final agreement signed. George Price and PUP lose the general election. Manuel Esquivel and UDP are elected.
1998	PUP win landslide general election: **Said Musa** is prime minister.

THE MAYA ACHIEVEMENT

For some three thousand years before the arrival of the Spanish, Maya civilization dominated Central America, leaving behind some of the most impressive and

mysterious architecture in the entire continent. At their peak, around 300 AD, Maya cities were far larger and more elaborate than anything that existed in Europe at the time. Their culture was complex and sophisticated, fostering the highest standards of engineering, astronomy, stone carving and mathematics, as well as an intricate writing system.

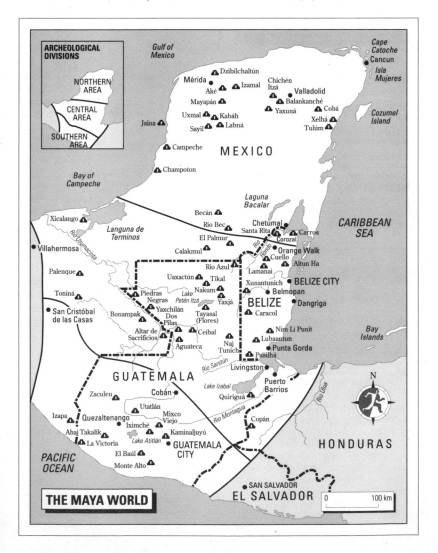

THE MAYA WORLD

To appreciate all this you have to see for yourself the remains of the great centres. Despite centuries of neglect and abuse they are still astounding, their main temples towering above the forest roof. Stone monuments, however, leave much of the story untold, and there is still a great deal that we have to learn about Maya civilization. What follows is the briefest of introductions to the subject, hopefully just enough to whet your appetite for the immense volumes that have been written on it.

MAYA SOCIETY

While the remains of the great Maya sites are a testament to the scale and sophistication of Maya civilization, they offer little insight into daily life in Maya times. To reconstruct the lives of ordinary people archeologists have turned to the smaller **residential groups** that surround the main sites, littered with the remains of household utensils, pottery, bones and farming tools. These groups are made up of simple structures made of poles and wattle-and-daub, each of which was home to a single family. The groups as a whole probably housed an extended family, who would have farmed and hunted together and may well have specialized in some trade or craft. The people living in these groups were the commoners, their lives largely dependent on agriculture. Maize, beans, cacao, squash, chillies and fruit trees were cultivated in raised and irrigated fields, while wild fruits were harvested from the surrounding forest. Much of the land was communally owned and groups of around twenty men worked in the fields together.

Maya **agriculture** was continuously adapting to the needs of the developing society, and the early practice of slash and burn was soon replaced by more intensive and sophisticated methods to meet the needs of a growing population. Some of the land was terraced, drained or irrigated in order to improve its fertility and ensure that fields didn't have to lie fallow for long periods, and the capture of water became crucial to the success of a site. The large cities, today hemmed in by the forest, were once surrounded by open fields, canals and residential compounds, while slash-and-burn agriculture probably continued in marginal and outlying areas. Agriculture became a specialized profession and a large section of the population would have bought at least some of their food in

markets, although all households still had a kitchen garden where they grew herbs and fruit.

Maize has always been the basis of the Maya **diet**, in ancient times as much as it is today. Once harvested it was made into *saka*, a cornmeal gruel, which was eaten with chilli as the first meal of the day. During the day labourers ate a mixture of corn dough and water, and we know that *tamales* were also a popular speciality. The main meal, eaten in the evenings, would have been similarly maize-based, although it may well have included meat and vegetables. As a supplement to this simple diet, deer, peccary, wild turkeys, duck, pigeons and quail were all hunted with bows and arrows or blowguns. The Maya also made use of dogs, both for hunting and eating. Fish were also eaten, and the remains of fish hooks and nets have been found in some sites, while there is evidence that those living on the coast traded dried fish far inland. As well as food, the forest provided firewood, and cotton was cultivated to be dyed with natural colours and then spun into cloth.

The main sites represent larger versions of the basic residential groups, housing the most powerful families and their assorted retainers. Beyond this these centres transcended the limits of family ties, taking on larger political, religious and administrative roles, and as Maya society developed they became small cities. The principal occupants were a small number of priestly rulers, but others included bureaucrats, merchants, warriors, architects and assorted craftsmen – an emerging middle class. At the highest level this **hierarchy** was controlled by a series of hereditary positions, with a single chief at its head.

The relationship between the cities and the land, drawn up along feudal lines, was at the heart of Maya life. The peasant farmers supported the ruling class by providing labour – building and maintaining the temples and palaces – food and other basic goods. In return the **elite** provided the peasantry with leadership, direction, protection and above all else the security of their knowledge of calendrics and supernatural prophecy. This knowledge was thought to be the basis of successful agriculture, and the priests were relied upon to divine the appropriate time to plant and harvest.

In turn, the sites themselves became organized into a hierarchy of power. At times a single city, such as Tikal or El Mirador, dominated vast areas, controlling all of the smaller sites, while at other times smaller centres operated independently. A complex structure of **alliances** bound the various sites together and there were periodic outbursts of open **warfare**. The distance between the larger sites averaged around 30km, and between these were myriad smaller settlements, religious centres and residential groups. The structure of these alliances can be traced in the use of emblem glyphs. Only those of the main centres are used in isolation, while the names of smaller sites are used in conjunction with those of their larger patrons. Trade and warfare between the large centres was commonplace as the cities were bound up in an endless round of competition and conflict.

THE MAYA CALENDAR

The cornerstone of all Maya thinking was an obsession with **time**. For both practical and mystical reasons the Maya developed a highly sophisticated understanding of arithmetics, calendrics and astronomy, all of which they believed gave them the power to understand and predict events. All great occasions were interpreted on the basis of the Maya calendar, and it was this precise understanding of time that gave the ruling elite its authority. The majority of carving, on temples and stelae, records the exact date at which rulers were born, ascended to power and died.

The basis of all Maya **calculation** was the vigesimal counting system, which used multiples of twenty. All figures were written using a combination of three symbols – a shell to denote zero, a dot for one and a bar for five – which you can still see on many stelae. When calculating calendrical systems the Maya used a slightly different notation known as the head-variant system, in which each number from one

---

MAYA TIME – THE UNITS

1 *kin* = 24 hours
20 *kins* = 1 *uinal*, or 20 days
18 *uinals* = 1 *tun*, or 360 days
20 *tuns* = 1 *katun*, or 7200 days
20 *katuns* = 1 *baktun*, or 144,000 days
20 *baktun* = 1 *pictun*, or 2,880,000 days
20 *pictuns* = 1 *calabtun*, or 57,600,000 days
20 *calabtuns* = 1 *kinchiltun*, or 1,152,000,000 days
20 *kinchiltuns* = 1 *alautun*, or 23,040,000,000 days

---

to twenty was represented by a deity, whose head was used to represent the number.

When it comes to the Maya **calendar** things start to get a little more complicated as a number of different counting systems were used, depending on the reason the date was being calculated. The basic unit of the Maya calendar was the day, or *kin*, followed by the *uinal*, a group of twenty days roughly equivalent to our month; but at the next level things start to get more complex as the Maya marked the passing of time in three distinct ways. The **260-day almanac** (16 *uinals*) was used to calculate the timing of ceremonial events. Each day was associated with a particular deity that had strong influence over those born on that particular day. This calendar wasn't divided into months but had 260 distinct day names. (This system is still in use among the Cakchiquel Indians who name their children according to its structure and celebrate fiestas according to its dictates.) A second calendar, the so-called "**vague year**" or *haab*, was made up of 18 *uinals* and five *kins*, a total of 365 days, making it a close approximation of the solar year. These two calendars weren't used in isolation but operated in parallel so that once every 52 years the new day of the solar year coincided with the same day in the 260-day almanac, a meeting that was regarded as very powerful and marked the start of a new era.

Finally the Maya had another system for marking the passing of history, which is used on dedicatory monuments. The system, known as the **long count**, is based on the great cycle of 13 *baktuns* (a period of 5128 years). The current period dates from 3116 BC and is destined to come to an end on December 10, 2012. The dates in this system simply record the number of days that have elapsed since the start of the current great cycle, a task that calls for ten different numbers – recording the equivalent of years, decades, centuries etc. In later years the Maya sculptors obviously tired of this exhaustive process and opted instead for the short count, an abbreviated version.

ASTRONOMY

Alongside their fascination with time the Maya were interested in the sky and devoted much time and energy to unravelling its patterns. Several large sites such as Copán, Uaxactún and Chichén Itzá have **observatories** carefully aligned with solar and lunar sequences.

The Maya showed a great understanding of **astronomy** and with their 365-day "vague year" were just half a day out in their calculations of the solar year, while at Copán, towards the end of the seventh century AD, Maya astronomers had calculated the lunar cycle at 29.53020 days, not too far off our current estimate of 29.53059. In the Dresden Codex their calculations extend to the 405 lunations over a period of 11,960 days, as part of a pattern that set out to predict eclipses. At the same time they had calculated with astonishing accuracy the movements of Venus, Mars and perhaps Mercury. Venus was of particular importance to the Maya as they linked its presence with success in war; there are several stelae that record the appearance of Venus prompting the decision to attack.

RELIGION

Maya **cosmology** is by no means straightforward as at every stage an idea is balanced by its opposite and each part of the universe is made up of many layers. To the Maya this is the third version of the earth, the previous two having been destroyed by deluges. The current version is a flat surface, with four corners, each associated with a certain colour; white for north, red for east, yellow for south, and black for west, with green at the centre. Above this the sky is supported by four trees, each a different colour and species, which are also sometimes depicted as gods, known as *Bacabs*. At its centre the sky is supported by a ceiba tree. Above the sky is a heaven of thirteen layers, each of which has its own god, while the very top layer is overseen by an owl. Other attested models of the world include that of a turtle (the land) floating on the sea. However, it was the underworld, Xibalba, "the Place of Fright", which was of greater importance to most Maya, as it was in this direction that they passed after death, on their way to the place of rest. The nine layers of hell were guarded by the "Lords of the Night", and deep caves were thought to connect with the underworld.

Woven into this universe the Maya recognized an incredible array of **gods**. Every divinity had four manifestations based upon colour and direction and many also had counterparts in the underworld and consorts of the opposite sex. In addition to this there was an extensive array of patron deities, each associated with a particular trade or particular class. Every activity from suicide to sex had its representative in the Maya pantheon.

RELIGIOUS RITUAL

The combined complexity of the Maya pantheon and calendar gave every day a particular significance, and the ancient Maya were bound up in a demanding **cycle of religious ritual**. The main purpose of ritual was the procurement of success by appealing to the right god at the right time and in the right way. As every event, from planting to childbirth, was associated with a particular divinity, all of the main events in daily life demanded some kind of religious ritual and for the most important of these the Maya staged elaborate ceremonies.

While each ceremony had its own format there's a certain pattern that binds them all. The correct day was carefully chosen by priestly divination, and for several days beforehand the participants fasted and remained abstinent. The main ceremony was dominated by the expulsion of all evil spirits, the burning of incense before the idols, a sacrifice (either animal or human) and blood-letting.

In divination rituals, used to foretell the pattern of future events or account for the cause of past events, the elite used various **drugs** to achieve altered states of consciousness. Perhaps the most obvious of these was alcohol, made either from fermented maize or a combination of honey and the bark of the balche tree. Wild tobacco, which is considerably stronger than the modern domesticated version, was also smoked. The Maya also used a range of hallucinogenic mushrooms, all of which were appropriately named, but none more so than the *xibalbaj obox*, "underworld mushroom", and the *k'aizalah obox*, "lost judgement mushroom".

ARCHEOLOGY

Like almost everything in Belize, archeology has made leaps and bounds in the last decade or so as researchers have unveiled a wealth of new material. The main text that follows was written by the late Winnel Branche, former Belize Museums Director, and illustrates the problems facing Belizean archeology as it emerges into the limelight, under siege from foreign expeditions and looters.

The ancient Maya sites of Belize have seen activity since the late nineteenth century. During these early times British amateur archeologists and both British and American museums kept up a lively interest in artefacts from these sites. Preservation of monuments was not yet "in" and techniques were far from subtle. In some cases dynamite was used to plunder the sites and Belizean artefacts often found their way, unmonitored, into museums and private collections worldwide.

Since 1894 the ancient monuments and antiquities of Belize have had loosely structured legislation to protect them, but it was not until 1952 that a civil servant was made responsible for archeology, and not until 1957 that a department was formed to excavate, protect and preserve these remains. Since then scientific excavation of hundreds of sites in Belize has been carried out, with prior agreement from the Department of Archeology, by universities, museums and scientific institutions from the US, Canada and, to a lesser extent, Britain.

The Belize Department of Archeology had grown from one member in 1957 to eight members of office staff by 1990. It monitors fieldwork and excavations carried out by foreign researchers in the country. It also performs small-scale salvage excavations in emergencies and is dedicated to the training of Belizeans to carry out all archeological work in the country. A vital task is to prevent looting activities, which have become rampant in recent years, but all these efforts are hampered by the lack of resources. The department also carries out educational activities including lectures, slide shows and travelling exhibitions in an attempt to sensitize the public on this part of their heritage. The responsibility of maintaining archeological sites, especially those open to the public, falls to the department, as has the safekeeping of the vast national collections in the absence of a museum in Belize. Since any immovable man-made structure over 100 years old and any movable man-made item over 150 years old are considered ancient monuments and artefacts respectively, the department is also in charge of all the non-Maya historical and colonial remains.

There are now at least sixteen archeological research teams visiting Belize annually, illustrating the fact that the Maya of Belize were not on the fringe of the Maya civilization, as had previously been thought, but were in fact a core area of the Maya culture. Evidence has been found of extensive raised-field agriculture and irrigation canals in northern Belize, and the oldest known site so far found in the Maya world is at Cuello, near Orange Walk. Even Tikal in Guatemala, once thought to be the centre of power of the lowland Maya, is now known to have been toppled at least once by Caracol, perhaps the largest site in Belize.

There has been increased interest lately in ancient Maya maritime trade, with coastal sites and those on the cayes receiving more attention. In addition, the extensive cave systems which form a network under inland Belize have shown much evidence of use by the Maya. In 1984 the longest cave system in Central America, containing the largest cave room in the western hemisphere, was discovered in Belize. It is known as the Chiquibul Cave System (p.142) and exploration here has revealed areas of concentration of Maya artefacts.

ARCHEOLOGY FIELD SCHOOLS AND PROJECTS IN BELIZE

Archeological research at Maya sites in Belize is at the cutting edge of the discipline. Many of the sites accept paying students (and often non-students): the average two- to four-week stint at a field school costs in the region of US$1500–2500. It's fascinating work but be prepared for some pretty arduous conditions.

In addition to the **schools and projects** listed below it's worth looking in the *Archaeology Fieldwork Opportunities Bulletin* (☎1-800/228-0810; US$10 to members), or in *Archaeology Magazine* (☎1-800/221-3148, Web site *www.archaeology.org*). Earthwatch (see p.42 for details) also has several archeological projects in Belize and throughout the region. Finally, the Web site at *www.serve.com/archaeology/america.html* has myriad useful links.

The Belize River Archaeological Settlement Survey (BRASS) has been working in the Belize River valley area since 1983 and at El Pilar since 1993. El Pilar, a major Maya centre straddling the Belize-Guatemala border (see p.136), forms the core of the new El Pilar Archeological Reserve for Maya Flora and Fauna. Preference is given to those with experience and skills in ceramics, drafting, computers and photography. Graduate students are preferred in student applications. Contact: Dr Anabel Ford, ISBER/MesoAmerican Research Center, University of California, Santa Barbara, CA 93106 (fax 805/893-2790, email *ford@alishaw.ucsb.edu* or *elpilar@btl.net*).

Blue Creek Archaeological Project of the Maya Research Program (MRP) has been conducting excavations in northwestern Belize since 1992. Contact: Thomas H. Guderjan, St Mary's University, San Antonio, Texas 78228 (☎210/431-2280, email *guderjan@netxpress.com*, Web site *www.mayaresearchprogram.org*).

The Belize Caracol Regional Archaeological Field School (BCRAFS) is designed to give students experience at one of the premier Maya sites of Belize (see p.141). Contact: Department of Archaeology, Ministry of Tourism and the Environment, Belmopan, Belize (☎08/22106, fax 23345, email *ceibelize@btl.net*, Web site *www.belize.gov.bz/doa*).

Mayflower Archaeology Project in Stann Creek District covers three Late Classic sites; Mayflower, Maintzunun and T'au Witz. The area was surveyed twenty years ago but, until recently, excavations have been virtually non-existent; much of the site is still covered in tropical forest. Students stay in Hopkins (see p.174). Contact: Wendy Brown, Social Sciences Division, A237, College of Lake County, Grayslake, IL 60030 (☎847/223-6601 ext 2608, email *wbrown@clc.cc.il.us*).

Ma'ax Na Regional Archaeology Project works in the Rio Bravo Conservation Area (see p.77). First discovered in 1995, Ma'ax Na is a large site – the ceremonial centre covers a one-kilometre-long hilltop. To date, 469 structures have been mapped within and around the centre and in several smaller centres to the east. Contact: Dr Leslie Shaw, New England Archaeology Institute, 14 Maine Street, Suite 210, Brunswick, ME 04011 (☎207/725-8402, email *lshaw@ime.net*, Web site *www.neai.org*).

With the wealth of Maya remains in the country, it is hardly surprising but most unfortunate that looting of sites and the sale of antiquities on the black market is still prevalent. In Belize all ancient monuments and antiquities are owned by the state, whether on private or government land or underwater. Residents are allowed to keep registered collections under licence, but the sale, purchase, import or export of antiquities is illegal and punishable under the law. Excavation and other scientific research can only be done with department permission after agreement on conditions. While intended to prevent looting and destruction, this law is also meant to keep the remains intact and within the country so that Belizeans and visitors can see the evidence of this splendid heritage.

LANDSCAPE AND WILDLIFE

For its size, Belize has a diverse range of environments: from the coral reefs and atolls of the Caribbean coast, through the lowland swamps and lagoons, up the valleys of pristine tropical rivers, to the exposed ridges of the Maya Mountains. Physically the land increases in elevation as you head south and west; the main rivers rise in the west and flow north and east to the Caribbean.

Away from the coast, which is entirely low-lying and covered by marine sediments for 10–20km inland, the country can be roughly divided into three **geological regions**: the **northern lowlands**, a continuation of the Yucatán Platform, with Cretaceous limestone overlain by deposits of alluvial sand; the **Maya Mountains**, where Santa Rosa quartz with granite intrusions rises to over 1000m to form the highest peaks in the country; and **southern Belize**, where more Cretaceous limestone hills with an impressive range of wonderfully developed **karst features**, including caverns, natural arches and sinkholes, give way to foothills and the coastal plain.

The **wildlife** is correspondingly varied; undisturbed forests provide a home to both temperate species from the north and tropical species from the south, as well as a number of indigenous species unique to Belize. In winter, the hundreds of native bird species are joined by dozens of migrant species from the eastern seaboard of North America. With its variety of tropical land and marine ecosystems Belize is increasingly a focus of scientific research.

THE TROPICAL FOREST

Over most of the country the natural vegetation is technically **tropical moist forest**, classified by average temperatures of 24°C and annual rainfall of 2000–4000mm; the only true **rainforest** lies in a small belt in the extreme southwest. More than 4000 flowering plant species can be found in Belize, including around 700 species of tree (about the same number as the whole of the US and Canada) and 200 varieties of orchid. So diverse is the forest that scientists have identified seventy different types, though these can be placed into three broad groups: thirteen percent is fairly open **pine savannah** (known in Belize as "pine ridge" regardless of the elevation); nineteen percent is **mangrove and coastal forest** (which includes the rarest habitat type in Belize, **caye littoral forest**); and the remaining 68 percent is **broadleaf forest** and *cohune* palm forest – the type commonly referred to as rainforest.

Belize still has around sixty percent of its **primary forest**: the combination of a year-round growing season, plenty of moisture and millions of years of evolution has produced a unique environment. While temperate forests tend to be dominated by a few species – for example, fir, oak or beech – it's diversity that characterizes the tropical forest, with each species specifically adapted to fit a particular ecological niche. This biological storehouse has yet to be fully explored, though it has already yielded some astonishing **discoveries**. Steroid hormones, such as cortisone, and diosgenin, the active ingredient in birth control pills, were developed from wild yams found in these forests, while tetrodoxin, derived from a species of Central American frog, is an anaesthetic 160,000 times stronger than cocaine.

But despite its size and diversity the forest is surprisingly **fragile**, forming a closed system in which nutrients are continuously recycled and decaying plant matter fuels new growth. The forest floor is a spongy mass of roots, fungi, mosses, bacteria and micro-organisms, in which nutrients are stored, broken down with the assistance of insects and chemical decay, and gradually released to the waiting roots and fresh seedlings. The thick canopy prevents much light from reaching the forest floor, ensuring that the soil remains damp but warm, a hotbed of chemical activity. The death of a large tree prompts a flurry of growth as new light reaches the forest floor and seedlings struggle. However, once a number of trees are removed the soil is highly vulnerable – exposed to the harsh tropical sun and direct rainfall, an area of cleared forest soon becomes prone to flooding and drought. Recently cleared land will contain enough nutrients for four or five years of good growth, but soon afterwards its usefulness declines rapidly and within twenty years it will be almost completely barren. If the trees are stripped from a large area soil erosion will silt the rivers and parched soils disrupt local rainfall patterns.

Belize's forests are home to abundant **birdlife** and in fact birds are the most visible of the country's wildlife, and a big draw for many visitors. Even if you've never had much of an interest in them, you'll be astonished at the sheer numbers of birds you can see just by sitting by a cabin in any one of the jungle lodges in Belize. Parrots, such as the **Aztec** and **green parakeets**, are seen every day, and if you're an expert you'll be aware of a range of otherwise scarce species that you might catch a glimpse of here, from the tiny **orange-breasted falcon** to the massive **harpy eagle**, the largest of Belize's raptors. Watching a jewel-like **hummingbird** feed by dipping its long, delicate bill into a heliconia flower as it hovers just inches in front of your eyes is a wonderful experience. Their names are as fascinating as their colours: the rufous-tailed, the little hermit, the white-bellied emerald and the violet sabrewing, to mention just a few.

Although Belize has 56 species of **snakes** many of which occur widely throughout the country, only nine are venomous and you're unlikely to see any snakes at all. One of the commonest is the **boa constrictor**, which is also the largest, growing up to 4m, though it poses no threat to humans. Others you might see are **coral snakes** (which are venomous) and **false coral snakes** (which are not); you'd need to be quite skilled to tell them apart.

Finally, one thing you'll realize pretty quickly is that you're never far from an **insect** in Belize. Mostly you'll be trying to avoid them or even destroy them, particularly the common (though

by no means ever-present) mosquitoes and sandflies. But the **butterflies** are beautiful, and you'll frequently see clouds of them feeding at the edges of puddles on trails; the caterpillars are fascinating and sometimes enormous. The largest and most spectacular are the gorgeous, electric-blue **blue morpho** and the **owl butterfly**, and you can see many more on a visit to one of a growing number of **butterfly exhibits** around the country. **Ants** are the most numerous insects on the planet; something you can easily believe here. Perhaps the most impressive are the **army ants**, called the "marchin' army" in Belize, as the whole colony ranges through the forest in a narrow column voraciously hunting for insects. Rest assured that, unlike their Hollywood movie counterparts, they can't overpower you and rip the flesh from your bones – though they will give you a nasty bite if you get too close. People in rural areas welcome a visit as the ants clear pests from their houses. **Leafcutter ants** (wee-wee ants) have regular trails through the forest along which they carry bits of leaves often much larger than themselves – which is how they get the name "parasol ants". The leaves themselves aren't for food, but they provide a growing medium for a unique type of fungus that the ants do eat.

Spiders are also very common: take a walk at night with a flashlight anywhere in the countryside and you'll see the beam reflected back by the eyes of dozens of **wolf spiders**. **Tarantulas** too, are found everywhere – the sharp fangs may look dangerous but tarantulas won't bite unless they're severely provoked.

THE MAYA MOUNTAINS

The main range of the **Maya Mountains** runs southwest to northeast across the whole of south-central Belize and straddles the border with Guatemala. This wild region, covered in dense forest and riddled with caves and underground rivers, has few permanent residents. The mountains form part of the great swathe of **national parks** and **forest reserves**, the most accessible of which are the **Mountain Pine Ridge** (p.137) and the **Cockscomb Basin Wildlife Sanctuary** (p.178), home of Belize's **jaguar reserve**.

The flora and fauna, though similar to those found in the tropical forests of Guatemala, are often more prolific here as there's much less pressure on the land. Though rarely seen, the

scarlet macaw, probably the country's most spectacular bird, is occasionally found in large flocks in the southern Maya Mountains and the Cockscomb Basin. All of Belize's cat species are found in the Maya Mountains. **Jaguars** (tiger in Belize) range widely over the whole country, but the densest population is found in the lower elevation forests of the west, while **pumas** (red tiger) usually keep to remote ridges. The two smaller species of spotted cats – the **ocelot** and the **margay** (both called tiger cat in Belize and slightly larger than a domestic cat) – are also found here, as is the **jaguarundi**, the smallest and commonest of Belize's cats – you might spot one on a trail since it hunts during the day. Belize's largest land animal, **Baird's tapir** (mountain cow), weighing up to 300kg, is usually found near water. Tapirs are endangered throughout most of their range, but are not rare in Belize, though you're unlikely to see one without a guide.

On the northern flank of the Maya Mountains, the **Mountain Pine Ridge** is a granite massif intruded into the sedimentary quartz and resulting in a ring of metamorphic rock around the granite. Many of the rivers rising here fall away to the Macal and Belize river valleys below in some of the most spectacular waterfalls in the country. On this nutrient-poor soil the dominant vegetation is the **Caribbean pine**, which covers sixty percent of the area in the largest stands anywhere in its range; bromeliads and orchids adorn the trunks and branches. It's a unique habitat in Belize, and home to several endemic species, including two frogs and a fish known only by their Latin names.

LOWLAND BELIZE

The forests of Petén extend into **northwestern Belize**, where the generally low-lying topography is broken by a series of roughly parallel **limestone escarpments**. The main ones – the Booth's River and Rio Bravo escarpments – each have a river below draining north to the Rio Hondo. Here the **Rio Bravo Conservation Area** (p.77) protects a huge area of forest. Further east the plain is more open; pine savannah is interspersed with slow-flowing rivers and lagoons, providing spectacular **wetland habitats** that continue to the coast. In the centre **Crooked Tree Wildlife Sanctuary** (see p.69) covers several freshwater lagoons, protecting over 200 bird species, including the nesting

sites of the rare **jabiru stork**. The tiny village of Sarteneja is the only settlement between Belize City and Corozal on the northeast coast – an important wetland area for **wading birds**, **crocodiles** and **turtles**, protected in the **Shipstern Nature Reserve** (p.80). In addition, almost all of the mammals of Belize – with the exception of monkeys but including jaguar, ocelot and tapir – can be found at this mosaic of coastal lagoons, hardwood forest and mangrove swamp. Other forest mammals you might see signs of include the **collared** and the **white-lipped peccaries** (warrie), **brocket** and **white-tailed deer**, **opossums**, **weasels**, **porcupines** and **armadillos**.

At the **Bermudian Landing Baboon Sanctuary** in the lower Belize River valley, (p.66), visitors can be almost guaranteed views of troops of **black howler monkeys** (baboons); you'll certainly hear the deep-throated roar of the males.

In the south there's only a relatively narrow stretch of lowland between the Maya Mountains and the coast, but heavy rainfall ensures the growth of lush rainforest. Along the coast and navigable rivers much of the original forest has been logged; some is in varying stages of regrowth after hurricane damage, and around human settlements it has been replaced by patches of agricultural land and coconut plantations. A boat journey along the **Burdon Canal Nature Reserve** (p.162), which connects the Belize and Sibun rivers to the Northern and Southern lagoons, is a good introduction to the wildlife to be found in the inland mangrove forests.

At night in the forest you'll hear the characteristic chorus of frog mating calls and you'll frequently find the **red-eyed tree frog** – a beautiful pale green creature about 2–3cm long – in your shower in any rustic cabin. Less appealing perhaps are the giant **marine toads**, the largest toad in the Americas, weighing in at up to 1kg and growing to over 20cm. These are infamous as the cane toad, which caused havoc with the native species when introduced into Australia; it eats anything it can get into its capacious mouth. Like most frogs and toads it has toxic glands and the toxin of the marine toad has hallucinogenic properties – a characteristic the ancient Maya employed in their ceremonies by licking these glands and interpreting the resultant visions.

Take a trip along almost any river and you'll see **green iguanas**, which, along with their very similar cousin the **spiny-tailed iguana** (wish-willy), are probably the most prominent of Belize's reptiles. Along the **New River** you'll see (or more likely be shown) **Morelet's crocodiles**, which are common in almost any body of water, and of no danger to humans unless they're very large – at least 3m long. Previously hunted to the brink of extinction they've made a remarkable comeback since being protected, and are now frequently spotted in the mangroves of Haulover Creek, immediately west of Belize City. Rivers also offer great bird-watching, including several species of **kingfisher**. One of the most common, the **belted kingfisher**, is also Belize's largest. There're herons and egrets too, including the **tri-colured heron**, the **boat-billed heron**, the **great egret** and occasionally the **jabiru stork**.

THE CARIBBEAN COAST AND THE BARRIER REEF

Belize's most exceptional environment is its **Caribbean coastline** and offshore barrier reef, dotted with hundreds of small islands and three atolls. The shoreline is still largely covered with **mangroves** which play an important role in the Belizean economy, not merely as nurseries for commercial fish species but also for their stabilization of the shoreline and their ability to absorb the force of hurricanes. For centuries the reef has been harvested by fishermen. In the past they caught manatees and turtles, but these days the **spiny lobster** and **queen conch** are the main catch. In the last two decades the fishing industry has boomed and the numbers of both species have now gone into decline.

Just inland from the mangroves along the coast and on the cayes the **littoral forest** occupies slightly higher ground. The vegetation here is salt tolerant, and many plants are characterized by their tough, waxy leaves which help conserve water. Species include red and white **gumbo limbo**, **black poison-wood**, **zericote**, **sea grape**, **palmetto** and of course the **coconut**, which typifies Caribbean beaches, though it's not actually a native. The littoral forest supports a very high density of fauna, especially migrating birds, due to the succession of fruits and seeds, yet it also faces the highest development pressure in Belize due to its higher coastal elevation; **caye littoral forest** is the smallest and most endangered habitat in the country.

The dominant species of the coastal fringe is the **red mangrove**, although in due course it undermines its own environment by consolidating the sea bed until it becomes more suitable for the less salt-tolerant black and white mangroves. Each kilometre of mangrove shoreline is valued at several thousand dollars per year. The cutting down of mangroves, particularly on the cayes, exposes the land to the full force of the sea and can mean the end of a small and unstable island.

The basis of the shoreline food chain is the nutrient-rich mud, held in place by the mangroves, while the roots themselves are home to **oysters** and **sponges**. Young **stingrays** cruise through the tangle of mangrove roots, accompanied by juvenile **snappers**, **bonefish** and small **barracudas**. The tallest mangrove forests in Belize are found along the Temash River, in the **Sarstoon-Temash National Park** (p.196), where the black mangroves reach heights of over 30m. From a canoe among the mangrove cayes and lagoons you can easily spot the **brown pelican**, **white ibis**, **roseate spoonbill** or even a **greater flamingo**. You might even see the American **salt-water crocodile**, rarer and much larger than the Morelet's crocodile.

The mangrove lagoons are also home to the **West Indian manatee**; Belize has the largest manatee population in the Caribbean, estimated to be somewhere between three hundred and seven hundred individuals. Manatees can grow up to 4m in length and 450kg in weight, but are placid and shy, moving between the freshwater lagoons and the open sea. Once hunted for their meat, they are now protected and the places where they congregate are tourist attractions. In shallows offshore, "meadows" of **seagrass beds** provide nurseries for many fish and invertebrates and pasture for conch, manatees and turtles. The extensive root system of seagrasses also protects beaches from erosion by holding the fragments of sand and coral together.

The **barrier reef** is the longest in the western hemisphere, an almost continuous chain of **coral** that stretches over 600km from northern Quintana Roo in Mexico to the far south of Belize. East of the barrier reef are the **atolls** (see p.110) – roughly oval-shaped reefs rising from the seabed surrounding a central lagoon. **Glover's Reef** atoll is considered by the scientific community to be one of the most pristine and important coral reef sites in the Caribbean.

Further south, the **Bay Islands** (see p.202) of Honduras are the peaks of underwater mountains, and are also surrounded by coral reefs.

Beneath the water is a world of astounding beauty, with fish and coral in every imaginable colour. Resembling a brilliant underwater forest, each coral is in fact composed of colonies of individual **polyps,** feeding off plankton wafting past in the current. There are basically two types of coral: hard, calcareous, reef-building corals, such as **brain coral** and **elkhorn coral** (known scientifically as the hydrocorals), and the soft corals such as **sea fans** and **feather plumes** (the ococorals). On the reefs you'll find the garish-pink **chalice sponge**, the appropriately-named **fire coral**, the delicate **feather-star crinoid**, and the **apartment sponge**, a tall thin tube with lots of small holes in it. In 1995 a major **coral reef bleaching** event occurred throughout the Caribbean. Bleaching occurs when the polyp loses some or all of the symbiotic **microalgae** (zooxanthellae) which live in its cells, usually in response to stress. The most common cause is a period of above average sea temperatures – the increased occurrence of coral bleaching may indicate that global warming is taking place.

The fish, including **angel** and **parrot fish**, several species of **stingrays** and **sharks** (the most common the relatively harmless nurse shark), **conger** and **moray eels**, **spotted goatfish** and the small striped **sergeant-major**, are just as unusual. The sea and islands are also home to grouper, **barracuda**, **marlin** and the magnificent **sailfish**. **Dolphins** are frequently seen just offshore, and will mostly be the Atlantic bottle-nosed dolphin, though further out large schools of the smaller spotted dolphin are sometimes found. In the autumn **whale sharks** pass by far out to sea.

Belize's three species of **marine turtles**, the **loggerhead**, the **green** and the **hawksbill**, occur throughout the reef, nesting on isolated beaches, but are infrequently seen as they are still hunted for food. Recent changes in legislation have provided them with greater protection, however.

Above the water the cayes are an ideal nesting ground for birds, providing protection from predators and surrounded by an inexhaustible food supply. At **Half Moon Caye**, right out on the eastern edge of the reef, there's a wildlife reserve designed to protect a breeding colony of 4000 **red-footed boobies**. Here you'll also see **frigate birds**, **ospreys**, **mangrove warblers** and **white-crowned pigeons**, among a total of 98 different species.

CONSERVATION

Recent additions to Belize's already impressive network of national parks, nature reserves and wildlife sanctuaries now bring over 35 percent of the land under some form of legal protection, an amazing feat for a developing country with a population of only 225,000. With such enlightened strategies to safeguard the nation's biodiversity Belize is gaining recognition as the most conservation-conscious country in the Americas. The success of these nature reserves, national parks and community wildlife sanctuaries (covered in detail in the relevant chapters), however, is due as much to the efforts of local communities to become involved in conservation as it is to governmental decisions.

CONSERVATION STRATEGY

The conservation of natural resources is the main plank in the government's declared policy to make "**ecotourism**" the focus of development and marketing in the nation's tourism industry. Ideally this is a community-based form of tourism, inspired primarily by the wildlife and landscape of an area and showing respect for local cultures. The theory is that by practising small-scale, nonconsumptive use of the country's natural resources, visitors will be contributing financially both to the conservation of protected areas and to local communities; it is hoped that this will aid sustainable development not only locally but in Belize as a whole.

LEGISLATION

Conservation legislation in Belize originally focused on forest reserves established by the colonial government to provide areas for timber exploitation, not primarily for nature preservation. In 1928, however, Half Moon Caye was established as a Crown Reserve to offer protection to the red-footed booby. Other bird and wildlife sanctuaries were established in the 1960s and 1970s, and in the period since independence the government has taken measures which have increased enormously the area of land and sea under protection. The passing of the **National Parks Act** in 1981 provided the legal basis for establishing national parks,

natural monuments and reserves, and the **Wildlife Protection Act** of 1981 (extended in 1991) created closed seasons for various endangered species, including marine and freshwater turtles, lobster, conch and black coral.

Another step in the right direction came with the 1992 **Environmental Protection Act**, intended to control pollution and promote environmental health by requiring companies to carry out an Environmental Impact Assessment before undertaking any proposed development. Low penalties for its contravention, though, compounded by the act's loosely worded definitions have dulled its impact. **Hunting**, which has for a long time been a means of supplementing diet and income, remains a real problem in almost all reserves and protected lands; the most popular species include iguana, armadillo, deer and the gibnut, or *tepescuintle*, a large rodent sometimes seen on menus. Needless to say you should avoid ordering these creatures in restaurants.

Belize is also a signatory to a number of important **international conservation agreements**, including the **Ramsar Convention** on wetlands of international importance, and the UNESCO **World Heritage Convention**. Seven reserves on the barrier reef, totalling over 90 square kilometres, were declared World Heritage Sites in 1996: Bacalar Chico National Park and Marine Reserve, Blue Hole and Half Moon Caye Natural Monuments, South Water Caye Marine Reserve, Glovers Reef Marine Reserve, Sapodilla Cayes Marine Reserve and Laughing Bird Caye National Park; all can be visited and details are in the relevant chapters of the *Guide*. These and other protected areas form the **Belize Barrier Reef Reserve System**, which has the ultimate aim of forming a continuous corridor of marine reserves from Mexico to Honduras. An important step towards this was taken in 1997 when the leaders of Belize, Guatemala, Honduras and Mexico signed the **Mesoamerican Caribbean Coral Reef System Initiative** (the Tulum Declaration) to promote conservation and sustainable use of the coral reef system shared by these four nations.

These countries are also members of the **Central American Commission on Environment and Development** (CCAD), an organization that encompasses all of the Central American nations and is planning the implementation of an even more ambitious

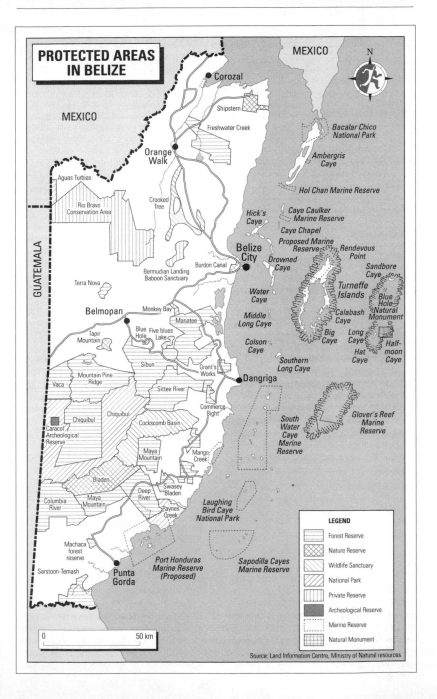

PROTECTED AREAS IN BELIZE

N

MEXICO

MEXICO

Corozal

Shipstern

Freshwater Creek

Bacalar Chico National Park

Orange Walk

Ambergris Caye

Aguas Turbias

Hol Chan Marine Reserve

Rio Bravo Conservation Area

Crooked Tree

Hick's Caye

Caye Caulker Marine Reserve

Caye Chapel

Proposed Marine Reserve

Rendevous Point

Belize City

Drowned Caye

Burdon Canal

Sandbore Caye

Bermudian Landing Baboon Sanctuary

Terra Nova

Water Caye

Turneffe Islands

Blue Hole Natural Monument

Belmopan

Monkey Bay

Middle Long Caye

Calabash Caye

Tapir Mountain

Blue Hole

Manatee

Five blues Lake

Colson Caye

Big Caye

Long Caye

Half-moon Caye

Sibun

Hat Caye

Vaca

Mountain Pine Ridge

Grant's Works

Southern Long Caye

Dangriga

Chiquibul

Sittee River

Chiquibul

Commerce Bight

Cockscomb Basin

South Water Caye Marine Reserve

Glover's Reef Marine Reserve

Caracol Archeological Reserve

Maya Mountain

Mango Creek

Bladen

Swasey Bladen

Columbia River

Maya Mountain

Deep River

Paynes Creek

Laughing Bird Caye National Park

Machaca forest reserve

Sarstoon-Temash

Punta Gorda

Port Honduras Marine Reserve (Proposed)

Sapodilla Cayes Marine Reserve

GUATEMALA

0   50 km

LEGEND

- Forest Reserve
- Nature Reserve
- Wildlife Sanctuary
- National Park
- Private Reserve
- Archeological Reserve
- Marine Reserve
- Natural Monument

Source: Land Information Centre, Ministry of Natural resources

CONSERVATION ORGANIZATIONS IN BELIZE

The following are just some of the national and international organizations either directly involved in conservation projects in Belize or providing support and funding to various projects. Several of these organizations welcome **volunteers** to help carry out a huge range of conservation work, from constructing trails and camping facilities in national parks to undertaking a survey of manatees. If you're interested, contact the organizations directly, but have a look first at the general information on volunteering in Belize given on p.41.

The Belize Audubon Society (BAS), founded in 1969, is the country's pre-eminent conservation organization and extremely well-respected both in Belize and internationally. While the name might suggest bird-watching as its main focus of activity, BAS is active in all aspects of nature conservation and manages many of the country's reserves. It also publishes a range of books, guides and fact sheets on the reserves it manages. Members receive a monthly newsletter about the progress of wildlife conservation in Belize. Call in at the office to find out how to get to the various nature reserves. For details of membership contact BAS, PO Box 1001, 12 Fort St, Belize City (☎ 02/34987, fax 34985, email *base@btl.net*, Web site *www.belizeaudubon.org*).

The Belize Zoo and Tropical Education Center (see p.116) is renowned throughout the conservation world for the quality of its educational programmes. The zoo encourages Belizean schoolchildren to understand the natural environment by visits and the Outreach Programme. If you wish to support its aims, individual membership is available: write to Sharon Matola (the zoo's director), PO Box 474, Belize City (☎ & fax 081/3004, Web site *www.belizenet.com/belizezoo.html*).

Conservation Corridors (CC) is a UK-based charity that works directly with Belize-based organizations to preserve migration routes by establishing wildlife corridors between larger reserves. CC arranges field-trip research for students up to PhD level (mainly in physical geography) and can provide partial funding for successful applicants. In Belize, research is currently undertaken at Monkey Bay Wildlife Sanctuary (see p.117). In the UK, contact Conservation Corridors of Central America, 96 Riversmeet, Hertford, Herts, SG14 1LE (☎01992/413412); in Belize, contact Matt Miller, MBWS, ☎08/23180, email *mbay@pobox.com*).

Green Reef is a private, non-profit organization dedicated to the promotion of sustainable use and conservation of Belize's marine and coastal resources. Operating in San Pedro, Belize's busiest tourist destination, Green Reef provides educational programmes for schools in Belize, and is about to open a visitor centre in the town to inform tourists about the management of Ambergris Caye's two marine reserves. Green Reef can accept volunteers: contact Mito Paz, 100 Coconut Drive, San Pedro, Ambergris Caye, Belize (☎ 026/-2838, fax 2766, email *greenreef@btl.net*, Web site *www.ambergriscaye.com*).

project: the **Mesoamerican Biological Corridor**. Also known as the *Paseo Pantera* – the Path of the Panther – it aims to connect an unbroken corridor of parks and refuges for wildlife throughout Central America. By linking the reserves and creating a network of protected areas spanning the isthmus, it is hoped that the *Paseo Pantera* will safeguard the entire region's biodiversity.

At the time of writing a thorough overview of Belize's environmental and wildlife protection legislation is nearing completion. Known as the **National Protected Areas Systems Plan for Belize**, it recognizes that a viable plan cannot be established on nationally owned lands alone, but will need cooperation from many private landowners.

THE ROLE OF GOVERNMENT

Three ministries in Belize shoulder between them most of the responsibility for drafting legislation relating to conservation and ensuring compliance with the relevant regulations: **the Ministry of Agriculture and Fisheries**, **the Ministry of Natural Resources** and **the Ministry of Tourism and the Environment**. They are staffed by very able, dedicated professionals, and Belize's reputation as a leader in protected areas management owes much to their expertise.

Apart from monitoring and enforcing fishing regulations, the **Fisheries Department** manages the country's increasing number of marine reserves. In 1990 the Coastal Zone Management Unit (CZMU) was established within the department to coordinate all of the

The Programme for Belize (PFB), initiated in 1988 by the Massachusetts Audubon Society and launched in Britain in 1989, manages over 250,000 acres in the Rio Bravo Conservation Area (see p.77). The programme has bought land, to be held in trust for the people of Belize, and is managing it for the benefit of wildlife. For information on visiting the sites in Belize contact PFB, 2 South Park St, PO Box 749, Belize City (☎02/75616, email *pfbel@btl.net*); in UK: World Land Trust, PO Box 99, Saxmundham, Suffolk IP17 2BR (☎01986/874222, email *worldlandtrust@btinternet.com*); in USA: Massachusetts Audubon Society, 208 Great South Rd, Lincoln MA 01773 (☎617/259-9500).

The Siwa-Ban Foundation (SBF) was formed in 1990 for the purpose of establishing a multi-habitat reserve and a marine reserve on Caye Caulker. Years of dedicated campaigning appeared to have been in vain when an airstrip was built in the area to the south of the village, proposed for the reserve. Undaunted, the Siwa-Ban members continued their efforts and in 1998 the Caye Caulker Marine Reserve (see p.107) was established, with the northern tip of the caye forming the terrestrial element, connected to several kilometres of the reef offshore. Contact Ellen McRae, PO Box 47, Caye Caulker, Belize (☎ 022/2178, fax 2239, email *sbf@btl.net*); in the US: Susan Scott, 143 Anderson, San Franciso, CA 94110.

The Wildlife Conservation Society (WCS) works with all the countries involved in the *Paseo Pantera* project (see opposite) to strengthen and improve management of parks and conservation lands, and to restore degraded habitat for migratory wildlife. Instrumental in developing plans to establish marine reserves throughout the barrier reef, it maintains a research station on Middle Caye, Glover's Reef, working closely with the Belize government to develop a coordinated research and management programme for the whole atoll (see p.178). Inland, in reserves in the western Maya Mountains, researchers are developing guidelines to preserve biodiversity. Contact WCS, 2300 Southern Blvd, Bronx, NY 10460-1099 (email *membership@wcs.org*, Web site *www.wcs.org*).

The World Wide Fund for Nature (WWF) works closely with the BAS and is also helping the Belize government to raise its capacity for environmental regulation and protected area management. WWF has for many years provided initial support for a number of projects in Belize, from the Community Baboon Sanctuary at Bermudian Landing (see p.66) to the Cockscomb Basin Wildlife Sanctuary (see p.178). One current project works with farmers in the buffer zones adjacent to the Maya Mountains to develop new technologies for profitable and sustainable agricultural systems. Contact 1250 24th St NW, Washington DC, 20037, USA (☎202/293-4800); 90 Eglinton Ave E, Toronto, Ontario M4P 2Z7, Canada (☎416/489-8800); or Panda House, Weyside Park, Godalming, Surrey GU7 1XR, UK (☎01483/26444). The excellent, well-organized Web site is packed with useful information: *www.panda.org*.

---

agencies and nongovernmental organizations (NGOs) involved in coastal zone issues. Belize's timber reserves (including all mangroves) have always been under the compass of the **Forest Department** of the Ministry of Natural Resources, though it now has a much greater role in forest conservation than the provision and regulation of hardwoods for export. Its Conservation Division, created in 1990, is responsible for the enforcement of the Wildlife Protection Act, but also has overall responsibility for the management of all terrestrial protected areas and the coordination of biodiversity management. A conservation officer has now been appointed to all forest reserves.

The Ministry of Tourism and the Environment covers a broad range of environmental issues: the **Department of the Environment** is responsible for implementing the Environmental Protection Act, while the **Belize Tourist Board**, apart from attracting tourists to Belize and providing them with information, also licenses the country's **tour guides** and arranges training courses for them: you'll find the guides in Belize highly motivated guardians of the environment. In addition, all **archeological sites** are reserves, also within the Ministry's remit.

In general, these government agencies have proved extremely successful in coordinating protection of the nation's reserves, almost always with the cooperation of the private sector and expert assistance from a range of NGOs (see p.248). However, the dramatic increase in the amount of protected land has posed the question of how such protection is to be financed. Following years of discussion between the government and various NGOs as to how best to raise the funds, the **Protected Areas Conservation Trust** (PACT) was established in 1996, levying an **exit tax** of Bz$7.50 per person, payable at all departure points. The revenue generated is shared between the government departments and voluntary organizations responsible for conservation, according to a pre-arranged formula. A percentage of the money raised (which could total Bz$1,000,000 a year) is invested in a trust fund to provide a long-term buffer against the vicissitudes of government funding. In addition, reserve and archeological site entry fees have been raised, and some new ones implemented.

NGOS AND VOLUNTARY ORGANIZATIONS

Various national and international **voluntary organizations** have been active in conservation in Belize for many years, building up experience through practical work and by attending and hosting environmental conferences. The organizations recently joined to present a united front known as the **Belize Association of Conservation NGO's (BACONGO)** in order to present their cause to government more effectively. This unity was recently demonstrated in the Lamanai Room Declaration (see below), which called into question the government's environmental and conservation policies.

The tourism industry is also playing its part in raising environmental awareness: **Belize Eco-Tourism Association (BETA)** is a small but growing number of hotels and lodges whose members agree to a code of ethics promoting sustainable tourism management. One of the agreed aims is to reduce (and eliminate) the use of disposable products from their businesses. If you're concerned about your hotel's impact on the environment ask if they're a member of BETA.

THE FUTURE OF CONSERVATION

If it sounds as if the Belize authorities and the NGOs are too closely linked to enable the latter to undertake proper scrutiny of proposals that might adversely affect the environment, the outcome of the **Lamanai Room Declaration** of August 1997 should put minds at rest.

Signed by over thirty NGOs, the declaration sent a strong message to the government of the time that it could not ignore their concerns, which, at that point, related to certain existing and proposed **developments** that they claimed indicated "disregard for the principles of sustainable development", and were "a possible violation of Belizean legislation . . . and terms of international agreements relating to the environment". These included damage to the reef by cruise ships, a "lobster ranching" scheme that took lobsters below legal size to raise on "farms", and the sale of logging concessions on Maya lands in Toledo District. But it was the proposal by a Mexican company to build a "dolphin park attraction" at Cangrejo Caye, southwest of San Pedro that caused alarm nationwide. Dolphins (imported from Mexico, as they are a protected species in Belize) were to be held in "semi-captivity" – a term no one was able to define satisfactorily – and resort cabañas built around the enclosure. So vehement was opposition that the government never issued the necessary licence (in any case it was unlikely that the proposal would have met the strictures of the requisite Environmental Impact Assessment). Further success came with the fining of a cruise ship (US$75,000, half of which was used to provide reef mooring buoys), and the dropping of all other proposals that had triggered the protests.

Had these projects gone ahead, Belize's shining reputation as an example of "ecotourism" forming part of a viable development strategy would have been severely tarnished, if not irreparably damaged. At the time of writing the new government was still formulating its environmental policy.

ETHNIC BELIZE

Belize has a very mixed cultural background, with the two largest ethnic groups, Creoles and Mestizos, which together form 75 percent of the total population (currently 225,000), themselves the descendants of very different ancestors.

Creoles, descended from Africans brought to the West Indies as slaves and early White settlers, comprise just under a third of the population. They make up a large proportion of the population of Belize City, with scattered settlements around the rest of the country. Creole is the common language in Belize, a form of English similar to that spoken in those parts of the West Indies that were once part of the British empire. Belizean Creole is currently undergoing a formalization similar to that taken by the Garífuna in the 1980s. A society has been formed to standardize written Creole and possibly produce a dictionary, and controversy rages in the press over whether or not Creole should become the country's official language and be taught in schools.

The largest group (44 percent) are **Mestizos**, descended from Amerindians and early Spanish settlers, who speak Spanish as their first language. They are mainly located in the north and on Ambergris Caye and Caye Caulker, with a sizable population in Cayo. Many of the ancestors of the present population fled to Belize during the Caste Wars of the Yucatán (see p.227). And in recent years, many thousands of refugees from conflicts and repression in El Salvador, Guatemala and Honduras have settled in Belize, probably adding permanently to the numbers of Spanish-speaking Mestizos.

The **Maya** in Belize are from three groups – the Yucatec, Mopan and Kekchí – and make up around eleven percent of the population. The Yucatecan Maya also entered Belize to escape the fighting in the Caste Wars and most were soon acculturated into the Mestizo way of life as small farmers. The Mopan Maya came to Belize in the 1880s and settled in the hills of Toledo and the area of Benque Viejo in the west. The last group, the Kekchí, came from the area around Cobán in Guatemala to work in cacao plantations in southern Belize. Small numbers still arrive in Belize each year, founding new villages in the southern district of Toledo.

The **Garífuna** (see p.170) form about seven percent of the population and live mainly in Dangriga and the villages on the south coast, such as Hopkins and Seine Bight. They are descended from shipwrecked and escaped African slaves who mingled with the last of the Caribs on the island of St Vincent and eventually settled in Belize in the nineteenth century. A Garífuna dictionary, published by the National Garífuna Council, is available within the country.

Another group is the **East Indians**. They are relatively recent immigrants as apparently none of the earlier East Indians, brought as servants for the British administrators, left any descendants.

During the 1980s, the arrival of an estimated 40,000 **Central American immigrants**, refugees from war and poverty, boosted Belize's population to more than 200,000. Those granted refugee status were settled in camps, mostly in Cayo, and allowed to farm small plots, though many, especially the undocumented refugees, provide convenient cheap labour in citrus and banana plantations. The immigrants are tolerated, if not exactly welcomed – few countries could absorb a sudden twenty percent increase in population without a certain amount of turmoil – and the official policy is to encourage the refugees to integrate into Belizean society. Though there is no question of an enforced repatriation scheme, anyone wanting to return is supported. The refugees are industrious agriculturists providing a variety of crops for the domestic market. However, despite official tolerance they are often referred to as "aliens" and blamed for a disproportionate amount of crime. Their presence means that Spanish is now the most widely spoken first language, causing some Creoles to feel marginalized. Without doubt this recent Hispanic influence represents the greatest shift in Belize's demography for centuries.

MUSIC

For such a tiny country, Belize enjoys an exceptional range of musical styles and traditions. Whether your tastes run to the ethereal harp melodies of the Maya or the up-tempo punta of the Garífuna, or to calypso, marimba, brukdown, soca or steelpan, Belize is sure to have something to suit. Some visitors still complain about the noisiness of Belizean society and the volume at which the music is played, but if you can get into it, it's one of the quickest ways to the heart of Belizeans and their culture.

ROOTS

Until the demise of the Maya civilization and the arrival of the Spanish, the indigenous **Maya** of Belize played a range of instruments drawn almost entirely from the flute and drum families. Drums were usually made from hollowed logs covered in goat skin. Rattles, gourd drums and the turtleshell provided further rhythmic accompaniment. Trumpets, flutes, bells, shells and whistles completed the instrumentation. Most music was ritual in character and could involve up to eight hundred dancers, although smaller ceremonial ensembles were more common.

However, as befits a nation of immigrants, each new group arriving – the Europeans, the Creoles, the Mestizos and the Garífuna – brought with them new styles, vigour and variety which today inform and influence popular culture.

Mestizo music combined elements of its two constituent cultures: Maya ceremonial music and new instruments from Spain, such as the classical guitar, violin and later brass band music. Mestizo communities (including the Mopan Maya) in the north and west of the country continue to favour **marimba** bands: half a dozen men playing two large, multi-keyed wooden xylophones, perhaps supported by a double bass and a drum kit. Up to half a dozen bands play regularly in the Cayo district: Elfigo Panti presides over the nation's pre-eminent marimba group, **Alma Beliceña**; **Los Angeles Marimba Band** is another popular group. Leading marimba bands occasionally pop over from Flores in Guatemala, and Mexican **mariachi** bands occasionally make an appearance too. Nonetheless, traditional Mestizo music remains under threat as the youth turn to rock, rap and punta.

The **Europeans** introduced much of the hardware and software for playing music: "Western" musical instruments and sheet music, and, much later, record players, compact discs and massive sound systems. The Schottische, quadrille, polka and waltz can be counted amongst their strictly musical innovations. From the mid-nineteenth century onwards, British colonial culture, through church music, military bands and the popular music of the time, was able to exert a dominant influence, over what was "acceptable" music in Belize.

From **Africa** (primarily from southeast Nigeria) via Jamaica an exciting melange of West African rhythms and melodies, as well as drums and stringed instruments, arrived in Belize as a result of the slave trade during the eighteenth century. However, given that the Baymen purchased slaves from Jamaica rather than directly from Africa it should be remembered that African influences arrived indirectly.

A new syncretic style, nurtured in the logging camps and combining "Western" instrumentation with specifically African musical inflections, emerged in the late nineteenth century to create a specifically Belizean musical tradition known as "**Brukdown**". Featuring a twentieth-century line-up of guitar, banjo, accordion, drums and the jawbone of an ass (rattling a stick up and down the teeth!), brukdown remains a potent reminder of past Creole culture. Although the style is slowly fading, as Creole society itself changes, there are still several bands playing in and around Belize City of which **Mr Peter's Boom and Chime** is the

Andy Palacio *Keimoun* (Beat On) and *Till Da Mawnin* (Stonetree Records). These two recent releases display a mastery of punta and a widening of scope to incorporate Cuban and Anglophone Caribbean influences.

Lugua and the Larubeya Drummers *Bumari* (Stonetree Records). Roots Punta at its strongest, Lugua et al. open a new chapter in the distinguished history of Garífuna percussion.

The Original Turtle Shell Band *Serewe* (Stonetree Records). This recent recording is a stunning and seminal collection of Garífuna rhythms from the pioneers of punta.

Mr Peter's Boom and Chime *Berry Wine Days* (Stonetree Records). A musical journey through Creole history from the undisputed king of brukdown.

Brother David Obi & Tribal Vibes *Raw* (Stonetree Records). Rock guitars overlaid on the new generic Belizean rhythm and lyrical wit combine to produce a satisfying run around the Cungo kingdom.

best. Generally though, brukdown is recreational music best enjoyed in the Creole villages of Burrell Boom itself, Hattieville, Bermudian Landing and Isabella Bank.

Brad Patico, an accomplished guitarist and singer-songwriter, similarly does his best to keep the Creole folk-song tradition alive; from his base in Burrell Boom he collects old material, composes new songs and performs regularly to highly appreciative audiences. Originating from the same cultural roots – and equally conscious of a disappearing musical past – is Brother David Obi, better known as **Bredda David**, the creator of **Cungo Beat** (Creole for "let's go with the music"), a mixture of musical styles that includes the traditional Creole music of Belize and the pulsating drum rhythms of Africa. David is an accomplished musician and songwriter and plays regularly in Belize City – his audience can be sure of enjoying a great performance. He regularly records new material and recently collaborated on an album with Mr Peter.

More recently, the "African" elements in Creole music have been expressed through wider **pan-Caribbean** styles like calypso, reggae, soca and rap. **Calypso** enjoyed a brief period of pre-eminence and is still usually associated with **Lord Rhaburn's Combo**, a band that can still be found performing regularly, though live appearances by Rhaburn himself are increasingly rare. Most other bands copy current hits with one or two original compositions thrown in: **Youth Connection**, **Gilharry 7** and **Santino's Messengers** all provide an excellent evening's entertainment.

PUNTA ROCK

If Maya, Mestizo and Creole styles retain only a fragile hold on popular musical consciousness, it's the **Garífuna** who have been catapulted to centre-stage over the last decade with the invention and development of **punta rock**. Descended from Carib Indians and African slaves, the Garífuna arrived in Belize in the early nineteenth century having been exiled from St Vincent by the British (see box on p.170). With a distinct language and a vibrant, living culture, the Garífuna suffered a century of discrimination in Belize before re-establishing their individuality in the cultural renaissance of the early 1980s.

The key musical developments were the amplification of several traditional drum rhythms (while keeping faith with other traditional instruments such as the turtleshell) and the almost universal aversion to singing in anything but Garífuna. Although many master musicians and cultural nationalists pushed Garífuna culture forward, pride of place must go to drummer and drum-maker **Isabel Flores** and the enigmatic singer, guitarist and artist **Pen Cayetano** in Dangriga. More than anyone else, Pen pioneered popular Garífuna music, inventing punta rock in the late 1970s and sparking off a new cultural assertiveness that saw dozens of younger musicians take up the challenge. Pen's **Turtle Shell Band** set the standard which hypnotized audiences, and within a few years other electric bands including **Sounds Incorporated, Children of the Most High, Black Coral, Titiman Flores, Jeff Zuniga** and above all, **Andy Palacio** (see box on p.253), had consolidated the popularity of punta: Palacio's satirical 1988 hit "Bikini Panti" remains a national favourite. The **Waribagabaga Drum and Dance troupe**, formed in 1964, remain the chief guardians of more orthodox arrangements and should on no account be missed when they perform in Dangriga. Other popular artists include **Peter "Poots" Flores**, **Alvin Paine** and **Bella Caribe**. The most popular band in Belize today is probably the **Garífuna Kids**.

VENUES AND ARTISTS

Thursday evening is widely considered to mark the start of the weekend, and weekends are the best time to catch bands and other entertainment in **Belize City**. The *Lumba Yaad*, *Lindbergh's Landing* and the *Calypso* usually offer live music, while bigger venues like *Bird's Isle* and the *Civic Auditorium* often host longer variety bills.

The larger **hotels** usually have something on offer as well; it's always worth checking the *Bellevue* and *Radisson Fort George* in Belize City, the *Pelican Beach* in Dangriga, and the *Victoria* in Orange Walk. It would be a pity to leave Belize without hearing one of the several **one-man bands** which, with an array of electronic equipment and virtuoso keyboard skills, provide enjoyable dance music in less crowded settings; the most popular performers remain **Davonix**, **Steve Babb** and the talented **Magaña**.

Caye Chapel offers live entertainment and beach barbecues on the last Saturday of every month, while neighbouring **San Pedro**, as the major tourist destination in Belize, guarantees some kind of entertainment throughout the tourist season. **Belmopan** is less well served. The *Bayman Inn's* disco changes hands with a disruptive regularity while *Ed's Bar* in nearby Roaring Creek, despite its enjoyable dance-hall ambience, can seldom guarantee a show. **San Ignacio**, capital of the Cayo district, presents far livelier options, and residents of Belmopan clearly prefer the west to Belize City when it comes to weekend fun. Bands regularly perform at the *San Ignacio Hotel*, *Cahal Pech Tavern* and the *Blue Angel*, while the delightful Obandos entertain guests at their family-owned resort at *Las Casitas*. **Pablo Collado**, of Benque Viejo, with two beautiful, evocative and much-sought-after flute and guitar instrumental albums, *Armonia en la Selva* and *Amancear*, to his credit, frequently plays at locations in Cayo; definitely worth getting to.

In **Dangriga**, the *Roundhouse Disco* provides regular live music while the **Turtleshell Band** can sometimes be found playing in the street in front of the art studio on a Friday night. Rural areas do occasionally come up trumps with unexpected and informal performances: Placencia, Hopkins, Succotz, Bullet Tree, Ladyville, Burrell Boom, Consejo and Maskall all still entertain in the traditional way; luck alone will determine whether anything is happening on the night you happen to be there.

SPECIAL EVENTS

Perhaps the best times to hear and see the full panoply of Belizean musical culture are the various **national events** which regularly punctuate the social calendar. Biggest and best are National Day (Sept 10) and Independence Day (Sept 21) – dates which mark almost two weeks of festivities as Belize City comes close to the spirit and atmosphere of Caribbean carnival. Block parties, "jump-ups" and late-night revelry characterize what are known locally as **"The Celebrations"**. On Independence Day, the main Albert and Regent streets are closed to traffic and there's a band or sound system on every corner.

In between these dates there's a genuine **Carnival**, established only since independence but a hugely popular event, with an enormous street parade, floats, a carnival queen attended by a bevy of princesses, and of course bands and sound systems. The **Costa Maya Festival**, held in San Pedro in the third week of July, is a celebration of dance, music and culture which attracts performers from Mexico and throughout Central America. **Garífuna Settlement Day** (Nov 19) brings huge crowds to Dangriga for a long weekend of late nights, rum and rhythm. Mestizo communities celebrate with a number of very Latin type **fiestas** – bands, funfairs, sports and competitions. They're usually held around Easter and are soon followed by the **National Agricultural Show** held just outside Belmopan, when up to fifty thousand people gather over three days for things both agricultural and recreational. All the country's top bands will appear at some stage during the weekend.

Occasionally, the scene is further enlivened by visits from **Belizean musicians based in the States**. Los Angeles is the favourite destination for many Belizeans' bands like Chatuye, Jah Warriors, Poopa Curly and Sounds Incorporated, who usually try to come at least once a year; Calypso Rose is a regular visitor.

RECORDINGS

With a tiny population, Belize has never been in a position to support a record industry from domestic sales alone and consequently very few discs of Belizean music were ever produced. With the advent of cassette recording in the 1970s, however, the situation improved dramatically as leading dance bands released annual compilations, and domestic recordings from the

ANDY PALACIO

For more than a decade, **Andy Palacio** has influenced, dominated and even helped produce the modern Belizean sound. As the country's only truly professional star he has succeeded in incorporating an enormous diversity of national and regional styles into a unique popular sound that appeals to all sections of the music market.

Born in Barranco, he grew up in the rural cosmopolitanity of Garífuna, Maya and Mestizo communities, integrating a diversity of cultural and linguistic influences from an early age. As a teenager in the 1970s, he experienced first hand the new Belizean cultural nationalism of the PUP (People's United Party), which brought the country to independence, introducing a broader ideological dimension to his inevitable cultural affinity with the Garífuna musical tradition. Though he then went on to train as a teacher, his guitar skills, compelling voice and penchant for a neat lyric marked him out for a very different kind of career.

The break came in 1987 when on an exchange visit to London, courtesy of Cultural Partnerships, he spent a year picking up the latest recording techniques and honing his musical and compositional skills. He returned triumphantly to Belize a year later with enough equipment to open a studio and run a small band. He also had several London recordings of the songs that would become huge hits back home, transforming the music scene and laying the first foundations of the new national sound. The biggest song was undoubtedly **Bikini Panti** an English–Garífuna, punta-rock satire on Belize's burgeoning tourist business, that set a new musical and lyrical standard for the entire country. But if Bikini Panti was the dancefloor killer, it was **Me Goin' Back** that provided the clear ideological expression of the new national sensitivity, as the almost calypsonian lyrics clearly demonstrate:

Now check this one from Belize
because it's hard like Caribbean breeze,
You know how we do it with ease.

Me goin back, yes me really goin back,
Cause it happened the same way
me no come here to stay

Time come now and me ha fe go back
long time since I left me country
Come in a London and live in a Hackney
What a life in a this your city
All kind a people, what a diversity
African, Afro-Caribbean
Asian and a European
Mek them know this is a Belizean
Come alive in this Ingalan

Me goin back, yes I'm really goin back
Happened same way, me no come here to stay
time come now and me ha fe go back

Set up the line for the Dangriga posse
Play a little rhythm for the Stann Creek posse
Mash up the place with the Cayo posse
Bruk down the house with the Belize posse
Control the area for the Orange Walk posse
Mek them know that me fresh and ready
Mek them know, me have the authority

Now don't burst your brains wondering what
I'm goin back to
So I'll mention just a few
Some old and some new

Rice n Beans and a Belikin
Friends FM and a dollar chicken
Pine Ridge and a Swing bridge
Brukdown, Punta Rock
Sunshine and a cashew wine
Belize Times and Amandala
Maya, Creole and the Garífuna
Mek them know that me fresh and ready
Mek them know me have the authority

Andy Palacio's recent collaboration with Stonetree Records (see above) has seen two releases to date (see box on p.251). **Till Da Mawnin** (1997) brings a new maturity and mastery to his music. Less mindful of public opinion and more comfortable in his national superstar status, he has established an enviable reputation as a musician capable of producing catchy melodies accompanied by articulate, astute and entertaining lyrics and underpinned by unique Garífuna rhythms.

radio began to document the passing of musical time. But it wasn't until the setting up of the **Sunrise Recording Studio** in 1987 that Belize saw a systematic approach to recording and preserving musical culture. In the years that followed, over a dozen original cassette recordings reached the market, including the classic compilation **Punta Rockers** (1988). The brainchild of Andy Palacio, the cassette featured recordings by Palacio himself and several other pioneers of punta rock. It sold several thousand copies, confirming punta as the country's pre-eminent party music and Andy Palacio as a pivotal figure in the production and distribution system. *Punta Rockers* and other Sunrise recordings from around the same time can occasionally be found hiding away behind the mahogany carvings in San Pedro gift shops.

The next major burst of recording activity began in 1995 with the establishment of **Stonetree Records**. This now thriving music house was set up by Cubola, Belize's foremost publishing house, to provide a platform for Belizean music of all genres, from melodic Maya harps through the African-born beat of punta and cungo to experimental fusion by such artists as Ivan Duran, founder of Free Access.

Other groups, like Brother David, Messengers and Sounds Incorporated, have also produced good local cassettes, and there are some signs that local record shops are beginning to respect the rights of musicians to also earn a living. On an official level, the government takes a lively interest in local arts with a revitalized Arts Council based at the Bliss Institute. *Radio Belize* does its best to promote local talent, but cable TV and pirate satellite stations steadily erode interest in local products.

Of course there are those who do not fit into any of the tidy musical categories outlined above. Both the **Police Band** and the **Belize Defence Force Band** perform regularly and creditably. The **All-Stars Steel Band** plough a lonely furrow but are well received wherever they play. There are also a number of small **jazz** outfits and some very gifted up-and-coming **female vocalists**. But on a national level, punta still holds sway and there is no question, given the richness of their traditional musical repertoire, that the Garifuna will continue to develop new styles for decades to come. For their part, several young musicians are now experimenting with more traditional Mestizo melodies and rhythms. Mestizo rock, anyone?

Ronnie Graham and Cindy Carlson
(with additional material adapted from
***The Rough Guide to World Music*)**

BOOKS

Belize under British rule didn't inspire much literature, but independence has prompted a handful of writers to publish works based on the transition to independence and the emergence of a national identity. There are a number of excellent wildlife guides and studies, and also some good travel accounts covering Belize. Most sociological or political works on Central America don't even mention Belize; some of those that do are reviewed here.

In the list given below, o/p means a book is out of print. See also the box on p.16 for specialist publishers.

TRAVEL

Aldous Huxley, *Beyond the Mexique Bay* (Flamingo, UK; o/p). Huxley's travels, in 1934, took him from Belize through Guatemala to Mexico, swept on by his fascination for history and religion, and sprouting bizarre theories on the basis of what he saw. There are some great descriptions of Maya sites and Indian culture, with superb one-liners summing up people and places.

Jeremy Paxman, *Through the Volcanoes* (Paladin, UK; o/p). A political travel account investigating the turmoil of Central America and finding solace in the calm of Costa Rica. Paxman's travels take him through all seven of the republics, including Belize, and he offers a good overview of the politics and history of the region.

John Lloyd Stephens, *Incidents of Travel in Central America, Chiapas, and Yucatán* (Dover, UK; Prentice Hall, US). Stephens was a classic nineteenth-century traveller. Acting as American ambassador to Central America, he indulged his own enthusiasm for archeology: while the republics fought it out among themselves he was wading through the jungle stumbling across ancient cities. In Belize he dines with high society and is given a naval gun salute from the superintendent, though he doesn't venture inland. His journals, told with superb Victorian pomposity punctuated with sudden waves of enthusiasm, make great reading. Some editions include fantastic illustrations by Catherwood of the ruins overgrown with tropical rainforest.

Ronald Wright, *Time Among the Maya* (Henry Holt, UK; Abacus, US). A vivid and sympathetic account of travels in the 1980s from Belize through Guatemala, Chiapas and Yucatán, meeting the Maya and exploring their obsession with time. The book's twin points of interest are the ancient Maya and the violence that took place in the 1980s. An encyclopedic bibliography offers ideas for exploration in depth, and the author's knowledge is evident in the superb historical insight he imparts throughout the book. Certainly one of the best travel books on the area.

BELIZEAN LITERATURE

Zee Edgell, *Beka Lamb* (Heinemann). A young girl's account of growing up in Belize in the 1950s, in which the problems of adolescence are described alongside those of the Belizean independence movement. The book also explores everyday life in the colony, describing the powerful structure of matriarchal society and the influence of the Catholic Church. *In Times Like These* is a semi-autobiographical account of personal and political intrigue set in the months leading up to Belize's independence.

Zoila Ellis *On Heroes, Lizards and Passion* (Cubola, Belize). Seven short stories written by a Belizean woman with a deep understanding of her country's people and their culture.

Felicia Hernandez, *Those Ridiculous Years* (Cubola, Belize). A short autobiographical book about growing up in Dangriga in the 1960s.

Emory King, *Belize 1798, The Road to Glory* (Tropical Books, Belize). Rip-roaring historical novel peopled by the characters involved in the Battle of St George's Caye. King's enthusiasm for his country's history results in the nearest thing you'll get to a Belizean blockbuster, yet it's based on meticulous research in archives on both sides of the Atlantic. Wonderful holiday reading. King is something of a celebrity in Belize (see box on p.56): his first book *Hey Dad,This is Belize*, a hilarious account of family life in Belize, became something of a minor classic and was followed up with *I Spent it all in Belize*, an anthology of witty, lightly satirical articles gently but effectively pricking the pomposity of officialdom. These and other books written by him are usually only available in Belize.

Shots From The Heart, (Cubola, Belize). Slim anthology of the work of three young Belizean poets: Yasser Musa, Kiren Shoman and Simone Waight. Evocative imagery and perceptive comment relate experiences of a changing society. Musa's *Belize City Poem* (published separately) is a sharply observed, at times vitriolic, commentary on the simultaneous arrival of independence and US-dominated television in Belizean society.

HISTORY, POLITICS AND SOCIETY

Tom Barry, *Inside Belize* (LAB; Resource Center). One of a series of up-to-date guides covering the history, politics, economy and society of Central America. Packed with accessible facts and analysis.

Nigel Bolland, *Colonialism and Resistance in Belize* (Cubola, Belize). Perhaps the most academic text on Belizean history, adopting a staunchly Marxist stance, and sweeping away many of the myths and much of the romance that surrounds the history of Belize.

Byron Foster, *Spirit Possession in the Garifuna Community of Belize* (Cubola, Belize). One of the few titles available on Garífuna culture in Belize, and by no means comprehensive, though admittedly the focus of the book is the experience of spirit possession as described by several Garífuna. Another of Foster's books – *The Baymen's Legacy: A Portrait of Belize City* (Cubola, Belize) – is a school text but offers an approachable and interesting history of the city.

Gerald S. Koop, *Pioneer Years in Belize* (self published). A history of the Mennonites in Belize, written in a style as stolid and practical as the lives of the pioneers themselves. A good read nonetheless. Available in Belize.

Ian Peedle, *Belize in Focus* (LAB, UK; Resource Center US). Latest in this excellent series: an up-to-date, easily digested overview of Belizean society and politics. Worth taking along if you're there for more than a few days.

Assad Shoman, *Thirteen Chapters of a History of Belize* (Angelus Press, Belize). A long overdue treatment of the country's history written by a Belizean who's not afraid to examine colonial myths with a detailed and rational analysis. Primarily a school textbook, but the style will not alienate non-student readers. Shoman, active in politics both before and since independence, also wrote *Party Politics in Belize*, a short but highly detailed account of the development of party politics in the country.

William David Setzekon, *A Profile of the New Nation of Belize, formerly British Honduras* (Ohio University Press, US). An approachable, easy-going Belize history; still available and worth a look but perhaps a little dated.

Colville Young, *Creole Proverbs of Belize* (Cubola, Belize). A wonderful compilation of oral folk-wisdom from Belize, written by the present governor general, who's also a distinguished linguist. Each saying or proverb is written in Creole, translated into English, and then has its meaning explained. A primer for street life.

A History of Belize – A Nation in the Making (Cubola, Belize). Straightforward and simple historical accounts, written for use in schools but providing a good, accurate background; available within Belize.

The Maya Atlas (North Atlantic Books, Berkeley). As much a collection of personal accounts compiled by the contemporary Maya of southern Belize as a geography book, this is a fascinating co-production between university researchers and the Maya of Toledo. Trained by Berkeley cartographers, teams of villagers surveyed their lands, completed a census and then wrote a history of each community. The regional maps accurately show the position of each village and drawings and photographs show scenes from everyday life. Available in Belize from the Toledo Maya Cultural Council, PO Box 104, Punta Gorda, Belize.

ARCHEOLOGY

Michael Coe, *The Maya* (Thames & Hudson). Now in its fifth edition, this clear and comprehensive introduction to Maya archeology is certainly the best on offer. Coe has also written several more weighty, academic volumes. His *Breaking the Maya Code* (Thames & Hudson), a very personal history of the decipherment of the glyphs, owes much to the fact that Coe was present at many of the most important meetings leading to the breakthrough. While his pointed criticism of J. Eric Thompson – much of whose work he describes as burdened with "irrelevant quotations", and his role in the decipherment of the Maya script as "entirely negative" – may provoke controversy, this book demonstrates that the glyphs did actually reproduce Maya speech.

William Coe, *Tikal: A Handbook to the Ancient Maya Ruins*. Superbly detailed account of the site, usually available at the ruins. The detailed map of the main area is essential for in-depth exploration.

Diego de Landa, *Yucatán Before and After the Conquest* (Dover). A translation edited by William Gates of the work written in 1566 as *Relación de las Cosas de Yucatán*. De Landa's destruction of almost all original Maya books as "works of the devil" leaves his own account as the chief source on Maya life and society in the immediate post-conquest period. Written during his imprisonment in Spain on charges of cruelty to the Indians (remarkable itself, given the institutional brutality of the time), the book provides a fascinating wealth of detail for historians. Although (as far as is known) Landa did not visit Belize, the vivid descriptions of Maya life and ceremony are applicable to the Maya of Chetumal, a province then extending into northern Belize.

Byron Foster (ed.), *Warlords and Maize Men – A Guide to the Maya Sites of Belize* (Cubola, Belize). An excellent handbook to fifteen of the most accessible sites in Belize compiled by the Association for Belizean Archeology and the Belize Department of Archeology.

Joyce Kelly, *An Archaeological Guide to Northern Central America* (University of Oklahoma). Detailed and practical guide to 38 Maya sites and 25 museums in four countries; an essential companion for anyone travelling purposefully through the Maya World. Kelly's "star" rating – based on a site's archeological importance, degree of restoration and accessibility – may affront purists but it does provide a valuable opinion on how worthwhile a particular visit might be. The most detailed guide available to the Maya sites of Belize.

Mary Ellen Miller, *The Art of Mesoamerica: From Olmec to Aztec* (Thames & Hudson). An excellent, wonderfully illustrated survey of the artisanship of the ancient cultures of Mexico, whose work reflects the sophistication of their civilizations.

Mary Ellen Miller and Karl Taube, *The Gods and Symbols of Ancient Mexico and the Maya: An Illustrated Dictionary of Mesoamerican Religion* (Thames & Hudson). A superb modern reference on ancient Mesoamerica, written by two leading scholars. Taube's *Aztec and Maya Myths* (British Museum Press, UK) is perfect as a short, accessible introduction to Mesoamerican mythology.

Jeremy A. Sabloff, *The New Archeology and the Ancient Maya* (Scientific American Library). Sabloff explains the "revolution" which has taken place in Maya archeology since the 1960s, overturning many firmly held beliefs and assumptions on the nature of Maya society, and stating how the study of archeology relates to current environmental problems.

Linda Schele and David Freidel (et al.). The authors, in the forefront of the "new archeology", have been personally responsible for decoding many of the glyphs. Their writing style, which frequently includes "recreations" of scenes inspired by their discoveries, is controversial in some areas, but has nevertheless inspired a devoted following. *A Forest of Kings: The Untold Story of the Ancient Maya* (Quill, US), in conjunction with *The Blood of Kings* (Braziller, UK; Thames & Hudson, US), by Linda Schele and Mary Miller, shows that far from being governed by peaceful astronomer-priests, the ancient Maya were ruled by hereditary kings, lived in aggressive city-states and engaged in a continuous entanglement of alliances and war. *The Maya Cosmos* (Quill, US) by Schele, Freidel and Joy Parker is perhaps more difficult to read, dense with copious notes, but continues to examine Maya ritual and religion in a unique and far-reaching way. *The Code of Kings* (Scribner, US), written in collaboration with Peter Matthews and illustrated with Justin Kerr's famous "rollout" photography of Maya ceramics, examines in detail the significance of the monuments at selected Maya sites (though none are in Belize). Schele's last book (she died in 1998), it is sure to become a classic of epigraphic interpretation.

Robert Sharer, *The Ancient Maya* (Stanford University). The classic, comprehensive (and weighty) account of Maya civilization, now in a completely revised and much more readable fifth edition, yet as authoritative as ever. Required reading for archeologists, it also provides a fascinating reference for the non-expert.

J. Eric S. Thompson, *The Rise and Fall of the Maya Civilization* (University of Oklahoma). A major authority on the ancient Maya, Thompson has produced many academic studies – this is one of the more approachable. *The Maya of Belize – Historical Chapters Since Columbus* (Cubola, Belize) is a very interesting book on the first two centuries of Spanish colonial rule – a little-studied area of Belizean history – and casts some light on the groups that weren't immediately conquered by the Spanish.

WILDLIFE AND THE ENVIRONMENT

Belize has a range of superb wildlife books and pamphlets, written by specialists with visitors, teachers and students in mind. Unfortunately, many are difficult to obtain outside the country; the best ones are available from the Belize Audubon Society (BAS; see p.246), who offer a mail order service.

Rosita Arvigo with Nadia Epstein, *Sastun: My Apprenticeship with a Maya Healer* (HarperCollins). A rare glimpse into the life and work of a Maya *curandero*, the late Elijio Panti of San Antonio (see p.132). Dr Arvigo has ensured the survival of generations of healing knowledge, and this book is a testimony both to her perseverance in becoming accepted by Mr Panti and the cultural wisdom of the indigenous people. Arvigo has also written or collaborated on several other books on traditional medicine in Belize: *Rainforest Remedies*; *One Hundred Healing Herbs of Belize* (Lotus Books), co-authored with Michael Balick of the New York Botanical Garden, is a detailed account of some of Belize's commonest medicinal plants and their uses. Both books are widely available in Belize

Louise H. Emmons, *Neotropical Rainforest Mammals* (University of Chicago). Highly informative and very detailed with colour illustrations by François Feer, it's written by experts for non-scientists. Local and scientific names are given, along with plenty of interesting snippets. Emmons is also the principal author of *The Cockscomb Basin Wildlife Sanctuary* (Producciones de la Hamaca, Belize; Orang-Utan Press, Gay Mills, Wisconsin), a comprehensive guide to the history, flora and fauna of Belize's

Jaguar Reserve. Though aimed at teachers and students, it's incredibly useful to any visitor and is available from the sanctuary and the BAS.

Carol Farnetti Foster and John R. Meyer, *A Guide to the Frogs and Toads of Belize*. Great book with plenty of photos and text to help you identify the many anurans you'll see – and hear – in Belize.

Steve Howell and Sophie Webb, *The Birds of Mexico and Northern Central America* (Oxford University Press). The result of years of research, this tremendous work is the definitive book on the region's birds. Essential for all serious birders.

John C. Kricher, *A Neotropical Companion* (Princeton University). Subtitled "An Introduction to the Animals, Plants and Ecosystems of the New World Tropics", this contains an amazing amount of valuable information for nature lovers. Researched mainly in Central America, so there's plenty that's directly relevant.

Alan Rabinowitz, *Jaguar* (Arbor House). Account of the author's experiences studying jaguars for the New York Zoological Society in the early 1980s and living with a Maya family in the Cockscomb Basin. Rabinowitz was instrumental in the establishment of the Jaguar Reserve in 1984.

SPECIALIST GUIDES

Kirk Barrett, *Belize by Kayak*. The most detailed book on this increasingly popular activity. Not widely available; contact Reef Link Kayaking, 3806 Cottage Grove, Des Moines, Iowa, US.

Emory King, *Emory King's Driving Guide to Belize* (Tropical Books, Belize). Worth a look if you're driving around. The maps are perhaps a little too sketchy for complete accuracy but the book is typically Belizean: laid-back and easy-going.

Ned Middleton, *Diving in Belize* (Aqua Quest). The most readable book on the subject, expertly written and illustrated with excellent photographs taken by the author. Covers in detail all the atolls and many of the reefs and individual dive sites. Also includes a section on Mexico's Banco Chinchorro, just north of Belize.

LANGUAGE

English is the official language of Belize and naturally enough it's spoken everywhere, though in fact it's the first language of only a small percentage of the population. For many people, particularly in the north and the west, English is the language spoken at home. That said, listening to any conversation can be confusing as they switch from Spanish to Creole to English and back – often in the same sentence. Without spending a lot of time in the Maya or Garífuna communities you're not going to be able to able to pick up more than a word or two of those languages. If you plan to cross the border into Guatemala to visit Tikal, some Spanish will be essential.

CREOLE

Creole is the *lingua franca* of Belize: whether their first language is Maya, Spanish, Garífuna or English, every Belizean can communicate with every other in Creole. It may sound like English from a distance and as you listen to a few words you'll think that their meaning is clear, but as things move on you'll soon realize that complete comprehension is just out of reach. It's a beautifully warm and relaxed language, typically Caribbean, and loosely based on English but including elements of Spanish and Maya. **Written Creole**, which you'll see in some newspaper columns and booklets, is a little easier to get to grips with, though you'll need to study it hard at first to get the meaning. There is a booklet available from some bookstores (designed for use by Peace Corps volunteers) which explains the grammar, and a dictionary may be available now, but Creole will always be much more of a spoken language than a written one.

Just to give you a taste of Belizean Creole here are a couple of simple phrases:

Bad ting neda gat owner – Bad things never have owners.

Better belly bus dan good bikkle waste – It's better that the belly bursts than good victuals go to waste.

Cow no business eena haas gylop – Cows have no business in a horse race.

If you're after more of these then get yourself a copy of *Creole Proverbs of Belize*, which is usually available in Belize City.

SPANISH

The **Spanish** spoken in both Guatemala and Belize has a strong Latin American flavour to it, and if you're used to the dainty intonation of Madrid or Granada then this may come as something of a surprise. Gone is the soft s, replaced by a crisp and clear version. If you're new to Spanish it's a lot easier to pick up than the native version.

The rules of **pronunciation** are pretty straightforward and, once you get to know them, strictly observed. Unless there's an accent, words ending in d, l, r and z are **stressed** on the last syllable, all others on the second last. All **vowels** are pure and short.

A somewhere between the "a" sound of back and that of father.

E as in get.

I as in police.

O as in hot.

U as in rule.

C is soft before "e" and "i", hard otherwise: *cerca* is pronounced serka.

G works the same way, a guttural "h" sound (like the *ch* in loch) before "e" or "i", a hard "g" elsewhere: *gigante* becomes higante.

H always silent.

J the same sound as a guttural "g": *jamón* is pronounced hamon.

L sounds like an English "y": tortilla is pronounced torteeya.

N as in English unless it has a tilde (accent) over it, when it becomes "ny": *mañana* sounds like manyana.

QU is pronounced like an English "k".

A SPANISH LANGUAGE GUIDE

BASICS

yes, no	*sí, no*	open, closed	*abierto/a, cerrado/a*
please, thank you	*por favor, gracias*	with, without	*con, sin*
where, when	*dónde, cuando*	good, bad	*buen(o)/a, mal(o)/a*
what, how much	*qué, cuanto*	big, small	*gran(de), pequeño/a*
here, there	*aquí, allí*	more, less	*más, menos*
this, that	*este, eso*	today, tomorrow	*hoy, mañana*
now, later	*ahora, más tarde*	yesterday	*ayer*

GREETING AND RESPONSES

Hello, goodbye	*¡hola!, adios*	I don't speak Spanish	*(No) Hablo español*
Good morning	*buenos días*	What (did you say)?	*Mande?*
Good afternoon/ night	*buenas tardes/noches*	My name is...	*Me llamo...*
How do you do?	*¿Qué tal ?*	What's your name?	*¿Como se llama usted?*
See you later	*Hasta luego*	I am English	*Soy inglés(a)*
Sorry	*lo siento/disculpeme*	...American	*americano(a)*
Excuse me	*Con permiso/perdon*	...Australian	*australiano(a)*
How are you?	*¿Cómo está (usted)?*	...Canadian	*canadiense(a)*
Not at all/	*De nada*	...Irish	*irlandés(a)*
You're welcome		...Scottish	*escosés(a)*
I (don't) understand	*(No) Entiendo*	...Welsh	*galés(a)*
Do you speak English?	*¿Habla (usted) inglés?*	...New Zealander	*neozelandés(a)*

NEEDS – HOTELS AND TRANSPORT

I want	*Quiero*	Can one...?	*¿Se puede...?*
Do you know...?	*¿Sabe...?*	...camp (near) here?	*¿...acampar aquí (cerca)?*
I'd like....	*quisiera... por favor*	Is there a hotel nearby?	*¿Hay un hotel aquí cerca?*
I don't know	*No sé*		
There is (is there?)	*Hay (?)*	How do I get to...?	*¿Por dónde se va a...?*
Give me...	*Deme...*	Left, right, straight on	*izquierda, derecha, derecho*
(one like that)	*(uno asi)*		
Do you have...?	*¿Tiene...?*	Where is...?	*¿Dónde está...?*
...the time	*...la hora*	...the nearest bank	*...el banco más cercano (ATM is cajero automático)*
...a room	*...un cuarto*		
...with two beds/	*...con dos*		
double bed	*camas/cama matrimonial*	...the post office	*...el correo (la oficina de correos)*
It's for one person	*Es para una persona*	...the toilet	*...el baño/sanitario*
(two people)	*(dos personas)*	Where does the bus	*¿De dónde sale el*
...for one night	*...para una noche (una*	to... leave from?	*camión para...?*
(one week)	*semana)*	What time does it	*¿A qué hora sale*
It's fine, how much is it?	*¿Esta bien, cuánto es?*	leave (arrive in...)?	*(llegaen...)?*
It's too expensive	*Es demasiado caro*	What is there to eat?	*¿Qué hay para comer?*
Don't you have	*¿No tiene algo más*	What's that?	*¿Qué es eso?*
anything cheaper?	*barato?*	What's this called in Spanish?	*¿Cómo se llama este en español?*

NUMBERS AND DAYS

1	un/uno/una	20	veinte	1996	mil novocientos
2	dos	21	veintiuno		noventa y seis
3	tres	30	treinta	first	primero/a
4	cuatro	40	cuarenta	second	segundo/a
5	cinco	50	cincuenta	third	tercero/a
6	seis	60	sesenta	fifth	quinto/a
7	siete	70	setenta	tenth	decimo/a
8	ocho	80	ochenta		
9	nueve	90	noventa		
10	diez	100	cien(to)	Monday	Lunes
11	once	101	ciento uno	Tuesday	Martes
12	doce	200	doscientos	Wednesday	Miércoles
13	trece	500	quinientos	Thursday	Jueves
14	catorce	700	setecientos	Friday	Viernes
15	quince	1000	mil	Saturday	Sábado
16	dieciséis	2000	dos mil	Sunday	Domingo

R is rolled, RR doubly so.

V sounds more like "b", *vino* becoming beano.

X is slightly softer than in English – sometimes almost "s" – except between vowels in place names where it has an "h" sound – i.e. México (Meh-Hee-Ko) or Oaxaca (Wa-ha-ka). (Note: in the Maya region "x" in Maya words is pronounced "sh", thus *Xel Ha* is ShelHa.)

Z is the same as a soft "c", so *cerveza* becomes servesa.

Although we've listed a few essential words and phrases here some kind of dictionary or **phrasebook** is a worthwhile investment: the *Rough Guide to Mexican Spanish* is the best practical guide, correct and colloquial, and certainly acceptable for most purposes travelling in Guatemala. One of the best small, Latin-American Spanish dictionaries is the University of Chicago version (Pocket Books), and the Collins series (published by HarperCollins) of pocket grammars and dictionaries is excellent.

INDEX

Stay in touch with us!

ROUGH*NEWS* **is Rough Guides' free newsletter.
In three issues a year we give you news, travel
issues, music reviews, readers' letters and the
latest dispatches from authors on the road.**

I would like to receive ROUGH*NEWS*: please put me on your free mailing list.

NAME . . . .

ADDRESS . . . .

Please clip or photocopy and send to: Rough Guides, 62–70 Shorts Gardens, London WC2H 9AB,
England or Rough Guides, 375 Hudson Street, New York, NY 10014, USA.